The Sierra Club
Green Guide

The Sierra Club Green Guide

Everybody's

Desk Reference to

Environmental

Information

by Andrew J. Feldman

Sierra Club Books
San Francisco

Library of Congress Cataloging-in-Publication Data

Feldman, Andrew J.
    The Sierra Club green guide : Everybody's Desk Reference to Environmental Information / by Andrew J. Feldman.
       p.   cm.
    Includes bibliographical references and index.
    ISBN 0-87156-402-5 (pbk.)
    1. Environmental sciences—Information services— United States—Directories. 2. Environmental sciences—Information services—Canada—Directories. 3. Environmental sciences—Research—Databases— Directories. I. Sierra Club. II. Title.
GE30.F45   1995
026'.363—dc20   95-2438
                                       CIP

Editorial Assistant: Steve Toub
Production by Janet Vail
Cover design by Bonnie Smetts Design
Book design by Mark Ong
Composition by Wilsted & Taylor

Printed on acid-free paper containing a minimum of 50% recovered waste paper of which at least 10% of the fiber content is post-consumer waste.

10 9 8 7 6 5 4 3 2 1

To my wife Lisa
and my parents Ronald and Frayda,
without whose love and encouragement
I could not have achieved this goal.

Contents

Preface

I first recognized the need for an environmental information guide while in college. I frequently became frustrated because I could not find the environmental information I needed. After speaking with many professionals in the field, it became clear that most people with environmental questions didn't know where to turn to find answers. The problem was not a lack of information, but rather an overwhelming abundance of information with no organized method of access.

Upon graduation, I continued to work in the environmental and energy fields. During these years I gained a more complete picture of the available sources of information and how they were being used. Because this experience confirmed my belief in the need for an environmental resource guide, I developed an independent project which, over three years, included intensive work by twenty-eight dedicated researchers. Upon being presented with a proposal and partial *Green Guide* manuscript, Sierra Club Books enthusiastically agreed to become the publisher. The result is *The Sierra Club Green Guide,* an easy-to-understand desk reference that will help you locate the resources you need to answer any environmental question.

By design, the *Green Guide* is not comprehen-sive; rather, it critically evaluates more than six hundred of the most vital sources of environmental information. Many of these references have been specifically selected because they will lead you to other sources of relevant information; for example, government clearinghouses that make referrals to experts and distribute documents; directories of local organizations; Internet sites and bulletin board systems that provide access to other online resources; and abstracts that describe articles and reports.

The sources of information evaluated in this book are as varied as the different reasons people need to gather environmental information. Browse through the chapters that interest you the most and begin to discover the fascinating resources that are readily available.

At least one member of my staff has talked to each organization, used each online resource, and reviewed each publication evaluated in this book. The accuracy of each description has been verified before publication; however, it is inevitable in a project of this nature that some information will have changed by the time you use this book. For updated information or to submit comments, send an e-mail message to **feld@interramp.com.**

Acknowledgments

Steven Toub is deserving of special recognition and thanks. He became dedicated to the *Green Guide* in its early stages and has worked tirelessly for two and a half years to ensure that the research and writing is as thorough and as focused as possible. His keen insight, eye for detail, and critical intellect have proven invaluable to the successful completion of this book.

This project would not have been possible without the help of numerous interns. My heartfelt appreciation to Alicia Boomer, Brian Bridgeford, Jeffrey Cadman, Kris Calori, Daryl Collette, Margaret (Magen) Delahanty, Britt Dionne, Traci Henry, Aimée Ipson, Serene Jweied, Casey Kern, Janice Kim, Jennifer LaPointe, Eric Linden, Regan Loyd, Nell Ma'luf, Kristen McArdle, Deborah Meisegeier, Beth Murphy, Colby Paino, Sonja Plesset, Derek Roberto, Fausto Rodriguez, David Rynn, Eric Schwager, and Ching Yeh.

I am indebted to my agent Anne Edelstein and to my editor Jim Cohee at Sierra Club Books for their interest and support, and to Heidi Reinberg for her advice and expert copy editing. And a special thank you to Sharon Gallagher, president of Distributed Art Publishers, for giving me the courage to tackle this project.

Finally, many people from hundreds of organizations and agencies have been enormously helpful and generous in answering questions and providing publications. My thanks to all of you.

Andrew J. Feldman

How to Use This Book

Parts and Chapters

This book is divided into two parts: **Environmental Issues** and **Green Living**. Part One, **Environmental Issues**, is composed of ten chapters, nine of which focus on a single broad environmental topic such as biodiversity, energy, or waste. The exception, Chapter 1, **General**, includes resources that cover many environmental issues.

Part Two, **Green Living**, includes eight chapters that cover topics that integrate environmental concerns into our everyday lives. For example, these chapters will help those who want to renovate a home in an environmentally sensitive manner, look for a job in an environmental field, garden organically, obtain a grant for an environmental project, invest in mutual funds that screen companies based on their environmental records, make environmentally sound purchasing decisions, or plan an environmental vacation.

In both parts, each chapter introduction defines those issues covered in the chapter and lists other relevant chapters in the book. A particular resource is described only once, in the chapter that best reflects its primary focus.

Types of Information Sources

Within each chapter, entries are grouped by type of information source in the following categories:

- **Government clearinghouses** include government-sponsored hotlines and clearinghouses that are set up specifically to answer questions and provide information to the public. A few government research centers and offices that distribute government documents are also included.

- **Organizations** include national nonprofit environmental advocacy and research organizations. Some coalitions of organizations, trade and professional associations, and companies that provide environmental information services are also described.

- **Internet sites** include World Wide Web and gopher sites. Internet mailing lists and Usenet newsgroups are not included.

- **Commercial online services** include fee-based computer information services that allow users to send and receive e-mail, use online databases, and view and download documents.

- **Bulletin boards** include free electronic bulletin board systems, to which users can dial in by modem to send and receive e-mail, use online databases, and view and download documents.

- **Directories** include resource guides that contain many different types of information sources, as well as directories of a single type of information source, such as organizations.

- **Bibliographies** include full-length, annotated guides to published literature. There are also several annotated book catalogs and bibliographies of Internet resources.

- **Reference handbooks** include atlases, almanacs, collections of statistics, manuals, guides, and other books that are used for reference, rather than read cover to cover.

- **Dictionaries and encyclopedias** are found under their own heading only in Part One, Chapter 1, **General**. In other chapters, dictionaries and encyclopedias are included with reference handbooks.

- **Introductory reading** includes recent books as well as classic works and landmark scientific reports that provide background information on the issues.

- **Abstracts and indices** include resources that summarize or provide citations of published literature, for example, journal articles, reports, and conference proceedings.

- **Periodicals** include magazines and organizational newsletters, especially those that provide news or help readers network (announce new resources, update legislative activities, provide a calendar of conferences, etc.). In general, academic journals and industry newsletters are not included.

Understanding Entry Numbers, Cross-references, and the Indices

Entry Numbers

Each information source described in this book has an entry number that appears next to the name of the resource. Occasionally, two or more resources are reviewed together. Also, some sources of information are only mentioned within the descriptions of other resources and do not have their own entry numbers. These resources supplement the entry that is being described.

Cross-references

Frequently, an entry will contain cross-references to other entries in the book (i.e., see entry 134). Cross-references can be found not only within the description of a specific resource, but also after groups of information sources. These cross-references point to resources that are described elsewhere in the book, but are particularly relevant to that group of information sources. For example, since the Indoor Air Quality Information Clearinghouse (IAQ INFO), which is described under Government Clearinghouses in Part One, Chapter 3, **Air**, is an outstanding source of information relevant to green building, there is a cross-reference to IAQ INFO following Government Clearinghouses in Part Two, Chapter 11, **Architecture**. Since resources in Part One, Chapter 1, **General**, apply to most other chapters in the book, they are generally not cross-referenced in this way.

Although these methods of cross-referencing provide a convenient way to discover resources that may be useful in locating information on a particular topic, they do not replicate the function of the indices.

Indices

Use the indices to find a particular name or title, or to search for information sources by keyword, for example, *pesticides, electromagnetic fields, global climate change,* or *socially responsible mutual funds.* The numbers in the indices refer to entry numbers, not page numbers.

Contact Information, Bibliographic Information, and Online Access Information

Contact Information

Government clearinghouses and organizations appear with their addresses, phone and fax numbers, e-mail addresses, and contact persons. All e-mail addresses are Internet e-mail addresses. The contact person listed is the person responsible for directing the activities of an organization, usually the group's executive director or president.

Bibliographic Information and Ordering Publications

Publications appear with their bibliographic information, such as the author, publisher, date of publication, number of pages, and price. The address and phone numbers of publishers—including publishers of diskettes and CD-ROMs—appear in **Appendix C, Publishers**. If an electronic resource is also available in print, the *Green Guide* reviews the print version and explains the best way in which to access the various electronic formats available.

Online Access Information

- ◆ **Database vendors:** For a fee, these services provide access to databases via modem. For contact information, see **Appendix B, Database Vendors**.
- ◆ **Bulletin boards:** Parameters for all bulletin boards are eight bits, no parity, one stop bit (8-N-1), unless otherwise indicated.
- ◆ **EcoNet:** For more information about EcoNet, see entry 58.
- ◆ **Internet:** Directions for accessing Internet sites are supplied largely from the perspective of those using browsing client software, such as gopher, or Mosaic for the World Wide Web. All listed ftp sites are anonymous.

Instructions for accessing or navigating online resources that are in *italic* refer to menu items that should be chosen (i.e., highlight the appropriate menu option and press enter), whereas instructions that are in **bold** refer to a command that must be typed exactly as it appears in the book, including spacing and punctuation. Those unfamiliar with online resources and related terminology should consult the essay that follows this section, "The Information Superhighway."

How to Get the Most Out of This Book

1. **Browse, browse, browse.** Even the best professional researchers must sometimes rely on "researcher's luck" to help them acquire the information they need. If you have ever used a card catalog to find a book in a library, then you have probably experienced "researcher's luck": You walk to the shelf to find the book you are looking for and your eye catches a different book that turns out to be even more appropriate than the book you originally wanted. While using the *Green Guide* to find information, browse, to increase *your* "researcher's luck."

2. **Many different types of information sources may be able to answer your question.** If you are looking for background information on a specific topic—for instance, you may initially think that you want a book, say, a reference book that you can use at your local library. But also keep in mind that a government clearinghouse may be able to supply the same information over the phone or by fax.

Or, if you have a computer and a modem, you may also be able to locate the information you need using an online resource.

3. **Use the entire book, not just the chapter most closely related to your topic of interest.** An organization, online resource, or publication in Part One, Chapter 1, **General**, can often lead you to the information related to energy just as easily as a similar resource in Part One, Chapter 5, **Energy**. You might also use other chapters in the book related to energy, for instance, Part One, Chapter 3, **Air**, because pollution associated with energy consumption is a major cause of air pollution, or Part Two, Chapter 11, **Architecture**, to find information on energy-efficient design.

4. **The *Sierra Club Green Guide* can lead you to any environmental information you may need, although sometimes the route may be indirect.** Although not every source of environmental information is to be found in this book, there are numerous resources included that steer users to other sources of information. Thus, by combining your creativity with the contents of the *Green Guide*, you will locate, efficiently and effectively, the environmental information you need. For example, if you want to contact an organization that works to protect the Hudson River, several resources can help you find an appropriate contact. You can track down a copy of the *River Conservation Directory* (see entry 480), or try to get a referral from organizations such as the River Network (see entry 469) or Save Our Streams (see entry 470) that provide support to river conservation groups. The information you need is available, and the *Green Guide* will help you find it.

The Information Superhighway

Though the popularized notion of the Information Superhighway, with its five hundred cable channels and interactive television, is more hype than reality, recent technological advances in digital telecommunications have revolutionized—and will continue to revolutionize—the ways in which people gather information. Through a modem, a device that allows computers to talk to each other over regular phone lines, and communications software, it is now possible to link your computer with other computers around the world—you can literally have a global electronic library at your desktop.

On your home or office computer, it is now possible to:

◆ send and receive electronic messages
◆ visit electronic conferences and subscribe to electronic mailing lists that cover thousands of specialized topics
◆ view and retrieve millions of documents such as organizational press releases and government reports
◆ receive electronic versions of magazines and newsletters as they are released, as well as search through the full text of back issues by keyword
◆ search card catalogs at the Library of Congress and thousands of other libraries around the world
◆ download free computer software
◆ receive technical support from computer software and hardware companies

A common first point of entry to the online world is through an electronic bulletin board system. A bulletin board, or BBS, usually serves a local audience and, in general, is free to all users. Most bulletin boards focus on a specific topic and limit user activity to exchanging messages with local users, participating in topical conferences, and viewing and downloading documents and software.

Also at the local level, many public and academic libraries provide free access to their computerized card catalogs via modem. The convenience of being able to search your public library's card catalog from your desk only hints at the power that awaits you once you have entered the online world.

Commercial online services like America Online, CompuServe, and EcoNet (see entry 58) are similar to bulletin boards, but they generally serve a national audience, provide information on a variety of topics, offer significantly more features, and charge a monthly fee (usually less than $10) in addition to an hourly rate for connection time. Users can check the weather, read the latest news from wire services, play games, join conferences on hundreds of special topics that are occasionally moderated by well-known individuals in a given field, or view and download thousands of files. Each online service offers a different mix of features, with some features available only from a particular service. On CompuServe, for example, it is possible to connect to a service that allows users to search more than eight hundred reference databases, such as *Books in Print* and the *Encyclopedia of Associations*. The variety of services offered continues to evolve rapidly.

The Internet, originally a U.S. Department of Defense computer network designed to help government scientists communicate and share information, is not a single service operated by one company, but rather a global network of computer networks. Like the telephone system, the Internet allows different parties all over the world to transmit information. In the case of the Internet, however, the transmitted information is not voices from phone to phone, but rather data (text, sound, graphic, video) from computer to computer. With more than twenty million users—government agencies, schools, companies, organizations, individuals—the

Internet serves as the foundation for the Information Superhighway of the future.

There are three basic Internet functions: e-mail; ftp (transferring of files); and telnet (logging on to other computers). Until the 1990s, using ftp or telnet involved arcane commands. Today navigating tools, like gopher, or Mosaic for the World Wide Web, automate these functions and make the Internet far easier to use. A gopher main menu or a World Wide Web home page at the Environmental Protection Agency (EPA) (see entry 56), for example, allows users, with a single keystroke or click of the mouse, to read daily EPA press releases, look for current job openings, or read EPA reports. Another stroke allows users to connect to other EPA Internet sites, such as the agency's national card catalog (see entry 60, EPA Online Library System) or a network of bulletin board systems that contain information on air pollution (see entry 245, Technology Transfer Network). The possibilities for finding information on any given topic are virtually endless.

Your company or school may have a direct connection, which is available for your use, to the Internet. Individuals without these affiliations can pay an Internet access provider for an account and can connect through a modem. The pricing structure is similar to commercial online services, though Internet providers are usually slightly more expensive. Different types of accounts allow different levels of access to the variety of services that are available on the Internet. Before choosing an account, educate yourself about the different types of Internet services and the different types of connections so you can select the options best suited to your needs.

At first the Internet can be confusing and intimidating. Don't let initial fears delay your eventual entry into the online world. Many books, written for users of all levels, explain basic concepts and provide how-to instructions. Although these books offer a good way to gain a basic understanding of what is available, there is no substitute for actually going online and exploring the terrain for yourself. Try out your modem—or borrow a friend's—to dial into a local bulletin board. Or join a commercial online service for a month—most have free trial memberships. If you have access to the Internet, by all means take advantage of the opportunity. The power of using a computer to exchange information with the global community, as millions of people have already seen, is a tool that those in search of environmental information should not be without.

Reference Sources That Will Help You Get Started Online

◆ *The Little ONLINE Book: A Gentle Introduction to Modems, Online Services, Electronic Bulletin Boards, and the Internet* (Alfred Glossbrenner. Peachpit Press, 1995) provides a thorough introduction to going online, including what to do once you are connected. *EcoLinking* (see entry 73) covers similar ground, focusing especially on environmental resources that exist online. Other books that are devoted to a specific topic, such as bulletin boards, commercial online services, or modems, are widely available.

◆ *The Whole Internet: User's Guide and Catalog* (2nd ed. O'Reilly and Associates, 1994), by Ed Krol, is an excellent Internet manual for those conducting research. Many local libraries and bookstores have this book and many other quality guides.

◆ InterNIC Information Services Reference Desk (619/455-4600; fax: 619/455-4640; e-mail: refdesk@is.internic.net), a clearinghouse for Internet information, supplies listings of Internet providers and recommends books and documents to assist organizations and individuals in getting connected to the Internet. For those who already have a connection, InterNIC Information Services' Internet sites provide beginners as well as advanced users with access to many valuable Internet tools and resources (gopher to **gopher.internic.net**; on the World Wide Web, the URL is **http://www.internic.net/**; then, at either site, choose *Information Services*).

◆ *Internet Web Text* (on the World Wide Web the URL is **http://www.rpi.edu/Internet/Guides/decemj/text.html**), written by John

December, is an excellent place for learning more about the Internet.

Glossary of Online Terms Used in This Book

baud rate The speed at which modems transmit data over phone lines. Baud rate is measured in bits per second (bps)—i.e., 2400bps, 4800bps, 9600bps. The higher the bits per second number the faster the transmission of data.

BITNET Links computers at universities and other educational facilities around the world.

bulletin board, or **BBS** An online arena through which computer users can share information and exchange files. Access is provided through a modem, and is usually free.

commercial online service A fee-based computer network that allows users to communicate and exchange information. America Online and CompuServe are two popular services.

communications software Computer software that enables computers to communicate and exchange information through modems.

conference An online discussion group through which users can exchange information via e-mail. Conferences are devoted to a specific topic and are free to join. On Usenet, conferences are called *newsgroups*. A conference in which messages are automatically distributed to the e-mail boxes of all conference participants is called a *mailing list*, or *list* for short. On BITNET, a mailing list is called a *listserv*.

database Refers to a storehouse of information available in an electronic format, usually online, but also on diskettes and CD-ROMs. Common databases include abstracts of literature and collections of statistical data.

database vendor A commercial online service that allows access to many different databases, particularly scientific, business, and legal abstracts, and the full text of periodicals. One popular database vendor is DIALOG.

download As a verb, it refers to copying a computer file from a computer network to your personal computer. As a noun, it is the file that has been retrieved.

e-mail, or **electronic mail** A file or message sent from one computer user to another over a network.

FidoNet A computer network that relays e-mail between thousands of local bulletin boards.

ftp Short for *file transfer protocol*, ftp is the Internet protocol for transferring files from one computer to another. An ftp site is a set of computer file directories (similar to DOS directories) where Internet users can "ftp" (download) files from the ftp site to their computers.

gopher A menu-driven system for finding and connecting to Internet resources. Gopher allows users to browse documents without using telnet or ftp commands. Users can choose items on a gopher menu to view files and other menus. To the user, all menu items have the same appearance, even though the files and menus exist on different computers all over the world.

home page A main menu on the World Wide Web.

html, or **hypertext markup language** The language in which hypertext documents are written.

http Short for *hypertext transfer protocol*, which allows users to access hypertext documents on the World Wide Web.

hypertext A hypertext document is an electronic document that contains connections to text in other locations. It is much like footnoting, in which the footnoted document appears instantly when, say, the mouse is clicked.

Internet The information infrastructure that allows communication between computer networks. Through the Internet, people can send e-mail all over the world, use ftp to download files, telnet to remote computers, or browse through gopher and the World Wide Web.

listserv A BITNET conference.

mailing list See *conference*.

menu A "place" online that allows users to choose different options. For example, the main menu on a bulletin board may allow users to *join a conference*, *send e-mail*, or *download a file*.

modem A computer hardware device that allows communication between computers through phone lines.

Mosaic A popular type of software that allows Internet users to browse the World Wide Web.

network Two or more computers that are linked so that they can share and exchange information.

online Using a computer and a modem to access information on another computer. Being online means being connected to another computer.

site A "place" on the Internet (e.g., gopher site, World Wide Web site, ftp site, telnet site).

system operator *Sysop* is a common abbreviation for system operator, the person responsible for maintaining a computer network.

telnet The Internet protocol that allows a user at one site to interact with a remote computer at another site. The verb *telnet* means to log in to a another computer.

URL, or **Uniform Resource Locator** A standard for specifying any item (e.g., ftp site, hypertext document, gopher main menu) on the Internet. Like a postal address, it allows Internet users to locate all different types of Internet resources.

Usenet A series of thousands of conferences, called *newsgroups,* that are widely used all over the world.

WAIS, or **Wide Area Information Search** Allows users to search for documents that have been indexed on the Internet.

World Wide Web, **WWW**, or **Web** A system that allows access to a wide array of Internet resources (e.g., anything available through gopher, through WAIS, at an ftp site, by telnet, on Usenet) through hypertext documents. A graphical WWW browser like Mosaic makes navigating the Internet relatively easy.

Environmental Issues

CHAPTER ONE

General

What This Chapter Covers

In contrast to the other chapters in Part One, each of which provides sources of information pertinent to a single issue such as **Air, Energy**, or **Water**, each entry in this chapter covers many environmental issues. (For example, *Environmental Profiles: A Global Guide to Projects and People* (see entry 76) covers air pollution, biological diversity, deforestation, energy, global warming, health, population, waste, and water quality.) Use this chapter to find general information about the environment or to supplement research on a specific issue covered in one of the other chapters in Part One.

Government Clearinghouses

1   **Global Change Research Information Office (GCRIO)**
United States Global Change Research Program
c/o Consortium for International Earth Sciences
Information Network
2250 Pierce Road
University Center, MI 48710

Phone: 517/797-2730. Fax: 517/797-2622.
E-mail: help@gcrio.org

Gerald Barton, Director

Internet: To connect to the GCRIO site, gopher to
gopher.gcrio.org.

The Global Change Research Information Office
(GCRIO) disseminates United States Global
Change Research Program (USGCRP) information on methods and technologies for mitigation
of and adaptation to global change. (USGCRP is
a federal interagency program that is working
to understand, assess, predict, and respond to
human-induced and natural processes of global
change—largely global climate change, but also
other global issues such as desertification, deforestation, land-use management, and preservation of ecosystems and biodiversity.) GCRIO,
operated by the Consortium for International
Earth Science Information Network (see entry
53) for USGCRP, informs users of the best ways
in which to obtain scientific and technical information—satellite data sets, results of scientific
research, information about applicable technologies, etc.—from U.S. government agencies, and
also refers users to appropriate government data
and information sources. Examples of questions
that GCRIO can answer are: What U.S. government agency has information on efficient home
energy technology? Where can I find salinity
and temperature data for shrimp aquaculture in
Nicaragua? Where can I find information about
replacements for CFC refrigerants? The GCRIO
Internet gopher has the full text of documents
on global change and USGCRP, and provides
access to other relevant Internet resources.

Though GCRIO was originally mandated to
serve foreign governments, businesses, institutions, and citizens, its services are also available
to users in the United States.

2   **Center for Environmental Research Information (CERI)**
Environmental Protection Agency
Office of Research and Development
26 West Martin Luther King Drive
Cincinnati, OH 45268

Phone (publications): 513/569-7562.
Fax (publications): 513/569-7566

Bulletin Board: To connect to the Environmental
Protection Agency's Research and Development
Electronic Bulletin Board System by modem, dial
513/569-7610. For technical support by phone,
call 513/569-7272.

The Center for Environmental Research Information (CERI) specializes in the referral and
distribution of technical documents from the
Environmental Protection Agency's (EPA) Office
of Research and Development (ORD). ORD and
its laboratories conduct research and development on various pollution issues, including
sources and control, transport and fate processes, health and ecological effects, measurement and monitoring, and risk assessment. CERI
helps produce technology transfer products such
as reports, design manuals, seminars, and training courses; it also distributes ORD documents,
such as *Landfill Leachate Clogging of Geotextile
(and Soil) Filters: Project Summary* and *Research
Plan for Monitoring Wetland Ecosystems*. ORD's
Research and Development Electronic Bulletin
Board houses a database that contains abstracts
of all ORD documents published since 1976; this
database can be used to order documents electronically. To contact EPA experts in environmental research and development, use ORD's
Technical Assistance Directory (see entry 91).

3   **EPA Public Information Center (PIC)**
Environmental Protection Agency
401 M Street, SW, Mail Code 3404
Washington, DC 20460

Phone: 202/260-7751. Fax: 202/260-6257

Internet: Many Environmental Protection
Agency (EPA) publications—as well as general
information about the agency—are available
on the EPA Internet sites (see entry 56).

An excellent source for free Environmental Protection Agency (EPA) publications—as well as

referrals to other sources of EPA information —the EPA Public Information Center (PIC) distributes brochures, posters, and publications appropriate for a general audience, although some technical documents are also available. Copies are free of charge but are only available while supplies last. If an item is not available at PIC, staff members will tell you how and where it can be acquired. While the EPA Personnel Locator (202/260-2090) provides phone numbers for EPA offices, PIC will guide callers to EPA's sources of public information, such as the National Center for Environmental Publications and Information (see entry 7), the Indoor Air Quality Information Clearinghouse (see entry 232), or the Office of Pesticide Programs. EPA phone numbers are also listed in the *EPA Headquarters Telephone Directory* (available from the Government Printing Office). For a complete guide to EPA clearinghouses and hotlines, dockets, libraries, and other public information contacts, use *Access EPA* (see entry 62); *Access Express*, a brief version of *Access EPA*, is available free of charge from PIC.

4   General Accounting Office (GAO)
Documents Distribution Center
P.O. Box 6015
Gaithersburg, MD 20884

Phone (orders): 202/512-6000. Fax (orders): 301/258-4066

The General Accounting Office (GAO) serves as the investigative arm of Congress. Since GAO's primary task is to independently audit the activities of federal agencies, it is an excellent source of information on the strengths and weaknesses of government programs; its testimony and reports are highly regarded. Environmentally relevant GAO titles include *Nuclear Energy: Consequences of Explosion of Hanford's Single-Shell Tanks Are Understated*; *Environmental Enforcement: Penalties May Not Recover Economic Benefits Gained by Violators*; and *Pesticides: Information Systems Improvements Essential for EPA's Reregistration Efforts*. The first copy of each GAO report is free; additional copies are $2 each. A list of GAO reports is compiled monthly and annually.

5   Government Printing Office (GPO)
Superintendent of Documents
P.O. Box 371954
Pittsburgh, PA 15250

Phone (orders): 202/783-3238. Fax (orders): 202/512-2250

Bulletin Board: GPO sponsors the Federal Bulletin Board. To connect by modem, dial 202/512-1387.

Internet: To access the Federal Bulletin Board (see above), telnet to **federal.bbs.gpo.gov**, port 3001.

The Government Printing Office (GPO) sells popular U.S. government documents. Although GPO sells far fewer environmental titles than the National Technical Information Service (see entry 8), GPO is more likely to have major reference publications and smaller booklets aimed toward a general audience. Titles available from GPO include *The United States Government Manual*; the *EPA National Publications Catalog* (see entry 7, National Center for Environmental Publications and Information); *Environmental Trends* (see entry 122, *Environmental Quality*); the *River Conservation Directory* (see entry 480); the *Guide to Federal Water Quality Programs and Information* (see entry 478); *A Citizen's Guide to Radon*; and *What You Can Do About Secondhand Smoke*. Most major environmental publications sold by GPO are described in GPO's *Catalog of Information Products on Environmental Science and Methods*. To order this free sixteen-page catalog, write to: Superintendent of Documents, Dept. SM, Washington, DC 20402. This and other GPO documents can be ordered from GPO's Federal Bulletin Board.

6   INFOTERRA/USA
United Nations Environment Programme
c/o Environmental Protection Agency
401 M Street, SW, Mail Code 3404
Washington, DC 20460

Phone: 202/260-5917. Fax: 202/260-3923

Emma J. McNamara, Manager

Internet: Some INFOTERRA information resides on the Central European Environmental Data Request Facility (CEDAR) site. Gopher to

pan.cedar.univie.ac.at; on the World Wide Web, the URL is **http://pan.cedar.univie.ac.at/**.

Most widely used by those in business and government, INFOTERRA/USA helps locate environmental information and provides referrals to free or low-cost scientific and technical information and resources to its users in the United States. INFOTERRA/USA is one of the more than 140 National Focal Points (NFPs) that make up the worldwide INFOTERRA network, sponsored by the United Nations Environment Programme (UNEP) (see entry 10). Each NFP has access to information sources covering more than one thousand topics relating to both social and physical environments, such as fermentation as an energy source; fish breeding in industrial waste; the mutagenic effects of pesticides; acid rain in Eastern Europe; and toxic-chemical legislation. INFOTERRA/USA can help locate relevant documents and bibliographies and can provide referrals to government agencies, international organizations, and environmental experts in all United Nations (UN) member countries. All services, with the exception of searches on some UN databases, are free to users. When requesting information, be as specific as possible in stating the type of information needed, what it will be used for, and the most appropriate format. INFOTERRA's database of international experts and archives of INFOTERRA's electronic discussion list are available on the Central European Environmental Data Request Facility (CEDAR) Internet site.

7   National Center for Environmental Publications and Information (NCEPI)
Environmental Protection Agency
P.O. Box 42419
Cincinnati, OH 45242

Fax: 513/489-8695

Bulletin Board: NCEPI's *EPA National Publications Catalog* is available on the EPA Online Library System (OLS) (see entry 60). At the main menu for OLS, type **NC** to search the catalog; or type **?NC** to find out how to contact primary distributors of the publications.

Internet: OLS (see "Bulletin Board," above) is available on the Internet.

The National Center for Environmental Publications and Information (NCEPI) is the national distribution center for EPA publications. More than four thousand current agency publications, documents, journals, and electronic information products are available through NCEPI. In 1994, NCEPI produced the premier edition of the annual *EPA National Publications Catalog* (available for a fee from the Government Printing Office or the National Technical Information Service), which identifies current agency publications and the source of availability. This catalog is searchable online on the EPA Online Library System (see entry 60). Members of the public can request one complimentary copy of NCEPI documents. Out-of-print or out-of-stock documents can usually be obtained, at cost, through the Government Printing Office (see entry 5) or the National Technical Information Service (see entry 8). Many EPA documents are also available at no charge from the EPA Public Information Center (see entry 3), an EPA hotline on a particular topic such as the Wetlands Information Hotline (see entry 461), or the sponsoring EPA office. Document requests should be made to NCEPI via mail or fax.

8   National Technical Information Service (NTIS)
Department of Commerce
5285 Port Royal Road
Springfield, VA 22161

Phone: 703/487-4650. Phone (subscriptions): 703/487-4630. Fax: 703/321-8547

Bulletin Board: NTIS maintains FedWorld (see entry 61).

The National Technical Information Service (NTIS) is the largest source of Environmental Protection Agency (EPA) and other federal documents pertaining to environmental issues. NTIS sells most scientific, technical, and engineering documents produced by U.S. government agencies. The *Government Reports Announcements & Index* (see entry 157)—known online as the *NTIS Bibliographic Database*—provides abstracts of government documents and serves as the comprehensive NTIS publications catalog. The abstracts in the database are packaged in a variety of ways, including a current awareness service on specific topics and a comprehensive catalog of EPA publications sold by NTIS, the *EPA Publications Bibliography* (see entry 157, *Government Reports Announcements & Index*). Two other specialized catalogs, both free, will be of particular interest to those in the environmental field: *NTIS Highlights: Environment*, which describes NTIS best-sellers, and *U.S. Government Environmental Datafiles and Software*. One particularly noteworthy product is a CD-ROM that includes the full text of all environmental regulations (Titles 29, 40, and 49); it is fully cross-referenced and updated quarterly. NTIS offers many useful services such as rush delivery and electronic ordering; request the *Catalog of Products and Services* for more information. Note that single copies of some EPA documents sold through NTIS are available to the public at no charge from the National Center for Environmental Publications and Information (see entry 7).

9 Small Business Ombudsman Hotline

Environmental Protection Agency
401 M Street, SW, Mail Code 1230-C
Washington, DC 20460

Phone: 800/368-5888; 703/305-5938. TDD: 703/305-6824. Fax: 703/305-6462

Karen V. Brown, Ombudsman

The Small Business Ombudsman Hotline works in a variety of ways to facilitate communications between the small business community and the Environmental Protection Agency (EPA). The hotline works with EPA personnel to increase their understanding of small business; investigates and resolves disputes between businesses and the EPA; and provides a convenient way for small businesses to get in touch with the EPA. Most callers—numbering more than a thousand each month—seek information that will enable them to comply with regulations. To answer these questions, the ombudsman's office holds training seminars, supplies referrals to other EPA contacts, and distributes information packets. Among the documents that the hotline can send are a summary of laws that the EPA administers, reprints of the *Federal Register*, and EPA documents such as *Safer Disposal for Solid Waste: The Federal Regulations for Landfills* and *Guidance for Preventing Asbestos Disease Among Auto Mechanics*. All products and services are free and confidential. Specialists are available on a

wide range of topics, including air issues, toxic substances and hazardous materials, water pollution, and asbestos. Both this hotline and the Toxic Substances Control Act Assistance Information Service (see entry 364) can supply information on asbestos.

10 United Nations Environment Programme (UNEP)

Regional Office for North America
UNDC Two Building, Room 0803
Two United Nations Plaza
New York, NY 10017

Phone: 212/963-8139. Fax: 212/963-7341

Internet: UNEP has space on the United Nations Development Programme gopher site. To connect, gopher to **gopher.undp.org**, choose *Other United Nations & Related Gophers*, then *United Nations Environment Programme (UNEP)*.

The United Nations Environment Programme (UNEP) is the division of the United Nations (UN) that specializes in environmental programs. Major UNEP programs include INFOTERRA (see entry 6), the Global Environment Monitoring System (GEMS), and the International Register of Potentially Toxic Chemicals (IRPTC). The New York UNEP office can provide UNEP's publications catalog, *Environment in Print*, but most of the actual publications must be ordered from UNEP's headquarters in Nairobi, Kenya. Many major UNEP-sponsored publications (e.g., *Environmental Data Report* [see entry 120], *World Resources* [see entry 134], *The World Environment 1972–1992* [see entry 133]) are, however, also available from other publishers. Many UN publications can be ordered from the UN publications department in New York City; call 800/253-9646 for a catalog. On the Internet, UNEP press releases, speeches, background information, databases, and an electronic version of *Environment in Print* are available from the United Nations Development Programme gopher.

11 World Bank Public Information Center (PIC)

1776 G Street, NW, Room GB1–300
Washington, DC 20433

Phone: 202/458-5454. Fax: 202/522-1500.
E-mail: pic@worldbank.org

Internet: The World Bank PIC has space on the World Bank Internet sites. To connect, gopher to **gopher.worldbank.org**; on the World Wide Web, the URL is **http://www.worldbank.org/**. Then, at either site, choose *Public Information Center.*

All environmental information that the World Bank sells to the public is available from the World Bank Public Information Center (PIC). On the Internet, the World Bank's PIC site provides bibliographic and ordering information for many environmental documents (e.g., *Environmental Assessments and Analyses, National Environmental Action Plans*) and includes the full text of others *(Environmental Data Sheets).*

For third-party criticism of international development bank policies and programs from an environmental viewpoint, read Bruce Rich's controversial *Mortgaging the Earth: The World Bank, Environmental Impoverishment, and the Crisis of Development* (Beacon Press, 1994) or consult the April/May 1994 issue (Volume 2, Number 6) of *The Green Disk* (see entry 176), which includes an extensive bibliography and background information on this topic. Other third-party information sources critical of the environmental policies and programs of international development banks include *BankCheck Quarterly* (published by International Rivers Network [see entry 467], $25 per year for individuals) and the Bank Information Center (202/466–8191), which monitors multilateral development bank activities and policies that have a negative impact on the environment. The Bank Information Center maintains a calendar of events for the "50 Years Is Enough" campaign against the World Bank and also offers *A Citizen's Guide to World Bank Environmental Assessment Procedures* and *A Citizen's Guide to the World Bank's New Information Disclosure Policy* free of charge.

Organizations

There are many different places to find out about environmental organizations. For descriptions of environmental organizations all over the world, including the United States, refer to *Environmental Profiles: A Global Guide to Projects and People* (see entry 76) or the *World Directory of Environmental Organizations* (see entry 95).

The *Conservation Directory* (see entry 65) and *GreenWorld's Almanac & Directory of Environmental Organizations* (see entry 83) provide descriptions of North American environmental organizations. Descriptions of only the largest U.S. organizations can be found in *The Nature Directory: A Guide to Environmental Organizations* (see entry 89) and *Your Resource Guide to Environmental Organizations* (see entry 90). For regional U.S. coverage, consult the *Harbinger File* (see entry 86) and the *Rocky Mountain Environmental Directory* (see entry 87). To find the names, addresses, and phone numbers of local environmental groups, refer to the *Directory of Environmental Organizations* (see entry 69) or *Who is Who in Service to the Earth* (see entry 93).

12 Canadian Environmental Network (CEN)
National Office
P. O. Box 1289, Station B
Ottawa, Ontario K1P 5R3 Canada

Phone: 613/563-2078. Fax: 613/563-7236.
E-mail: cen@web.apc.org

Eva Schacherl, Executive Director

The Canadian Environmental Network (CEN) provides a forum through which Canadian public-interest environmental organizations can share information and expertise. In addition to its national office, CEN maintains eleven regional offices and organizes several caucuses on specific issues, such as oceans and waste avoidance. The national office can provide referrals and answer questions about Canadian organizations and public policy. CEN publishes a monthly newsletter and *The Green List: A Guide to Canadian Environmental Organizations*, a bilingual directory of more than two thousand Canadian grassroots environmental organizations, associations, and agencies.

13 Center for Environmental Citizenship (CEC)
1400 16th Street, NW, Box 24
Washington, DC 20036

Phone: 202/939-3316. Fax: 202/797-6646.
E-mail: campaign@cec.org

Lista Lincoln, Executive Director

Internet: CEC cosponsors Campus EarthNet, a resource on the Brown Is Green World Wide Web site at Brown University. The URL for Campus EarthNet is **http://www.envstudies.brown.edu/environ/earthnet/homepage.html**.

An excellent resource for student activists, the Center for Environmental Citizenship (CEC) provides students with the training and information necessary to make them leaders in the environmental movement—especially in the political process. One CEC project, Campus Green Vote, trains students to conduct voter registration and education campaigns and offers day- and week-long training sessions on organizing, honing legislative skills, and working with the media. Another project, the Shadow Congress Information Network, provides semiweekly e-mail updates of activities in congressional subcommittees; this allows students and activists to respond quickly at key moments in the legislative process. Campus EarthNet, a World Wide Web site on the Internet, is a joint project of CEC and the Brown Is Green program at Brown University. It includes detailed case studies of campus environmental programs and "how-to" information for student activists, as well as a directory of student environmental groups, recycling and environmental coordinators, and environmental studies directors from hundreds of campuses. CEC, which also publishes the *Student Environmental Organizing Guide*, is an excellent resource for student activists.

14   Center for Environmental Information (CEI)
50 West Main Street
Rochester, NY 14614

Phone: 716/262-2870. Fax: 716/262-4156

William Wagner, Executive Director

A nonprofit organization not affiliated with any state or national group or agency, the Center for Environmental Information (CEI) was established in 1974 to collect and disseminate information on all environmental topics. While much of CEI's work is at the local and state levels, the organization has the capacity to serve a national audience. CEI's library includes books and periodicals on all environmental issues, though there is a particular focus on acid rain and global climate change. CEI responds to thousands of requests each year from students and others who need environmental information. These requests—

whether made in person, through the mail, or on the phone—are answered directly by CEI staffers or referred to more appropriate sources. Staff members can provide bibliographies and photocopies of articles at cost, plus postage. CEI publishes the *Global Climate Change Digest: A Guide to Current Information on Greenhouse Gases and Ozone Depletion* (see entry 261) as well as a directory of environmental agencies and organizations in the Rochester, N.Y., area. The center also sponsors regional seminars and national conferences on atmospheric issues. Though services have been scaled back in recent years, CEI is still a good place for laypeople to begin an environmental information search.

15   Center for Policy Alternatives (CPA)
1875 Connecticut Avenue, NW, Suite 710
Washington, DC 20009

Phone: 202/387-6030. Fax: 202/986-2539.
E-mail: cfpa@capaccess.org

Linda Tarr-Whelan, President

The Center for Policy Alternatives (CPA) promotes creative policy leadership at the state level on issues related to public capital, governance, sustainable development, and women's economic justice. The organization coordinates networks of progressive state leaders; sponsors conferences; and provides policy research, model legislation, and other publications. CPA's sustainable development program produces publications on agriculture (*Database of State Alternative Agriculture Laws* [see entry 207]); energy and transportation (*Energywise Options for State and Local Governments* [see entry 332, *The Renewable Source*]); environmental justice (*Environmental Justice: Annotated Bibliography* [see entry 354]); solid waste (*Model Solid Waste Management Bidding Reform Act*); and other issues (*An Ounce of Toxic Pollution Prevention, Unfunded Mandates: Clarifying the Debate*). CPA also publishes *Guidelines for State Level Sustainable Development* and the annual *Policy Alternatives on the Environment: A State Report*.

16 Co-op America

1612 K Street, NW, Suite 600
Washington, DC 20006

Phone: 202/872-5307. Fax: 202/331-8166

Alisa Gravitz, Executive Director

Co-op America actively works to build a sustainable economy based on peace, justice, cooperation, and the health of the environment. This nonprofit believes that change can be achieved if enough consumers vote with their dollars. Current interests involve building green businesses, fighting corporate irresponsibility, empowering consumers and investors, and building sustainable communities. Co-op America provides assistance to businesses through the Co-op America Business Network (CABN). Individual and business memberships include a subscription to *Co-op America Quarterly*, an outstanding magazine that features articles on sustainability issues, news updates on businesses and products, and status reports on current consumer boycotts. Each issue is devoted to a particular theme—e.g., confronting environmental racism; exploring the possibilities for establishing sustainable communities; exposing the hidden agenda of the wise-use movement—and includes extensive resource lists. Other Co-op America publications include the *Socially Responsible Financial Planning Handbook* (see entry 586) and *Co-op America's National Green Pages: The Yellow Pages for People and the Planet* (see entry 593), a directory of businesses that are members of CABN. Co-op America also sells socially responsible consumer products, and, through its business partners, provides socially responsible financial planning (i.e., credit cards, insurance, and investment) and consumer (i.e., travel and long-distance) services.

17 CONCERN

1794 Columbia Road, NW
Washington, DC 20009

Phone: 202/328-8160. Fax: 202/387-3378.
E-mail: concern@igc.apc.org

Susan Boyd, Executive Director

CONCERN strives to promote environmental literacy and action by training individuals to be effective community advocates for policies and programs that improve environmental quality and public health. CONCERN's primary activity is the publication and distribution of widely praised, in-depth reports, each of which clearly analyzes a different environmental issue—drinking water; farmland; global warming and energy issues; household waste; pesticides; solid and hazardous waste—and contains suggestions for individual and group action, as well as a select list of relevant local and national organizations, directories, books, and reports. Each report costs $4 and averages thirty pages in length. CONCERN also provides personalized assistance to local environmental groups that need additional help in implementing effective programs. In addition, CONCERN maintains the *Building Sustainable Communities Database*, which contains information on more than one thousand projects and publications on community sustainability. CONCERN staff will conduct regional or subject searches of the database upon request.

18 Earth Day USA

P.O. Box 470
Peterborough, NH 03458

Phone: 603/924-7720. Fax: 603/924-7855

Bruce Anderson, President

Earth Day USA facilitates hundreds of regional and local Earth Day organizing activities and promotes the annual public observance of Earth Day on April 22nd. Educators and organizers can request information packets and may purchase the brief *Earth Day Organizer's Manual* ($10) and the bimonthly *Earth Day USA News* ($10 per year). The organization also maintains a hotline so that callers can find out how they can get involved in the Earth Day movement (900/933-7999; $1 per minute, one-minute minimum). All hotline proceeds benefit the organization and local Earth Day organizers across the country. For Earth Day organizers looking for contacts and assistance, or for those who want to sponsor their own Earth Day program, Earth Day USA is the place to call.

19 Earth Island Institute (EII)
300 Broadway, Suite 28
San Francisco, CA 94133

Phone: 415/788-3666. Fax: 415/788-7324.
E-mail: earthisland@igc.apc.org

John Knox and Dave Phillips, Executive Directors

The Earth Island Institute (EII) provides technical, financial, communications, and networking support for twenty-eight grassroots environmental projects. EII was founded by David R. Brower—the first executive director of Sierra Club (see entry 45) and founder of both Friends of the Earth (see entry 29) and the League of Conservation Voters (see entry 37)—in order to develop innovative projects for the conservation, preservation, and restoration of the global environment. Many of the projects link activists and lead coalitions of organizations in environmental advocacy campaigns. EII projects focus especially on endangered species and threatened ecosystems—e.g., the International Marine Mammal Project, the Preserve Appalachian Wilderness Network (PAW Net), the Sea Turtle Restoration Project—but the organization supports efforts on all global issues, especially those that bridge the gap between the environment and other concerns such as human rights, economic development in the Third World, economic conversion from militarization to peaceful production, and poverty in inner-city communities. Some past EII projects—the International Rivers Network (see entry 467), the Rainforest Action Network (see entry 276), the Arctic to Amazonia Alliance (802/765–4337)—have become independent nonprofit organizations; EII continues to invite proposals for new projects. Its outstanding quarterly magazine, the *Earth Island Journal* (see entry 165), serves as a forum for public outreach for the various projects. EII is on the leading edge of many environmental issues and is an excellent medium for networking within the grassroots community.

20 Earth Share
3400 International Drive, NW, Suite 2K
Washington, DC 20008

Phone: 800/875-3863; 202/537-7100.
Fax: 202/537-7101

Kalman Stein, President and Executive Director

Earth Share is a coalition of forty-one nonprofit environmental organizations that enables charitable giving through payroll deduction programs. Member organizations include well-known national advocacy organizations such as American Rivers (see entry 462), the Citizen's Clearinghouse for Hazardous Waste (see entry 423), Environmental Defense Fund (see entry 24), National Wildlife Federation (see entry 39), The Nature Conservancy (see entry 275), Pesticide Action Network (see entry 193), and the Union of Concerned Scientists (see entry 47). Millions of employees of companies (e.g., Time Warner, Nissan, Turner Broadcasting, Levi Strauss), universities (e.g., Southern Methodist University, Tufts University), and state governments (e.g., Maine, Massachusetts) contributed almost $10 million to Earth Share in 1993. Employees can contribute either directly to Earth Share—which then redistributes the funds to the member organizations—or to one of Earth Share's member organizations. Contact Earth Share to place an environmental option on an employer's payroll deduction program.

21 Ecoline
Together Foundation for Global Unity
130 South Willard Street
Burlington, VT 05401

Phone: 802/862-2030

The Ecoline hotline, a project of the Together Foundation for Global Unity, a nonprofit organization that operates the TogetherNet (see entry 59) computer network, ceased to exist in the fall of 1994. However, the Ecoline database, which contains basic contact information for sixty thousand individuals, projects, and organizations working at the grassroots level for environmental and social change, is still available on TogetherNet. The database, primarily an expanded version of *Who is Who in Service to the Earth* (see entry 93), can be searched by name as well as keyword so users can identify, for example, all of the forestry organizations in the Pacific Northwest.

22 Environmental Action (EA)
6930 Carroll Avenue, Suite 600
Takoma Park, MD 20912

Phone: 301/891-1100. Fax: 301/891-2218.
E-mail: eaf@igc.apc.org

Margaret Morgan-Hubbard, Executive Director

Founded by the organizers of the first Earth Day, Environmental Action (EA) provides grassroots movements with a strong national voice on energy, pollution, and environmental justice issues. EA is a leader in organizing national coalitions and campaigns both on pollution prevention (the Solid Waste Alternatives Project; the Toxics Project) and sustainable-energy issues (the Energy Conservation Coalition). EA works directly to shape public policy and provides educational, legal, technical, and organizing assistance to grassroots environmental organizations. EA publishes two excellent periodicals, *Environmental Action* magazine (see entry 171) and *Wastelines*, as well as policy reports, activist handbooks, action papers, fact packets (clippings of articles on topics such as bottle bills and styrofoam), fact sheets, and bibliographies. The organization accepts no corporate contributions.

23 Environmental and Energy Study Institute (EESI)
122 C Street, NW, Suite 700
Washington, DC 20001

Phone: 202/628-1400. Fax: 202/628-1825.
E-mail: eesi@igc.apc.org

Ken Murphy, Executive Director

As a nonpartisan, nonprofit public policy research, analysis, and education organization, the Environmental and Energy Study Institute (EESI) serves as both catalyst and consensus builder for federal legislation. The institute was established in 1984 by the leaders of Environmental and Energy Study Conference (EESC), the largest U.S. congressional caucus, to promote informed national debate on environmental and energy issues and to generate innovative public policy responses. EESI currently has programs in

energy, global climate change, international cooperation on the environment, and water. EESI provides information and technical assistance to members of Congress, though the organization also sponsors and organizes educational briefings, workshops, and conferences. EESI's highly regarded and widely read publications include the annual *Briefing Book on Environmental and Energy Legislation* (see entry 115); the essential *Weekly Bulletin*, which provides summaries of recent and expected congressional action on proposed legislation; *Floor Briefs*, which addresses major legislation as it reaches the Senate and House floors and alerts members of Congress about possible amendments; and special reports that analyze emerging issues and provide periodic updates on major legislation. EESI is an excellent resource for information on current federal legislation affecting environmental issues.

24 Environmental Defense Fund (EDF)
257 Park Avenue South
New York, NY 10010

Phone: 212/505-2100. Phone (membership line): 212/505-2383. Fax: 212/505-2375.
E-mail: members@edf.org

Fred D. Krupp, Executive Director

A leader in developing market-based approaches to protecting the environment, the Environmental Defense Fund (EDF) links science, economics, and law to create innovative, economically viable solutions to environmental problems. In the 1980s, EDF gained notoriety and stirred controversy by forming partnerships with companies, particularly General Motors and McDonalds, to find market-oriented strategies for dealing with issues like automobile pollution and excessive and environmentally harmful fast-food packaging. Since adopting this strategy of cooperation rather than confrontation, EDF has grown steadily and now has more than 250,000 members and more than fifty full-time scientists, engineers, lawyers, and economists working in its six offices around the nation. During the current decade, EDF is seeking to control global warming; preserve wetlands; halt ozone depletion; achieve 50 percent recycling by the year 2000; stop acid rain; guarantee clean water for the future; clean up toxic waste; safeguard wildlife and habitats; and save tropical rainforests. In addition to numerous books, reports, and fact sheets, EDF produces the *EDF Letter*, an eight-page monthly newsletter on its current activities.

25 Environmental Law Alliance Worldwide (E-LAW)

U.S. Office
1877 Garden Avenue
Eugene, OR 97403

Phone: 503/687-8454. Fax: 503/687-0535.
E-mail: elaw.usoffice@conf.igc.apc.org

Bern Johnson, Executive Director

EcoNet: E-LAW maintains the *elaw.public.interest* conference.

The Environmental Law Alliance Worldwide (E-LAW) is the United States branch of an international network of public-interest environmental attorneys who share information with each other. Although E-LAW only provides direct assistance to lawyers in countries outside of the United States, the U.S. office plays a critical role in the network by providing U.S. legal and scientific databases and resources that are unavailable in other countries. E-LAW will either answer questions with information it has in the office or make referrals to attorneys and scientists who will offer assistance free of charge. For example, when advocates in Peru were drafting a new constitution and requested model language that would guarantee strong environmental protection, E-LAW advocates in Sri Lanka, Ecuador, Japan, and the United States provided provisions from the constitutions of their own (and other) countries. The U.S. E-LAW office also helps U.S. public-interest lawyers learn of model environmental-protection approaches from other nations. Most E-LAW communication is performed electronically, through computer networks affiliated with the Association for Progressive Communications (see entry 58, EcoNet). For more information on E-LAW, contact its U.S. office or see the *elaw.public.interest* conference on EcoNet (see entry 58).

26 Environmental Law Institute (ELI)

1616 P Street, NW, Suite 200
Washington, DC 20036

Phone: 202/328-5150. Fax: 202/328-5002

J. William Futrell, President

The Environmental Law Institute (ELI), a leading resource for environmental law information, was created in 1969 by the environmental community to serve as an independent research and education center involved in developing national and international environmental laws and policies. Although ELI provides information to the general public, its research and services are geared toward professionals (lawyers, economists, scientists, and environmentalists) and businesses, citizens groups, universities, and government agencies. ELI does no advocacy work; it neither litigates cases nor lobbies Congress or government agencies. Instead, it conducts professional education courses, administers numerous educational outreach programs, organizes conferences on environmental law topics, consults with government agencies and organizations on the development of environmental legislation, and produces a library of highly regarded and widely used publications. Some of ELI's more prominent publications include the *Practical Guide to Environmental Management*, *Law of Environmental Protection*, the *Environmental Law Deskbook*, and the *Superfund Deskbook*. The institute also publishes several periodicals: *Environmental Law Reporter* (see entry 121), an authoritative update service on environmental laws, cases, and news; *The Environmental Forum*, a policy journal with in-depth analysis of environmental issues; and the *National Wetlands Newsletter*, which focuses on science, management, and policy.

27 Environmental Support Center (ESC)

1825 Connecticut Avenue, NW, Suite 220
Washington, DC 20009

Phone: 202/328-7813. Fax: 202/265-9419.
E-mail: envsc@igc.apc.org

James W. Abernathy, Executive Director

The Environmental Support Center (ESC) works to meet the managerial and administrative needs of regional, state, and local grassroots organizations working on environmental issues. It gives preference to organizations with budgets of less than $250,000 or to organizations that serve people of color and/or low-income constituents (ESC does not assist individuals or international, governmental, or national organizations or their local chapters). ESC provides training and technical assistance—including subsidies for a portion of the costs—for organizational development, including fundraising, organizing, financial management, board development, communications, coalition building, planning, marketing and public relations, leadership development, and computer applications. The organization also seeks equipment donations—especially computer equipment and software—for distribution to local environmental groups. ESC promotes the creation of environmental federations that use workplace solicitation as a fundraising tool and assists these federations in their relationships with EarthShare (see entry 20), a fundraising federation for national organizations. All grassroots groups that meet ESC's guidelines should take advantage of its outstanding services.

28   Environmental Working Group (EWG)
1718 Connecticut Avenue, NW, Suite 600
Washington, DC 20009

Phone: 202/667-6982. Fax: 202/232-2592.
E-mail: ewg@igc.apc.org

Ken Cook, President

The Environmental Working Group (EWG) issues reports on national environmental policy issues. Prior to July 1993, this nonprofit research organization was the Policy Studies Program of the Center for Resource Economics/Island Press. Currently, EWG produces reports in two major areas: environmental aspects of U.S. agriculture policy (e.g., *Pesticides in Children's Food*; *Subsidizing Soil Loss: USDA's Lax Enforcement of Federal Conservation Compliance Policy*), and federal budget and appropriations policy related to the environment (e.g., *Annual Review of the U.S. Environmental Protection Agency: Program Evaluation, Budget Analysis, and Funding Recommendations*). In addition, EWG operates the Clearinghouse on Environmental Advocacy and Research (CLEAR), which serves as a resource and information center for environmental groups that are

fighting anti-environment wise-use campaigns. CLEAR collects and provides background information on local wise-use groups and their leadership, and helps environmental groups develop strategies for using the media and organizing campaigns to combat wise-use activists.

29   Friends of the Earth—United States (FOE-US)
218 D Street, SE
Washington, DC 20003

Phone: 202/544-2600. Fax: 202/543-4710.
E-mail: foedc@igc.apc.org

Jane Perkins, President

The U.S. affiliate of Friends of the Earth International (FOE), Friends of the Earth—United States (FOE-US) is one of fifty-two FOE affiliates around the globe. FOE is one of the largest global networks of grassroots activists, focusing on such international issues as global warming, depletion of the ozone layer, and destruction of the world's rainforests. FOE-US is one of the more radical of the large environmental advocacy organizations that are headquartered in Washington, D.C.; the organization works on national issues from nuclear weapons production to coastal erosion and is a leader in holding corporations accountable for the environmental impact of their practices. Past FOE-US reports include *Earth Budget: Making Our Tax Dollars Work for the Environment* (a critique of federal environmental spending), and *Hold the Applause!* (an investigative report of DuPont's environmental record). Periodicals include the monthly *Friends of the Earth* newsmagazine and several newsletters: *Atmosphere*, *Groundwater News*, and *Community Plume*.

30   Global Action and Information Network (GAIN)
740 Front Street, Suite 355
Santa Cruz, CA 95060

Phone: 408/457-0130. Fax: 408/457-0133.
E-mail: info@gain.org

Bill Leland, Executive Director

EcoNet: GAIN maintains several conferences, including *gain.alerts*, *gain.ecosystem*, *gain.justice*, *gain.infobase*, *gain.resources*, and *gain.toxics*.

Internet: GAIN makes many of its postings available by e-mail. To receive a catalog of items that can be received automatically by e-mail, send a message to **almanac@gain.org** with the words **send EnvIssues catalog** in the body of the message.

The Global Action and Information Network (GAIN) is an outstanding, must-use resource for anyone taking action on environmental and sustainability issues. GAIN provides background data, analysis, and up-to-date status reports on current or past environmental legislation, as well as action alerts. Though the organization's current focus is on helping activists stay on top of pending federal legislation, GAIN also serves as a clearinghouse for other information useful for environmental activists (e.g., success stories and ideas, referrals to other resources). GAIN gathers the most relevant materials from a wide range of sources and compiles it in concise, easy-to-use formats. Network membership includes subscriptions to GAIN's periodicals, both of which are published three times a year: *Gaining Ground* magazine, and *The GAIN Packet*, a comprehensive update of major environmental legislation tracked by GAIN. GAIN posts much of its information on EcoNet (see entry 58) and America Online, as well as its own e-mail site on the Internet.

GAIN has plans for other projects, including a database of case studies of successful communities and a comprehensive national directory of environmental organizations that will consist of *The Harbinger File* (see entry 86), the *Rocky Mountain Environmental Directory* (see entry 87), and other regional directories.

31 Global Tomorrow Coalition (GTC)

1325 G Street, NW, Suite 1010
Washington, DC 20005

Phone: 202/628-4016. Fax: 202/628-4018

Donald R. Lesh, President

The Global Tomorrow Coalition (GTC) strives to make sustainable development the cornerstone of decision making in the United States by the year 2000. This coalition of more than one hundred organizations serves as a nonpartisan forum for environmental, educational, corporate, and political leaders seeking to build consensus on practical goals and strategies concerning seemingly disparate issues: trade, jobs, the economy, poverty, social equity, population growth, biological diversity, water and waste management, air quality, and global warming. GTC has both participating members who can vote in elections (e.g., the Environmental Defense Fund [see entry 24], Rodale Press [see entry 555], Turner Broadcasting System) and Business Alliance Partners that GTC feels respect its goals (e.g., BankAmerica, Church & Dwight Company, Dow Chemical, Waste Management). GTC trains local leaders to develop and monitor sustainable-development projects; organizes a national conference each year called GLOBESCOPE; and sponsors an ongoing series of discussions, called "21st Century Dialogues," between key business and environmental leaders. The organization also coordinates other educational and networking activities, such as the *Race to Save the Planet*, a well-received ten-part series that aired on PBS in 1990, and the *Global Ecology Handbook* (Beacon Press, 1990), a companion volume to that series.

32 Greenpeace

1436 U Street, NW
Washington, DC 20009

Phone (switchboard): 202/462-1177.
Phone (public information): 202/319-2444.
Fax: 202/462-4507

Barbara Dudley, Executive Director

EcoNet: For a searchable version of Greenpeace's press releases, choose *Online Databases*, then *News Services*, then *Greenpeace Press Releases*. These press releases are also available in the *gp.press* conference.

Bulletin Board: Greenpeace maintains the Environet Bulletin Board System. To connect at 2400 baud, dial 415/512-9108. To connect at 14,400 baud, dial 415/512-9120.

Internet: Greenpeace International maintains a site on the Internet. Gopher to **gopher.greenpeace.org**; on the World Wide Web, the URL is **http://www.greenpeace.org/**.

Greenpeace seeks to draw attention to environmental destruction in an effort to force the world to confront environmental problems and consider environmental solutions. Greenpeace activists work to prevent nuclear war; preserve forests and rainforests; stop the threat of global warming and ozone depletion; reduce toxic pollution; ban the international trade in toxic waste; and halt the slaughter of whales, dolphins, seals, and other endangered animals. Greenpeace believes that to stop environmental atrocities, direct, nonviolent action must be taken. In the past, Greenpeace members have used high-speed inflatable rafts to interfere with whalers; scaled factory smokestacks to hang banners; and plugged the discharge pipes of chemical polluters. Information about environmental issues and the organization's campaigns is communicated to the public through reports (e.g., *Breast Cancer and the Environment: The Chlorine Connection*; *Climate Change and the Insurance Industry: Solidarity Among the Risk Community?*), periodicals (e.g., *Toxic Trade Update* [see entry 453]), videotapes (e.g., *Why Our Landfills Leak*), and books (e.g., *The Greenpeace Guide to Anti-Environmental Organizations* [see entry 82]), as well as fact sheets, press releases, and a catalog of news clippings. All publications are available from the organization's public information coordinator, including a biannual publications catalog ($2).

33   The Greens/Green Party USA

P.O. Box 30208
Kansas City, MO 64112

Phone: 816/931-9366. Fax: 816/931-0014.
E-mail: gpusa@igc.apc.org

Susan Whitmore, Coordinator

Internet: The Greens/Green Party USA posts information on GreenGopher, which is available on EcoGopher (see entry 54, EcoSystems). Choose *The Library*, then *General*, then *GreenGopher, A Greens Resource*.

The Greens/Green Party USA is a grassroots national political party committed to the following values: ecological wisdom, social justice, grassroots democracy, nonviolence, decentralization, community-based economics, feminism, a respect for diversity, personal and global responsibility, and a focus on the future. The Kansas City office can provide lists of Green groups, individuals who have contacted the clearing-

house, organization and media contacts, and Green contacts working on particular issues of focus, such as toxics, native solidarity, and alternative energy. This office also serves as the first point of contact for those interested in the party, and provides support for its 450 local groups in 46 states. In addition, it offers do-it-yourself kits for starting a Green local and three quarterly Greens publications: *Green Politics*, an organizational newsletter; *Groundwork*, a newsmagazine covering social and environmental justice; and *Synthesis/Regeneration*, which contains essays and analysis. On the Internet, information about the Greens, including their party platform and a directory of local groups, is available on the GreenGopher.

34   INFORM

120 Wall Street
New York, NY 10005

Phone: 212/361-2400. Fax: 212/361-2412.
E-mail: inform@igc.apc.org

Joanna Underwood, President

INFORM, known for its high-quality reports on a range of environmental issues, is a nonprofit research organization that currently focuses on pollution prevention. Though INFORM staffers are currently working on air-quality and energy issues (past focus issues have included land and water conservation), much of the organization's current research centers around municipal solid waste and chemical hazards prevention. INFORM's publications analyze policy and case studies (*Paving the Way to Natural Gas Vehicles*; *Germany, Garbage, and the Green Dot: Challenging the Throwaway Society*; *Environmental Dividends: Cutting More Chemical Wastes*) or serve as planning guides for communities (*Preventing Industrial Toxic Hazards: A Guide for Communities* [see entry 445]; *Making Less Garbage: A Planning Guide for Communities*), though the group also publishes *Tackling Toxics in Everyday Products: A Directory of Organizations* (see entry 380) and offers several free fact sheets. A quarterly newsletter that announces new INFORM publications is included with membership.

35 Institute for Conservation Leadership
2000 P Street, NW, Suite 413
Washington, DC 20036

Phone: 202/466-3330. Fax: 202/659-3897

Michele Frome, Executive Director

The Institute for Conservation Leadership trains and empowers volunteer conservation leaders and helps build volunteer institutions that protect and preserve the environment. The institute offers a broad range of training and other custom-designed services in many areas of organizational development, including board development, fundraising, strategic planning, leadership training, conflict management, organizational structure, time management, executive director training, and meeting facilitation. It has served more than two hundred local (Albany County Conservation Alliance), state (Environmental Council of Rhode Island), regional (Chesapeake Bay Foundation) and national (World Wildlife Fund) conservation organizations since 1988.

36 The Izaak Walton League of America (IWLA)
National Office
707 Conservation Lane
Gaithersburg, MD 20878

Phone: 301/548-0150. Fax: 301/548-0146

Maitland Sharpe, Executive Director

One of the country's oldest conservation organizations, The Izaak Walton League of America (IWLA) works to conserve the nation's soil, air, woods, waters and wildlife, primarily through public education and lobbying programs. IWLA's 53,000 members are conservationists who hunt, fish, hike, or pursue other outdoor recreational activities. IWLA currently maintains the following major programs: Save Our Streams Program (see entry 470), Wetlands Watch, Midwest Energy Efficiency Program, Outdoor Ethics, and the Carrying Capacity Project. IWLA offers newsletters for its outdoor ethics, volunteer water monitoring, and population programs; all members receive *Outdoor America*, a conservation magazine. Other IWLA publications include a report on the decline and restoration of the Mississippi River, a survey of hunter behavior, and a curriculum guide on population issues. Free pub-

lic education brochures like *Common Sense, Common Courtesy, Common Interests: A Boater's Guide to Ethics on the Water* and *Wildlife and Global Climate Change: An Uncertain Future* are also available.

37 League of Conservation Voters (LCV)
1707 L Street, NW, Suite 550
Washington, DC 20036

Phone: 202/785-8683. Fax: 202/835-0491.
E-mail: lcv@igc.apc.org

Jim Maddy, President

The League of Conservation Voters (LCV) is a nonpartisan political arm of the environmental movement. Representatives from more than twenty environmental organizations sit on the league's board of directors and its Political Advisory Committee. The organization's goal is to change the balance of power in Congress by helping to elect candidates who will vote to protect our citizens' health, our country's resources, and our planet. During election years, LCV targets key congressional races by endorsing candidates and providing support in the form of direct contributions, media assistance, canvassing, and voter education. LCV's flagship publication, the annual *National Environmental Scorecard* (see entry 129), rates all 535 members of Congress based on their commitment to environmental protection. The League occasionally produces other publications that rate congressional committees or profile presidential candidates. The national LCV office can put people in touch with its affiliates and other organizations working on environmental politics at the state and local levels.

38 National Audubon Society (NAS)
Headquarters
700 Broadway
New York, NY 10003

Phone: 212/979-3000. Fax: 212/979-3188

Peter A. A. Berle, President

The National Audubon Society (NAS) is one of the oldest, largest, and most powerful nature appreciation and conservation organizations in the country. While it is known especially for its educational programs related to birds, NAS works on a broad range of concerns related to the protection of the world's ecosystems: preserving wetlands; population planning; eliminating acid rain and reducing air pollution; promoting environmental justice; conserving biological diversity; and protecting water quality. NAS also maintains more than one hundred wildlife sanctuaries and coordinates the activities of more than five hundred local chapters and ten regional offices and education centers. NAS provides its half a million members, most of them dedicated naturalists, with the tools they need to assume an activist role in protecting natural ecosystems; at the same time, the organization itself lobbies intensively for stronger state and federal conservation laws. NAS publishes many nature field guides and educational materials as well as the *Audubon* (see entry 161), *Audubon Activist*, and *American Birds* periodicals. Interested individuals should contact a local NAS chapter for detailed information on local ecosystems and other activities. Contact the Washington, D.C., office (202/547-9009) for national legislative and policy information.

39 National Wildlife Federation (NWF)

1400 16th Street, NW
Washington, DC 20036

Phone: 202/797-6800. Fax: 202/797-6646

Jay D. Hair, President

With several million members, the National Wildlife Federation (NWF) is certainly the largest—and one of the most influential—conservation organizations in the U.S. Though NWF began as a support network for hunters, its membership now includes hunting opponents, and the organization has widened its focus to include pollution control (e.g., water conservation and quality, hazardous-waste cleanup, pesticide runoff) and the sustainable use of natural resources (e.g., wetlands conservation, preservation of tropical forests, mining reform) through public education, lobbying, and research initiatives. Among its many programs are Cool It!, which provides technical assistance to campus environmental activists, and the Corporate Conservation Council, a forum through which leaders of blue-chip corporations can discuss environmental issues. NWF produces several well-known publications, including the *Conservation Directory* (see entry 65) and *National Wildlife* magazine (see entry

162), as well as numerous other pieces for activists, educators, researchers, and other professionals. Titles include *Poisoned Profits: Cyanide Heap Leach Mining and its Impact on the Environment*; *Biotechnology's Bitter Harvest*; *EnviroAction* (a newsletter that summarizes events on Capitol Hill); the NatureScope educational curriculum series; and fact sheets that outline issues and NWF's position on them. NWF also operates a dedicated phone line (202/797–6655) that provides up-to-date information on pending environmental legislation in Congress.

40 Natural Resources Defense Council (NRDC)

40 West 20th Street
New York, NY 10011

Phone: 212/727-2700. Fax: 212/727-1773

John H. Adams, Executive Director

EcoNet: NRDC posts press releases and news items to the *nrdc.news* conference.

Known as a group of tough litigators and environmental watchdogs, the Natural Resources Defense Council (NRDC) monitors government agencies, brings legal action to preserve natural resources—especially in cases with widely applicable precedents—conducts policy research, and disseminates information concerning damage to the environment. NRDC's primary mission is to protect human health and the environment while simultaneously fostering sustainable global economic growth. Areas of organizational interest include energy; population; air pollution; health (especially pesticide safety); water quality and management; and protection of the inner-city environment. NRDC is known and respected for its well-researched reports; representative titles include *The Harvest of Hope: The Potential for Alternative Agriculture to Reduce Pesticide Use*; *After Silent Spring*; and *Defending the Earth: Abuses of Human Rights and the Environment*. NRDC also publishes *The Amicus Journal* (see entry 160), an environmental magazine that updates members on current programs.

41 Redefining Progress

116 New Montgomery Street, Suite 209
San Francisco, CA 94105

Phone: 415/543-6511. Fax: 415/543-9687

Ted Halstead, Executive Director

Redefining Progress promotes the idea that the social and environmental problems facing society are not atypical defects within a properly functioning system, but rather the result of an economic, political, and social system that prioritizes economic growth at the expense of human communities and the natural environment. This nonprofit research and advocacy organization was established to challenge the basic tenets and purposes of growth-based economics and to contribute to the development of an alternative ideological and institutional economic framework.

Redefining Progress has developed a comprehensive alternative to the Gross National Product (GNP), named the Genuine Progress Indicator (GPI), which measures the socioeconomic well-being and sustainability of the U.S. from 1950 to 1992 by accounting for a series of social and ecological costs. The group is initiating a series of projects based on the GPI with the purpose of broadening understanding of how economic well-being is currently measured. Another major program consists of promoting a fundamental shift in tax structures that would create a more just and sustainable society. The aim of the project is to show how a new tax structure that shifts revenue generation from labor and capital to the use of natural resources could serve the dual purpose of enhancing employment and equity (by reducing taxes on human resources) while simultaneously increasing environmental conservation (by raising taxes on natural resources). Additionally, the organization is developing literature designed to clarify for the general public how the policies of GNP-driven economies serve to undermine "our common good."

There are several publications that further explore the principles espoused by Redefining Progress. For a thorough introduction to the subject, consider *Ecological Economics: The Science and Management of Sustainability* (Robert Costanza. Columbia University Press, 1992); *For the Common Good: Redirecting the Economy Toward Community, the Environment, and a Sustainable Future* (Herman E. Daly and John B. Cobb. Beacon Press, 1989); *Paradigms in Progress: Life Beyond Economics* (Hazel Henderson. Knowledge Systems, 1991); or *Saving the Planet: How to Shape an Environmentally Sustainable Global Economy* (Lester R. Brown, Christopher Flavin, Sandra Postel. W. W. Norton & Company, 1991).

42 Renew America

1400 16th Street, NW, Suite 710
Washington, DC 20036

Phone: 202/232-2252. Fax: 202/232-2617

Kenneth Brown, Executive Director

Renew America seeks out and promotes successful environmental programs that offer positive, constructive models for other communities, governments, and businesses. Renew America evaluates programs in terms of their effectiveness and replication potential as well as for their economic feasibility and sustainability. Analyses of successful programs are found in the annual *Environmental Success Index* directory (included with membership; $25 for nonmembers) and database. *Index* entries include a city ordinance to ban polystyrene; a farmer who uses no-till methods on cotton crops; a state wastewater operator training center; and a volunteer tree-planting organization. Each year Renew America, in conjunction with the National Environmental Awards Council, honors the twenty most innovative and effective programs in the *Index*. In addition to the *Environmental Success Index*, the organization publishes environmental resource guides that include lists of model programs.

43 Resources for the Future (RFF)

1616 P Street, NW
Washington, DC 20036

Phone: 202/328-5000. Fax: 202/939-3460

Robert W. Fri, President

Resources for the Future (RFF) is a think tank that focuses on long-term natural resource and environmental-quality issues, particularly with respect to social, political, and economic realities. RFF is highly respected among policymakers for its objective scholarly research. RFF staffers and fellows are currently conducting research in the areas of mitigation and adaptation to climate change; world oil markets and energy security; renewable resource management; the economic resources of outer space; cost-benefit analyses of regulations; analyses of industry's response to government regulation; strategies for toxic waste management; methodology of risk assessment; and evaluation and development of policy tools for managing environmental risks and determining priorities. Reports of ongoing research, called discussion papers (e.g., *Accelerated Vehicle Retirement to Reduce Emissions: An Economic Analysis of the Delaware Program; Regulatory Review of Environmental Policy: The Potential Role of Health-Health Analysis*), are distributed by RFF's External Affairs office. RFF's books and studies (e.g., *Public Policies for Environmental Protection; America's Renewable Resources: Historical Trends and Current Challenges*) are distributed by The Johns Hopkins University Press. The organization also sponsors conferences, colloquia, and occasional policy briefs for members of Congress.

44 Rocky Mountain Institute (RMI)

1739 Snowmass Creek Road
Snowmass, CO 81654

Phone: 303/927-3851. Fax: 303/927-4178.
E-mail: orders@rmi.org

L. Hunter Lovins, President

Internet: RMI has space on Solstice, the Center for Renewable Energy and Sustainable Technology (see entry 321) site. From the gopher main menu, choose *Energy Efficiency*, then *general*, then *Rocky Mountain Institute information*. From the World Wide Web home page, choose *Rocky Mountain Institute*.

The Rocky Mountain Institute (RMI), through its research and consulting programs, fosters the efficient and sustainable use of resources as a path to global security. Founded in 1982 by energy pioneers Amory and Hunter Lovins, RMI has played a leading role in convincing utilities and policymakers of the value of the "end-use/least-cost" approach to conservation and of the "soft-path" philosophy of energy use (which blends efficient energy use with sustainable sources of energy). RMI's Green Development Services program works with architects, builders, developers, and property managers to encour-

age cost-effective, state-of-the-art construction—thereby saving energy, water, and materials. The organization also has programs in transportation, water efficiency, sustainable communities, and global security. Among its many publications are *The Efficient House Sourcebook* (see entry 513); *The Energy-Efficient Home* (see entry 514, *Consumer's Guide to Home Energy Savings*); *Water-Efficient Technologies: A Catalog for the Residential/Light Commercial Sector;* and the *Economic Renewal Guide*, a practical guide to sustainable community development.

RMI has also formed a for-profit consulting service, called E Source, which serves as a subscription-based clearinghouse that supplies detailed information on electric efficiency to utilities, governments, and manufacturers in thirty-five countries.

45 Sierra Club

National Headquarters
730 Polk Street
San Francisco, CA 94109

Phone: 415/776-2211. Fax: 415/776-0350

Carl Pope, Executive Director

Sierra Club is the most progressive of the large mainstream conservation organizations. Though Sierra Club influences public policy decisions—legislative, administrative, legal, and electoral—through lobbying, expert testimony, grassroots activism, and public education, the organization is also active in planning wilderness trips and helping people enjoy the outdoors. Current advocacy campaigns focus primarily on the protection of biodiversity and wilderness areas, especially from an ecosystem-based perspective, but the organization works on many other issues including economics, energy, population, waste, and water. Cofounded by John Muir in 1892, Sierra Club now has 63 chapters, 396 local groups, and more than 500,000 members in the United States and Canada. The national office produces the bimonthly magazine *Sierra* (see entry 163) and a monthly activist newsletter; there are also a variety of publications centered around specific Club campaigns (for instance, *Public Lands* and *Population Report*). All Sierra Club chapters, including many of the group's local affiliates, produce their own newsletters.

Request the *Mail-Order Service Guide* for an extensive catalog of nature guides, travel guides, and other books sold by Sierra Club. Request the *Sourcebook* for a list of Sierra Club fact sheets, brochures, videos, and other available public information; most of these materials are sent free of charge, though a donation of $2 to cover the costs of printing and postage is requested.

The Sierra Club Legal Defense Fund (415/627-6700), an affiliated organization, is a public-interest law firm that argues cases on behalf of Sierra Club and other environmental organizations.

46   Student Environmental Action Coalition (SEAC)

National Office
P.O. Box 1168
Chapel Hill, NC 27514

Phone: 800/700-7322; 919/967-4600.
Fax: 919/967-4648.
E-mail: seac@igc.apc.org

Miya Yoshitani, Executive Director

Internet: SEAC sponsors a series of electronic-mailing lists called SEACnet. SEACnet is archived on EcoGopher (see entry 54, EcoSystems). To view these archives, choose *Archives of Environmental Electronic Mailing Lists*, then *SEACnet*.

The Student Environmental Action Coalition (SEAC) is a national network of high school and college organizations and activists dedicated to building power among students and youth involved in environmental and social justice action. (SEAC's People of Color Caucus, for example, is active on environmental racism issues.) SEAC promotes networking opportunities among its member groups, provides organizing assistance, offers information on environmental issues, and furnishes speakers on environmental issues. Among SEAC's publications are *Campus Ecology: A Guide to Assessing Environmental Quality & Creating Strategies for Change* (April Smith and SEAC. Living Planet Press, 1992); *The SEAC High School Organizing Guide*; and a variety of action guides, including *Starting a Campus Waste Reduction and Recycling Program* and *How to Start or Revive a Local Group*. Members can communicate through SEACnet, a series of electronic conferences, or they can stay in touch through SEAC's monthly magazine, *Threshold*. SEAC is also part of Action for Solidarity, Equality, Environment and Development (ASEED), a network of student environmental groups in fifty-three countries.

47   Union of Concerned Scientists (UCS)

National Headquarters
2 Brattle Square
Cambridge, MA 02238

Phone: 617/547-5552. Fax: 617/864-9405

Howard Ris, Executive Director

The Union of Concerned Scientists (UCS) began as a group of faculty and students at the Massachusetts Institute of Technology who joined together to protest the misuse of science and technology—especially as it related to defense research at universities. UCS has more than forty full-time staff members in three offices, and more than 75,000 members. The group now advocates responsible public policy in all areas where technology plays a critical role: energy, transportation, arms, and sustainable agriculture. UCS conducts technical studies and public education campaigns, and seeks to influence government policy at all levels. Two networks are available for individuals who wish to become more involved with UCS's programs: the Concerned Citizens Action Network and the Scientists Action Network. The organization's publications include books such as *Cool Energy: Renewable Energy Solutions to Environmental Problems* (see entry 339, *Renewable Energy: A Concise Guide to Energy Alternatives*); reports, including *A Program for World Nuclear Security*; free introductory brochures like *World Scientists' Warning to Humanity* and *Solar Power: Energy for Today and Tomorrow*; and free briefing papers, such as *Environmental Impacts of Renewable Energy Technologies* and *U.S. Consumption and the Environment*.

48   United States Public Interest Research Group (U.S. PIRG)

215 Pennsylvania Avenue
Washington, DC 20003

Phone: 202/546-9707. Fax: 202/546-2461

Gene Karpinski, Executive Director

The United States Public Interest Research Group (U.S. PIRG) is the national lobbying and research office for state Public Interest Research Groups (PIRGs): nonpartisan, nonprofit environmental and consumer advocacy organizations active in more than thirty states (CALPIRG, Florida PIRG, MASSPIRG, etc.). The PIRGs concentrate on organizing grassroots campaigns and educating policymakers, both locally and in Washington, D.C., about necessary environmental reforms, consumer rights, and government accountability. U.S. PIRG has helped to strengthen the Clean Air Act, the federal Superfund program, and the Safe Drinking Water Act in addition to its campaigns against unsafe consumer products and unfair credit-card, banking, and insurance practices. Through its numerous publications, including the quarterly newsletter *U.S. PIRG Citizen Agenda*, individuals can stay on top of U.S. PIRG's well-respected research findings. Recent U.S. PIRG reports include *Avoiding Toxic Consumer Products*; *Below Regulatory Concern, But Radioactive and Carcinogenic*; *Energy Drain: Special Interest Money & National Energy Legislation*; and *Ten Ways to Save Energy, Money and the Environment*. A publications catalog is available. Free one-page fact sheets concerning current legislation outline eco- or consumer-friendly bills before Congress; in addition to providing details of the legislation, the papers cite the bill's opposition and any recommended action for PIRG members. U.S. PIRG is a highly regarded and reliable source of grassroots consumer information. For assistance, or to become more involved, contact your nearest state PIRG or the national office.

49 **Women's Environment and Development Organization (WEDO)**
845 Third Avenue, 15th Floor
New York, NY 10022

Phone: 212/759-7982. Fax: 212/759-8647.
E-mail: wedo@igc.apc.org

Susan Davis, Executive Director

Internet: WEDO has space on the Institute for Global Communications (see entry 57) gopher. From the main menu, choose *Women*, then *Women's Environment & Development Organization (WEDO)*.

Established in 1989, the Women's Environment and Development Organization (WEDO) works on an international level to empower women to play an active and equal role in decision making on environmental, development, peace, and social justice issues. WEDO's mandate is twofold: to put women's issues on the United Nations agenda and to link women from around the world who are interested in achieving a powerful collective voice. Almost twenty thousand active members are already in WEDO's database. The organization operates in a nonhierarchical, decentralized manner, encouraging the free exchange of information among networks. WEDO recently began a new campaign in conjunction with Greenpeace (see entry 32), called Women, Cancer and the Environment: Action for Prevention, that raises awareness of the growing link between breast cancer and women's exposure to human-made pollutants. WEDO also produces publications, including the newsletter *News & Views* and numerous briefing packets (e.g., "Women, Health & the Environment" ; "Fourth World Conference on Women" ; "Women for a Healthy Planet Kit").

The WorldWIDE Network (202/347–1514) is another decentralized international organization dedicated to creating networks among women environmentalists and providing them with support. Its major ongoing project is the *WorldWIDE Directory of Women in the Environment*, which provides information about two thousand women involved in environmental work around the world.

50 **World Resources Institute (WRI)**
1709 New York Avenue, NW, Suite 700
Washington, DC 20006

Phone: 202/638-6300. Phone (publications): 800/822-0504; 410/516-6998. Fax: 202/638-0036.
E-mail: info@wri.org
E-mail (publication requests): pub-info@wri.org

Jonathan Lash, President

EcoNet: WRI maintains the *wri.news* conference.

The World Resources Institute (WRI) is an esteemed think tank that studies both environmental problems threatening the economic and environmental interests of all nations and problems particular to developing countries. Specific areas of research include biological resources, economics, population, climate, energy, technology, and environmental institutions. WRI also develops environmental indicators and accounting methods that allow policymakers to more accurately evaluate the health of the environment. The institute's 105-member staff often collaborates with other organizations, governments, and intergovernmental agencies, and provides technical assistance to professionals in developing countries. Most WRI publications are geared toward a professional audience—e.g., the authoritative *World Resources* (see entry 134); *Biodiversity Prospecting: Guidelines for Using Genetic and Biochemical Resources Sustainably and Equitably*; *Green Fees: How a Tax Shift Can Work for the Environment and the Economy*; and the *Directory of Country Environmental Studies* (see entry 66). However, WRI also publishes several excellent books for educators and the public—for example, the *Information Please Environmental Almanac* (see entry 128); *Trees of Life: Protecting Tropical Forests and Their Biological Wealth*; and the *Teachers Guide to World Resources*.

51 Worldwatch Institute
1776 Massachusetts Avenue, NW
Washington, DC 20036

Phone: 202/452-1999. Fax: 202/296-7365.
E-mail: worldwatch@igc.apc.org

Lester R. Brown, President

EcoNet: The Worldwatch Institute maintains the *worldwatch.new* conference.

Researchers at the Worldwatch Institute, a leading think tank on the environment and sustainability, frame issues such as climate change, forest cover, population, poverty, food production capacity, water resources, and biological diversity in a global context while writing in a style that all audiences will readily understand. Institute staffers record global environmental data, analyze and interpret trends, and highlight the most effective strategies for making progress toward a sustainable society. The most comprehensive treatment of a particular topic will be found in a *Worldwatch Paper* (e.g., *Empowering Development: New Energy Equation*; *Indigenous Peoples and Health of the Earth*; *Costly Tradeoffs: Reconciling Trade and Environment*). This series of bimonthly reports averages fifty to

one hundred pages each. Adaptations of the research done for these reports are found in both *State of the World* (see entry 130), the institute's annual flagship publication, and *World Watch* magazine (see entry 180). The organization also compiles another annual publication, *Vital Signs: The Trends That Are Shaping Our Future* (see entry 132), and several books, including *Last Oasis: Facing Water Scarcity* (see entry 492) and *How Much is Enough? The Consumer Society and the Future of the Earth* (see entry 618). Annual membership includes *State of the World* and six *Worldwatch Papers*. A database for all Worldwatch statistical information, including tables and charts found in *State of the World* and *Vital Signs*, is available directly from the Worldwatch Institute for $89.

52 Zero Population Growth (ZPG)
1400 16th Street, NW, Suite 320
Washington, DC 20036

Phone: 202/332-2200. Fax: 202/332-2302.
E-mail: zpg@igc.apc.org

Susan Weber, Executive Director

Zero Population Growth (ZPG) works to bring human population and its activities back into balance with Earth's resources and the environment. ZPG, which coordinated the U.S. participation of nongovernmental organizations at the 1994 United Nations International Conference on Population and Development held in Cairo, also sponsors classroom education programs and conducts citizen, media, and legislative outreach campaigns. Publications include an annotated bibliography (*Selected Resources on Population*); teaching materials (*Earth Matters: Studies for Our Global Future; For Earth's Sake: Lessons in Population and the Environment*), reports (e.g., *USA by Numbers: A Statistical Portrait of the United States; Environmental Stress Index*) and numerous fact sheets (e.g., *Where Will All the Forests Go?: Deforestation Deeply Rooted in Population Growth; Population and the Greenhouse Effect*). ZPG also publishes the monthly *ZPG Reporter* and the quarterly *ZPG Activist* newsletter.

Many large environmental organizations have programs on the interrelationship between population growth and the environment. For starters, check with the National Audubon Society (see entry 38) and Sierra Club (see entry 45).

Other Organizations

- ◆ The International Institute for Sustainable Development (see entry 166, *Earth Negotiations Bulletin*)
- ◆ The World Conservation Union (see entry 280)
- ◆ The World Wildlife Fund (see entry 282)

Internet Sites

To find out about additional sites on the Internet, consult *A Guide to Environmental Internet Resources* (see entry 104), the *Internet Environmental Resources Guide* (see entry 105), the *Selected Bibliography of Sources of Environmental Information on the Internet* (see entry 106), and the *Guide to Online Resources for the Conservationist* (see entry 107).

53   Consortium for International Earth Science Information Network (CIESIN)

Internet: To access CIESIN Internet sites, ftp to **ftp.ciesin.org** or gopher to **gopher.ciesin.org**; on the World Wide Web, the URL is **http://www.ciesin.org/**.
    For technical support by phone, call CIESIN User Services at 517/797-2727. For technical support by e-mail, send an e-mail message to **ciesin.info@ciesin.org**.

Anyone interested in global change, particularly in its socioeconomic implications, should familiarize him- or herself with the Consortium for International Earth Science Information Network (CIESIN) Internet site. The network was established in 1989 to advance the understanding of the human dimensions of global change, largely by providing access to and enhancing the use of information. CIESIN's Internet site provides access to an enormous amount of data on all global change issues. Through the online catalog service, users can search descriptions of data sets, look at sample data, view data graphically, and order data sets online from CIESIN's own archives, from similar directories (such as NASA's *Global Change Master Directory*), and from partners in CIESIN's Information Cooperative

(including the Agency for Toxic Substances and Disease Registry, the World Conservation Monitoring Centre of the World Conservation Union [see entry 280] and the United Nations Environment Programme [see entry 10]). In addition to providing access to satellite and other types of data on global change, the CIESIN Internet site contains publications on the socioeconomic aspects of global change. Two particularly noteworthy features of the site are the CIESIN Electronic Bookshelf, which includes many public policy and other reference documents, and Thematic Guides, excellent overviews of key topics and issues that pertain to the human interactions in global environmental change. Through the CIESIN Internet site, it is possible to access other CIESIN projects, like the Global Change Research Information Office (see entry 1) gopher, the Human Dimensions of Global Environmental Change Programme gopher, and the Classroom Earth BBS, a resource for environmental educators.

54   EcoSystems

Maintained by the University of Virginia's Division of Recoverable and Disposable Resources.

Internet: EcoSystems is comprised of EcoGopher and EcoWeb. To access EcoGopher, gopher to **ecosys.drdr.virginia.edu**. To access EcoWeb, the URL is **http://ecosys.drdr.virginia.edu/EcoWeb.html**.
    For technical support by e-mail, send an e-mail message to **gopher@ecosys.drdr.virginia.edu** or **www@ecosys.drdr.virginia.edu**.

EcoSystems is an outstanding collection point and access site for environmental information. Owned and operated by the University of Virginia's Division of Recoverable and Disposable Resources (DRDR), EcoSystems contains statistical information about recycling on the University of Virginia campus. However, EcoSystems' other services—comprising a gopher site (EcoGopher) and a World Wide Web site (EcoWeb)—appeal to a much wider audience. EcoGopher and EcoWeb are two of the best places to begin an Internet search on environmental issues; of all the Internet sites specializing in environmental information, these are certainly the best maintained.

EcoGopher includes directories of organizations, archives of environmental mailing lists, and features that allow WAIS searches and real-time chat. Its list of other environmental gophers and Internet resources is one of the best available anywhere. EcoGopher also serves as the home of SEACnet (see entry 46, Student Environmental Action Coalition) and the GreenGopher (see entry 33, The Greens/Green Party USA). EcoWeb, on the other hand, contains one of the most comprehensive lists of environmental Web sites on the Internet. Gopher users can browse EcoWeb in hypertext through EcoSystems' public lynx client (from the main menu on EcoGopher, choose *EcoLynx*).

55   The EnviroLink Network

Internet: The EnviroLink Network maintains EnviroGopher, EnviroWeb, and EnviroFreenet. To access EnviroGopher, gopher to **envirolink.org**. To access EnviroWeb, the URL is **http://envirolink.org/**. To access EnviroFreenet, telnet to **envirolink.org**.

For technical support by e-mail, send an e-mail message to **admin@envirolink.org**.

The EnviroLink Network aims to provide a central location for all environmental information on the Internet. This grassroots organization is entirely volunteer run and supported by individual donations; the organization hopes to remain free of corporate or foundation funding. EnviroLink's information is available from three different viewing formats: EnviroGopher (gopher), EnviroWeb (World Wide Web), and EnviroFreenet (panda). EnviroGopher includes a hodgepodge of message postings, directories of environmental resources, and access to many other environmental resources on the Internet, including archives of electronic-mailing lists and periodicals. EnviroWeb provides extensive access to Internet resources on environmental issues in hypertext and with graphics. It also serves as the home for other projects (e.g., Animal Defense Network, NativeWeb, World Species List) that were formed in partnership with EnviroLink. EnviroFreenet gives Internet users an e-mail address and the ability to access EnviroLink's bulletin boards and Usenet newsgroups. The EnviroLink Network also offers users the ability to chat in real time with other users and sponsors eleven Internet mailing lists (for more informa-

tion, send an e-mail message to **listproc@envirolink.org** with the words **help** and **list** in the body of the message on separate lines). To contact The EnviroLink Network by phone, call 412/268-7187.

56   Environmental Protection Agency (EPA)

Internet: To access the Environmental Protection Agency sites, ftp to **ftp.epa.gov** or gopher to **gopher.epa.gov**; on the World Wide Web, the URL is **http://www.epa.gov/**.

Not surprisingly, the Environmental Protection Agency (EPA) Internet site provides the best access to electronic EPA information sources. The gopher and World Wide Web sites provide access to other EPA resources on the Internet, including the EPA Online Library System (see entry 60). Electronic versions of essential EPA directories, including *Access EPA* (see entry 62), the *Information Systems Inventory* (see entry 88), a directory of offices and regions, and an EPA people locator are available and searchable by WAIS. The full text of many other publications—e.g., press releases; policy and strategy documents; standards; rules, regulations, and legislation; the *EPA Journal* (see entry 174)—are also available here, as well as an EPA calendar, announcements, and information about grants, contracts, and jobs. In addition, the gopher and Web sites provide access to other government and environmental Internet resources.

For more information about EPA publications and expertise, consult the EPA Public Information Center (see entry 3) or *Access EPA* (see entry 62).

57   Institute for Global Communications (IGC)

Internet: To access IGC sites, ftp to **ftp.igc.apc.org**; gopher to **gopher.igc.apc.org**; on the World Wide Web, the URL is **http://www.igc.apc.org/**.

The Institute for Global Communications (IGC) Internet sites are excellent sources for information on all progressive issues, including those that pertain to the environment. In contrast to EcoNet (see entry 58), PeaceNet, and other commercial online services operated by IGC, which are fee-based services that contain many electronic conferences, the IGC Internet sites are available free to anyone with access to the Internet. These sites also serve as excellent resources for learning about (and connecting to) EcoNet. For example, the ftp site contains brochures about IGC networks and a list of all conferences available, in addition to many other publications. Since the IGC Internet gopher and World Wide Web sites have comprehensive subject trees of Internet information sources, EcoNet subscribers and nonsubscribers alike will find them useful for a beginning exploration of the Internet. In addition, these Internet sites include some resources (e.g., the EcoJustice Network [see entry 352]; the hypertext version of the League of Conservation Voters' *National Environmental Scorecard* [see entry 129]) that are not available directly on EcoNet.

Other Internet Sites

- ◆ The Global Change Research and Information Office (see entry 1)
- ◆ The Global Action and Information Network (see entry 30) makes documents available via e-mail
- ◆ Linkages (see entry 166, *Earth Negotiations Bulletin*)
- ◆ The United Nations (see entry 10, United Nations Environment Programme)

Commercial Online Services

58   EcoNet
Institute for Global Communications
18 De Boom Street
San Francisco, CA 94107

Phone: 415/442-0220. Fax: 415/546-1794.
E-mail: support@igc.apc.org

EcoNet: To connect to EcoNet by modem, dial 415/322-0284 or 800/777-9454. In addition, local access numbers are available in hundreds of cities. New users will need a credit card; type **new** at the log-in prompt, then hit <return> at the password prompt. Prices vary depending on modem number used. Contact the Institute for Global Communications for further details on connecting to the system.

Internet: To access EcoNet, telnet to **igc.apc.org**.

The environmental movement's computer network of choice, EcoNet is an extraordinary tool for communication, advocacy, education, and research, especially among grassroots activists and nonprofit organizations. EcoNet is a commercial service of the Institute for Global Communications (IGC), a division of the Tides Foundation. Subscriptions to EcoNet allow access to the other IGC networks—PeaceNet, ConflictNet, LaborNet—and to similar computer networks in other countries that are members of the Association for Progressive Communications (APC). Access to EcoNet is available by direct dial; through SprintNet; or through the Internet.

EcoNet has three main features: mail, conferences, and databases. Subscribers can send and receive electronic mail to and from almost any e-mail address in the world via the Internet. The heart and soul of EcoNet is its conferences, which number in the hundreds. They cover every environmental issue imaginable—e.g., *climate.news, energy.bikes, env.alaska, env.ecolinking, env.journalism, greenleft.news, green.travel, haz.pulpmills, rainfor.worldbank, trade.strategy.* Conferences perform a variety of functions: They can be devoted to a single type of message (e.g., action alerts, press releases); contain the full text of periodicals, directories, or other publications (e.g., the *Conservation Directory* [see entry 65], the *Earth Negotiations Bulletin* [see entry 166]); or they may simply be a forum through which users can ask questions and share information on a particular topic. Some conferences are quite active—more than five messages a day—but others contain only a handful of messages in a given year. Many Internet conferences and mailing lists are available on EcoNet; some EcoNet conferences are available on the Internet. There are also several searchable EcoNet databases, including: the *People of Color Environmental Groups* directory (see entry 353), press releases from the United Nations, Greenpeace's *Toxic Trade Update* (see entry 453), and a calendar of events. In addition, EcoNet users have access to the Internet through the Institute for Global Communications (see entry 57) Internet site.

Reviewing information on current legislation and then faxing a personal response to Congress; sending an e-mail message to environmental organizations; reading newsletters; or searching directories for environmental information—these are only a few of the many creative uses for EcoNet. Everyone associated with the environmental movement should explore EcoNet to see the ways in which it can best meet their needs.

59 TogetherNet

Together Foundation for Global Unity
130 South Willard Street
Burlington, VT 05401

Phone: 802/862-2030. Fax: 802/862-1890

Database Vendor: Contact the Together Foundation for Global Unity for details on connecting to TogetherNet.

Internet: Contact the Together Foundation for Global Unity for details on connecting to TogetherNet.

TogetherNet is a communications network that provides information on issues related to the environment, sustainable development, and the United Nations. The fee-based service, run by the nonprofit Together Foundation for Global Unity, began operation in late 1992. TogetherNet is similar to EcoNet (see entry 58) in both mission and features; though TogetherNet contains far fewer conferences than EcoNet and is used by fewer environmental organizations.

TogetherNet currently offers a user-friendly graphical interface, available for both Macintosh and Windows. TogetherNet is accessible by direct dial and through SprintNet. Internet users can access TogetherNet through telnet, but cannot use the graphical interface.

TogetherNet users can send and receive electronic mail to and from nearly every e-mail address worldwide via the Internet. (TogetherNet does not allow subscribers Internet access beyond electronic-mail privileges. Internet users may access some TogetherNet information on the Together Foundation's gopher: gopher to **gopher.together.org**.) Subscribers can also chat with each other electronically, in real time. There are eighteen TogetherNet conferences and roughly two hundred Usenet newsgroups and archives of Internet electronic-mailing lists. At the main TogetherNet window, there are several icons that can be double-clicked to begin exploring the network. For example, the library icon contains many documents of interest, including background papers on issues, maps, government documents such as the North American Free Trade Agreement (NAFTA), *A Guide to Environ-*

mental Resources on the Internet (see entry 104), the United Nations Environment Programme (see entry 10) publications catalog, and original directories compiled by TogetherNet's staff, including a directory of environmental funding sources arranged by state and a directory of environmental products and services. Another particularly noteworthy icon leads to United Nations information: background information, press releases, the daily UN newspaper, and the full text of many documents, including the official *AGENDA 21* (see entry 112). Among the searchable databases on TogetherNet are the extensive Ecoline (see entry 21) database, *Who's Who at the Earth Summit* (see entry 93, *Who is Who in Service to the Earth*), a directory of toxic waste sites in the United States, and a directory of alternative health-care providers. Other items on TogetherNet include clippings of electronic postings, periodicals such as *The Earth Times* (see entry 167), and a calendar of events that are of interest to subscribers.

Though TogetherNet is less well known than EcoNet, it is an excellent medium for environmental communication and information exchange.

Bulletin Boards

To find out about other environmental bulletin boards, consult *Eco-Data: Using Your PC to Obtain Free Environmental Information* (see entry 71), the *Environmental and Related BBS List* (see entry 72), and the *Green BBS List for Environmental Bulletin Board Systems* (see entry 81).

60 EPA Online Library System (OLS)

Maintained by the Environmental Protection Agency.

Bulletin Board: To connect to OLS by modem (7-1-E), dial 919/549-0720. Choose *EPA OLS*.

Internet: To access OLS, telnet to **epaibm.rtpnc.epa.gov**, choose *Public*, then *OLS*.

A variety of searchable Environmental Protection Agency (EPA) databases can be accessed through the EPA Online Library System (OLS). Available OLS databases include a catalog of all EPA documents published in the past year (see entry 7, the National Center for Environmental

Publications and Information) and a searchable version of *Access EPA* (see entry 62), which contains descriptions of EPA public information sources. Also available is a card catalog system that includes the holdings of all EPA libraries (from the OLS main menu, choose *National Catalog*); there is a separate card catalog system on OLS for the contents of the EPA's Hazardous Waste Superfund Collection (from the OLS main menu, choose *Hazardous Waste*) (see entry 451, Hazardous Waste Superfund Database).

61   FedWorld

Maintained by the National Technical Information Service.

Bulletin Board: To connect to FedWorld by modem, dial 703/321-8020. To connect to FedWorld's GateWay from the main menu, choose *GateWay System*. Then, from FedWorld's GateWay, choose *Connect to Gov't sys/database* to connect directly to another government bulletin board system, then choose the number code for the bulletin board of your choice.

For technical support by phone, call the FedWorld Help Desk at 703/487-4608.

Internet: To access FedWorld, telnet to **fedworld.gov**.

A government bulletin board that allows users to connect directly to other federal bulletin boards, FedWorld is a free service of the National Technical Information Service (NTIS) (see entry 8). Several of the more than one hundred total bulletin boards available through FedWorld's GateWay are in the environmental subject category, including the Cleanup Information Bulletin Board (see entry 433), the Pesticide Information Network (see entry 199), and the Nonpoint Source Electronic Bulletin Board (see entry 474). Within the GateWay feature, users can list all available bulletin boards, search descriptions of bulletin boards by keyword, or list bulletin boards by subject category. Although access to the FedWorld bulletin board is free and unrestricted, some bulletin boards accessible through FedWorld's GateWay system have restricted access or charge a fee.

Other FedWorld areas let users search databases (e.g., the *Catalog of Federal Domestic Assistance*), find out more about NTIS and order selected NTIS documents, look for federal jobs, participate in electronic conferences on finding government information, or download files. Two environmental bulletins are among the most popular: the NTIS publications catalog entitled *U.S. Government Environmental Datafiles and Software* and the Superfund Early Bird Announcement Window, which announces new publications. The FedWorld user's guide, which is available online and downloadable, describes other federal bulletin boards not available through FedWorld.

There is also a FedWorld World Wide Web site on the Internet (the URL is **http://www.fedworld.gov/**); it provides telnet access to the FedWorld bulletin board and is a good place for government information available on the Internet.

Other Bulletin Boards

◆ The Right-To-Know Network (see entry 378)
◆ The Federal Bulletin Board (see entry 5, Government Printing Office)

Directories

62   Access EPA

Environmental Protection Agency, 1993; available from the Government Printing Office and the National Technical Information Service. Updated irregularly. 645p. $24.00 (paper).

Bulletin Board: Available on the EPA Online Library System (OLS) (see entry 60). Choose *A* to search the *Access EPA* database.

Internet: OLS (see above) is available on the Internet.

Access EPA is also available, in a chapter-by-chapter format, on the Environmental Protection Agency (see entry 56) gopher. Choose *EPA Information Locators*, then *Access EPA*.

One of the most useful environmental reference works, the essential *Access EPA* contains lengthy descriptions of all publicly available information sources maintained by the Environmental Protection Agency (EPA). Resources are organized by type of information source: clearinghouses, databases, major dockets, scientific models, EPA libraries, or records management programs.

Within these sections the resources are further divided by issue. Each entry is accompanied by complete contact information, including primary contact person and hours of availability, and a detailed mission statement. In addition, *Access EPA* contains a listing of state environmental and federal depository libraries as well as a select list of acronyms and detailed author, title, and subject indices. *Access Express* (14p. Free from the EPA Public Information Center [see entry 3]) provides listings, without descriptions, of the most useful EPA information sources.

63 Air, Waste and Environmental Management Research Faculty Profile Directory

1st ed. Air & Waste Management Association and Synergistic Technologies, 1993. 378p. $79.95 (paper).

Diskette: Available from Synergistic Technologies for $495.00.

The *Air, Waste and Environmental Management Research Faculty Profile Directory* describes the research activities of twelve hundred North American university researchers, primarily from the United States and Canada. By using this resource, researchers can more easily determine if their work is redundant, companies can more efficiently locate researchers who are working in specific areas, and government agencies can more effectively determine where scarce funding should be directed. Listed are faculty members from more than 350 institutions with expertise in a broad range of areas, including: aerosol science and engineering, air pollution control, asbestos, biological treatment, pollution prevention, risk assessment, and water quality and analysis. Information for this directory was gathered through questionnaires; each entry includes: name and title; address; telephone and fax numbers; e-mail address; general and specific research interests; funding sources; courtroom/litigation experience; staff size and qualifications; desire to collaborate with industry; and commercial applications of research. Entries are organized by country and further divided by state or province. There are three indices: expertise, treatment/control, and name.

64 Canadian Environmental Directory

Edited by Peter Asselstine. Canadian Almanac and Directory Publishing Company, 1994. Annual. 1,322p. $215.00 (hardcover).

The *Canadian Environmental Directory* is an outstanding and comprehensive guide to Canadian sources of environmental information. A broad range of topics and different types of resources are thoroughly covered, including government agencies (federal, provincial, municipal); Canadian and international organizations; research laboratories; special libraries; attorneys and law firms; journalists; and products and services. Also included are an extensive, briefly annotated bibliography of directories, databases, and both books and newsletters (business, legal, general interest, technical, and political). Each entry includes the bibliographic information necessary to successfully locate a resource, as well as enough descriptive information to understand the resource. In addition to these resource lists, the directory provides a chronology of the past year's most significant environmental events, an analysis of legislative and regulatory changes and trends, and summaries of relevant acts and regulations. Numerous specialized indices allow the different types of resources to be easily located by name, location, and subject. While this book is far and away the best place to begin a search for Canadian environmental information, it is also useful as a general reference to U.S. and international resources.

For those looking for information on Canadian grassroots organizations, the Canadian Environmental Network (see entry 12) publishes *The Green List: A Guide to Canadian Environmental Organizations*.

65 Conservation Directory: A List of Organizations, Agencies, and Officials Concerned with Natural Resource Use and Management

39th ed. National Wildlife Federation, 1994. Annual. 477p. $20.00 (paper).

EcoNet: For a searchable version, choose *Online Databases*, then *Directories*, then *NWF Conservation Directory*. The full text is available in the *nwf.consdirect* conference.

The *Conservation Directory* is the first place to look for accurate contact information for conservation organizations in the U.S. and Canada. This directory provides extensive lists of key personnel and brief descriptions of almost 3,000 government and private state, national, and international organizations, including more than 16,000 staff members. The 578 entries for international, national, and regional organizations provide phone numbers, addresses, and contact names for both local and regional offices. Useful appendices include lists of colleges and universities that have conservation programs, online networks and database services, fish and game commissioners and directors, state coordinators for environmental education, national wildlife refuges, national forests, national parks, selected periodicals and directories, and sources of audio-visual materials. There are two indices: a name index that lists all of the individuals, organizations, and publications mentioned in the directory; and the much-improved subject index, which covers almost 90 environmental areas and now includes organization names. The *Conservation Directory* is an essential component of environmental reference collections, both personal and public.

66 Directory of Country Environmental Studies

Edited by Daniel Tunstall and Mieke van der Wansem. 2nd ed. World Resources Institute in cooperation with the International Institute for Environment and Development and The World Conservation Union, 1993. Updated irregularly. 230p. $19.95 (paper).

Diskette: Available from the World Resources Institute for $49.95.

The *Directory of Country Environmental Studies* is an excellent source of information on the content and availability of more than 325 studies of environmental and natural resource conditions in the developing world. The directory can help analysts identify and gain access to reports in English, Spanish, French, and Portuguese for more than 130 countries; it can also be used to identify organizations currently preparing reports. Over 90 percent of the studies were prepared between 1987 and 1992, with most focusing on development issues as they relate to the

environment. For each study, the directory provides a detailed, half-page abstract and cites the title, author, sponsoring and collaborating organizations, publication date, and information for obtaining the study. Studies include *Ghana: Environmental Action Plan* and *Brazil Atlantic Coastal Forests*. Because of the depth of the descriptions, this unique resource allows readers, without actually viewing the studies, to gain an understanding of environmental conditions in the developing world.

67 Directory of Environmental Attorneys

3rd. ed. Prentice Hall Law & Business, 1994. Annual. 1,756p. $195.00 (hardcover).

CD-ROM: Available from Prentice Hall Law & Business.

The *Directory of Environmental Attorneys* describes 9,265 attorneys from 4,494 U.S. law firms, public-interest groups, companies, and regulatory agencies. Law firm profiles include office address, number of offices maintained by the firm, the number of attorneys who practice in the area of environmental law, and the total number of attorneys. Attorney profiles, which appear directly below their firms' profiles, are much more detailed. They include biographical information (e.g., education, state bar admissions and years, previous affiliations, professional affiliations), areas of concentration, types of clients represented, representative clients, significant representations, regulatory agencies for whom the lawyer has worked and/or appeared before, types of cases and capacities in which the attorney has appeared as an expert witness, and publications authored. The directory is arranged by city and state. The detailed indices (law school, areas of concentration, regulatory agency experience, firm and organization, and name of attorney) also make it easy to find the right attorney for a particular matter.

68 Directory of Environmental Information Sources

Edited by Thomas F. P. Sullivan. 4th ed. Government Institutes, 1992. Updated irregularly. 300p. $78.00 (paper).

The *Directory of Environmental Information Sources* is an excellent resource for professionals in industries regulated by environmental law. This directory describes more than seventeen hundred environmental, health, and safety resources that can help professionals comply with and remain up to date on current regulations. Resources are organized by type: federal and state government agencies and offices; professional, scientific, and trade organizations; newsletters, magazines, and journals; and databases and data services. Complete bibliographic information and insightful one- to three-sentence descriptions accompany each resource—with the exception of government resources, which have no descriptions. The guide contains a detailed table of contents and an alphabetical index, but no subject index. Readers will find this work similar in content to the *Gale Environmental Sourcebook: A Guide to Organizations, Agencies, and Publications* (see entry 80) but with a more narrowly defined focus and more insightful descriptions of far fewer resources.

69 Directory of Environmental Organizations

Edited by Nancy Pearlman and Lynn Cason. Educational Communications, 1980–. Updated several times each year. 300p. $30.00 (velobound).

Diskette: Available from Educational Communications.

The *Directory of Environmental Organizations* provides addresses and phone and fax numbers for more than 5,700 environmental organizations. All U.S. regions are well represented, though there is a particular emphasis on Southern California; some international organizations are also included. The directory is a printout of the contact database of Educational Communications, a grassroots organization that administers a number of environmental projects, including the production of radio and television series, documentaries, and public service announcements, and a speaker's bureau. The database is printed a number of times annually in alphabetical order, zip code order, and subject order ($30 each). Versions on an IBM-compatible diskette ($300) or on mailing labels ($200) are also available. Those who need addresses for smaller organizations will want to consider purchasing this directory. Despite its occasional double listings, and some

outdated and partial information, this is the most current and complete directory of U.S. environmental organizations.

70 A Directory of European Environmental Organizations

Edited by Mireille Deziron and Leigh Bailey. Blackwell Publishers, 1993; first published in England in 1991. 177p. $59.95 (hardcover).

A Directory of European Environmental Organizations contains descriptions of broad-based national and international environmental groups that have a strong influence on policy in Europe. Each entry includes contact name, phone and fax numbers, and an address as well as the purpose, activities, publications, and sources of funding for each organization. In addition to being a standard directory with name and country indices, this directory also explains how environmental policies are developed and how problems are handled within the European Community.

For detailed information, including e-mail addresses, for more than three hundred libraries and environmental information centers in Poland, Hungary, Bulgaria, Romania, and the Czech and Slovak Republics, consult *Libraries and Environmental Information Centers in Central Eastern Europe* (Wladyslaw Poniecki Foundation, 1994. $27.50). This directory, updated regularly, is also available on the Poniecki Foundation gopher on the Internet (gopher to **poniecki.berkeley.edu** and choose *EcoDirectory*).

71 Eco-Data: Using Your PC to Obtain Free Environmental Information

Edited by Roland W. Schumann III. Government Institutes, 1994. 128p. $45.00 (paper).

72 Environmental and Related BBS List

Electronic document. Compiled by Judy Trimarchi. Updated irregularly. Free.

Bulletin Board: Available on the Nonpoint Source Electronic Bulletin Board (NPS BBS) (see entry 474). To download, search for the "BBS####.ZIP" file, where #### is the month and year it was updated, e.g. "BBS0994.ZIP."

Internet: NPS BBS (see above) is available on the Internet via FedWorld.

Eco-Data: Using Your PC to Obtain Free Environmental Information and the *Environmental and Related BBS List* are annotated directories that will be useful to those looking for environmental bulletin boards. *Eco-Data* describes sixty-seven bulletin boards operated by individuals, associations, universities, and companies in the private sector as well as forty governmental boards. The September 1994 version of the *Environmental and Related BBS List* provides short descriptions of eighty-five bulletin boards, roughly half of which are governmental. It also describes some twenty-five commercial online services and government hotlines. The two directories have thirty-eight bulletin boards in common. *Eco-Data* has more complete information for each bulletin board—access limitations, likely audience, initial time limit, whether or not there are conferences and downloadable files, and insightful comments by the editor that highlight certain features. It also includes a short, generic essay about the Internet, which describes several environmental, health, and safety Internet resources. The *Environmental and Related BBS List* contains enough information to allow users to access each bulletin board as well as a one- or two-sentence description of each resource, and the date the information was last verified. It is only available electronically, and is usually updated once a year.

Another electronic document that lists environmental bulletin boards, the *Green BBS List for Environmental Bulletin Board Systems* (see entry 81), is updated and verified quarterly. In addition, the FedWorld (see entry 61) bulletin board provides access to many government bulletin board systems.

73 EcoLinking: Everyone's Guide to Online Environmental Information

Don Rittner. Peachpit Press, 1992. 352p. $18.95 (paper).

EcoLinking is an introductory guide to the online world as well as a directory of environmental online resources. It contains chapters on: Fido-Net, BITNET, Usenet, Internet, bulletin boards, America Online, CompuServe, EcoNet, GEnie, The Well, commercial online databases, CD-ROMs, and sources of environmental news. Each chapter provides a short overview, including history, contact and log-in information, and screen printouts, which makes it easy for the beginner to see the differences between systems without logging on to each one. In each chapter there are annotated descriptions of scientific, environmental, and recreational resources, such as EcoNet conferences and government bulletin boards. Corrections and additions to *EcoLinking* are made available electronically on the Environmental Forum on America Online, where *EcoLinking* author Don Rittner is the host. Another good directory of online environmental resources is the *Guide to Online Resources for the Conservationist* (see entry 107), which is available electronically at no charge.

74 Encyclopedia of Environmental Information Sources

Edited by Sarojini Balachandran. 1st ed. Gale Research, 1993. Triennial. 1,850p. $125.00 (hardcover).

Diskette: Available from Gale Research.

The *Encyclopedia of Environmental Information Sources* lists both environmental and general reference sources that environmental professionals will find useful. Within more than one thousand environmental subject categories, resources are organized by type of information source—abstracts and indices, almanacs, bibliographies, directories, dictionaries and encyclopedias, governmental organizations, handbooks and manuals, online databases, periodicals, research centers, statistical sources, or trade and professional associations. Each subject heading contains an average of fifty information sources. However, a particular resource, such as the *Cambridge Encyclopedia of Life Sciences*, may be found in more than one category, and many resources are listed in more than twenty categories. Subject categories cover a broad range of specialized topics, such as botanical ecology, buffer species, chelating agents, dioxin, population growth, vegetation mapping, water analysis, and women in the environment. All entries include complete contact information. Although some resources include one- to three-sentence descriptions, many lack descriptions altogether.

Each entry is repeated in an alphabetical section that follows the subject listings.

For information on less technical resources, readers may want to consult the *Gale Environmental Sourcebook: A Guide to Organizations, Agencies, and Publications* (see entry 80).

75 Environmental Management SourceBook

3rd ed. Environment Today, 1994. Annual. 362p. $29.95 (paper).

The *Environmental Management SourceBook* is the most comprehensive directory of environmental resources of interest to environmental managers. The majority of the book's pages are devoted to a directory of companies that offer environmental products and services. Each main subject category (e.g., wastewater and sludge treatment, site remediation equipment, environmental consulting/engineering services, environmental liability insurance) is further divided into subcategories. For example, under the heading of air emissions control equipment, subheadings include air pumps, electrostatic precipitators, and scrubbers. Entries detail a company's name, address, phone and fax numbers, contact person for purchasing, and cross-references to other subcategories. Compared to the *World Environment Directory* (see entry 96), another directory of companies offering environmental goods and services, the *Environmental Management SourceBook* has slightly fewer entries but is just as descriptive, and it is available at a fraction of the cost. Another section of the *Environmental Management SourceBook*—the section on more than twelve hundred education and information resources, each with a one-sentence description—is incredibly useful. For environmental managers, it is the most complete listing of professional associations, newsletters, magazines and journals, electronic databases, reference works, and training courses. The *SourceBook*—which is actually the annual August issue of *Environment Today*, a monthly newsmagazine for environmental managers—also includes an alphabetical directory of all companies listed, a summary of trends in the field of environmental management, and an index to articles that have appeared in the past year's *Environment Today*.

76 Environmental Profiles: A Global Guide to Projects and People

Edited by Linda Sobel Katz, Sarah Orrick, and Robert Honig. Garland Reference Library of Social Science series. Garland Publishing, 1993. 1,083p. $125.00 (hardcover).

Environmental Profiles provides informative summaries—the most detailed available—on more than 1,500 environmental organizations in 115 countries. More than a third of the directory describes organizations in the United States. Within each country section, entries are divided into four categories: government organization, nongovernment organization, private organization, or university. Each entry includes complete contact information, organizational history, details about staff members and ongoing projects, and resources, both available and needed. Descriptions range in length from half a page to more than two dense pages. An appendix lists organizations by broad subject area: air quality, biodiversity, deforestation, energy, global warming, health, population, transportation, waste, and water quality. A detailed index identifies people, issues, species, legislation, and organizations. This highly recommended guide provides broader coverage and more detailed descriptions than any other environmental directory.

77 Environmental Software Directory

3rd ed. Donley Technology, 1993. Biannual. 446p. $75.00 (spiral-bound).

The *Environmental Software Directory* is an outstanding collection of more than nine hundred commercial and government databases, software, and bulletin board systems that simplify environmental compliance or improve access to technical information. The systems are organized by topic: hazardous substances, waste management, water and wastewater, groundwater and soils, mapping, air pollution, ecology, and others. Each description provides an overview of a resource's objectives and coverage as well as information about system format, developer, distributor, hardware and software requirements, and cost; most of this information is taken directly from user's manuals and promotional materials. Cited resources are readily accessible and useful to a relatively broad audience. The directory contains four indices: software developers and distributors, software, keyword, and computer system, which lists the software that must be run on a particular computer (for example, IBM-compatible or Apple Macintosh). The *Environmental Software Report* (8 issues per year. $95), also published by Donley Technology, is outstanding too. This twenty-four-page newsletter analyzes trends in the environmental software and online industries and reports on new and upgraded software packages, databases, and bulletin board systems. The format alternates between special focus issues and news and analysis. Donley Technology also publishes the *Environmental Code Book Software Report* (see entry 119), which compares twenty-five systems that provide environmental, health, and safety regulations electronically.

78 Environmental Telephone Directory

Government Institutes, 1994. Annual. 256p. $65.00 (paper).

The *Environmental Telephone Directory* is an essential resource for anyone who needs to contact state or federal officials about environmental laws, regulations, policies, and court decisions. This extensive directory contains more than fifteen hundred contacts divided into five sections: U.S. senators and representatives and their environmental aides; U.S. Senate and House committees and subcommittees dealing with environmental issues; Environmental Protection Agency offices and staffers; other federal agencies dealing with the environment; and state environmental agencies. Each section does much more than simply list contact information; for example, readers will find: the jurisdiction, specific meeting times, chairperson, majority and minority members, and complete listings of professional staff members of each congressional committee; maps of EPA regional offices and their jurisdictions; and details on each state's organizational structure for dealing with environmental matters. This highly recommended directory makes it easy to reach the appropriate government official.

79 The Environmentalists: A Biographical Dictionary From the 17th Century to the Present

Alan Axelrod and Charles Phillips. Facts on File, 1993. 258p. $45.00 (hardcover).

The Environmentalists is an annotated directory of people who are significant to the environmental movement in some way. Some five hundred individuals from the U.S. and abroad are included, as well as nearly one hundred major environmental organizations and agencies. To be included, "an individual must either be significantly representative of a significant point of view or methodology or must have exercised significant influence on the study of ecology or on environmental policy." These criteria allow for the inclusion of scientists (Charles Darwin), conservationists (John Muir), activists (Petra Kelly), government administrators (Al Gore), and writers (Barry Lopez). Also featured are some individuals whose significance is not necessarily positive (Saddam Hussein, James Watt). Each detailed entry contains a summary of the individual's major achievements, thoughts, and writings. Entries are often followed by recommendations for further reading. This directory includes many photographs and an index. American conservationists not found here may be located in *National Leaders of American Conservation* (Smithsonian Institution Press, 1985).

80 Gale Environmental Sourcebook: A Guide to Organizations, Agencies, and Publications

Edited by Donna Batten. 2nd ed. Gale Research, 1994. Triennial. 934p. $80.00 (hardcover).

Diskette: Available from Gale Research.

The *Gale Environmental Sourcebook* offers the most comprehensive depth of coverage for the largest variety of U.S. environmental information sources. The resources in this directory cover the full range of environmental issues and are organized by type of information source: 703 associations and organizations; 249 foundations and other funding sources; 396 federal agencies; 1,002 state agencies; 569 national parks, forests, and wildlife refuges; 1,976 commercial, government, nonprofit, and university research facilities; 228 publishers; 652 books; 349 directories;

873 magazines, newspapers, and newsletters; 875 videos; 167 online databases; 381 consultants; 89 clearinghouses and hotlines; 606 libraries; 1,239 environmental corporate contacts; and 432 environmental products. For most sections, information has been lifted from other Gale directories, such as the *Encyclopedia of Associations* (annual) and the *Research Centers Directory* (annual). Some entries lack descriptions (state agencies), while others are described in up to ten sentences (research centers); however, most are two to three sentences in length. The sourcebook contains a glossary, a thorough index, and lists of endangered wildlife and plants and Environmental Protection Agency Superfund cleanup sites. All audiences will find this directory useful as a library reference.

The following directories are similar to the *Gale Environmental Sourcebook*: The *Encyclopedia of Environmental Information Sources* (see entry 74) is targeted toward scientific and engineering professionals and is arranged in subject order; the *Directory of Environmental Information Sources* (see entry 68) is much more selective and will be of interest to business professionals; the *European Environmental Information Sourcebook* (Gale Research, 1994) describes 1,900 European organizations, government agencies, and publications.

81 Green BBS List for Environmental Bulletin Board Systems

Electronic document. Compiled by Bob Chapman. Quarterly. Free.

Bulletin Board: Available on the Earth Art BBS. To connect by modem, dial 803/552-4389. To view, choose *Bulletin Listing*, then *The Latest International GREEN BBS List! (It's Become A "Worldwide Hit"!)*.

The *Green BBS List for Environmental Bulletin Board Systems* lists bulletin boards related to the environment. Available only as an electronic document, the list focuses primarily on local bulletin boards run by home enthusiasts, though some government boards and larger commercial services are included. The list is divided into the following categories: U.S. and Canada boards, toll-free boards, additions since last quarter, boards with temporary problems, verified international boards, unverified boards, those sched-

uled to open soon, and green bulletin boards no longer in operation. Each entry lists the bulletin board name, a one- or two-word comment, access number, highest baud speed, hours of operation, system operator, and type of software the bulletin board runs on. In addition, symbols represent other essential information, such as whether there is a subscription charge and if the parameters are not the standard 8-N-1 (eight bits, no parity, one stop bit). Although various versions of the list are widely uploaded to other bulletin boards and the Internet (look for "GBBS####.ZIP" or "GREENBBS.ZIP" files), the most current version is always available on the Earth Art BBS, where Bob Chapman is system operator. Earth Art BBS, in addition to being the home of GreenNet, which relays messages between environmental bulletin boards, has a GREEN BBS door where users can add to, update, or download this list.

For descriptions of other environmental bulletin boards, especially governmental and industry boards, see *Eco-Data: Using Your PC to Obtain Free Environmental Information* (see entry 71).

82 The Greenpeace Guide to Anti-Environmental Organizations

Edited by Carl Deal. Real Story series. Sponsored by Greenpeace. Odonian Press, 1993; distributed to bookstores and book wholesalers by Publishers Group West. 110p. $5.00 (paper).

The Greenpeace Guide to Anti-Environmental Organizations describes fifty-four organizations that Greenpeace has determined are working against environmental protection. These organizations include public relations firms, corporate front groups, think tanks, legal foundations, endowments and charities, and wise-use groups. Many of the groups (e.g., Alliance for a Responsible CFC Policy, The Sea Lion Defense Fund) have names many consider to be misleading. Entries include contact information; a description of the organization's philosophy, history, and tactics; names of officers; and, most important, a partial list of funding sources. The directory also includes two short essays that provide background on the anti-environmental movement and describe the different categories of groups. This slim guide is a tremendous help not only to activists who need to know what they're up against, but for contributors to environmental causes who want to make sure their support is going to the right place.

83 GreenWorld's Almanac & Directory of Environmental Organizations: Volume One: United States & Canada

1st ed. GreenWorld Environmental Publications, 1994. 326p. $49.95 (paper).

The full-color *GreenWorld's Almanac & Directory of Environmental Organizations* provides detailed descriptions of roughly seven hundred environmental organizations in the U.S. and Canada. Each entry includes contact information, pertinent facts (e.g., date of incorporation, number of members), mission statement, annual fees, description of programs, selected publications, and names of key people who work at the organization. *GreenWorld's* includes all major national organizations and many regional ones as well. The book's twenty-one chapters (e.g., "Urban Environment," "Atmosphere & Climate • Global Warming") cover all environmental topics. Short essays introduce each chapter, and many pages include relevant tables and charts. There are alphabetical and geographical indices as well as cross-references within chapters.

84 A Guide to Selected National Environmental Statistics In The U.S. Government

3rd ed. Environmental Protection Agency, Environmental Statistics and Information Division, 1993. Updated irregularly. 92p. Free (paper).

Diskette: Available from the Environmental Protection Agency, Environmental Statistics and Information Division, free. The information on the diskette was updated in May 1994.

A Guide to Selected National Environmental Statistics In The U.S. Government is a directory of U.S. government programs that regularly compile and distribute national environmental statistics. It includes programs on environmental quality (National Contaminant Biomonitoring Program), natural resources (Timber Sale Information System), human activities that affect the environment (Toxic Releases Inventory), and responses to environmental problems (National Wild and Scenic Rivers System). Each entry is over

a page in length, and includes a description of the program, its data coverage, collection methods, collection frequency, geographic coverage, contact information, and information about its publications and databases. The guide helps analysts, political aides, consultants, scientists, students, and others obtain federal environmental statistics and statistical publications as well as locate experts who are knowledgeable about the data. The version available on diskette updates a few phone numbers and addresses and includes some data tables.

85 Guide to State Environmental Programs

3rd ed. Bureau of National Affairs, 1994. Updated irregularly. 750p. $75.00 (paper).

The *Guide to State Environmental Programs* is an invaluable reference tool for environmental managers. The first part of this guide—fewer than forty pages—outlines federal environmental laws and programs, including the Clean Air Act, the Clean Water Act, and the Resource Conservation and Recovery Act; the remainder of the book profiles, state by state, agencies involved in environmental regulation. The profiles provide remarkable insight into the attitudes and management styles of the different states and even into the different agencies. At a minimum, each chapter includes the following information: a statement of a state's organizational scheme, with applicable agency names, addresses, and telephone numbers, including most effective first point of contact; summaries of a state's major programs; its regulatory priorities and unique characteristics; detailed spill reporting information; and a brief summary of its permit fee structure. Two appendices provide telephone directories of the Environmental Protection Agency and Army Corps of Engineers as well as state and local directories for economic development agencies and other individual state agencies. A useful bibliography is also included.

86 The Harbinger File

8th ed. Harbinger Communications, 1994. Biannual. 365p. $18.50 (paper).

Diskette: Available from Harbinger Communications, with names and addresses only, for $75.00.

EcoNet: For a searchable version, choose *Online Databases*, then *Directories*, then *Harbinger File*.

87 Rocky Mountain Environmental Directory

2nd ed. Harbinger Communications, 1994. Biannual. 427p. $20.00 (paper).

Diskette: Available from Harbinger Communications, with names and addresses only, for $75.00.

EcoNet: For a searchable version, choose *Online Databases*, then *Directories*, then *Rocky Mtn. Environmental Directory*.

The Harbinger File and the *Rocky Mountain Environmental Directory* are the first two volumes of the Global Action and Information Network (GAIN) (see entry 30) National Environmental Directory Project. Eventually there will be a multi-volume comprehensive directory of citizen groups, government agencies, and others concerned with environmental education and environmental action, which will include a volume for every region in the country. GAIN oversees the project, but the research is done by regional organizations. *The Harbinger File* includes 1,560 organizations in California; the *Rocky Mountain Environmental Directory* contains information on 1,840 groups in the states of Colorado, Idaho, Montana, Utah, and Wyoming. (Research for the first volumes covering the Northeast, Southeast, and Great Lakes regions are currently under way.) In all directories, entries include the following: address, phone number, and contact person; a succinct mission statement; national affiliation; year first active; principal geographic focus; up to five keywords; primary activities (for example, education, litigation, or research); services offered (for example, speaker's bureau, grants, or training); sources of funding; membership demographics; number of employees; publications; and specific environmental education programs. Organizations are arranged in alphabetical order by state; they can also be located using the keyword and educational program indices. Geographical indices, mailing labels, and special sorts are also available upon request.

88 Information Systems Inventory

Environmental Protection Agency, Office of Information Resources Management, 1994; distributed by the National Technical Information Service. Annual. 200p. $36.00 (paper).

Diskette: Available from the National Technical Information Service (see entry 8).

Internet: Available as a single file on the Environmental Protection Agency gopher (see entry 56). Choose *EPA Information Locators*, then *Information Systems Inventory*.

The *Information Systems Inventory* is the definitive source of information about the Environmental Protection Agency's (EPA) computer-based information systems and applications. It describes more than five hundred systems, including some models and databases. Although businesses and the general public may find this directory useful, EPA personnel and consultants will find it invaluable because many of the systems are small and meant solely for internal administrative purposes. In addition to a brief—one to four sentences—but informative description, each information system entry includes the sponsoring office, contact person, legislative authorities, database descriptors, access information, necessary hardware and software, keywords, and an indication of whether a system is widely relied upon or only used by a single individual or small group. This directory is organized by sponsoring office—for instance, all of the systems maintained by the Office of Air and Radiation are listed together—and includes both system name and acronym indices. An IBM-compatible version on diskette allows for more powerful searching capabilities. In June 1994, Government Institutes published the same information found in the *Information Systems Inventory* under the title *EPA Database Book* ($68). For descriptions of information systems that are more readily available to the public, refer to the *Environmental Software Directory* (see entry 77) and *Access EPA* (see entry 62).

89 The Nature Directory: A Guide to Environmental Organizations

Susan D. Graham-Lanier. Walker & Company, 1991. 190p. $22.95 (hardcover), $12.95 (paper).

90 Your Resource Guide to Environmental Organizations

Edited by John Seredich. Smiling Dolphin Press, 1991. 514p. $15.95 (paper).

The Nature Directory and *Your Resource Guide to Environmental Organizations* provide detailed descriptions of large and small national environmental organizations. Each entry is one to three pages in length—although *Your Resource Guide* tends toward lengthier descriptions—and includes the purpose, programs, accomplishments, volunteer opportunities, publications, and membership benefits of each non-profit organization. *The Nature Directory* contains 120 entries, while *Your Resource Guide* cites 150, with 71 organizations appearing in both. Both books contain thorough indices. These two directories can serve as outstanding starting points for individuals wishing to select organizations through which they can become more intensely involved with environmental issues. Most of the organizations highlighted in these two directories can also be found in the *Conservation Directory* (see entry 65), though descriptions in that publication tend to be less detailed.

91 Technical Assistance Directory

Environmental Protection Agency, Office of Research and Development, 1993; distributed by the Center for Environmental Research Information. 98p. Free (paper).

The *Technical Assistance Directory* provides detailed contact information for hundreds of experts working in conjunction with the Environmental Protection Agency's Office of Research Development (ORD). All ORD offices and laboratories—twenty-six are found in this directory—are outstanding sources of scientific and technical information. Some of the more prominent laboratories included in this directory are the Atmospheric Research and Exposure Assessment Laboratory, the Health Effects Research Laboratory, and the Robert S. Kerr Environmental Research Laboratory. Each entry provides a photograph and biography of the director, an organizational chart, a one-page program description, and an extensive list of contact people, with telephone numbers and one-line descriptions of their areas of expertise (the book contains an area-of-expertise index). If additional help is needed to locate the appropriate EPA expert, contact the EPA Office of Science, Planning, and Regulatory Evaluation (202/260-7669).

92 U.S. Energy and Environmental Interest Groups: Institutional Profiles

Lettie McSpadden Wenner. Greenwood Press, 1990. 358p. $59.95 (hardcover).

U.S. Energy and Environmental Interest Groups offers insightful analysis of groups that lobby in the fields of environmental and energy policy. This directory begins with an introduction exploring the goals and tactics of the three different types of lobbying groups: trade associations, public-interest groups, and professional, research, and governmental groups. This is followed by entries on 140 organizations, covering history, membership, sources of funding, organizational structure, policy concerns, and tactics for each. The descriptions provide hard-to-find information on membership and goals, including those bills for which the organizations have lobbied. Descriptions provide addresses but not phone numbers. Even though the information is based on surveys and telephone and personal interviews conducted in 1987 and 1988, the background information on the trade and professional groups remains valuable.

93 Who is Who in Service to the Earth

Edited by Hans Keller. 2nd ed. VisionLink Education Foundation, 1993. Updated irregularly. 375p. $30.00 (paper).

Who is Who in Service to the Earth offers a great way to find phone numbers and addresses for both well-known and obscure environmental activists and their organizations. It also includes many peace, New Age, feminist, vegetarian, and other alternative groups. A majority of entries are from the United States. The tremendously expanded second edition, now with more than eight thousand listings, is organized alphabetically by organization name. For each entry, the name of an individual comes first and is followed by the name of the organization he or she represents, complete contact information, and the name of a specific project, including a brief one- to three-sentence description. There are three indices, all useful: people, project, and country, with the United States entries listed by state. Much of the information found in this directory can be obtained from the Ecoline (see entry 21) database which is available on TogetherNet (see entry 59), a computer network.

Hans Keller and the VisionLink Education Foundation have also produced *Who is Who at the Earth Summit, Rio de Janeiro, 1992* ($8.95), which provides contact information for more than twenty-five thousand participants in the Earth Summit; it is organized by country and has name and organization indices.

94   Who's Who Environmental Registry

4th ed. Citation Directories, 1993. 995p. $100.00 (hardcover).

The *Who's Who Environmental Registry* provides biographical sketches for some eight thousand environmental professionals. The focus is on consultants and engineers, but individuals from all fields are represented, including conservationists, scientists, lawyers, and journalists. Individuals are arranged alphabetically within each subject category (e.g., environmental insurance services, environmental marketing, public utilities). Biographies include most items found on a resume: contact information, education, and professional experience, as well as titles, awards, and achievements. All information was provided by the registrants themselves. Other sections include basic information for associations and organizations, universities with environmental programs, and companies. There is a geographical index.

95   World Directory of Environmental Organizations: A Handbook of National and International Organizations and Programs—Governmental and Non-governmental—Concerned with Protecting the Earth's Resources

Edited by Thaddeus C. Trzyna. 5th ed. California Institute of Public Affairs in cooperation with Sierra Club and the World Conservation Union, 1995. Updated every two or three years. 250p. $55.00 (paper).

More than twenty-eight hundred organizations in more than two hundred countries are clearly described in the highly regarded and heavily relied upon *World Directory of Environmental Organizations*. It is the best directory for United Nations organizations, other intergovernmental organizations, and major international organizations. Descriptions clearly convey the strengths of—and differences between—organizations. Organizations that influence policy or that are major sources of information are also included, but receive significantly shorter descriptions. A name index includes all international organizations, but only selected national groups. Two separate sections list all organizations by geographic region and area of interest (e.g., air quality, appropriate technology, economic aspects, forests, land use, noise). The directory also includes a glossary, a chronology of landmark events, and a useful appendix of directories related to environmental protection; directories of organizations in individual countries are provided with the country listings. Contact INFO-TERRA/USA (see entry 6) for additional help in locating international organizations or organizations in other countries, or consult *Environmental Profiles: A Global Guide to People and Projects* (see entry 76).

96   World Environment Directory

7th ed. Business Publishers, 1995. Annual. 800p. $300.00 (paper).

The *World Environmental Directory* offers a way to find North American companies that provide environmental products and services. It is published by Business Publishers, which produces many weekly and biweekly environmental newsletters (e.g., *Air Toxics Report, Solid Waste Report*) that cover regulatory issues and other news items of interest to businesses. Targeted toward those in the industry, the *World Environmental Directory* includes more than seven thousand product manufacturers and professional services in the United States. Each entry includes address, phone and fax numbers, names of a group's president and other key personnel, date of incorporation, and number of employees. Entries also include a set of codes that inform readers of the company's specialties (e.g., LU-7 means Land Use–Environmental Impact). This directory also provides contact information for thousands of federal and state agencies, professional associations, corporate environmental officials, and educational institutions. A separate section includes this same information for Canada. Another good—and less expensive—directory of companies that sell environmental products and provide environmental services is the *Environmental Management SourceBook* (see entry 75). A third directory, *The Green Pages: A Directory of U.S. Suppliers of Environmental Products and Services*, which is produced annually by the Department of Commerce and the Environmental Protection Agency (EPA) in order to boost exports, contains listings for more than one thousand companies; it is available free from the EPA Public Information Center (see entry 3).

97 World Environmental Research Directory

Edited by Susan Farrell. Pira International, 1992; distributed by Gale Research. 300p. $120.00 (paper).

The *World Environmental Research Directory* lists the research projects of industrial, academic, governmental, and private research organizations in twenty-three industrialized countries, including the United States and Canada. Within fourteen subject areas (e.g., energy, management, contaminated land, air pollution, wildlife conservation) organizations are grouped by country. Each organization is listed only under its primary research area; cross-references appear throughout the book under other appropriate subject headings. Entries contain addresses and phone and fax numbers, research project titles, research personnel, length of project, funding, and papers published since 1988. All information has been taken verbatim from questionnaires. There are three indices: project leader, subject, and organization.

Bibliographies

98 Beacham's Guide to Environmental Issues and Sources

5 vols. Beacham Publishing, 1993. 3,335p. $240.00 (hardcover).

Beacham's Guide to Environmental Issues and Sources is a comprehensive bibliography of

books and magazine and journal articles— largely from 1988 through 1993—on all environmental topics. Items are grouped in detailed categories on every environmental topic imaginable (e.g., Earth Day, global warming law and diplomacy, water supply in the former Soviet Union, low-level radiation and electromagnetic fields, light rail, siting hazardous waste facilities, Arctic National Wildlife Refuge). Within each category, resources are grouped by type: books, general interest periodical articles, environmental and professional journal articles, law journal articles, reports, federal government reports, or conference proceedings. Many sections also contain entries in the following categories: technical books, bibliographies, reference, databases, books for young adults, and videos. Roughly one-third of the resources include some sort of annotation—a list of chapter titles, an excerpt, or a third-party summary. *Beacham's Guide* will be most useful to students, particularly those working on term papers, but because it covers so much territory more advanced researchers may also find it helpful. There are no title or author indices, only a keyword index. *Beacham's Guide* also includes the full text of the 1992 edition of *Environmental Quality: Annual Report of the Council on Environmental Quality* (see entry 122).

99 Core List For An Environmental Reference Collection

Environmental Protection Agency, Office of Information Resources Management, Information Access Branch, 1993; distributed by the Environmental Protection Agency's Public Information Center. Updated irregularly. 35p. Free.

The *Core List For An Environmental Reference Collection* lists reference publications that are most often used by Environmental Protection Agency (EPA) librarians. Though most titles listed here are described fully in the *Green Guide*, the *Core List* includes many technical and regulatory reference books the *Green Guide* has chosen to omit. Headings include subject areas (e.g., air, laboratory practices, pesticides) and types of information sources (e.g., dictionaries and glossaries, directories, encyclopedias). A directory of publishers and distributors is also included. This bibliography was not meant for widespread distribution, but copies are available at the EPA Public Information Center (see entry 3) or at regional EPA libraries. There are plans to update and annotate the *Core List*.

100 Ecophilosophy: A Field Guide to the Literature

Donald Edward Davis. R. & E. Miles, 1989. 137p. Out of print.

Ecophilosophy is a comprehensive annotated bibliography of almost three hundred multidisciplinary books related to deep ecology, social ecology, environmental ethics, natural philosophy, and the philosophy of science. Coverage also spans political, scientific, religious, and psychological issues. Descriptive annotations are about six sentences each in length. Appendices include shorter descriptions of more than fifty periodicals and organizations. For research on issues related to environmental philosophy, particularly in the 1970s and 1980s, this is an outstanding resource.

101 Environmental Studies: An Annotated Bibliography

Diane M. Fortner. Magill Bibliographies series. Scarecrow Press and Salem Press, 1994. 157p. $29.50 (hardcover).

Environmental Studies is ideal for high school, undergraduate, and other lay readers interested in learning more about environmental issues. This bibliography describes widely available, full-length books that explore environmental issues in depth; it also includes some technical works. Most of the roughly five hundred resources were published between 1985 and 1990, though many classics and several more recent volumes are also included. Books are arranged by topic: nature and nature writing, environmental history and general studies, atmospheric and climate change, biodiversity, ocean pollution, acid rain and groundwater pollution, household garbage and toxic industrial waste, ambient and indoor air pollution, and the environment and the future. Descriptions range from fifty to two hundred words in length and provide good summaries of each work. *Environmental Studies* is an outstanding source of introductory reading on environmental issues.

102 The Environmentalist's Bookshelf: A Guide to the Best Books

Edited by Robert Merideth. G. K. Hall & Company, 1993. 272p. $40.00 (hardcover).

The Environmentalist's Bookshelf provides information on five hundred of the most acclaimed environmental books, as selected by 236 environmental leaders who responded to a survey. Selections tend to be books that are influential and thought provoking rather than scholarly works, though all types are included. The top five vote getters are Aldo Leopold's *A Sand County Almanac*, Rachel Carson's *Silent Spring* (see entry 216), the Worldwatch Institute's *State of the World* (see entry 130), Paul Erlich's *The Population Bomb*, and Thoreau's *Walden*. Books are arranged alphabetically by author within each of three sections: 100 "core" books (recommended by four or more people); 250 "strongly recommended" books (recommended by two or three people); and 150 "other recommended" books. Many classics are included, although the latter two sections include some books from 1991 and 1992 chosen by editor Robert Merideth. Annotations for the first 350 selections usually exceed 150 words in length and also include comments from survey respondents. The last 150 books listed receive either one-sentence annotations or single comments. This well-indexed book, which contains an appendix that includes an essay on sources for further reference, is good for research and enjoyable to browse. Merideth also compiled the environmental section of *The Reader's Adviser* (R. R. Bowker, 1994), a guide to the best books on a wide range of topics.

103 The Free Market Environmental Bibliography

3rd ed. Competitive Enterprise Institute, 1994. 87p. $10.00 (paper).

The Competitive Enterprise Institute is a nonprofit organization committed to advancing the principles of free enterprise and limited government. Its Environmental Studies Program promotes free-market environmentalism as an alternative to government-mandated solutions to environmental problems, and strives to develop and legitimize an approach to environmental protection that relies upon private property and voluntary contractual arrangements rather than political management. *The Free Market Environmental Bibliography,* an unannotated bibliography, provides citations to books and journal articles that support this ideology. Many citations are from libertarian literature (e.g., "Animal Rights Are an Individual Responsibility" in the *Freeman,* "Law, Property Rights, and Air Pollution" in the *Cato Journal*), although mainstream publications (e.g., "Partnerships for Today and Tomorrow" in the *Nature Conservancy Magazine;* "The Environment: Risk and Reality" in the *Detroit News*) are also cited. Most references date from the early 1980s through 1993. For students and advocates of free-market environmentalism, this bibliography is a good starting point for research.

104 A Guide to Environmental Resources on the Internet

Electronic document. Compiled by Carol Briggs-Erickson and Toni Murphy. 2nd ed. 1994. Free.

Internet: Available on Clearinghouse of Subject-Oriented Resource Guides sites at the University of Michigan.

To view the hypertext version, the URL is **http://www.lib.umich.edu/chhome.html**. Choose *HTML versions,* then *Environment; T. Murphy, C. Briggs-Erickson.*

To view the text version, choose *All Guides,* then *Environment; T. Murphy, C. Briggs-Erickson.* The URL is **gopher://una.hh.lib.umich.edu/00/ inetdirsstacks/environment%3amurphybriggs**.

To retrieve the text version by ftp, the URL is **ftp://una.hh.lib.umich.edu/inetdirsstacks/ environment%3amurphybriggs**.

105 Internet Environmental Resource Guide

Electronic document. Compiled and edited by Janet Dombrowski. A cooperative project of the Washington D. C. Environment and Resources Management Group of the Special Libraries Association. 1993. Free.

Internet: Available via e-mail. To request a copy, send an e-mail message to Janet Dombrowski at **natgeo2@capcon.net** with the words **send environmental guide** in the subject line.

106 Selected Bibliography of Sources of Environmental Information on the Internet

Electronic document. Compiled by Anda Phelps. University of British Columbia, School of Library, Archival and Information Studies. 1994. Free.

Internet: Available on the Clearinghouse of Subject-Oriented Resource Guides sites at the University of Michigan.

At the gopher menu, choose *All Guides,* then *Environment; A. Phelps.* The URL for this document is **gopher://una.hh.lib.umich.edu/00/ inetdirsstacks/environment%3aphelps**.

To retrieve by ftp, the URL for this document is **ftp://una.hh.lib.umich.edu/inetdirsstacks/ environment%3aphelps**.

All three of these documents—*A Guide to Environmental Resources on the Internet,* the *Internet Environmental Resource Guide,* and the *Selected Bibliography of Sources of Environmental Information on the Internet*—inform Internet users about gopher sites, electronic journals, mailing lists, and other Internet resources that pertain to the environment. *A Guide to Environmental Resources on the Internet* is the most comprehensive of the three; its editors promise to issue updates every six months. It contains some short descriptions and is arranged largely by subject. The *Internet Environmental Resource Guide* is more selective, arranged by type of information source, and contains more insightful descriptions. The *Selected Bibliography of Sources of Environmental Information on the Internet,* also arranged by type of information source, contains the longest and most insightful descriptions, but it covers the fewest number of resources.

The Clearinghouse for Subject-Oriented Internet Resource Guides at the University of Michigan is a good Internet source for new bibliographies of Internet resources. In late 1994, this clearinghouse not only contained the *Guide to Environmental Resources on the Internet* and the *Selected Bibliography of Sources of Environmental Information on the Internet* but also the *Guide to Online Resources for the Conservationist* (see entry 107), *International Biodiversity Information Available on the Internet Gopher System* (compiled by Sean Gordon, 1994. On the Clearinghouse it is called "Biodiversity (Gophers); S. Gordon"), and an annotated list of ecology and environmental studies electronic-mailing lists (compiled by Leslie Haas, 1994. On the Clearinghouse it is called "Ecology & Environmental Studies; L. Haas").

107 Guide to Online Resources for the Conservationist

Electronic document. Compiled by Dan Wendling and J. Scott Christianson. 2nd ed. 1993. Updated irregularly. Free.

Bulletin Board: Available on the Coin of the Realm bulletin board. To connect by modem, dial 301/585-6697. Choose *Bulletins*. It is also available as a downloadable file.

Internet: To retrieve by ftp, the URL for this document is **ftp://nic.sura.net/pub/nic/conservation-guide.11–93.txt**.

To view by gopher, go to the Clearinghouse of Subject-Oriented Resource Guides gopher site at the University of Michigan, choose *All Guides*, then *Conservation*. The URL for this document is **gopher://una.hh.lib.umich.edu:70/00/inetdirsstacks/conservation%3awendling**.

The *Guide to Online Resources for the Conservationist* is an outstanding bibliography of all types of online resources on conservation and environmental issues. The guide, which is only available electronically, is geared toward academic researchers, but it will be helpful to everyone. Though many entries are related to the biological sciences, the guide also has excellent coverage of other environmental science topics such as geology and toxicology, as well as other related topics like green politics, home energy conservation, and government publications. Arranged by type of information source, it provides descriptions of hundreds of resources both on the Internet (lists, electronic publications, gopher sites, Usenet newsgroups, and bulletin boards) and non-Internet resources (open access dial-up bulletin boards and online services, FidoNet and RIMEnet networked bulletin boards, general interest commercial online services, and database vendors). Online research tips and information about how the bibliography was compiled are found throughout the document.

108 In Praise of Nature

Edited by Stephanie Mills. Island Press, 1990. 258p. $29.95 (hardcover), $16.00 (paper).

In Praise of Nature provides a good introduction to environmental thought, via descriptions and excerpts of books on a variety of environmental themes. Selections are largely classics (*A Sand County Almanac, Small Is Beautiful, Walden*) relating to nature appreciation or environmental philosophy, although some reference books— *State of the World* (see entry 130), *The Forest and the Trees* (see entry 292)—and other works recent at the time of publication are also included. Five thematic sections (earth, air, fire, water, spirit) include ten to twelve books or profiles of authors each; a short essay introduces each section's theme. Roughly two pages—informal reviews and/or excerpts—are devoted to each entry. A sixth section includes shorter descriptions of more than one hundred other relevant books. *In Praise of Nature* is not meant to be comprehensive, but rather to introduce readers to environmental ideas and to suggest materials for further reading.

109 The Island Press Bibliography of Environmental Literature

Compiled by Joseph A. Miller, Sarah M. Friedman, David C. Grigsby, and Annette Huddle. Sponsored by The Yale School of Forestry and Environmental Studies. Island Press, 1993. 396p. $48.00 (hardcover).

The Island Press Bibliography of Environmental Literature describes most of the major technical environmental materials published in the 1980s. It was produced to survey the extent of available literature, and will be of most use to scientists and policymakers though lay readers will also find it helpful. The bibliography covers all ecological, natural resource, and environmental issues: e.g., conservation biology, fisheries, land degradation, endangered plants, forest management, society and environment, nature writing and thought, U.S. laws and legislation, economic costs and benefits, public health, and environmental control technology. Books and reports are most often cited, but journals, indices, and other reference materials are also included. Each entry has an insightful two-sentence annotation.

Most of the 3,084 entries date from the 1980s through 1991, though some older classics are included. Most publications are from the U.S., though many significant British and other foreign works are also cited. The book's indices and cross-references are excellent.

110 Island Press Environmental Sourcebook: Books for Better Conservation and Management

Island Press, 1995. Annual. 32–48p. Free (paper).

The *Island Press Environmental Sourcebook* is a selective book catalog of the best recent environmental books. Some two hundred popular, academic, and reference books from a variety of publishers and organizations are described. Many entries—though not all—are published by Island Press, one of the largest publishers of books on conservation and environmental issues. Topics covered include wetlands, biodiversity, ecological restoration, water quality and use, toxics and hazardous waste, and nonprofit administration. All items described in the sourcebook are sold through Island Press. This is one of the best sources for finding out about the newest and best environmental publications—everyone should have a copy of this sourcebook. Another excellent annotated environmental book catalog is *Books of the Big Outside* (see entry 285), which focuses on wilderness, biodiversity, and environmental thought.

111 Reading About the Environment: An Introductory Guide

Pamela E. Jansma. Libraries Unlimited, 1993. 252p. $27.50 (paper).

Reading About the Environment offers annotations of books and articles for the nonspecialist. The 786 entries are from the 1960s through the early 1990s, though a majority of the works were published earlier than 1987. Symbols note whether a source is a good overview of the chapter topic, a scholarly work, or an excellent factual source. The section on air pollution is representative of most sections: It includes a book chapter from 1965, an activist handbook from 1975, a book from 1982, and a 1989 *Scientific American* article; however, no special symbols are included in this chapter. For a more selective annotated

guide to introductory reading on environmental issues, consult *Environmental Studies: An Annotated Bibliography* (see entry 101).

Other Bibliographies

◆ The *EPA National Publications Catalog* (see entry 7, National Center for Environmental Publications and Information)

Reference Handbooks

112 AGENDA 21: The Earth Summit Strategy to Save Our Planet

Edited by Daniel Sitarz. EarthPress, 1993. 321p. $24.95 (hardcover), $15.95 (paper).

AGENDA 21: The Earth Summit Strategy to Save Our Planet is an abridged version of *AGENDA 21*, the final report of the United Nations Conference on Environment and Development (UNCED)—better known as the 1992 Earth Summit. Adopted by 172 nations on June 14, 1992, in Rio de Janeiro, *AGENDA 21* is a blueprint for achieving sustainable development in the coming years. This book includes the full text of the preamble of the actual *AGENDA 21*; the forty chapters of that document were rearranged, condensed, and clarified in this book's seven chapters: "The Quality of Life on Earth"; "Efficient Use of the Earth's Natural Resources"; "The Protection of Our Global Commons"; "The Management of Human Settlements"; "Chemicals and the Management of Waste"; "Sustainable Economic Growth"; and "Implementing AGENDA 21." This volume is much easier to read than the often convoluted language of the actual document, and loses very little of the original meaning. The text of the actual *AGENDA 21* and other official Earth Summit documents are available in print and on CD-ROM from United Nations Publications. They are also available and searchable electronically on the United Nations Development Programme Internet gopher—gopher to **gopher.undp.org**, choose *United Nations Conferences*, then *United Nations Conference on Environment & Development (UNCED)*. The text of *AGENDA 21* and other nongovernmental organizations' documents related to the Earth Summit can be delivered from the NGONET library automatically by electronic mail; to receive a complete catalog of these documents, send an e-mail message to **ngonet-lib@chasque.apc.org** with the words **send catalog** in the body of the message.

113   Atlas of the Environment

Edited by Geoffrey Lean and Don Hinrichsen. 2nd ed. Sponsored by the World Wildlife Fund. HarperPerennial, 1994. Updated irregularly. 192p. $20.00 (paper).

The *Atlas of the Environment* is an excellent global environmental atlas loaded with maps, charts, and graphs. The book's forty-two chapters feature topics on environmental and natural resource issues such as fuelwood shortage and ocean mineral resources, as well as topics necessary to understanding environmental issues, like education and Gross National Product. Each chapter contains two full pages of text and a well-designed, two-page spread of color maps, charts, graphs, and tables. The combination of short essays and authoritative statistics from the United Nations, the Worldwatch Institute (see entry 51), The World Conservation Union (see entry 280), World Wildlife Fund (see entry 282) and other sources makes this a solid reference book on the status of humanity's impact on the environment. A more simplistic quick-reference atlas, *The State of the Earth Atlas* (Joni Seager. Touchstone, 1990), contains thirty-seven maps coded with icons, and is aimed at a more popular audience.

114   Atlas of United States Environmental Issues

Robert J. Mason and Mark T. Mattson. MacMillan Publishing Company, 1990. 264p. $95.00 (hardcover).

The *Atlas of United States Environmental Issues* provides an excellent introduction to national environmental issues. This atlas is divided into eighteen chapters on such issues as forests, noise pollution, and water use and quality. It is divided equally between essays and 130 graphics—maps, photographs, charts, tables, and diagrams. The text does not explain the data contained in the graphics, but rather effectively describes and analyzes U.S. policy and legislation. Each map—e.g., "Generation of Industrial Hazardous Waste per Capita"—shades all fifty states based on their rel-

ative environmental standing. Tables and charts also show a state-by-state analysis. Page-long case studies of events like the Mount St. Helens eruption, the 1988 Yellowstone fires, and the Exxon Valdez oil spill are also included. Backmatter includes a selected bibliography, an index, a glossary, and a summary of national environmental laws (1785–1988).

115   Briefing Book on Environmental and Energy Legislation

Compiled by Environmental and Energy Study Conference. Environmental and Energy Study Institute, 1995. Annual. 230p. $75.00 (paper).

The *Briefing Book on Environmental and Energy Legislation* is prepared especially for members of Congress and their staffs, though it is also widely used by activists, scientists, students, and businesspeople who need overviews of federal environmental laws and background on environmental issues. The first large section devotes two to four pages each to more than thirty environmental issues, providing background on scientific knowledge, defining current policy issues, and summarizing recent congressional action. The second section provides summaries—averaging four pages each—of fourteen major laws and paragraph-long descriptions of all other federal environmental and natural resource laws. Shorter sections include a directory of related congressional committee jurisdictions and memberships, a primer on the budget process, and a twenty-five-page glossary of terms related to environmental science, law, and policy. The book's purchase price includes updates at summer recess and a year-end wrap-up.

For up-to-date, behind-the-scenes coverage of environmental legislation in the Senate and House of Representatives, readers should consult the Environmental and Energy Study Institute's (see entry 23) *Weekly Bulletin* (published every Monday when Congress is in session, 32–40 p., $395 per year).

116   The Environment Encyclopedia and Directory

1st ed. Europa Publications, 1994; distributed in the United States by Gale Research. 416p. $325.00 (hardcover).

The Environment Encyclopedia and Directory is a multipurpose sourcebook of international environmental information. It is divided into five sections: twenty world and regional maps that highlight environmental issues; definitions of one thousand terms and events; descriptions of environmental organizations from around the world; an extensive annotated bibliography of periodicals; and biographical details for key individuals in the environmental movement. The bulk of the sourcebook is devoted to the directory of organizations. Each entry provides contact information and a brief description of relevant activities and publications of both governmental and nongovernmental organizations working on environmental issues.

117   Environment Online: The Greening of Databases

Edited by Paula Hane. Eight Bit Books, 1992. 88p. $19.95 (paper).

Environment Online is a guide for both beginners and experts searching commercial databases for environmental information. The book is a collection of reprinted articles from *DATABASE* magazine. The three main articles, subtitled "General Interest Databases" (August 1991), "Scientific and Technical Databases" (October 1991), and "Business and Regulatory Information" (August 1992), describe the general coverage and useful features of each database (e.g., *Books in Print, PR Newswire, General Science Index, Public Opinion Online, Pollution Abstracts, Teratogen Information System, Environmental Information Networks*) in roughly a paragraph; database vendors are also listed. These three articles also include general searching tips and a number of sidebars, including a list of environmental terms and phrases, a list of full-text newsletters available from commercial online vendors, and descriptions of thirty environmental bulletin board systems. (These articles are updated each year in the December issue of *DATABASE* magazine.) The book also includes reprints of six *DATABASE* and *ONLINE* columns that are cited in the above articles: "Material Safety Data Sheets: Online and CD-ROM Sources," "TOXLINE Search Tips," "Searching the Federal Register," "Online Access to Legal Articles Indices," "Researching Federal Legisla-

tive Histories Online," and "Current State Legislation Information Online."

118   Environment Reporter

Bureau of National Affairs, 1970–. Weekly. $1,113/year for 38 binders and a looseleaf subscription service. Other prices vary depending on the service.

CD-ROM: Available as part of *BNA's Environmental Library on CD* from the Bureau of National Affairs.

Database Vendor: Available on LEXIS/NEXIS and WESTLAW.

Environment Reporter is a comprehensive subscription service on environmental laws, regulations, and policy. *Environment Reporter* is the most well known environmental publication of the Bureau of National Affairs (BNA), a publishing company that specializes in regulatory affairs. The complete service includes thirty-eight three-ring binders. Thirty-six of these binders serve as reference, and are updated as necessary. These include: nine binders that contain the full text of federal laws, regulations, and other executive agency documents; twenty-four binders that contain the full text of laws and regulations from many states in the areas of air, water, solid waste, and land use; and three binders of federal and state laws and regulations on mining issues. The contents of the final two binders— "Decisions" and "Current Developments"—are issued every week. "Decisions" contains the full text of significant court decisions affecting environmental management and pollution control. "Current Developments" is an outstanding way to keep up with all environmental news, mostly related to pending legislation, regulations, agency actions, and litigation. There are roughly forty articles each week, averaging over a page in length each. "Current Developments" also includes news briefs, reprints of the *Federal Register*, announcements of executive agency activities, and a calendar of events. The contents of "Current Developments" are either expanded or condensed in other BNA publications; among these are *BNA's Daily Environmental Report*, which includes more than fifty pages every business day, and *BNA's National Environment Watch,* an eight-page weekly briefing for executives. BNA also offers other subscription services similar to *Environment Reporter* (e.g., *Chemical Regulations Reporter, International Environment Reporter, Toxics Law Reporter, California Environment Reporter*). The entire *Environment Reporter,* and most other related BNA publications, are available and updated daily online on Dialog, LEXIS, and WESTLAW. Parts of *Environment Reporter* and *Chemical Regulations Reporter* are also available on *BNA's Library on CD,* a CD-ROM. The full text of items summarized in BNA publications, as well as other research services, are also available through the BNA Plus service (contact BNA for subscription information). For current news, legal research, and regulatory reference, *Environment Reporter* and its various sister publications are unparalleled. See also *Environmental Law Reporter* (see entry 121), a similar subscription service from the Environmental Law Institute.

119 Environmental Code Book Software Report

Donley Technology, 1994. 60p. $89.00 (paper).

Environmental Code Book Software Report, a special report from the publishers of the *Environmental Software Directory* (see entry 77), is a must-have resource for anyone who references environmental, health, or safety regulations online, or on diskette or CD-ROM. It explains the different types of systems that are available and the key features of each. Twenty-five systems are profiled; tables compare the systems head to head on their coverage of federal, state, and international laws and regulations, hardware and software requirements, viewing and printing features, search methods, and price and update options. Contact information for distributors is also included. For anyone who is choosing software with which to view environmental regulations, this report will make the decision-making process easier.

120 Environmental Data Report

4th ed. Prepared for United Nations Environment Programme by the GEMS Monitoring and Assessment Research Centre in cooperation with the World Resources Institute. Blackwell Publishers, 1993. Biannual. 408p. $74.95 (paper).

The *Environmental Data Report* is the most comprehensive and current collection of country-by-country environmental statistical data. All United Nations Environment Programme (UNEP) (see entry 10) member countries are included. Each biannual report supplies tables and charts, with most data from 1970 to the present in the following chapter categories: environmental pollution, climate, natural resources, population and development, human health, energy, industry and transport, waste, and international cooperation. Most data sets within these categories are repeated in each report with updated information. Text explains the data sets and provides other technical background information important to understanding and interpreting environmental trends.

Many other resources provide environmental statistical data. Lay readers may want to use *The Information Please Environmental Almanac* (see entry 128). Those looking for more information on data in developing countries should refer to the *Directory of Country Environmental Studies* (see entry 66). Those looking for data in developed countries should consult *OECD Environmental Data: Compendium* (Organization for Economic Cooperation and Development, Biannual).

121 Environmental Law Reporter (ELR)

Environmental Law Institute, 1970–. Weekly. $995.00/year for 7 binders and a looseleaf subscription service.

Database Vendor: Available on LEXIS/NEXIS and WESTLAW.

The *Environmental Law Reporter (ELR)* is a subscription service on recent developments pertaining to environmental law. Widely used by lawyers, *ELR* is similar in concept to the Bureau of National Affairs' *Environment Reporter* (see entry 118), but with a few minor differences. The two main binders that are issued monthly are "Litigation" and "News and Analysis." "Litigation" provides the full text of significant court decisions, roughly the same number in a year as *Environment Reporter*'s "Decisions" binder. "News and Analysis"—roughly 50 pages a month—contains twenty pages of paragraph-long news briefs and other updates; it also contains two or three in-depth articles that provide legal analysis, and a bibliography of recent environmental articles in legal literature. A four-page newsletter, *Update*, has its own binder and is issued on the three weeks of the month that these two regular services are not. There are four other continuously updated reference binders: pending litigation, federal statutes, federal agency documents, and an index. ELR lacks *Federal Register* reprints and information from state agencies. All items not published in full text are available from the *Environmental Law Reporter*'s Document Service.

122 Environmental Quality: Annual Report of the Council on Environmental Quality

Council on Environmental Quality. 23rd ed. Government Printing Office, 1994. Annual. 472p. $16.00 (paper).

Environmental Quality is an important reference book of federal environmental information. It has been published annually since 1970 by the Council on Environmental Quality (CEQ), an independent office of the Executive Branch, and is meant to serve as the official "State of the Environment" report of the federal government. Topic areas vary widely in each edition, focusing on areas of particular importance in the past year. In general, *Environmental Quality* summarizes the state of environmental quality in the United States and recommends changes in federal policy and management strategies. The publication also includes a section of statistical tables with data from various federal sources. In 1981 and 1989 this statistical information was expanded and published as a separate document entitled *Environmental Trends* (Government Printing Office).

123 The Environmental Sourcebook

Edith Carol Stein. Lyons & Burford, 1992; in cooperation with the Environmental Data Research Institute. 264p. $16.95 (paper).

The Environmental Sourcebook serves as an introduction to environmental issues as well as a bibliography of environmental information sources for nonspecialists. Each of the book's twelve chapters is divided into two parts. One part describes an environmental issue (agriculture, biodiversity, oceans, etc.), providing a good summary of the causes, effects, and extent of environmental degradation as well as insight on how a particular environmental problem can be solved. The latter two-thirds of each chapter is a bibliography, which covers books and reports, periodicals, and organizations. Also in each chapter, the ten foundations that donated the most money to that issue in 1990 are listed, along with dollar amounts given and number of grants awarded.

124 Environmental Viewpoints

Edited by Marie Lazzari. 3rd ed. Gale Research, 1994. Annual. 400p. $49.95 (hardcover).

Environmental Viewpoints provides excerpts and reprinted essays from more than eighty popular and professional periodicals and recent books and government publications. Each edition—or "volume" as the publisher refers to them—contains twenty topical chapters that cover virtually every environmental topic, from acid rain and alternative fuels to wetland preservation and the world water supply. The essays presented in each fifteen- to twenty-page chapter include both historical and current information that clearly illustrates several sides of each issue. Each essay is accompanied by full bibliographic information and each chapter concludes with a select list of additional readings. Essays require no special technical background; they are intended for adult lay readers as well as high school and entry-level college students. There are subject and keyword indices. Future editions will continue to incorporate new developments in each topic area as well as relevant new topics. This annual series serves as an excellent primer to current environmental issues and debates.

125 Gale Environmental Almanac

Edited by Russ Hoyle. 1st ed. Gale Research, 1993. Triennial. 689p. $79.95 (hardcover).

The *Gale Environmental Almanac* is an unusual but useful reference book. Hidden among twelve essays is a grab bag of extensive environmental reference information: a chronology of major U.S. environmental events; biographical descriptions of key historical figures, modern leaders, and environmental scientists; voting records for the 102nd Congress; summaries of U.S. legislation and international treaties; a bibliography of periodicals and reference books; and directories of national and state parks, organizations, contacts at federal agencies, congressional committees, international agencies, environmental science research centers, law firms, colleges and universities, and contacts at major corporations. While each of these features can be found in more detail elsewhere, the *Gale Environmental Almanac* is meant for the public or school library that wants all of this information in one book. However, it is difficult to use this almanac for quick reference because none of the features listed above are included in its main table of contents. Essays—three chapters on U.S. environmental history and one each on government, scientific uncertainty, business and the environment, international issues, environmental communications, climate change, biodiversity, energy, and toxics and health—are written by experts and are surprisingly insightful. All information was current in mid-1993.

126 Green Globe Yearbook of International Co-operation on Environment and Development

Edited by Helge Ole Bergesen and Georg Parmann. 3rd ed. Sponsored by the Fritjof Nansen Institute, Norway. Oxford University Press, 1994. Annual. 354p. $45.00 (hardcover).

The *Green Globe Yearbook of International Co-operation on Environment and Development* is an excellent quick-reference book on international environmental policy. The first half of the book features essays showing how the international community has been solving specific environment and development issues, what the main obstacles to effective international solutions are, and what is needed to overcome the barriers. The book's second part provides essential at-a-glance information on major environmental treaties, summarizing such information as the time and place of adoption, number of parties that have signed a treaty, how the finances are arranged, how the treaty is monitored and implemented, and related publications. The yearbook's third part provides information (e.g., contact information, publications, summary of activities, organizational structure, finances) on relevant intergovernmental organizations (e.g., Food and Agriculture Organization, World Health Organization) and major international nongovernmental organizations (e.g., Greenpeace International, Third World Network).

127 Green Index: A State-By-State Guide to the Nation's Environmental Health

Bob Hall and Mary Lee Kerr. Sponsored by the Institute for Southern Studies. Island Press, 1991. Updated irregularly. 162p. $29.95 (hardcover), $19.95 (paper).

Diskette: Available from the Institute for Southern Studies.

The *Green Index* serves as a good starting point for those wishing to get a sense of how states compare in terms of pollution. Tables rank each state by 256 indicators such as carbon dioxide emissions, number of Superfund sites, persons per motor vehicle, and amount of energy generated from renewable sources. Tables and shaded maps offer at-a-glance comparisons of states and regions; the book's text gives background on the issues and summarizes the trends reflected by the numbers in the tables. The first chapter ranks the best and worst performers, highlighting areas in which each state leads and lags behind. More sophisticated users should not rely solely on the rankings, but rather should interpret the data for themselves; complete data sets are available on diskette. A new edition is planned for release in summer 1995. It will include all of the information found in the first edition, plus several new features, including data for change over time, environmental justice indicators, and interviews with individuals involved with specific struggles. The new data will also be available on diskette; contact the institute for details about the new edition.

128 The Information Please Environmental Almanac

Compiled by the World Resources Institute. 3rd ed. Houghton Mifflin, 1994. Annual. 704p. $11.95 (paper).

The Information Please Environmental Almanac is an excellent quick-reference tool aimed at a popular audience. Its coverage of current national and international statistical data is excellent. There is one page of data, for each U.S. state and Canadian province, that covers selected topic areas: solid waste generated per capita, total water used per day per capita, etc. For more than 150 countries, there are two-page spreads that describe the country's major environmental problems and provide such statistical data as the percentage of all land that is protected and the country's share of world greenhouse emissions. The almanac also has many other components: background essays on environmental issues, the year in review, news articles and case studies, directories of organizations and state agencies, summaries of recent books, and statistical facts and rankings for U.S. metropolitan areas. All essays include a variety of charts and tables. Essay topics change annually; most environmental issues are covered in each volume. This reference work is current, authoritative, and inexpensive.

129 National Environmental Scorecard

Edited by Sarah Anderson, Betsy Loyless, and Peter L. Kelley. League of Conservation Voters, 1994. Annual. 51p. $6.00 (paper).

Internet: Available in hypertext on the Institute for Global Communications (see entry 57) World Wide Web site; the URL for this document is **http://www.econet.apc.org/lcv/scorecard.html**.

The *National Environmental Scorecard* rates members of Congress based on key votes on environmental issues. The guide records congressional votes and calculates the percentage of times each representative and senator was aligned with the position of the League of Conservation Voters (LCV) (see entry 37). The 1994 edition bases its ratings on twelve votes and four co-sponsorships in the Senate and fourteen votes and six co-sponsorships in the House of Representatives. Text summarizes the intent of the legislation, its history, and whether a vote of yes or no is considered pro-environmental. Charts record the votes of each senator and representative individually, and give LCV ratings for the current year as well as the two previous congressional sessions. A hypertext version is available on the Internet. *Vote for the Earth: the League of Conservation Voters' Election Guide* (Earth Works Press), an adaptation of the *Scorecard* for a popular audience, was published in 1992.

130 State of the World: A Worldwatch Institute Report on Progress Toward a Sustainable Society

Edited by Lester R. Brown. Sponsored by the Worldwatch Institute. 12th ed. W. W. Norton & Company, 1995. Annual. 265p. $23.00 (hardcover), $11.95 (paper).

State of the World is one of the most respected guides to the health of the planet. This flagship publication of the Worldwatch Institute (see entry 51) was created to be a single integrated analysis of issues regularly found in annual reports from United Nations agencies: *State of the World Environment* (United Nations Environment Programme), *State of World Population* (United Nations Population Fund), *State of Food and Agriculture* (Food and Agriculture Organization), *World Development Report* (World Bank), and *World Economic Survey* (International Monetary Fund). Essay topics vary with each edition, and are often excerpts or adaptations of recent and forthcoming *Worldwatch Papers*. Chapter titles for the 1994 edition are: "Carrying Capacity: Earth's Bottom Line," "Redesigning the Forest Economy," "Safeguarding Oceans," "Reshaping the Power Industry," "Reinventing Transport," "Using Computers for the Environment," "Assessing Environmental Health Risks," "Cleaning Up After the Arms Race," "Rebuilding the World Bank," and "Facing Food Insecurity." More than 100,000 English-language copies of *State of the World* are sold annually; the book is also translated into 25 other languages.

131 Statistical Record of the Environment

Edited by Arsen J. Darnay. 2nd ed. Gale Research, 1993. 855p. $105.00 (hardcover).

Diskette: Available from Gale Research.

The *Statistical Record of the Environment* is the best single resource of technical and popular statistical data on national environmental issues. The book's 851 charts, graphs, and tables are grouped into the following sections: air, water, land; pollutants and wastes; effects; costs, budgets, and expenditures; tools, methods, and solutions; pollution control industry; general industry and government data; cities, states, regions, and nations; laws and regulations; and politics and opinions. Representative entries include: "Tree Planting in the U.S.," "State Land-fill Capacity," and "Used Beverage Can Pricing." Data is taken from more than 150 governmental and nongovernmental sources, which are well cited. Both the table of contents and keyword index are detailed. This book is a tremendously useful source for students and politicians, or anyone who needs U.S. data at a glance.

132 Vital Signs: The Trends That Are Shaping Our Future

Lester R. Brown, Hal Kane, and Ed Ayres. Sponsored by Worldwatch Institute. 3rd ed. W. W. Norton & Company, 1994. Annual. 160p. $22.00 (hardcover), $10.95 (paper).

Diskette: Data from *Vital Signs* is available on a diskette that contains statistical information from several Worldwatch Institute publications. It is available from the Worldwatch Institute for $89.00.

Vital Signs serves as a succinct and authoritative introduction to international environmental trends over the last forty years. This small book presents trends that measure progress toward a sustainable world in a way that can be readily grasped by all audiences. Coverage includes not only natural resource and environmental issues such as grain harvest and solar cell production, but also economic and social indicators such as income distribution, cigarette consumption, and military expenditures. Each trend—e.g., "Cumulative Generation of Irradiated Fuel From Commercial Nuclear Plants, 1965–1990"—is presented in a two-page spread: the left side summarizes and analyzes the data that the right side presents in tabular and graphical form. Though some topics change from year to year, the focus is more consistent than *State of the World* (see entry 130). *Vital Signs* offers an excellent way to gain a broad, historical perspective on planetary environmental trends.

133 The World Environment 1972–1992: Two Decades of Challenge

Edited by Mostafa K. Tolba and Osama A. El-Kholy in association with E. El-Hinnawi, M. W. Holdgate, D. F. McMichael, and R. E. Munn. Chapman & Hall, on behalf of the United Nations

Environment Programme, 1992. 884p. $89.95 (hardcover), $39.95 (paper).

An authoritative guide to global environmental issues, supplemented by statistical tables and graphs, *The World Environment 1972–1992* is largely a summary of environmental trends, with many citations to the world's most authoritative studies. The book's first ten chapters summarize trends for major environmental issues, from air pollution to toxic chemicals to hazardous wastes. The second set of chapters reviews how different sectors of the economy—e.g., agriculture and fisheries, energy, tourism—have affected the human environment. Final chapters summarize public perceptions and attitudes, tools for environmental understanding and management, national and international responses, and future challenges and opportunities. Not meant to be read cover to cover, this influential document is valuable for quick reference. Similar volumes were published in 1982 *(The World Environment 1972–1982)* and 1987 *(State of the Environment).* The United Nations Environment Programme (see entry 10) also publishes *State of the World Environment* reports annually, which are harder to locate and less useful, since each report focuses on only one or at best a few environmental themes.

134 World Resources

A report by the World Resources Institute in collaboration with the United Nations Environment Programme and the United Nations Development Programme. Oxford University Press, 1994. Biannual. 416p. $35.00 (hardcover), $21.95 (paper).

Diskette: Available from World Resources Institute for $99.95.

World Resources is one of the most authoritative sources available of global environmental statistical data and information. Most of the book presents trends in many major global natural resource areas, including food and agriculture, forests and rangelands, biodiversity, energy, water, and climate. In each edition, a few special themes are also highlighted; this edition spotlights resource consumption, population growth, and women, and also contains essays on China and India. These essays are complemented by case studies and are supplemented by many graphs and tables on specific topics or regions. The remainder of the book provides more than fifty comprehensive statistical tables that compare most every country in the world on a variety of issues. Many of these tables ("Mortality and Nutrition 1970–1995," "Freshwater Resources and Withdraws") are updated biannually. This work is well annotated and very up to date. Two companion publications—a guide for high school teachers ($5.95) and a tremendously useful IBM-compatible diskette that expands upon the data in the print edition—are also sold by the World Resources Institute (see entry 50).

Other Reference Handbooks

◆ The *Global Ecology Handbook* (see entry 31, Global Tomorrow Coalition)

◆ *Green Essentials: What You Need to Know About the Environment* (see entry 148)

Dictionaries and Encyclopedias

135 The Concise Oxford Dictionary of Ecology

Edited by Michael Allaby. Oxford University Press, 1994. 420p. $35.00 (hardcover), $12.95 (paper).

136 The Dictionary of Ecology and Environmental Science

Edited by Henry W. Art. Reference Book series. Produced by Storey Communications. Henry Holt, 1993. 640p. $60.00 (hardcover).

137 Facts on File Dictionary of Environmental Science

Edited by L. Harold Stevenson and Bruce Wyman. Science Dictionaries series. Facts on File, 1991. 294p. $24.95 (hardcover), $12.95 (paper).

These three dictionaries feature clear, concise definitions of thousands of terms from the fields of ecology, biology, chemistry, geology, oceanography, toxicology, and climatology. In addition to covering the same topic areas, the dictionaries target the same audience: students, professors, businesspeople, environmental managers, and all interested nonspecialists. *The Concise Dictionary of Ecology* and *The Dictionary of Ecology*

and Environmental Science provide five thousand and eight thousand brief definitions, respectively, which rarely exceed one hundred words, while the *Facts on File Dictionary* covers nearly four thousand terms with slightly more detailed definitions. All three contain extensive cross-references. For more in-depth treatment of environmental science terms, consult the *Encyclopedia of Environmental Science and Engineering* (see entry 141) or the *McGraw-Hill Encyclopedia of Environmental Science and Engineering* (see entry 149).

138 Dictionary & Thesaurus of Environment, Health & Safety

Department of Energy, Office of Environment, Safety and Health. CRC Press, 1992. 510p. $75.00 (paper).

The *Dictionary & Thesaurus of Environment, Health & Safety* is more useful as a thesaurus than as a dictionary. The publication contains more than five thousand terms commonly used in government documents. Although this resource focuses heavily on environmental safety and health terms in the energy field, it also covers a broad spectrum of other terms, such as "greenhouse effect," "grenade launchers," "fugitive emissions," "non-attainment areas," "end box ventilation system," and "best available retrofit technology." Each term is followed by synonymous terms, related terms, broader terms, and narrower terms as well as the source or subject category of the term (i.e., *Environmental Protection Agency Glossary* or air pollution), and a one- to two-sentence definition. Two appendices—a listing of all thesaurus acronyms and a listing of all terms under the broader subject terms—are particularly valuable. This unique resource is essential for government employees and others who need to decipher government environmental safety and health materials.

139 Dictionary of Environment and Development: People, Places, Ideas and Organizations

Andy Crump. 1st ed. MIT Press, 1993. 272p. $40.00 (hardcover), $16.95 (paper).

The *Dictionary of Environment and Development* provides lengthy definitions for eight hundred popular terms in two now-complementary fields: environment and development. Author Andy Crump, an ecologist at the World Health Organization in Geneva, has produced an encyclopedia for those in the environmental field who need background on international development terms. International organizations (International Monetary Fund, Three Gorges Project), treaties (International Commodity Agreement, Treaty of Brussels), people (Idi Amin, U Thant), and events (International Drinking Water Supply and Sanitation Decade, Three Mile Island) are particularly well covered. Broad terms in the fields of health (diabetes), peace (disarmament), agriculture (dustbowl), international economics (debt swap), and the environment (dioxins) are also included. Entries are much longer than those in a standard dictionary, averaging over a third of a page in length. This first edition was originally published in London by Earthscan Publications in 1991.

140 A Dictionary of Environmental Quotations

Edited by Barbara K. Rodes and Rice Odell. Simon & Schuster, 1992. 288p. $35.00 (hardcover).

A Dictionary of Environmental Quotations offers approximately 3,700 quotations taken from books, articles, speeches, and bumper stickers. The quotes are divided into 143 scientific (deforestation, ocean pollution), philosophical (aesthetics, quality of life), and other related topic categories (automobiles, citizen action, economic growth, zoning). Each quotation includes the name of the author, occasion or publication title, and date. There is a good mix of historical and recent selections; quotes are arranged in chronological order within topic categories. Authors include famous and obscure politicians, philosophers, and poets. There are author and subject indices; topic categories are cross-referenced. This reference book is both fun to browse and useful for writing speeches, term papers, and articles.

141 Encyclopedia of Environmental Science and Engineering

Edited by James R. Pfafflin and Edward N. Ziegler. 3rd ed. 2 vols. Gordon & Breach Science Publishers, 1992. 1,884p. $545.00 (hardcover).

The *Encyclopedia of Environmental Science and Engineering* contains eighty encyclopedic essays, by leading international authorities, covering the fields of environmental science and technology. This well-edited work is primarily for environmental scientists and engineers and public officials, managers, and attorneys, but lay readers will also find it useful. The work does not provide concise, working definitions of terms and ideas; rather, it explains many related concepts within lengthy chapters—from four to fifty pages in length. This format permits the editors to draw connections between related concepts and enables the reader to better comprehend how an idea fits into a particular area of study. Chapter titles are broad and include such areas as acid rain, community health, desalination, ecosystem theory, energy sources, hydrology, legal aspects, statistical methods, noise, and pesticides. Each well-cited essay includes drawings, tables, charts, and graphs. An outstanding index allows users to easily locate a specific topic within the chapters.

For standard one- to four-page encyclopedic definitions of terms in these fields, consult the *McGraw-Hill Encyclopedia of Environmental Science and Engineering* (see entry 149).

142 The Encyclopedia of Environmental Studies

William Ashworth. Facts On File, 1991. 470p. $60.00 (hardcover).

143 Environmental Encyclopedia

Edited by William Cunningham, Terence Ball, Terence Cooper, Eville Gorham, Malcolm Hepworth, and Alfred Marcus. 1st ed. Gale Research, 1994. Biannual. 981p. $195.00 (hardcover).

Meant for a lay audience, both *The Encyclopedia of Environmental Studies* and the *Environmental Encyclopedia* provide clear definitions and discussions of every aspect of the interdisciplinary field of environmental studies. Both works include coverage of important environmental organizations, federal agencies, places, disasters, key individuals, major legislation, public policy topics, economic issues, and chemicals, along with terms from various scientific disciplines including botany, geology, seismology, oceanography, and ecology. *The Encyclopedia of Environ-*

mental Studies contains three thousand entries averaging ten sentences in length; some annotations are a single sentence while others are longer than a page in length. The twelve hundred descriptions in the *Environmental Encyclopedia* range from one paragraph to more than two pages in length. Both works have extensive cross-references, contact information for organizations, numerous charts and diagrams that help explain processes, and detailed indices—rare in this type of work. However, the *Environmental Encyclopedia* has black-and-white photographs of many people and places and, in general, considerably more in-depth descriptions that provide greater insight into the term or topic being discussed. In addition, longer entries include suggestions for further reading. In comparison, *Environmental Studies* has a single six-page bibliography at the end of the book. A third encyclopedia, *The Encyclopedia of the Environment* (Ruth Eblen and William Eblen. Houghton Mifflin, 1994. 846p. $49.95), sponsored by the René Dubos Center for Human Environments, is a similar work that provides lengthy, in-depth explanations—few entries are less than a page in length—of more than 550 basic scientific and environmental terms and concepts; entries focus particularly on the social and spiritual aspects of environmental problems.

144 Environmental Dictionary

Compiled by James J. King. 2nd ed. Executive Enterprises Publications, 1993. 977p. $89.95 (hardcover).

145 Environmental Regulatory Glossary

Edited by Thomas F. P. Sullivan. 6th ed. Government Institutes, 1993. 544p. $68.00 (hardcover).

146 Natural Resources Glossary

Government Institutes, 1991. 259p. $59.00 (paper).

All three of these publications—the *Environmental Dictionary*, the *Environmental Regulatory Glossary*, and the *Natural Resources Glossary*—provide legal definitions for environmental terms. All definitions in the *Environmental Dictionary* are taken directly from the *Code of Federal Regulations*, Title 40 (*40 CFR*)—the section that covers pollution control—and include the specific location in the *CFR* from which the definition came. The last 350 pages of this work outline the sections of *40 CFR*. The *Environmental Regulatory Glossary* has roughly the same number of definitions and takes the large majority of its definitions from *40 CFR*, but this book also includes definitions from *29 CFR*—the section that covers occupational safety and health—as well as from Environmental Protection Agency documents, and occasionally from the statutes themselves. Terms are coded to indicate each definition's source.

The *Natural Resources Glossary* also selects terms from a similar range of resources as its sister publication, the *Environmental Regulatory Glossary*, but the *Natural Resources Glossary* covers terms related to mineral resources, navigable waters, public lands, fish and wildlife, and endangered species. All three sourcebooks provide explanations of relevant abbreviations and acronyms.

147 The Green Encyclopedia: An A–Z Sourcebook of Environmental Concerns—and Solutions

Edited by Irene Franck and David Brownstone. Prentice Hall, 1992. 486p. $35.00 (hardcover), $20.00 (paper).

The Green Encyclopedia: An A–Z Sourcebook of Environmental Concerns—and Solutions provides concise, nontechnical descriptions of one thousand social, economic, political, and scientific environmental terms—in addition to plenty of information for concerned citizens wishing to take further action to save the Earth. The encyclopedia's coverage focuses on several categories related to environmental conservation, including individuals, organizations, philosophies, legislation, national parks, endangered species, and major disasters. Major topics such as acid rain, hazardous waste, nuclear energy, and the ozone layer are supplemented with "action guides": brief annotated directories of organizations and lists of a few reference books. Many of the entries, which range in length from half a page to three pages, include cross-references to other relevant entries and phone numbers for environmental organizations and government agencies.

Appendices provide additional "action guides" for animal rights and welfare, ecotourism, and forests, as well as lists of endangered species, wetlands, biosphere reserves, toxic chemicals, Superfund sites, and a glossary of acronyms. This encyclopedia is highly recommended as an affordable ready reference for concerned citizens and activists.

148 Green Essentials: What You Need to Know About the Environment

Geoffrey C. Saign. Mercury House, 1994. 528p. $16.95 (paper).

For the person who wants to begin to learn about environmental issues, *Green Essentials* is a perfect place to start. Although it is marketed as a dictionary, this book is more useful as a quick-reference guide to environmental issues. Each of the book's fifty-five entries covers a different environmental problem (e.g., deforestation, incineration, warfare effects on the environment). Though entries, averaging eight pages in length, begin with a dictionary-style definition of the problem, they also include the following at-a-glance information: a summary of the environmental impacts of the problem; descriptions of the major causes of the problem; background information on the extent of the problem; a survey of the human impacts of the problem; suggestions on what individuals can do; and a guide to what industry and government have done and should do. Entries are cross-referenced, and the book includes an extensive glossary. Other appendices include a directory of environmental groups and agencies and a bibliography of books and magazines for further reading.

149 McGraw-Hill Encyclopedia of Environmental Science and Engineering

Edited by Sybil P. Parker and Robert A. Corbitt. 3rd ed. McGraw-Hill, 1993. 749p. $85.00 (hardcover).

The *McGraw-Hill Encyclopedia of Environmental Science and Engineering* contains encyclopedic entries for some 220 environmental science and engineering terms. The publication is an excellent quick-reference tool for scientists, engineers, and others concerned about the environment. The encyclopedia's entries—each one to four dense pages in length—define terms within the fields of ecology, geophysics, geochemistry, forestry, public health, meteorology, agriculture, oceanography, and soil science as well as in the mechanical, mining, civil, petroleum, chemical, and power engineering fields. Bibliographies follow each entry; hundreds of drawings, tables, charts, graphs, and photographs are included. The encyclopedia is cross referenced and has an outstanding index. Most entries are taken verbatim from the acclaimed twenty-volume *McGraw-Hill Encyclopedia of Science and Technology* (7th ed. McGraw-Hill, 1992). For longer essays on a broader variety of topics, see the *Encyclopedia of Environmental Science and Engineering* (see entry 141); while the *Environmental Engineering Dictionary* (C. C. Lee. 2nd ed. Government Institutes, 1992) provides short definitions of more than twelve thousand engineering and related terms.

150 VNR Dictionary of Environmental Health and Safety

Edited by Frank S. Lisella. Van Nostrand Reinhold, 1994. 356p. $49.95 (hardcover).

The *VNR Dictionary of Environmental Health and Safety* furnishes more than seven thousand easy-to-understand definitions of terms from the fields of agronomy, biosafety, biostatistics, ecology, environmental law, epidemiology, general sanitation, hazardous-materials control, industrial hygiene, microbiology, radiation, and safety. This work should be useful not only for health and safety experts but also for professionals outside these fields who need a ready reference for core terms in these areas of study. Definitions for common environmental terms (such as "chlorofluorocarbons" and "greenhouse effect") that can be found easily in many dictionaries receive brief descriptions, while terms more closely related to environmental health (such as "chromatography" and "brucellosis") are usually defined in greater detail. Multiple definitions are supplied for terms that have different meanings in different fields, and many of the terms are cross referenced.

Introductory Reading

There are an overwhelming number of books that introduce readers to environmental issues. Some of the best are described in the following bibliographies: *Environmental Studies: An Annotated Bibliography* (see entry 101), *The Environmentalist's Bookshelf: A Guide to the Best Books* (see entry 102), and *In Praise of Nature* (see entry 108). Also, the annual *Island Press Environmental Sourcebook: Books for Better Conservation and Management* (see entry 110) describes new and recent environmental books.

Abstracts and Indices

151 Biological and Agricultural Index (BAI)

H. W. Wilson Company, 1964–. Monthly.

CD-ROM: Available from SilverPlatter and Wilson.

Database Vendor: Available on OCLC EPIC, OCLC FirstSearch, and WILSONLINE.

The *Biological and Agricultural Index (BAI)* covers more than 225 important English-language periodicals in the biological and agricultural sciences. Book reviews, chapters in annual research reviews, and journal supplements are indexed in addition to articles; however, publications of government agencies and university research facilities are not indexed. This widely available index adds more than 55,000 records each year, covering a wide range of subjects, including agricultural chemicals, biochemistry, biology, botany, ecology, entomology, environmental science, fishery science, food science, forestry, marine biology, and zoology.

152 Ecological Abstracts

Elsevier/Geo Abstracts, 1974–. Monthly.

CD-ROM: Available as part of *GeoBase* from SilverPlatter.

Database Vendor: Available as part of *GeoBase* on DIALOG.

153 Ecology Abstracts

Cambridge Scientific Abstracts, 1978–. Monthly.

CD-ROM: Available as part of the *Life Sciences Collection* from SilverPlatter.

Database Vendor: Available as part of the *Life Sciences Collection* on DIALOG.

Both *Ecological Abstracts* and *Ecology Abstracts* —the major abstracts on ecological topics— cover the international academic literature on the interaction of organisms with their environments and with one another. Pollution and conservation are covered to a lesser extent. *Ecological Abstracts* is arranged by ecosystem and includes subject, organism, and regional indices; *Ecology Abstracts* is arranged both by ecosystem and taxonomic divisions and includes subject, taxonomic, geographic, and author indices.

154 EIS: Digests of Environmental Impact Statements

Cambridge Scientific Abstracts, 1972–. Bimonthly.

CD-ROM: Available from SilverPlatter.

EIS: Digests of Environmental Impact Statements provides abstracts of all draft and final Environmental Impact Statements (EIS) filed with the Environmental Protection Agency (EPA)— roughly five hundred each year. Each abstract includes bibliographic information for the EIS, legal mandates, and lengthy summaries of the purpose of each project and its positive and negative environmental impacts. *EIS* also includes subject, legal, geographic, agency, EIS number/title, and EPA/EIS agency indices. Cambridge Scientific Abstracts also publishes an annual cumulative volume of these abstracts, and sells the full text of EIS documents on microfiche.

To keep up with current Environmental Impact Statements, consult the *Federal Register*. For referrals to sources of information on environmental impact statements and copies of EPA comments published in the *Federal Register*, contact EPA's Office of Federal Activities (202/260–5083).

155 Environment Abstracts

Congressional Information Service, 1971–. Monthly.

CD-ROM: Available as *Enviroline* from Congressional Information Service.

Database Vendor: Available as *Enviroline* on DIALOG.

Environment Abstracts, the premier environmental abstract, summarizes articles on environmental sciences, conditions, and issues from more than eight hundred English-language scientific journals. It also includes conference papers and proceedings, special reports, and articles from popular magazines. More than five thousand records are added annually. *Environment Abstracts* is published monthly in two separate volumes: the first contains only abstracts while the second contains subject, author, source, and title indices. All abstracts and indices are cumulated in hardbound volumes annually. When publishing responsibilities transferred from Bowker to the Congressional Information Service (CIS) in 1994, *Energy Information Abstracts*, formerly a separate abstract, became a part of *Environment Abstracts*. CIS publishes a CD-ROM version of *Environment Abstracts* as well as a version on microfiche—*Envirofiche*—which includes the full text of most articles. All full-text articles on *Envirofiche* are also available through CIS's Environment Abstracts Documents on Demand service (800/227-2477).

Refer also to *Pollution Abstracts* (see entry 158), the premier pollution-related abstract.

156 Environmental Periodicals Bibliography (EPB)

Environmental Studies Institute of the International Academy at Santa Barbara, 1973–. Bimonthly.

CD-ROM: Available from the National Information Services Corporation.

Database Vendor: Available as *Environmental Bibliography* on DIALOG.

The *Environmental Periodicals Bibliography (EPB)* lists the titles of articles found in popular, technical, and scientific environmental magazines and journals. Some four hundred interdis-

ciplinary periodicals are grouped within the following major subject headings: air; energy; land resources, conservation, preservation, wildlife, and nature; agriculture; marine and freshwater resources; water management, effluents, sewage, and pollution; and nutrition and health. Each periodical entry includes the issue date, and the title, author, and page number for each major article. *EPB* is known for the quality of its subject indexing. Approximately 25,000 citations are added annually. *EPB*'s publishers, the Environmental Studies Institute (805/965-5010), can conduct customized searches for $20 per search, plus 25¢ for each citation more than twenty.

157 Government Reports Announcements & Index

National Technical Information Service, 1964–. Biweekly.

CD-ROM: Available as the *NTIS Bibliographic Database* from DIALOG and SilverPlatter.

Database Vendor: Available as the *NTIS Bibliographic Database* on DIALOG.

The *Government Reports Announcements & Index* abstracts nearly all scientific and technical documents published by the U.S. government and selected foreign governments. Abstracted items are available for sale from the National Technical Information Service (NTIS) (see entry 8). The abstracts are published in print in the *Government Reports Announcements & Index*, but it is far easier to retrieve the same information online from the *NTIS Bibliographic Database*. The database currently contains more than two million records; more than thirteen hundred titles are added weekly. To stay current with new additions to the database from all government agencies, there are biweekly *NTIS Alerts* on specific topics such as energy and environmental pollution and control. *NTIS Alerts* can be customized for particular subtopics, such as solar energy or pesticide pollution and control. NTIS also publishes many topical subsets of the *Government Reports Announcements & Index*. One such subset, the quarterly *EPA Publications Bibliography*, includes abstracts of all Environmental Protection Agency documents cataloged by NTIS. *Government Reports Announcements & Index* and its subsets provide the most comprehensive coverage of environmental documents produced by U.S. government agencies.

158 Pollution Abstracts

Cambridge Scientific Abstracts, 1970–. Monthly.

Database Vendor: Available on DIALOG.

Pollution Abstracts offers outstanding coverage of environmental pollution research and related engineering studies. It abstracts articles from more than 250 international journals in the following topic areas: air pollution, marine pollution, freshwater pollution, sewage and wastewater treatment, waste management, land pollution, toxicology and health, and governmental action. Approximately eleven thousand records are added annually. A separate section lists papers presented at recent conferences.

Another widely used abstract, *Environment Abstracts* (see entry 155), includes entries on wildlife, population, pollution, and the environmental movement, and also abstracts articles from popular periodicals.

Periodicals

159 Ambio: A Journal of the Human Environment

Royal Swedish Academy of Sciences, 1972–; distributed by Allen Press. 8 issues per year. 70p. $61.00/year.

Ambio is a peer-reviewed journal that puts into perspective significant developments in environmental research and policy. All environmental issues are covered, though there is more coverage of environmental science than environmental studies. Occasional special issues are devoted to a single topic, such as the economics of biodiversity loss. *Ambio* includes articles (overviews of an issue or a project) and reports (published findings of scientific research), both of which are abstracted on the journal's back cover. *Ambio's* articles are easily understood by students, decision makers, and interested laypeople, but its reports are more technical, similar to those found in other academic journals. Top international scientists write and edit the articles and

reports. *Ambio* is one of the most respected and authoritative academic journals on global environmental issues.

160 The Amicus Journal: A Publication of the Natural Resources Defense Council

Natural Resources Defense Council, 1979–. Quarterly. 55p. $10.00/year.

Amicus Journal provides a good mix of essays, news analysis, and features for the general public on environmental affairs, especially those related to national policy. The publication's in-depth feature articles are thorough and usually revolve around a particular theme, such as environmental justice, drinking water, green spirituality, or population and consumption. Poetry, black-and-white drawings and photographs, and at least three environmental book reviews are also included in every issue, as are news of Natural Resources Defense Council's (NRDC) (see entry 40) programs and initiatives, profiles of NRDC staff members, and a catalog of NRDC publications and gifts. *Amicus* does not accept advertising.

161 Audubon

National Audubon Society, 1900–. Bimonthly. 120p. $20.00/year.

162 National Wildlife

National Wildlife Federation, 1963–. Bimonthly. 50p. $16.00/year.

163 Sierra

Sierra Club, 1893–. Bimonthly. 120p. $15.00/year.

Audubon, *National Wildlife*, and *Sierra* are the large-circulation magazines of the nation's largest conservation organizations. While all have a nature or wildlife focus, there are always many articles on other environmental issues, such as water pollution, nuclear waste, or the relationship between international trade and the environment. Each of the three magazines includes three or four feature articles, news shorts, organizational news, and plenty of color photographs. *Audubon* and *Sierra* are practically indistinguishable: widely available on newsstands, glossy finish, many advertisements, and even similar layouts. *Sierra* has slightly more coverage of environmental issues than the other two publications and is more progressive politically. It also advertises travel opportunities for outdoorspeople and naturalists, and includes a resource section at the end of each article. *National Wildlife* is not as slick as the other two publications and contains no advertisements. This magazine offers the greatest number of articles on wildlife and nature; photograph captions cite type of camera and film used. All three magazines contain good coverage of environmental issues, nature, and outdoor life.

164 E: The Environmental Magazine

Earth Action Network, 1990–. Bimonthly. 64p. $20.00/year.

Internet: A sample copy of *E* is available on the Electronic Newsstand. To view, gopher to **gopher.enews.com**, then choose *Magazines, Periodicals, and Journals (all titles)*, then *Titles Arranged by Subject*, then *Science—Ecology, Gardening, General*, then *Ecology*, then *E, the Environmental Magazine*.

E: The Environmental Magazine aims to keep mainstream environmentalists informed. Though not directly affiliated with any advocacy organization, *E* is published by the nonprofit Earth Action Network. Feature articles—usually four per issue—are either original articles or adaptations of recent books, and cover all environmental topics. The magazine is also filled with news shorts that profile people and organizations in the environmental movement, or that announce new projects, environmental products and services, or publications. Reading these sections regularly is one of the best ways to keep up with news about the environmental community. *E* includes among its regular features columns for shoppers and homeowners, and advertisements from environmentally sensitive companies.

165 Earth Island Journal

Earth Island Institute, 1986–. Quarterly. 45p. $25.00/year.

The *Earth Island Journal* offers outstanding original coverage, from a grassroots perspective, of international environmental news. The *Jour-* *nal*—the first U.S. publication to be made out of kenaf, a tree-free paper—is literally packed with paragraph- to page-long news shorts from around the world, including articles on Earth Island Institute (EII) (see entry 19) projects. Longer articles—each two pages in length—are written by those working on EII projects; past articles have covered topics such as indigenous people, endangered species, trade, urban issues, and a host of other environmental subjects. Most articles are followed by contact information for further action or information. The *Journal* contains few advertisements.

166 Earth Negotiations Bulletin (ENB)

International Institute for Sustainable Development. Updated irregularly. Free.

Diskette: A complete archive is available from the International Institute for Sustainable Development (IISD).

EcoNet: Available in the *enb.library* conference.

Internet: To subscribe to free electronic delivery, send an e-mail message to **listserver@ciesin.org** with the words **subscribe enb <your name>** in the body of the message.
   Archives of back issues are available on IISD's Linkages site. On the World Wide Web, the URL is **http://www.iisd.ca/linkages/**. Choose *Environmental Negotiations Bulletin*.
   Archives of back issues are also available on the Institute for Global Communications (see entry 57) gopher. Choose *EcoNet—Environment*, then *Publications and News Services on EcoNet*, then *Environmental Negotiations Bulletin*.

The *Earth Negotiations Bulletin (ENB)* is an independent reporting service that provides coverage of major United Nations (UN) negotiations on the environment and development. Editions of different volumes (e.g., vol. 5: *The United Nations Commission on Sustainable Development*; vol. 6: *The International Conference on Population and Development*; vol. 9: *The Convention on Biological Diversity*) of the *Earth Negotiations Bulletin* are distributed concurrently whenever major UN negotiations take place. Each edition summarizes in detail who spoke and what was discussed. During negotiations *ENB* is distributed daily to participants, who use it to follow the meetings they are not able to attend and as an official record of events. Special summary reports provide more background than the daily editions. The periodical—along with other background information on international environmental diplomacy—is archived in hypertext on Linkages, the World Wide Web Internet site of the International Institute for Sustainable Development (IISD), a nonprofit organization that focuses on international trade, business strategies, national finances, and communications and partnerships that support sustainable development. *ENB*'s funding comes from IISD, as well as governments (Norway, Australia), intergovernmental organizations (United Nations Environment Programme (see entry 10), the World Bank (see entry 11), and private foundations (the Pew Charitable Trusts, The John D. and Catherine T. MacArthur Foundation). The *Bulletin* is an excellent means of following international environmental diplomacy as it happens.

167 The Earth Times

Earth Times Foundation, 1992–. Biweekly. 24p. $36.00/year.

EcoNet: Available in the *earthtimes* conference.

The Earth Times is a newspaper that provides good coverage of international sustainable-development issues, including the environment, human rights, population, and trade. Each issue contains dozens of features, editorials, and news articles and analyses written either by the newspaper's staff or leaders of nongovernmental organizations. The primary emphasis is on United Nations (UN) activities and conferences—occasional special issues are devoted entirely to UN conferences—but there is also coverage of United States culture, science, and issues. Articles are posted electronically on EcoNet (see entry 58), TogetherNet (see entry 59), and America Online. *The Earth Times* is an excellent source for up-to-date information on UN activities related to sustainable development.

168 The Ecologist

Ecosystems, 1970–; distributed by MIT Press. Bimonthly. 70p. $34.00/year for individuals, $85.00/year for institutions.

Best known for challenging mainstream thinking, *The Ecologist* falls somewhere between an

academic journal and a magazine. Though similar to *Environment* (see entry 170), *The Ecologist* is exclusively international in scope, editorially radical, and does not contain articles on hard science. Each issue includes four or five articles that investigate the social, economic, and political aspects of humanity's impact on the environment, particularly Third World development issues. These features are scholarly and well referenced, but they are also readable by non-specialists. Editors Edward Goldsmith, Nicholas Hildyard, Peter Bunyard, and Patrick McCully also write fiery editorials and do not hesitate to condemn such institutions as the World Bank and the International Monetary Fund. Each issue contains several book reviews as well as information about specific letter-writing campaigns.

169 Electronic Green Journal

Electronic document. University of Idaho Library, 1994–. Updated irregularly. Free.

Internet: Available at the University of Idaho sites. Gopher to **gopher.uidaho.edu**; on the World Wide Web, the URL is **http://gopher.uidaho.edu/**. Then, at either site, choose *University of Idaho's Electronic Publications*, then *Electronic Green Journal*.
   The *Journal* is also available by ftp from **ftp.uidaho.edu** in the following directory: **pub/docs/publications/EGJ**.

The *Electronic Green Journal* is an academic journal that covers sources of environmental information. The new electronic format of the periodical—Volume 1, Issue 1 was released in mid-1994—replaces the now-defunct print *Green Library Journal: Environmental Topics in the Information World*. Each *Electronic Green Journal* issue includes many in-depth articles on information sources (e.g., "NTIS and Environmental Topics," "INFOTERRA: Gateway to International Environmental Information"); bibliographies ("Local Recycling Information Online," "Environmental Education Resources: Government Agencies," "Research Facilities," and "Professional Associations"); and both in-depth reviews and short announcements of new resources. Though articles are written by and for librarians and other information specialists interested in research on environmental issues, they are readily understood by anyone who needs environmental information. Both this publication and the newsletter of the Environmental and Resource Management Division of the Special Libraries Association (SLA)—subscription to the newsletter is a benefit of SLA membership—are outstanding resources for learning about new and existing environmental information sources.

170 Environment

Heldref Publications, 1958–. 10 issues per year. 45p. $31.00/year for individuals, $62.00/year for institutions.

Read by professionals from a variety of environmental disciplines, *Environment* is more comprehensible than most journals, but more rigorous than most magazines. The three feature articles in each issue summarize scientific research and provide the factual information professionals need to evaluate current and proposed policy. Features, often written by leading scientists, contain many tables, graphs, and charts and are well referenced; they are, however, readable by non-experts since they contain little technical jargon and few equations. All national and international issues are covered, but the emphasis is on science and policy pertaining to the United States. Regular departments include news shorts; excerpts from other environmental periodicals; profiles of both environmental organizations and legal issues; and several book reviews. *Environment* contains few advertisements.

171 Environmental Action

Environmental Action, 1970–. Quarterly. 40p. $15.00/year for students, $25.00/year for other individuals or organizations.

Environmental Action stands out for its no-nonsense reporting of grassroots environmental issues. Its content generally reflects the chief concerns of Environmental Action (see entry 22) (hazardous and solid waste, environmental justice, community organizing) but the magazine occasionally features pieces on other issues, such as classroom education or sustainable agriculture. Each issue's theme incorporates several feature articles that often show how abstract environmental issues affect people's lives. These articles always include an excellent page-long bibliography of resources. The magazine also

includes news shorts, activist alerts, and news about Environmental Action's activities. There are black-and-white photographs and few advertisements. *Environmental Action* contains well-written, well-researched information for activists.

172 Environmental Information Networks

119 South Fairfax Street
Alexandria, VA 22314

Phone: 703/683-0774. Fax: 703/683-3893

Database Vendor: All periodicals published by Environmental Information Networks are available on LEXIS/NEXIS and NewsNet.

Internet: Delivery is available via electronic mail. Contact Environmental Information Networks for details.

Environmental Information Networks offers four daily, one-page clipping services on issues pertaining to the Clean Air Act and the National Energy Policy Act. Each newsletter *(Global Warming Network Online Today, Ozone Depletion Network Online Today, Clean Air Network Online Today, Alternative Energy Network Online Today)* includes summaries of three articles that have been selected from more than thirty newspapers and fifty wire services, as well as many other periodicals and press releases. The emphasis is on regulations, research, and other relevant information for business executives. In addition to LEXIS/NEXIS and NewsNet, newsletters are delivered via fax, SprintNet, or e-mail through the Internet; a monthly review is available in print form. Prices vary depending on the number of newsletters subscribed to and the delivery method; via fax, for example, newsletters are $75 per month each or $150 for all four.

173 Environmental News Briefing (ENB)

Environmental News Network, 1993–. Monthly. $125.00/year.

Bulletin Board: Available on Environmental News Network (ENN) Online. To connect by modem, dial 208/726-2651.

Internet: Available at the University of Idaho sites. Gopher to **gopher.uidaho.edu**; on the World Wide Web, the URL is **http://gopher.uidaho.edu/**. Then, at either site, choose *University of Idaho's Electronic Publications*, then *Environmental News Network*.

ENB is also available by ftp from **ftp.uidaho.edu** in the following directory: **pub/docs/publications/ENN**.

Though *Environmental News Briefing (ENB)* provides current environmental news and announcements for its targeted audience of environmental professionals in Washington, Oregon, Idaho, Montana, Utah, Nevada, and Wyoming, the majority of its articles are relevant to a broad national audience. *ENB*—started in 1993—is divided into the following topics: government and politics; legal; hazardous materials; waste management; technology; energy; agriculture and ranching; flora and fauna; public land; air; water; business; education; and lifestyle. Each of these sections has at least five paragraph-long news briefs gathered from news wires, government agencies, industry, organizations, and original submissions from journalists and scientists. Other sections announce new publications and organizations, outline upcoming events, and summarize environmental highlights from the current *Federal Register*.

Environmental News Network (ENN) Online, a companion bulletin board system, contains not only current and back issues of *Environmental News Briefing*, but also expanded coverage of items found in the newsletter, including the full text of legislation.

174 EPA Journal

Environmental Protection Agency, 1975–; distributed by the Government Printing Office. Quarterly. 48p. $7.50/year.

Database Vendor: Available as part of the *Academic Index* on DIALOG, and as *EPA Journal* on LEXIS/NEXIS.

Internet: Available on the Environmental Protection Agency (see entry 56) gopher. Choose *Newsletters and Journals*, then *EPA Journal*.

The *EPA Journal* is not flashy, but it does provide steady, noncontroversial coverage of environmental science and policy. The large majority of *Journal* articles are one to two pages in length, and provide perspectives from experts in the fields of government, business, science, and advocacy. These articles may be speeches, reprints, or original articles covering any environmental theme. The publication also contains some essays, book reviews, and EPA news. All in all, the *Journal* is an inexpensive way to stay on top of environmental issues.

175 Garbage: The Independent Environmental Quarterly

Dovetale Publishers, 1989–1994.

At the beginning of 1994 *Garbage: The Independent Environmental Quarterly* changed its frequency from bimonthly to quarterly, doubled its price, and stopped accepting advertising; in the fall of that year it ceased publication. *Garbage* was known for having a strong editorial stance that questioned conventional environmental wisdom.

176 The GreenDisk Paperless Environmental Journal

Electronic document. The GreenDisk, 1992–. Bimonthly. Contains the equivalent of 350p.

Diskette: Available from The GreenDisk for $45/year.

Internet: Available by ftp for $35/year. Contact the publisher for directions and password.

The GreenDisk Paperless Environmental Journal is an excellent source for a wealth of environmental information. Each issue comes as a set of computer files (either on an IBM-compatible or Macintosh disk; the *GreenDisk* can also be downloaded from the Internet or America Online). The files can be used with all word-processing software, and an additional software application (included with subscriptions) allows users to search the *GreenDisk* by keyword. Each issue has a theme—e.g., pesticides, conserving biodiversity, computer networking—that may be addressed by the full text of a report, such as a *Worldwatch Paper* (see entry 51, the Worldwatch Institute), and an extensive bibliography. *GreenDisk* editors also put together a hodgepodge of other information on all environmental topics; these pieces may be items that organizations and activists have contributed or bits that the editors themselves have compiled or downloaded from online conferences and publications. Examples include recent press releases, action alerts, and news from organizations (e.g., Global Action Information Network (see entry 30), Save America's Forests (see entry 278), Greenpeace (see entry 32); the *Biological Conservation Newsletter* (see entry 306); lists of articles appearing in current environmental periodicals; recent environmental publications and their ordering information; calendars; and employment and internship listings. The *GreenDisk* is a unique and easy source for information, news, and announcements of new environmental information resources.

177 Greenwire

Electronic document. American Political Network, 1991–. Daily. 12p. $795.00/year for nonprofits, $1,495/year for a single-point subscriber, $3,000/year for multiple-point subscribers.

Database Vendor: Available on LEXIS/NEXIS the following day.

Bulletin Board: Available on the *Greenwire* database. Contact the American Political Network for more information.

Internet: Delivery is available via electronic mail. Contact the American Political Network for more information.

Greenwire is a daily briefing that covers all aspects of environmental news, with a focus on environmental politics and business. This clipping service summarizes stories from more than one hundred newspapers, broadcast news programs, and periodicals. *Greenwire* occasionally includes original articles. In each issue there are roughly twenty-five stories, each of which includes a citation of the source of the original information. Available after 10:30 a.m. Monday–Friday, most *Greenwire* subscribers receive issues via electronic mail or by downloading a copy from the *Greenwire* database; fax delivery is also available at additional cost. All back issues can be searched by keyword by dialing into the *Greenwire* database (for subscribers: 80¢ per minute; for nonsubscribers: $1.60 per minute with a fifteen-minute minimum, plus a $100 annual entrance fee).

178 The New Environmentalist: The Journal of Practical Sustainability

Electronic document. The New Environmentalist Magazine, 1994–. Monthly. Free.

Internet: Gopher to **manning.cais.com**, or, on the World Wide Web, the URL is **http://manning.cais.com/**.

The New Environmentalist concentrates on the actions and choices of individuals to help or harm the environment. Each issue contains three feature articles on individuals, communities, and companies that are making a positive impact on the environment. News shorts, book reviews, a column on gardening, and job postings are also included in each issue. The *New Environmentalist* is not available by subscription; rather, it is a browsable site on the Internet. The World Wide Web version is interactive, allowing readers to take part in online surveys and to post questions and comments online. The *New Environmentalist* is sustained by advertisements for environmentally sound products and services. The magazine is copyrighted and any electronic reproduction without consent is prohibited.

179 The Workbook

Southwest Research and Information Center, 1974–. Quarterly. 50p. $12.00/year for individuals, $25.00/year for institutions.

The Workbook is primarily a collection of in-depth book reviews that covers a wide variety of social and environmental volumes. The publisher of *The Workbook*, the Southwest Research and Information Center (505/262-1862), is a grass-roots organization that performs research and provides support to activists; it works locally in the southwestern United States on water, waste, and toxics issues, and nationally on oil and gas, mining, and nuclear waste issues. Each issue of the periodical includes two-page summaries of more than twenty reference handbooks and academic books. Categories of coverage (e.g., agriculture, corporations and business, government and military, land use, pollution and environment) are broad but will be of interest to anyone working on social-change issues. Because the reviews summarize each book's content so well, reading *The Workbook* cover to cover will keep those interested in social and environmental change up to date with new ideas in the field—even without reading the books that are reviewed.

A different magazine, the *Whole Earth Review: Access to Tools and Ideas* (Point, 1973–. Quarterly. $27 per year for individuals, $35 per year for institutions) is another good resource for those wanting to keep up with new books, periodicals, software, and products; the reviews—which, like *The Workbook*, cover not only issues of environmental concern but a variety of topics from digital encryption to organizational behavior—are short but insightful, and often include lengthy excerpts of the work being reviewed.

180 World Watch

Worldwatch Institute, 1989–. Bimonthly. 40p. $15.00/year.

World Watch targets policymakers, researchers, and concerned citizens with well-researched summaries of environmental, social, and political issues related to global sustainability. All articles are written by the staff of the Worldwatch Institute on themes from recent or future *Worldwatch Papers* (see entry 51, Worldwatch Institute). Sample feature articles include: "Men, Sex, and Parenthood in an Overpopulating World" ; "It Comes Down to the Coasts" ; and "Power Move: The Nuclear Salesmen Target the Third World." In addition to three six- to nine-page feature articles in each issue, *World Watch* includes news shorts, updates on past articles, excerpts from *Vital Signs: The Trends That Are Shaping Our Future* (see entry 132), and one or two in-depth book reviews. Articles from the magazine are distributed weekly by the Los Angeles Times Syndicate to nearly one hundred newspapers. *World Watch* does not accept advertising.

Other Periodicals

- ◆ The "Current Developments" section of *Environment Reporter* (see entry 118)
- ◆ The *Daily Environmental Report* (see entry 118, *Environment Reporter*)
- ◆ *Environment Today* (see entry 75, *Environmental Management SourceBook*)
- ◆ *Gaining Ground* (see entry 30, Global Action and Information Network)
- ◆ The *Global Environmental Change Report* (see entry 263)
- ◆ The "News and Analysis" section of *Environmental Law Reporter* (see entry 121)
- ◆ *Weekly Bulletin* (see entry 23, Environmental and Energy Study Institute)

Agriculture

What This Chapter Covers

This chapter focuses on the environmental impact of conventional agricultural practices, including pesticide use, as well as all aspects of sustainable agriculture (also known as organic or alternative agriculture). Food safety and food labeling are also covered.

For More Information

◆ See **General** for resources on all environmental issues, including those related to agriculture.
◆ See **Health and Toxics** for resources on pesticides and other toxic substances.
◆ See **Gardening** for resources on home gardening, lawn care, and pest control.

Government Clearinghouses

181 Alternative Farming Systems Information Center (AFSIC)
Department of Agriculture
National Agricultural Library
10301 Baltimore Boulevard, Room 304
Beltsville, MD 20705

Phone: 301/504-6559. Fax: 301/504-6409.
E-mail: afsic@nalusda.gov

Jane Potter Gates, Coordinator

Bulletin Board: AFSIC has a sub-board on the Agricultural Library Forum (ALF) (see entry 197). From the main menu, choose *Join Conferences*, then *Alternative Farming Systems (LISA, etc)*.

Internet: ALF (see above) is available on the Internet via FedWorld's GateWay (see entry 61). Choose *2* for *ALF (USDA)*.

In addition, AFSIC has space on the National Agricultural Library (NAL) (see entry 183) gopher. From the NAL gopher, choose *NAL Information Centers*, then *Alternative Farming Systems Information Center*.

The Alternative Farming Systems Information Center (AFSIC) provides inexpensive and invaluable access to scientific and popular sustainable agriculture information. AFSIC was established by Congress to "encourage research, education, and information delivery about farming systems that preserve the natural resource base while maintaining economic viability, especially sustainable, low-input, regenerative, biodynamic or organic farming, and gardening." The center's staff serves as a sustainable agriculture researcher's initial gateway to the Department of Agriculture and the National Agricultural Library (see entry 183). Staff members can supply bibliographies (e.g., *Sustainable Agriculture in Print: Current Books* [see entry 205]; *Societal Impacts of Adoption of Alternative Agricultural Practices*; *Drip, Trickle and Surge Irrigation*) and directories (e.g., *Educational and Training Opportunities in Sustainable Agriculture: A Directory*); recommend books and reports; make referrals to organizations and experts; perform brief complimentary searches on the *AGRICOLA* (see entry 221, *Bibliography of Agriculture*) database or exhaustive searches on a cost-recovery basis; and provide photocopies of hard-to-find articles and

reports. AFSIC is a reliable clearinghouse for experienced or novice farmers, researchers in need of a specific report, organizations concerned with the ecological effects of agriculture, or individuals interested in gardening and organic food.

182 Appropriate Technology Transfer For Rural Areas (ATTRA)
Department of the Interior
National Biological Survey
P.O. Box 3657
Fayetteville, AR 72702

Phone: 800/346-9140; 501/442-9824.
Fax: 501/442-9842.
E-mail: root@ncatfyv.uark.edu

Jim Lukens, Program Manager

Appropriate Technology Transfer For Rural Areas (ATTRA) is an outstanding source of practical sustainable agriculture information and guidance. This free government-sponsored service is geared toward farmers implementing sustainable technology, but ATTRA will assist anyone who calls or writes; staffers regularly answer questions as basic as "What is sustainable agriculture?" In response to information requests, technical specialists review publications in the ATTRA library, confer with other experts, and search databases and computer networks. Within two to four weeks of contacting ATTRA callers receive a written summary of the organization's findings accompanied by supporting literature; follow-up phone calls are encouraged. ATTRA has numerous free information packages and resource lists that provide in-depth background information and leads for additional research, including "Sustainable Hydroponics," "Integrated Pest Management," "Organic Certification," and "Sustainable Agriculture Organizations and Publications." ATTRA's four–page newsletter, *ATTRAnews*, provides research updates, book reviews, and announcements of new reference materials.

183 National Agricultural Library (NAL)
Department of Agriculture
10301 Baltimore Avenue
Beltsville, MD 20705

Phone (general information desk): 301/504-5755.
Phone (reference desk): 301/504-5479.
Fax (reference desk): 301/504-6927

Bulletin Board: NAL maintains the Agricultural Library Forum (ALF) (see entry 197).

Internet: ALF (see bulletin board above) is available on the Internet.
   To access the NAL gopher, gopher to **gopher.nalusda.gov**.

The National Agricultural Library (NAL) is the largest agricultural library in the world. The most user-friendly way to approach NAL is through its eleven information centers on specialized topics such as alternative farming systems (see entry 181), water quality (see entry 460), aquaculture (301/504-5558), biotechnology (301/504-5340), food and nutrition (301/504-5719), or animal welfare (301/504-6212). These clearinghouses provide referrals to other sources of information; preprinted bibliographies from the NAL Quick Bibliography Series (which includes free, specific-topic bibliographies comprising citations taken from the *AGRICOLA* [see entry 221, *Bibliography of Agriculture*] database); complimentary or fee-based database searches; and user support for the *AGRICOLA* database. Much of the full-text information provided by NAL information centers is available on NAL's outstanding Agricultural Library Forum (ALF) (see entry 197) bulletin board system. Through the NAL reference desk, the NAL information centers, ALF, and the NAL gopher on the Internet, individuals have easy access to the overwhelming amount of research and information collected and disseminated by the Department of Agriculture.

184   National Pesticide Telecommunications Network (NPTN)

Environmental Protection Agency
Texas Tech University
Health Sciences Center
Lubbock, TX 79430

Phone: 800/858-7378; 806/743-3091.
Fax: 806/743-3094

Anthony B. Way, Chairman

The National Pesticide Telecommunications Network (NPTN) provides pesticide information and emergency assistance to the general public and to the medical and business communities. NPTN, largely funded by the Environmental Protection Agency (EPA), is uniquely qualified to report and interpret federal regulatory information on pesticides, particularly *Pesticide Fact Sheets*, *Material Safety Data Sheets* (see entry 389, *New Jersey Department of Health Fact Sheets*), and pesticide product labels. Since most callers are homeowners without a background in pesticides, the hotline caters to those who need technical information interpreted in easy-to-understand language. NPTN specialists consult an extensive internal library of technical reference materials and databases to provide information about the health and environmental effects of pesticides and cleanup and disposal procedures.

Other Government Clearinghouses

◆   The Water Quality Information Center (see entry 460)

Organizations

For descriptions of additional organizations involved in sustainable agriculture, consult *Healthy Harvest: A Global Directory of Sustainable Agriculture and Horticulture Organizations* (see entry 200). To contact professionals in the field, consult the *Sustainable Agriculture Directory of Expertise* (see entry 203).

185   agAccess

603 4th Street
Davis, CA 95616

Phone: 916/756-7177. Phone (distribution): 800/235-7177. Fax: 916/756-7188.
E-mail: agaccess@igc.apc.org

David Katz, Director

A remarkable resource for sustainable agriculture researchers, the fee-based agAccess is dedicated to supplying and uncovering any information remotely related to agriculture; it produces its own publications, distributes virtually every agriculture book in print, and performs custom research. agAccess's Research and Document Delivery Service can be contracted on a project or hourly basis to research specific topics or answer technical questions, or to retrieve documents, articles, and publications. Staff experts will answer quick questions free of charge. agAccess offers the most comprehensive and personalized service for sustainable agriculture information searches; the organization's extensive book catalog is available free of charge.

186 Bio-Dynamic Farming and Gardening Association
P.O. Box 550
Kimberton, PA 19442

Phone: 610/935-7797. Fax: 610/983-3196

Charles Beedy, Executive Director

Since 1938, the Bio-Dynamic Farming and Gardening Association has been considered the definitive source of information on biodynamic agricultural practices: those producers that emphasize the use of environmentally and nutritionally beneficial forms of agriculture. This organization offers numerous services, but its primary vehicle for communication among its members is its bimonthly journal, *Biodynamics*. *Biodynamics* keeps members up to date on recent research, new resources, success stories, new practices, and much more. The association also publishes books and videos (e.g., *What is Biodynamic Agriculture?*; *Biodynamic Farming Practices*; *Biodynamic Gardening: A How-To Video*); offers a biodynamic advisory service for farmers; supports farmer training programs; sponsors conferences and lectures; funds research projects; certifies farms, gardens, and processed foods; and supplies biodynamic sprays and other farming products. In addition, it serves as a clearinghouse for Community Supported Agriculture (CSA). Consumers nationwide can call 800/516-7797 to request a list of community supported or biodynamic farms and gardens in their area.

For additional information about Community Supported Agriculture, consult *Community Supported Agriculture (CSA): An Annotated Bibliography and Resource Guide* (Alternative Farming Systems Information Center, 1993). The publication is free and available in hard copy from AFSIC or online on the Agricultural Library Forum (see entry 197)—(download the "AT93-02.TXT" file).

187 The Bio-Integral Resource Center (BIRC)
P.O. Box 7414
Berkeley, CA 94707

Phone: 510/524-2567. Fax: 510/524-1758.
E-mail: birc@igc.apc.org

Sheila Daar, Executive Director

A leading authority on Integrated Pest Management (IPM), the nonprofit Bio-Integral Resource Center (BIRC) has earned its reputation through extensive field research and ongoing exhaustive reviews of international research literature on least-toxic pest control. For a fee, municipalities, farms, businesses, homeowners, and gardeners can consult with BIRC staff members for hands-on advice and research assistance, or they can purchase BIRC's publications. In addition to the encyclopedic *Common-Sense Pest Control: Least-Toxic Solutions for Your Home, Garden, Pets and Community* (see entry 557), BIRC publishes a *Directory of IPM Products and Services* and many shorter documents on least-toxic methods for controlling cockroaches, mosquitoes, termites, aphids, weeds, raccoons, fleas, ticks, and all other garden, home, lawn, pet, and people pests. BIRC membership includes one free telephone consultation on a pest problem and a subscription to one of BIRC's magazines, either *The IPM Practitioner* (which is geared toward pest control professionals), or the *Common Sense Pest Control Quarterly* (which is targeted toward the general public).

188 Food & Water
R. R. 1, Box 114
Depot Hill Road
Marshfield, VT 05658

Phone (information packet): 800/328-7233.
Phone: 802/426-3700. Fax: 802/426-3711

Michael Colby, Executive Director

Food & Water has emerged as the leading activist organization in the fight against food irradiation. Food & Water's staff is knowledgeable about irradiation and can answer almost any question on the subject. This grassroots membership organization recently started a project on pesticide residues and can help with requests for information on all food-safety issues. Those calling the organization's toll-free number will receive a packet of basic information in about two weeks. Food & Water offers a number of fact packs ("Meat and Poultry Irradiation Packet"), audio- and videotapes, and publications (*No Denial!: A Handbook for Becoming a Socially, Environmentally, and Personally Responsible Citizen*). Membership includes a subscription to *Safe Food News*, an excellent quarterly (whose editors are not afraid to question conventional beliefs) on all food-safety issues.

Another good source of information on food irradiation, particularly for beginning researchers, is *Food Irradiation Overview: A Select Annotated Bibliography*; this bibliography was originally published in Volume 1, Number 1 (1993) of the *Journal of Agricultural and Food Information* (Haworth Press), but is also available from the National Agricultural Library's (see entry 183) Food and Nutrition Information Center (301/504-5719).

189 Henry A. Wallace Institute for Alternative Agriculture

9200 Edmonston Road, Suite 117
Greenbelt, MD 20770

Phone: 301/441-8777. Fax: 301/220-0164

I. Garth Youngberg, Executive Director

The Henry A. Wallace Institute for Alternative Agriculture serves as a bridge between the scientific and policy communities in the area of sustainable agriculture: In fact, this nonprofit membership organization is recognized as the premier sustainable agriculture policy analyst and lobbyist group. The institute promotes research and education on low-cost, resource-conserving, economically viable, and environmentally sound farming systems. Experts affiliated with the institute frequently testify at congressional hearings and provide information to government agencies. In addition to the highly regarded *American Journal of Alternative Agriculture* (see entry 223), the institute produces two newsletters: *Alternative Agriculture News*—a four–page monthly on scientific, legislative, and other developments concerning alternative agriculture—and the *Alternative Agriculture Resources Report*—geared toward the agriculture education, extension, research, and conservation communities. The institute should be consulted with questions concerning current agriculture policy initiatives.

190 Institute for Agriculture and Trade Policy (IATP)

1313 5th Street, SE, Suite 303
Minneapolis, MN 55414

Phone: 612/379-5980. Fax: 612/379-5982. E-mail: iatp@igc.apc.org

Mark Ritchie, Executive Director

EcoNet: The institute maintains several conferences, including *susag.news*, *susag.calendar*, *env.biotech*, *agri.farmbill*, *trade.news*, *trade.strategy*, and *trade.library*.

The Institute for Agriculture and Trade Policy (IATP) works to create environmentally and economically sustainable communities through sound trade policy, particularly agricultural policy. IATP helps public-interest organizations effectively influence both domestic and international policymaking by providing technical assistance, building coalitions, and monitoring current events. IATP also analyzes data to determine the potential economic and ecological implications of both current and proposed policies and develops alternative policy options. To educate and influence policymakers, other opinion leaders, and the public at large, the institute distributes a variety of educational materials, including *Can the States Live Happily After NAFTA?*; *Environment and International Trade: At Odds!*; *Trading Away the Family Farm: GATT and Global Harmonization*; and a newsletter, *Sustainable Agriculture Week* (see entry 228). In addition to the above, IATP maintains a number of electronic conferences and databases on EcoNet (see entry 58), including several related to sustainable agriculture that comprise the World Sustainable Agriculture Network—Sustainable Agriculture Bulletin (*susag.news*), Sustainable Agriculture Library (*susag.library*), Calendar of Events (*susag.calendar*), Biotechnology Bulletin (*env.biotech*), and the 1995 Farm Bill Strategy Conference (*agri.farmbill*). The institute is a leading source of analysis on the environmental implications of international trade, particularly its effects on agricultural practices.

191 National Coalition Against the Misuse of Pesticides (NCAMP)

701 E Street, SE, Suite 200
Washington, DC 20003

Phone: 202/543-5450. Fax: 202/543-4791.
E-mail: ncamp@igc.apc.org

Jay Feldman, Executive Director

The National Coalition Against the Misuse of Pesticides (NCAMP) links grassroots pesticide activists around the country. NCAMP focuses on public education, in addition to monitoring and lobbying the federal government. The organization can handle phone requests regarding the hazards of pesticides and alternative pest management strategies, and will provide callers with chemical profiles for specific pesticides. NCAMP offers several informative publications such as *Pesticides and Schools: A Collection of Issues and Articles*; the *Guide to Challenging Emergency Exemptions in Your State*; and *Safety at Home: A Guide to the Hazards of Lawn and Garden Pesticides and Safer Ways to Manage Pests*. The organization also publishes two periodicals: *Pesticides and You* (see entry 226) and *Technical Report*, a four-page monthly digest of federal news related to pesticides.

192 Northwest Coalition for Alternatives to Pesticides (NCAP)
P.O. Box 1393
Eugene, OR 97440

Phone: 503/344-5044. Fax: 503/344-6923.
E-mail: ncap@igc.apc.org

Norma Grier, Executive Director

The Northwest Coalition for Alternatives to Pesticides (NCAP) seeks to reduce pesticide use through policy reform and education concerning pesticide hazards and alternatives. NCAP's policy emphasis and grassroots support programs, including its training program, were created largely for organizations in the northwestern states; however, the staff is fully prepared to handle nationwide information requests and to provide direct assistance or referrals for pesticide exposure victims. Brochures are complimentary, but there is a charge for anything photocopied from NCAP's files. Membership includes the quarterly *Journal of Pesticide Reform* (see entry 225).

193 Pesticide Action Network (PAN)
North America Regional Center
116 New Montgomery Street, Suite 810
San Francisco, CA 94105

Phone: 415/541-9140. Fax: 415/541-9253.
E-mail: panna@igc.apc.org

Monica Moore, Executive Director

EcoNet: PAN maintains a searchable version of *The Pesticide Information Service (PESTIS)*. Choose *Online Database*, then *News Services*, then *Pesticide Information Service (PESTIS)*.

PAN also posts the full text of *The Pesticide Action Network North America Updates Service (PANUPS)* in the *panna.panups* and *haz.pesticides* conferences.

Internet: PAN posts *The Pesticide Information Service (PESTIS)* and *The Pesticide Action Network North America Updates Service (PANUPS)* on the Institute for Global Communications (see entry 57) gopher site. Choose *EcoNet—Environment*, then *Pesticides & Sustainable Agriculture*, then *Pesticide Action Network*, then either *Pesticide Information Service* or *Pesticide Action Network North America Updates Service*. Both can also be received via e-mail, by sending a short e-mail message to **pestdesk@igc.apc.org**.

The Pesticide Action Network (PAN) is the best source of information on international pesticide issues, especially those affecting developing countries. As one of seven regional PAN coordinating centers that link more than three hundred pesticide reform groups in sixty countries, the North America Regional Center specializes in research information services. It responds to information requests with subject bibliographies; fact sheets; referrals to or photocopies of reports, articles, and books; and referrals to other organizations, agencies, and experts. This regional office concentrates on providing information that is otherwise unavailable to the requester and handles requests in the following priority order: regions of the world with limited access to information; PAN affiliates; requests concerning international issues; all others. (Regardless of priority order, most requests are filled within two weeks.) Those who receive information will be billed only for a portion of actual costs. PAN's North America Regional Center also distributes numerous pesticide-related books and its quarterly newsletter, *Global Pesticide Campaigner* (see entry 224). In addition, PAN offers two valuable electronic resources on EcoNet (see entry 58) and the Internet: *The Pesticide*

Information Service (PESTIS), a full-text database of more than four hundred news items, action alerts, newsletter articles, and fact sheets, and *The Pesticide Action Network North America Updates Service* (PANUPS), a weekly news service.

194 Public Voice for Food and Health Policy
1001 Connecticut Avenue, NW, Suite 522
Washington, DC 20036

Phone: 202/659-5930. Fax: 202/659-3683

Mark Epstein, Executive Director

Public Voice for Food and Health Policy conducts public education, media outreach, and legislative advocacy campaigns on all issues related to safer, healthier, more affordable food. Pesticides, seafood safety, sustainable agriculture, meat and poultry inspection, and nutrition are currently high priorities. The staff, however, is also knowledgeable about other topics: food labeling, biotechnology, school lunches, rural poverty, and commodity policy. Public Voice members receive the monthly *Advocacy Update* newsletter and a discount on all other publications, such as *Seafood Roulette: The Victims' Stories*; *A Blueprint for Pesticide Policy: Changing the Way We Safeguard, Grow and Market Food*; and *Resources for Consumer Action: A Guide to Food and Nutrition Organizations*.

195 Sustainable Agriculture Network (SAN)
c/o Alternative Farming Systems Information Center
National Agricultural Library
10301 Baltimore Boulevard, Room 304
Beltsville, MD 20705

Phone: 301/504-6425. Fax: 301/504-6409.
E-mail: ghegyes@nalusda.gov

Gabriel Hegyes, SANlink Coordinator

Internet: Many of SAN's electronic information sources are available at the North Carolina Cooperative Extension Service gopher at North Carolina State University. To access these documents, gopher to **twosocks.ces.ncsu.edu**, then choose *National CES Information*.

SAN makes many of its files available by e-mail from the North Carolina Cooperative Extension Service site. For more information on receiving items automatically by e-mail, send an e-mail message to **almanac@ces.ncsu.edu** with the words **send guide** in the body of the message. Subscriptions to SAN's mailing list ("sanet-mg") are also available from this site; to subscribe, send an e-mail message to **almanac@ces.ncsu.edu** with the words **subscribe sanet-mg** in the body of the message.

The Sustainable Agriculture Network (SAN) is an informal network of individuals and institutions united in their interest to share and exchange information on sustainable agriculture. SAN is a decentralized organization that encourages its members to communicate directly with one another; its organizers and cosponsors—the Department of Agriculture's Sustainable Agriculture Research and Education and the Environmental Protection Agency's Agriculture in Concert with the Environment programs—simply work to facilitate this process. SANlink, the public information arm of SAN, helps participants contact each other and coordinates activities and publications. SAN's publications include the *Sustainable Agriculture Directory of Expertise* (see entry 203) and *The Showcase of Sustainable Agriculture Information and Education Materials*, which provides detailed descriptions of books, periodicals, and organizations. SAN's electronic-mailing list on the Internet, "sanet-mg," is a valuable source of information, with regular listings of new resources and calendars of relevant events as well as the full text of periodicals, news clippings, and reports. Request the brochure "Getting Started Electronically with the Sustainable Agriculture Network" for more information about SAN's electronic components.

Other Organizations

- The International Alliance for Sustainable Agriculture (see entry 201, *The Humane Consumer and Producer Guide*)
- The Land Institute (see entry 211, *Farming in Nature's Image*)
- Rodale Press (see entry 555)

Internet Sites

196 Extension Toxicology Network (EXTOXNET)

A cooperative effort of the University of California at Davis, Oregon State University, Michigan State University, and Cornell University.

Internet: EXTOXNET is available from the Oregon Extension Service gopher and World Wide Web sites. To access by gopher, gopher to **sulaco.oes.orst.edu**, choose *Oregon Extension Service Projects and Programs*, then *EXTOXNET—EXtension TOXicology NETwork.* On the World Wide Web, the URL is **http://www.oes.orst.edu/**; choose *EXTOXNET—EXtension TOXicology NETwork.*

To receive a catalog of items on EXTOXNET that can be distributed automatically by e-mail, send an e-mail message to **almanac@sulaco.oes.orst.edu** with the words **send extoxnet catalog** in the body of the message.

The Extension Toxicology Network (EXTOXNET) is an outstanding resource for locating toxicological information about pesticides and for communicating with experts in pesticide-related fields. EXTOXNET's information is primarily provided through two types of documents: *Pesticide Information Profiles (PIPs)* on the health and environmental effects of specific pesticides; and *Toxicology Information Briefs (TIBs)*, short descriptions of pesticide-related issues that help users better understand the PIPs. A third type of document, *Toxicology Issues of Concern (TICs)*, discusses pesticide-related issues in the context of the most sound scientific data available. EXTOXNET also provides access to pertinent newsletters, glossaries, mailing groups, and an abundance of other electronic toxicological resources. Individual *PIPs* can be delivered automatically to any Internet e-mail address by sending an e-mail message (e.g., **send extoxnet pips aldicarb.asc**) to an electronic-mail server. For detailed pesticide information in hard copy, consult the *Basic Guide to Pesticides: Their Characteristics and Hazards* (see entry 206) or the *Handbook of Pesticide Toxicology* (see entry 208).

Other Internet Sites:

♦ The National Agricultural Library (see entry 183)

♦ The North Carolina Cooperative Extension Service (see entry 195, Sustainable Agriculture Network)

Bulletin Boards

197 Agricultural Library Forum (ALF)

Maintained by the Department of Agriculture's National Agricultural Library.

Bulletin Board: To connect to ALF by modem, dial 301/504-6510. For technical support by phone, call the system operator, Karl Schneider, at 301/504-5113 or his assistant, Becky Thompson, at 301/504-6908. For technical support by e-mail, send an e-mail message to **kschneid@nalusda.gov** or **bthompson@nalusda.gov**.

Internet: ALF is available via FedWorld's GateWay (see entry 61). Choose *2* for *ALF (USDA).*

The Agricultural Library Forum (ALF) is an in-depth source of information on a wide range of agricultural topics. ALF includes a list of agriculturally related bulletin board systems; titles of available Quick Bibliography Series (see entry 183, the National Agricultural Library) guides and other reference documents, many of which are available for downloading; lists of upcoming conferences; bulletins, which often cover various aspects of alternative agriculture; and more than fifteen conferences, including *AFS (Alternative Farming Systems)*, *AWF (Animal Welfare User's Forum)*, *BT (Biotechnology User's Forum)*, *AGRAD (Graduate School—Online Education)*, and *WIN (Water Quality Information Network)*. First-time callers can register online. A detailed user's guide is available online (look for the file called "ALFGUIDE.TXT") or in hard copy from the system operator.

198 IPMnet

A joint project of the Consortium for International Crop Protection and the Department of Agriculture's National Biological Impact Assessment Program.

Internet: To access IPMnet, telnet to **cicp.biochem.vt.edu**. For technical support or more information, contact the system operator by phone at 703/231-3747 or by e-mail at **cicp@vt.edu**.

IPMnet is a bulletin board system—available only on the Internet—that houses current information on Integrated Pest Management (IPM) techniques. IPMnet allows for worldwide discussion and debate among researchers, agriculture extension agents, technical specialists, producers, and others interested in strengthening and fostering IPM. In addition, IMPnet provides institutions and individuals with access to a body of information that would otherwise be difficult and expensive to collect. IPMnet offers access to databases; a forum and message center; special reports; *IPMnet NEWS*, which contains research summaries, technical studies, and expert opinions; *Resistant Pest Management*, a newsletter that concentrates on increased pest resistance to well-known methods of pest management; and other sources of technical information. For those with access to the Internet, there are no charges or restrictions to use the system.

Another outstanding source of IPM information is the Bio-Integral Resource Center (see entry 187).

199 Pesticide Information Network (PIN)

Maintained by the Environmental Protection Agency's Office of Pesticide Programs.

Bulletin Board: To connect to PIN by modem (7-1-E), dial 703/305-5919. For technical support by phone, call 703/305-7499. Support is also available by fax at 703/305-6309.

Internet: PIN is available via FedWorld's GateWay (see entry 61). Choose *77* for *PIN BBS (EPA)*.

The Pesticide Information Network (PIN) is a bulletin board system used to collect and disseminate pesticide monitoring and regulatory information. PIN is used by the Environmental Protection Agency, other federal and state agencies, pesticide-associated industries, environmental consultants, and anyone involved with pesticide manufacturing, use, regulation and enforcement, and research. Its primary databases include the *Pesticide Monitoring Inventory (PMI)*, the *Restricted Use Products File (RUP)*, and the *Chemical Index*. *PMI* is a database of projects that monitor pesticide usage, including efforts by federal, state, and local governments and private institutions. The files contain a short synopsis of each project—including chemicals being monitored, substrates, and location—as well as contact information for each project. The *RUP* file contains a list of restricted pesticides, associated products, and reasons for restriction; the file is updated each month. The *Chemical Index* file contains a cross-referenced list of all chemical names, synonyms, and CAS numbers contained in the *PMI* and *RUP* files. Consulting the *Chemical Index* as a first step upon entering PIN will provide the chemical name under which the databases must be searched.

The following files are expected to be added to the *PMI* system in the near future: Pesticide Applicator Training system; Environmental Fate and Effects Data Summaries; additional regulatory information; and a contacts directory.

Directories

200 Healthy Harvest: A Global Directory of Sustainable Agriculture and Horticulture Organizations

5th ed. agAccess, 1995. Updated every 2 or 3 years. 200p. $19.95 (paper).

Healthy Harvest is an invaluable reference to fourteen hundred sustainable agriculture groups worldwide, most of which are based in the United States. The entries are organized alphabetically; each entry includes complete contact information and a description, which ranges from brief (one or two sentences) to extensive (more than a page). The subject index features thirty-three topics, including apprenticeships, conferences, direct action groups, funding, gardening, publications, and pest control. An additional index lists each organization by state and country. This virtually comprehensive compilation is an important networking tool that will help individuals decide which sustainable agriculture organizations would be most beneficial to them in their information search.

201 The Humane Consumer and Producer Guide: Buying and Producing Farm Products for a Humane Sustainable Agriculture

1st ed. The Humane Society of the United States and the International Alliance for Sustainable Agriculture, 1993. Biannual. 368p. $15.00 (paper).

The Humane Consumer and Producer Guide profiles more than four hundred farmers and ranchers who raise animals based on principles of humaneness and sustainability. An additional one thousand entries describe research and educational organizations, restaurants, stores, and publications that support humane agricultural practices. Although this directory's primary goal is to help consumers locate humane, ecologically sound producers and to find out where their products are available, it is equally useful to professionals (e.g., researchers, educators, consultants, farmers, entrepreneurs) as a guide to experts and the humane agriculture industry. Resources are listed alphabetically, each with a detailed description (one-third to one-half page) that varies in nature depending on the type of resource. For instance, entries for farmers and ranchers focus on animals raised and practices employed, while entries for restaurants and other retailers describe their services and supply standards. The guide has four indices: state; activity in animal agriculture; type of animal; and contact name. In addition, the guide contains a wealth of other valuable information, such as a state-by-state guide to retailers and restaurants; state contact points for locating farmers' markets, and a discussion of recommended humane principles for raising farm animals.

For additional information about humane agriculture, contact the International Alliance for Sustainable Agriculture (612/331-1099).

202 National Organic Directory: A Guide to Organic Information and Resources

11th ed. Community Alliance with Family Farmers, 1994. Annual. 356p. $38.95 (paper).

The *National Organic Directory* is a valuable resource for anyone growing, marketing, or seeking wholesale organic produce or products. This directory, formerly the *Organic Directory of Wholesalers*, details the activities of more than a thousand organic farmers, certification groups, food wholesalers, farm suppliers, and distributors in North America, as well as key buyers internationally. The information on each company includes phone and fax numbers; address; region of operation; services available; certification of business; and distinctive features. There is also a yearbook section that updates state and federal organic legislation, National Organic Standards Board activities, and other noteworthy news from the past year. The usefulness of the listings is enhanced by the easy-to-use indices that allow users to focus quickly on a specific commodity, type of supply, or service.

Consumers who wish to purchase organic products in smaller quantities should consult *Green Groceries: A Mail-Order Guide to Organic Foods* (see entry 596).

203 Sustainable Agriculture Directory of Expertise

Compiled by Appropriate Technology Transfer for Rural Areas. 2nd ed. Sustainable Agriculture Network, 1994; distributed by Sustainable Agriculture Publications. Updated irregularly. 400p. $14.95 (paper).

Diskette: Available from Sustainable Agriculture Publications.

Internet: Available on the North Carolina Cooperative Extension Service site at North Carolina State University. To access this document, gopher to **twosocks.ces.ncsu.edu**; choose *National CES Information*, then choose either *Search Sustainable Ag. Directory* to search via WAIS, or *Sustainable Ag. Directory* to browse alphabetically.

A list of entries found in the *Sustainable Agriculture Directory of Expertise* is also available by e-mail from the North Carolina Cooperative Extension Service site. For more information, send an e-mail message to **almanac@ces.ncsu.edu** with the message **send sust-ag-dir catalog** in the body of the message.

The *Sustainable Agriculture Directory of Expertise* is an indispensable directory of a broad range of individuals and organizations willing to share their expertise in sustainable agriculture. Funded by the U.S. Department of Agriculture's Sustainable Agriculture Research and Education (SARE) program, it is an extraordinarily useful resource for farmers and extension workers, but anyone who needs information about sustainable agriculture will also appreciate its depth of coverage. Users can contact people and groups for advice about building soil health, broadening pest control, applying for organic certification, or any other related topic. Each detailed entry in the directory provides complete contact information, including preferred method of contact (mail, phone, fax, e-mail); sustainable agriculture roles (e.g., grower, research, government policy development); major areas of expertise, a description of work in progress, information services available; and products available. When the directory was first released in 1993, in both electronic and printed forms, it contained seven hundred contacts. In September 1994 an update on diskette added an additional five hundred contacts; an updated hard-copy version with all twelve hundred entries is planned for 1995.

In addition to this directory, the Sustainable Agriculture Network (see entry 195) sponsors a number of other excellent sustainable agriculture reference sources.

Other Directories

- ◆ *The Showcase of Sustainable Agriculture Information and Education Materials* (see entry 195, Sustainable Agriculture Network)

Bibliographies

204 The Socioeconomics of Sustainable Agriculture: An Annotated Bibliography

Edited by Gary Goreham, David Watt, and Roy Jacobsen. Garland Press, 1992. 334p. $53.00 (hardcover).

The Socioeconomics of Sustainable Agriculture contains more than one thousand annotated references to publications that focus primarily on the impact of sustainable agriculture on North American farms, farm families, communities, and the U.S. agricultural production system. This comprehensive bibliography is intended for researchers, policymakers, legislators, farm program administrators, and farm organization officials. Entries are limited to books and book chapters, periodical articles, and government documents. One- to two-sentence annotations succinctly summarize the content of each resource. Author and subject indices are also included.

205 Sustainable Agriculture in Print: Current Books

Special Reference Brief series. Alternative Farming Systems Information Center, May 1994. Updated irregularly. 35p. Free (paper).

Bulletin Board: Available on the Agriculture Library Forum (ALF) (see entry 197). Download file "SRB94-04.BIB" for the May 1994 edition.

Internet: ALF is available via FedWorld's GateWay (see entry 61). Choose *2* for *ALF (USDA)*.
    This document is also available on the Alternative Farming Systems Information Center (see entry 181) gopher. To access this document from the gopher menu, choose *Sustainable Agriculture in Print: Current Books*.

Sustainable Agriculture in Print provides insight into nearly one hundred sustainable agriculture books published between 1989 and 1994. For anyone interested in this topic, *Sustainable Agriculture in Print* will be a valuable part of a personal reference collection. This selective bibliography supplies citations and descriptions for an equal number of overviews (*The Environmental Gardener: The Solution to Pollution for Lawns and Gardens; Toward A Sustainable Agriculture: A Teacher's Guide*) and more specialized works (*Alternative Agriculture: Federal Incentives and Farmers' Opinions; The Comparative Economics of Alternative Agricultural Production Systems*) including numerous reference works and bibliographies. Works cited in this bibliography are available from the National Agricultural Library (see entry 183) through interlibrary loan.

Another free bibliography, *Tracing the Evolution* (Alternative Farming Systems Information Center, 1988), provides brief descriptions of fifty classic sustainable agriculture books, articles, and reports published between 1980 and 1986.

Other Bibliographies

- ◆ The NAL Quick Bibliography Series (see entry 183, National Agricultural Library)

Reference Handbooks

206 Basic Guide to Pesticides: Their Characteristics and Hazards

Edited by Shirley Briggs and the Rachel Carson Council. Hemisphere Publishing, 1992; distributed by Taylor and Francis. 283p. $42.00 (hardcover).

The *Basic Guide to Pesticides* is a valuable resource for both the layperson who has basic questions about pesticides and the specialist in need of in-depth references. The guide fills a long-neglected niche by providing detailed information—information that is excruciatingly difficult to acquire—about the toxic nature of specific chemicals utilized in pesticides. The core of the book presents, in easy-to-interpret tables, the known facts about more than seven hundred of the most hazardous and widely used chemical ingredients found in pesticides. For each ingredient, the guide supplies common and trade names, class, and CAS number as well as information about use, persistence in the environment, toxicity in mammals, and physical properties. Since the information is organized in tables, it is easy to see all that is still unknown about specific chemicals. The *Basic Guide to Pesticides* also discusses how to choose and apply a pesticide if alternative methods are not appropriate, and includes articles that summarize the environmental and economic impacts of pesticide use, methods of testing for cancer-causing products, basic principles of Integrated Pest Management (IPM), and federal pesticide regulations.

207 Database of State Alternative Agriculture Laws

Edited by Whitney Chamberlin, John Sullivan, and Nan Kim. The Center for Policy Alternatives, 1994. 155p. $22.00 (paper).

Internet: Available on the North Carolina Cooperative Extension Service site at North Carolina State University. To access the database, gopher to **twosocks.ces.ncsu.edu**; choose *National CES Information*, then choose either *Search Sustainable Ag. State Laws* to search by WAIS, or *Sustainable Ag. State Laws* to browse by state.

The *Database of State Alternative Agriculture Laws* is a comprehensive abstract database of innovative state laws pertaining to alternative agricultural practices. Included in each entry is the law's title, citation, year enacted, purpose, and a brief summary of the law's elements. Laws enacted for the following purposes are included: research, public health, farmer safety, water quality, soil conservation, pesticide reduction, financial assistance, energy conservation, farmland preservation, technical assistance, organic food production, general sustainable agriculture, environmental protection, and synthetic nutrient reduction. Because the database's focus is on innovation, the Center for Policy Alternatives (see entry 15) deliberately excluded laws that are found in every state. For example, laws establishing soil conservation districts or pesticide registration are not included unless they incorporate a unique or innovative twist. The directory is available both in hard copy, indexed by the purpose of the law, and on the Internet, where users may retrieve laws by title, citation, purpose, or any word appearing in the entry. In addition, clauses that specifically encourage alternative practices are italicized in the hard copy of the directory. Users are encouraged to make comments and additions as new laws are enacted.

208 Handbook of Pesticide Toxicology

Edited by Wayland J. Hayes, Jr. and Edward R. Laws, Jr. 3 vols. Academic Press, 1991. 1,576p. $395.00 (hardcover).

An extensive reference source on human pesticide toxicology, the *Handbook of Pesticide Toxicology* is suitable for interested laypeople, farmers, lawyers, policymakers, government regulators, pest control operators, scientific researchers, and physicians dealing with poison. The three volumes of this handbook, written by thirty-two experts, combine and thoroughly update two standard reference works by Wayland J. Hayes, *Toxicology of Pesticides* (Williams & Wilkinson, 1975) and *Pesticides Studied in Man* (Williams & Wilkinson, 1982). Volume 1 covers various types of toxicity; nature of injuries; reversibility; metabolism of toxins; factors affecting toxicity; absorption and elimination; as well as most other general toxicological topics. Volumes 2 and 3 contain information on individual pesticides (e.g., identity, uses, chemical name, structure, physical and chemical properties) followed by detailed information on toxicity, including what is known about absorption, distribution, dose response, and tissue damage. This work also includes references at the end of each chapter, informative graphs and tables, and a subject index. The compounds found in this work are limited to those that have been studied in humans, 258 in all.

209 Increasing Organic Agriculture at the Local Level: A Manual for Consumers, Grocers, Farmers, and Policy Makers

Maren Hansen and the Santa Barbara County Safe Food Project, with Phil Boise and Jim Hagen. Community Environmental Council, 1992. 100p. $18.00 (paper).

Increasing Organic Agriculture at the Local Level is a step-by-step guide to increasing support for and the supply of organic food within local communities. Based on its experience, the Safe Food Project provides personal insight into planning community forums, designing signs and brochures, creating newspaper ads, and writing letters and government proposals. In each case, examples of actions taken by other groups are described, and contact information is usually provided. This manual is an indispensable resource for food activists, organic farmers and growers interested in improving their marketability, or anyone else who is serious about promoting organic agriculture.

Introductory Reading

210 Alternative Agriculture

National Research Council, 1989; distributed by the National Academy Press. 448p. $25.00 (paper).

Alternative Agriculture is an authoritative report that helped make sustainable agriculture a viable policy option. The five-year study was commissioned by the National Research Council to explore ways in which alternative agricultural methods can help solve many of the problems currently facing American agriculture. As clearly stated in the executive summary, the report demonstrates that moving toward organic agriculture will benefit the producer, the consumer, and the environment. The four chapters in Part I review the evolution of agriculture since World War II, with particular emphasis on the effect of current federal policies; the economic and environmental consequences of conventional agricultural practices; the scientific research that supports alternatives to conventional farming, such as crop rotation, Integrated Pest Management (IPM), and biological pest control; and the economic potential of alternative systems. Part II includes eleven case studies of fifteen alternative farms. Some terminology may be difficult to understand for those who are not agricultural scientists or economists; nonetheless, this landmark report remains required reading for anyone who wants to understand the issues surrounding agriculture and the environment.

211 Farming in Nature's Image: An Ecological Approach to Agriculture

Judith D. Soule and Jon K. Piper. Island Press, 1992. 290p. $34.95 (hardcover), $19.95 (paper).

Farming in Nature's Image is a critique of modern agriculture and a review of sustainable alternatives. Through clearly written, scientific documentation, authors Judith D. Soule and Jon K. Piper (researchers at the Land Institute [913/823–5376], the leading research center for perennial polyculture) argue that merely fine-tuning conventional agricultural practices will not result in agriculture that is sustainable—either economically or environmentally. The first half of the book examines the social, economic, and environmental inadequacies of modern industrial farming and critically evaluates alternative policies. The book's second half describes alternative farming methods that are feasible, economical, and sustainable over the long term, particularly perennial polyculture: a farming model that mimics local ecosystems. This modern classic is suitable for both lay researchers and professionals in the field.

212 Integrating Sustainable Agriculture, Ecology, and Environmental Policy

Edited by Richard K. Olson. Food Products Press, 1992. 161p. $32.95 (hardcover), $25.95 (paper).

Integrating Sustainable Agriculture, Ecology, and Environmental Policy is a concise summary of views presented by major participants at a conference sponsored by the Environmental Protection Agency and the Henry A. Wallace Institute for Alternative Agriculture (see entry 189), at which internationally recognized ecologists, economists, sociologists, soil scientists, and government policymakers discussed the ways in which ecology should and could address agricultural sustainability. Each fact-based, nonemotional paper supports the notion that agriculture, as currently practiced in the U.S., cannot continue to increase in productivity without such extensive environmental damage that it will significantly limit agriculture's ability to meet expanding population needs. Topic coverage includes incentives and disincentives of federal policies; soil nutrient processes; landscape ecology; informational needs required to support sustainable agriculture policies; and the reduction of agriculture's impact on the environment. Ecological and agricultural scientists will be most interested in this compilation, but others interested in expert views on the viability of widespread sustainable agriculture will also gain valuable insight.

213 The Pesticide Question: Environment, Economics, and Ethics

Edited by David Pimentel and Hugh Lehman. Chapman & Hall, 1993. 441p. $45.00 (hardcover).

The Pesticide Question is an extensive, well-referenced collection of essays that focus on the economic, environmental, ethical, and health issues associated with international pesticide use and policies. Eighteen essays by thirty-nine contributors are divided into five sections: the social and environmental effects of pesticides; the methods and effects of reducing pesticide use; government policy; the history, public attitudes, and ethics of pesticide use; and the benefits and risks of pesticides. Almost every essay calls for dramatic changes in pesticide policy, but a few support conventional programs. This stimulating book manages to mix scientific and socioeconomic issues with ease, and although written for policymakers and agricultural professionals, it is accessible to the lay reader. *The Pesticide Question* serves as a good introduction to pesticide issues.

214 Save Three Lives: A Plan for Famine Prevention

Robert Rodale. Sierra Club Books, 1991. 256p. $20.00 (hardcover).

Save Three Lives is a highly recommended, folksy narrative that provides an overview of the real-world importance of sustainable farming practices—it is filled with facts, insightful analysis, and history. Author Robert Rodale, a leading proponent of sustainable agriculture, explores the devastating effects of Western agricultural practices on African ecosystems and describes indigenous and new alternative agricultural methods that prevent environmental catastrophes. He systematically yet captivatingly explains his theory that famine is a threat to everyone, and he presents his plan for implementing policy solutions. Though this book, finished just before Rodale's death, is aimed at a lay audience, it will also be enjoyed by sustainable agriculture professionals.

215 Shattering: Food, Politics, and the Loss of Genetic Diversity

Cary Fowler and Pat Mooney. The University of Arizona Press, 1990. 278p. $29.95 (hardcover), $14.95 (paper).

Shattering presents the scientific and political issues surrounding the loss of agricultural genetic diversity. The authors, who work at the Rural Advancement Fund International, have been instrumental in bringing this issue to the spotlight; this book provides an overview of the issue for a general audience. *Shattering*'s first five chapters provide a good summary of the origins of agriculture, the importance of genetic diversity and the threats it now faces, and what all of this means to the world food supply. The next two chapters detail the increasing role of transnational petrochemical companies in the seed industry and the dangers posed by biotechnology. The last chapters describe recent conservation efforts and propose alternative strategies to preserve crop diversity. Well referenced and a pleasure to read, this is an excellent primer on a lesser-known but important environmental crisis.

Another excellent book on this topic, marketed for a lay, rather than academic, audience, is *Seeds of Change: The Living Treasure: The Passionate Story of the Growing Movement to Restore Biodiversity & Revolutionize the Way We Think About Food* (HarperSanFrancisco, 1994).

216 Silent Spring

Rachel Carson. Houghton Mifflin, original edition, 1962; anniversary edition, 1993. 368p. $11.00 (paper).

Through her classic *Silent Spring*, Rachel Carson, highly respected scientist in her day and grandmother of modern environmentalism, is credited with making the general public keenly aware of the adverse health and environmental effects of chemicals, such as pesticides. Controversial when first released, this well-documented, poetic standard has withstood the attacks of both the chemical industry and time. It remains an enjoyable, relevant read.

217 The Unsettling of America: Culture and Agriculture

Wendell Berry. Sierra Club Books, original edition, 1977; revised edition, 1986. 228p. $9.00 (paper).

The Unsettling of America is the most widely cited book by Wendell Berry, one of America's most eloquent farmer-philosophers. Weaving history and philosophy in a series of independent essays, Berry mourns the loss of spirituality and affinity to the Earth caused by the rise of agribusiness and America's increased industrialization and urbanization. Berry's vision of recultivating a strong bond with nature to correct many of society's problems continues to

serve as the philosophical foundation of the sustainable agriculture movement. Anyone interested in the principles and philosophies of sustainable agriculture will find this poetic classic a valuable primer.

Other interesting works by Berry include *Home Economics* (North Point Press, 1987); *The Gift of Good Land: Further Essays, Cultural and Agricultural* (North Point Press, 1981); and *Meeting the Expectations of the Land: Essays in Sustainable Agriculture and Stewardship* (North Point Press, 1984).

218 Unwelcome Harvest: Agriculture and Pollution

Edited by Gordon Conway and Jules Pretty. Earthscan Publications, 1991. 645p. $24.95 (paper).

Unwelcome Harvest is a comprehensive, authoritative review of the negative health effects and environmental dangers attributed to agricultural pollutants: pesticides, fungicides, herbicides, nitrates, methane, ammonia, and nitrous oxide. Also considered in this in-depth analysis are the negative effects of this pollution on agricultural productivity. The authors present and describe an almost overwhelming number of studies and reports, including extensive reference lists, to support their claims and add credibility to their proposed solutions. This is an ideal starting point for those interested in acquiring a detailed understanding of the pollution problems associated with pesticide use and the technology currently available for dealing with these problems.

219 The Violence of the Green Revolution: Third World Agriculture, Ecology and Politics

Vandana Shiva. Zed Books, 1991. 264p. $49.95 (hardcover), $17.50 (paper).

The Violence of the Green Revolution offers unique documentation of the consequences suffered by a rural region during the Western-imposed "Green Revolution"—the growth of chemical-based, industrialized agriculture following World War II. Author Vandana Shiva cites the ongoing hardships of Punjab, India, to represent the various ecological and social costs of both monoculture farming and a particular region's forced reliance on pesticide use. *The Violence of* the *Green Revolution* clearly documents the failures of the "Green Revolution" and makes a passionate argument for changing the focus and direction of international agricultural policy. Each chapter contains figures, tables, quotations, and references.

Abstracts and Indices

220 Agrindex

Food and Agriculture Organization of the United Nations, 1975–. Monthly.

CD-ROM: Available as *AGRIS* from SilverPlatter.

Database Vendor: Available as *AGRIS* on DIALOG.

The *Agrindex* is the most comprehensive bibliographic index to both published and unpublished foreign agricultural literature. Although the *Agrindex*, the print version of the *International Information System for Agricultural Science and Technology (AGRIS)* database, includes some American entries, there is little overlap with the primarily North American *Bibliography of Agriculture* (see entry 221). Citations are prepared cooperatively by more than one hundred national and multinational agricultural research centers. In addition to journal articles, the *Agrindex* includes materials not indexed anywhere else, such as unpublished scientific and technical reports, theses, conference papers, and government publications. Writings related to sustainable agriculture are well represented.

221 Bibliography of Agriculture

Compiled by the Department of Agriculture, National Agricultural Library. Oryx Press, 1942–. Monthly.

CD-ROM: Available as *AGRICOLA* from SilverPlatter.

Database Vendor: Available as *AGRICOLA* on DIALOG, OCLC EPIC, and OCLC FirstSearch.

The *Bibliography of Agriculture* is the most comprehensive bibliographic index to United States–published literature in agriculture and allied fields. The *Bibliography of Agriculture* is the print version of the National Agricultural

Library's (see entry 183) *AGRICOLA* database. The bibliography is arranged by broad subject, including administration and legislation; plant science; natural resources; aquatic sciences and fisheries; and pollution. Literature pertaining to alternative agriculture and pest control is also comprehensively represented. The majority of citations are for U.S. government materials; only those international citations not found in the *Agrindex* (see entry 220) are found here. In addition to journal articles, the bibliography covers books, how-to pamphlets, software, reports, and audiovisual materials, including numerous publications produced by the Department of Agriculture, state agricultural experiment stations and extension services, and the Food and Agriculture Organization (FAO). There are three indices: corporate author, personal author, and subject. *AGRICOLA* provides more than three million citations from 1970 to the present; contact the Alternative Farming Systems Information Center (see entry 181) for a free copy of *Searching AGRICOLA for Low Input/Sustainable Agriculture* and ask about the NAL Quick Bibliography Series (see entry 183, National Agricultural Library)—free bibliographies compiled from *AGRICOLA*. In addition, AFSIC conducts brief, personalized searches of *AGRICOLA* free, and mails the results.

222 CAB Abstracts

CAB International, 1972–; distributed in the United States by University of Arizona Press. Monthly.

CD-ROM: Available as *CABCD* from SilverPlatter.

Database Vendor: Available on DIALOG.

CAB Abstracts is the only comprehensive agricultural database in which most of the citations—i.e., more than 85 percent—include descriptions. This database, which contains more than three million citations, combines the contents of more than fifty specialized abstract journals. It is best to use *CAB Abstracts'* electronic formats since it is difficult to determine which print abstracts to consult, and harder still to locate them. Coverage includes all branches of agricultural science and related areas. Sample journal titles include: *Forestry Abstracts*; *Fava Bean Abstracts*; *Soil and Fertilizers*; *Review of Agricultural Entomology*; and *Nutrition Abstracts and Reviews*. *CAB Abstracts* is particularly important due to its coverage of low-input agriculture in Third World countries. Because of the large number of abstracts *CAB Abstracts* contains, many users will find this database more helpful than *AGRICOLA* (see entry 221, *Bibliography of Agriculture*) or *AGRIS* (see entry 220, *Agrindex*)—but also more expensive.

Other Abstracts and Indices

- ◆ *Biological Abstracts* (see entry 303)
- ◆ The *Biological and Agricultural Index* (see entry 151)

Periodicals

223 American Journal of Alternative Agriculture

Henry A. Wallace Institute for Alternative Agriculture, 1986–. Quarterly. 50p. $24.00/year for individuals, $44.00/year for libraries and organizations.

The *American Journal of Alternative Agriculture* is a multidisciplinary, peer-reviewed journal that publishes studies on alternative agriculture methods. Although the articles are meant for farmers, educators, and students in the field of alternative agriculture, nonexperts will also find them easy to understand. Specialized terms are defined, and both the significance of statements and the reasoning behind conclusions are clearly spelled out. Each article includes an abstract, introduction, and conclusion, as well as keyword listings and references. Representative articles include "An Economic Comparison of Conventional and Reduced-Chemical Farming Systems in Iowa" and "Sustainable Agriculture: the Wildlife Connection." The journal is highly recommended and respected in the field.

224 Global Pesticide Campaigner

Pesticide Action Network, 1989–. Quarterly. 20p. $15.00/year for low-income individuals, $25.00/year for individuals and nonprofits, $50.00/year for small businesses, government agencies, and public libraries, $100.00/year for corporations.

An essential resource for pesticide activists, the *Global Pesticide Campaigner* is primarily concerned with international pesticide issues as they pertain to policy, politics, and trade. Most issues contain five eye-opening feature articles—each of them one to four pages in length—on current topics such as "Market Potential of Organically Grown Cotton" ; "Methyl Bromide: Time to Stop the Killing" ; "Organic vs. Conventional: Considering the Costs" ; or "U.S. Pesticide Traffic: Exporting Banned and Hazardous Pesticides." Each article provides contacts for further research. Original news shorts, numerous reviews of new resources, and excerpts from other publications are also included in each issue of the *Campaigner*. In addition, the periodical provides regular updates on Pesticide Action Network's (see entry 193) Dirty Dozen Campaign, which focuses on pesticides that have been targeted for replacement with safer alternatives.

225 Journal of Pesticide Reform

Northwest Coalition for Alternatives to Pesticides, 1979–. Quarterly. 24p. $25.00/year.

226 Pesticides and You

National Coalition Against the Misuse of Pesticides, 1981–. Quarterly. 30p. $15.00/year for low-income individuals, $25.00/year for other individuals, $30.00/year for organizations without paid staff, $50.00/year for organizations with paid staff.

Similar in appearance and content, both the *Journal of Pesticide Reform* and *Pesticides and You* are practical magazines well suited to the needs of pesticide activists. The writing style in both is engaging, and articles explain the effects of toxic substances in terms anyone can understand; however, this does not deter either publication from tackling and unraveling complicated issues. Both contain articles, speeches, human-interest essays, book reviews, resource lists, updates on organizational activities, analyses of scientific reports, and news shorts on pesticide issues and related topics, such as the environmental movement, sustainable agriculture, environmental justice, and activist strategies. Representative articles include "Toxic Timebombs on the Road: For-Export-Only Pesticides" ; "Incidental Contamination: Organic Farming Standards Shouldn't Punish the Victim" ; "Toxic Chemicals & Behavior: What You Eat Could Affect How You Act" ; and "Least Toxic Control of Carpenter Ants." Most articles contain extensive footnotes. The subtle differences between these two periodicals are due to the differences in philosophy and areas of focus of their sponsoring organizations, the National Coalition Against the Misuse of Pesticides (NCAMP) (see entry 191) (*Pesticides and You*) and the Northwest Coalition for Alternatives to Pesticides (see entry 192) (*Journal of Pesticide Reform*).

Individuals interested in news on federal agency pesticide-related activities should read NCAMP's *Technical Report*, a four-page monthly digest.

227 Journal of Sustainable Agriculture

Haworth Press, 1990–. Quarterly. 120p. $36.00/year for individuals, $48.00/year for institutions, $60.00/year for libraries.

The *Journal of Sustainable Agriculture* is geared toward agricultural professionals and academics concerned with the study and application of sustainable agriculture. While some of the five or six articles presented in each issue are philosophical in tone, most of them present fact-based scientific research on innovative practices, new technology, Integrated Pest Management (IPM), organic farming, and energy use. Representative features include an economic study of alternative feeds in midwestern beef cattle, an insightful analysis of the evolution of farming through the year 2031, and an upbeat look at government policies and proposals involving cattle and sustainable agriculture. The *Journal* consistently forecasts a positive future for sustainable agriculture.

228 Sustainable Agriculture Week

Institute for Agriculture and Trade Policy, 1993–. Weekly. 4p. $35.00/year by mail, $100.00/year by fax.

EcoNet: Available in the *susag.news* conference.

Internet: To be placed on the electronic-mailing list, send name, electronic-mail address, and a brief e-mail message to Michelle Thom at **mthom@igc.apc.org**.

Sustainable Agriculture Week offers an outstanding way for individuals in the sustainable agriculture community to remain up to date on current developments in this field. Each issue of the newsletter provides detailed summaries of headline-making news concerning the agricultural and chemical industries, the status of legislation and regulations, scientific developments, and new sustainable agriculture projects. Full citations to the original source of each news story are always included. Most issues provide brief descriptions of new sources of sustainable agriculture information.

Other Periodicals

◆ *Alternative Agriculture News* (see entry 189, Henry A. Wallace Institute for Alternative Agriculture)

◆ *ATTRAnews* (see entry 182, Appropriate Technology Transfer for Rural Areas)

◆ *Technical Report* (see entry 191, National Coalition Against the Misuse of Pesticides)

◆ *The Pesticide Action Network North America Updates Service* (see entry 193, Pesticide Action Network)

◆ "sanet-mg" (see entry 195, Sustainable Agriculture Network)

CHAPTER THREE

Air

What This Chapter Covers

This chapter covers local air pollution and global atmospheric issues, including stratospheric-ozone depletion and climate change. Acid rain and indoor air pollution are also included.

For More Information

- ◆ See **General** for resources on all environmental issues, including those related to air.
- ◆ See **Energy** for resources on energy conservation and renewable energy sources, both of which help prevent air pollution.
- ◆ See **Health and Toxics** for resources on the health effects of specific air pollutants, including radon and asbestos.
- ◆ See **Health and Toxics** and **Architecture** for resources on indoor air quality.
- ◆ See **Waste** for resources on incineration and pollution prevention.

Government Clearinghouses

229 Acid Rain Hotline
Environmental Protection Agency

Phone: 202/233-9620

In 1991, the Environmental Protection Agency's Acid Rain Program created the automated Acid Rain Hotline to respond to technical questions, provide general information, and disseminate documents on the subject of acid rain. There is no better resource for learning about regulatory rules, regulatory impact predictions, and compliance requirements related to this topic. The hotline can also handle economic, scientific, and technological questions, as well as requests for fact sheets, brochures, *Federal Register* notices, and educational materials. Callers are encouraged both to request documents—for the current list, press "1" at the main menu—and to leave detailed messages for acid rain experts in one or more of five subject areas: general information, continuous emissions monitoring, permitting, allowance systems, or conservation and renewable energy. Questions should be well thought out and focused to ensure that the most qualified expert is assigned to fill the request. Calls to the hotline are generally returned within twenty-four hours. This service is a great starting point for anyone—the regulated business community, environmental groups, or concerned citizens—with questions about acid rain.

230 Air Risk Information Support Center (Air RISC)
Environmental Protection Agency
Office of Air Quality Planning and Standards
Research Triangle Park, NC 27711

Phone: 919/541-0888. Fax: 919/541-5661

The Air Risk Information Support Center (Air RISC) provides technical information on toxic air pollutants, especially those aspects related to health, exposure, and risk assessment. The hotline primarily caters to state and local air pollution control agencies and Environmental Protection Agency regional offices. Air RISC offers three levels of service. The first, called the hotline, is the only one regularly used by those outside the government. The hotline is designed to provide a quick response—from several min-

utes to several days—by matching callers with an appropriate expert. Callers can receive a wide range of information, from air pollution levels in a particular region to guidance in determining whether a manufacturing facility is using the appropriate control technology. The second service offers more in-depth evaluation—several weeks to several months—such as interpretations of toxicological data or reviews of site-specific exposure assessments. The final service provides funding for projects of broad national interest, including workshops, videos, and documents like the *Directory of Information Resources Related to Health, Exposure, and Risk Assessment of Air Toxics* (see entry 246).

231 Carbon Dioxide Information Analysis Center (CDIAC)
Department of Energy
Oak Ridge National Laboratory
P.O. Box 2008, Mail Code 6335
Building 1000
Oak Ridge, TN 37831

Phone: 615/574-0390. Fax: 615/574-2232.
E-mail: cdp@ornlstc.gov

Internet: CDIAC has space on the Oak Ridge National Laboratory's World Wide Web site. The URL is **http://www.esd.ornl.gov/programs/cdiac/cdiac.html**.
　　To access CDIAC's ftp files directly, ftp to **cdiac.esd.ornl.gov**, then choose *pub*.

The Carbon Dioxide Information Analysis Center (CDIAC) supports the data needs of researchers studying the relationship between atmospheric carbon dioxide (CO_2) levels and climate, carbon cycling processes, and natural resources. It also produces information suitable for educators, students, industry managers, congressional staffers, and science writers. CDIAC gathers information from university, government, and industry research centers and then analyzes and integrates the data into easy-to-understand graphics and reports. All publications are free; titles include *Atmospheric CO_2 Concentrations: 1958–1991; Global Surface–Air Temperature Variations: 1851–1984; Historical Sunshine and Cloud Data in the United States*; and the practical *Carbon Dioxide and Climate Glossary* (see entry 249, *Dictionary of Global Climate Change*). *CDIAC Communications* is another well-respected free publication offered by CDIAC; it is released three times a year and includes short articles and reports on global climate change activities around the world. CDIAC has a well-established referral network to specialized information sources outside the center's scope of expertise.

The National Climactic Data Center (704/271-4800) of the National Oceanic and Atmospheric Administration is an even better source than CDIAC for historical climate data such as daily average temperatures and precipitation rates for a specific city or region; fees are based on the complexity of the request.

232 Indoor Air Quality Information Clearinghouse (IAQ INFO)
Environmental Protection Agency
Indoor Air Division
P.O. Box 37133
Washington, DC 20013

Phone: 800/438-4318; 301/585-9020.
Fax: 301/588-3408

A primary contact for consumers and professionals, the Indoor Air Quality Information Clearinghouse (IAQ INFO) provides free information from the Environmental Protection Agency on the health effects of indoor air pollutants; procedures for testing, measuring, and controlling pollutants; the construction and maintenance of homes and buildings to minimize air-quality problems; and air-quality standards, guidelines, and legislative and regulatory information. IAQ INFO information specialists can perform searches on the bibliographic database of commercial and government literature, or callers can receive referrals to local public and private organizations. Examples of publications that IAQ INFO can send include: *Biological Pollutants in Your Home*; *Compendium of Methods for the Determination of Air Pollutants in Indoor Air: Project Summary*; and fact sheets about such topics as office ventilation, residential air cleaners, and carpets. A thirty-six-page pamphlet, *The Inside Story: A Guide to Indoor Air Quality*, is an excellent introduction to the effects of harmful indoor pollutants and strategies for controlling and preventing them.

233 National Center for Atmospheric Research (NCAR)
Communications Office
P.O. Box 3000
Boulder, CO 80307

Phone: 303/497-8601. Phone (personnel locator): 303/497-1000. Fax: 303/497-8610

Internet: To access NCAR sites, gopher to **gopher.ucar.edu**; or, on the World Wide Web, the URL is **http://http.ucar.edu/**.

The National Center for Atmospheric Research (NCAR), founded in 1960 by the University Committee for Atmospheric Research under the financial sponsorship of the National Science Foundation, pursues cutting-edge atmospheric research and supports university research. NCAR's research focuses on four basic areas: atmospheric chemistry, climate and its relationship to other environmental systems, solar physics, and meteorology. The Environmental and Societal Impacts Group (ESIG) is the NCAR program most relevant to environmental issues. In addition to distributing the *Network Newsletter* (see entry 264), ESIG works on issues pertaining to the interrelationship between human activities and the atmosphere, and on developing new methods for assessing societal responses to climate-related impacts. Since NCAR is a research institute that caters to a somewhat closed network of scientists, it does not have hotlines that facilitate access to information. However, NCAR's Internet sites offer members of the public an easy way to tap into the center's extensive data and expertise. For educational materials, publications, and other general information, contact the NCAR's communications office.

234 Stratospheric Ozone Information Hotline
Environmental Protection Agency
c/o The Bruce Company
501 3rd Street, NW, Suite 260
Washington, DC 20001

Phone: 800/296-1996. Fax: 202/783-1066

The Stratospheric Ozone Information Hotline is the best place to turn for information about regulations and requirements under Title VI of the Clean Air Act, which covers the production, use, and safe disposal of ozone-depleting chemicals. Most calls come from mechanics, the air-conditioning and -cooling industry, and manufacturers who are concerned about the production phaseout of ozone-depleting chemicals, alternative substances, recycling and emission reduction, product labeling, and the ban on nonessential chlorofluorocarbons (CFCs). Although not its primary focus, the hotline also serves as a distribution center and point of referral for all topics related to stratospheric-ozone depletion and protection; some of this information is suitable for the layperson interested in introductory materials. The hotline houses hundreds of relevant reports, articles, fact sheets, and policy and science documents, as well as contact lists. Although a publications list is not available, hotline staff members will recommend and supply relevant documents free of charge.

Organizations

235 American Lung Association (ALA)
1740 Broadway
New York, NY 10019

Phone: 800/586-4872; 212/315-8700.
Fax: 212/265-5642

John Garrison, Managing Director

Most widely known for its fight against tobacco use, the American Lung Association (ALA) is dedicated to eliminating lung diseases. ALA's programs work to prevent and control all types of indoor and outdoor air pollution—everything from secondhand smoke to low-level ozone. Through its more than 120 local chapters, the ALA works with citizen groups and government agencies to implement pollution control and educational programs. Contact the nearest local chapter (the New York headquarters can provide referrals to local affiliates) for basic educational materials—posters, booklets, fact sheets—on a variety of topics, such as radon, asbestos, car care, agricultural lung hazards, and exercise considerations. One report worth a special mention, *The Health Costs of Air Pollution*, is a sixty-two-page survey of studies published between 1984 and 1989 analyzing the physical and economic costs of air pollution.

236 The Atmosphere Alliance
P.O. Box 10346
Olympia, WA 98502

Phone: 206/352-1763. E-mail: ccarrel@igc.apc.org

Rhys Roth and Chris Carrel, Project Co-directors

237 Ozone Action
1621 Connecticut Avenue, NW, Suite 400
Washington, DC 20009

Phone: 202/265-6738. Fax: 202/332-4865.
E-mail: cantando@essential.org

John Passacantando, Director

Both the Atmosphere Alliance and Ozone Action have a similar mission: to build activist networks and to provide citizens with the skills and information they need to help protect the global atmosphere. Ozone Action focuses specifically on stratospheric-ozone depletion, while the Alliance covers the full range of climate change issues, though the group does place particular emphasis on the buildup of greenhouse gases. While neither group has an extensive national education program, respective staff members are extraordinarily knowledgeable about the field and can help activists reach scientists and other experts, find articles and reports, set up local education programs, and remain up to date on important issues and controversies. The Atmosphere Alliance publishes an indispensable quarterly newsletter, *No Sweat News: Journal of Grassroots Action to Protect the Atmosphere* (see entry 265) and has other useful information on action citizens can take to protect the atmosphere. Any citizen concerned about the effects of global climate change and ozone depletion should definitely be in touch with both groups.

238 Center For Clean Air Policy
444 North Capitol Street, Suite 602
Washington, DC 20001

Phone: 202/624-7709. Fax: 202/508-3829

Ned Helme, Executive Director

The Center for Clean Air Policy is an outstanding resource for regulatory decision makers, environmental groups, and industry representatives with an interest in potential air pollution control strategies, particularly in relation to air toxins, acid rain, energy conservation, transportation issues, and global climate change. The center's primary mission—for which it has been widely praised—is to work closely with parties that have competing interests in order to develop market-based solutions that balance political, economic, and environmental realities. Although the center consistently demonstrates that it regards the protection of the environment as critically important, it is officially neutral, favoring neither industry nor environmentalists, and recognizes the need for compromise. Those at the center believe that inaction due to disagreements is often more environmentally destructive than action based on carefully considered compromises. So far, the center has had great success in convincing industry that it can benefit financially by instituting programs that pollute the air less. Many of the center's strategies, both proposed and adopted, are outlined in reports, through which groups and individuals can best tap into the center's expertise. A few of the most influential ones include *Acid Rain: Road to a Middleground Solution*; *The Untold Story: The Silver Lining for West Virginia in Acid Rain Control*; and *Electric Utilities and Long-Range Transport of Mercury and Other Toxic Air Pollutants*.

239 Clean Air Network (CAN)

c/o Natural Resources Defense Council
1350 New York Avenue, NW, Suite 300
Washington, DC 20005

Phone: 202/624-9388. Fax: 202/783-5917.
E-mail: clairnet@igc.apc.org

Jayne Mardock, Coordinator

EcoNet: The Clean Air Network maintains the *env.cleanair* conference.

The independent, grant-funded Clean Air Network (CAN) facilitates the implementation of coordinated strategies to affect clean air policies and serves as an information clearinghouse to enhance these efforts. CAN is made up of more than eight hundred representatives from local, state, and national nonprofit organizations working on air pollution issues. CAN offers its own reports and publications (e.g., *Why NO$_x$—Talking Points for Reductions*; *Pollution Taxes for Roadway Transportation*; *CAN Fact Sheets on Acid Rain and Allowance Trading*) as well as copies of relevant portions of the *Federal Register* and

Environment Reporter (see entry 118); all photocopies are 10¢ per page. CAN will also provide callers with referrals to members of the network; its database is updated every six months. The network's quarterly newsletter, *CANnections*, provides news, action alerts, updates from member groups, announcements of new resources, and a list of all CAN publications.

240 Climate Institute

324 4th Street, NE
Washington, DC 20002

Phone: 202/547-0104. Fax: 202/547-0111.
E-mail: climateinst@igc.apc.org

John Topping, President

A respected and influential voice working to shape international policy on global climate change, the Climate Institute focuses on climate issues that are especially relevant to developing countries. By linking scholars with key decision makers, this nonprofit organization has been able to foster the development of effective international programs that limit the risks associated with climate change. The institute sponsors conferences and produces papers, books, and videos, as well as the newsletter *Climate Alert* (10 issues per year, $95). Because the institute focuses on networking and information dissemination, it has become an outstanding resource for referrals to climate change experts and literature.

241 The Global Climate Coalition (GCC)

1331 Pennsylvania Avenue, NW, Suite 1500
North Tower
Washington, DC 20004

Phone (executive director): 202/637-3158. Phone (press office): 202/628-3622. Fax (executive director): 202/638-1043. Fax (press office): 202/639-8685

John Shlaes, Executive Director

The Global Climate Coalition (GCC) is the leading voice for industry on the greenhouse effect, particularly in the area of carbon dioxide emissions. Its members include the major coal, oil, auto, paper, and chemical industry associations. GCC works to convince decision makers that because of the inherent uncertainties surrounding global warming predictions, only extremely limited action should be taken to prevent future climate alterations. The coalition promotes scientific research, analyzes the economic and societal impacts of policy options, encourages the transfer of technology to developing countries, and works to ensure that U.S. corporations are not hurt by inequitable international agreements. The organization's four-page monthly newsletter, *Climate Watch*, provides commentary from GCC's executive director, news updates, announcements of meetings and conferences, and recommended reading lists. This is the place to turn for information that asserts that global climate change is not a significant threat.

242 U.S. Climate Action Network (U.S. CAN)

c/o Natural Resources Defense Council
1350 New York Avenue, NW, Suite 300
Washington, DC 20005

Phone: 202/624-9360. Fax: 202/783-5917.
E-mail: uscan@igc.apc.org

Jennifer Morgan, U.S. CAN Coordinator

The U.S. Climate Action Network is part of the international Climate Action Network, a loose affiliation of more than one hundred nongovernmental organizations around the world. The ultimate goal of the international network is to promote governmental and individual action in order to keep human-induced climate change at ecologically sustainable levels. U.S. CAN acts as a clearinghouse for activists and helps coordinate the advocacy efforts of United States member organizations, including the Alliance to Save Energy (see entry 317), Greenpeace (see entry 32), Sierra Club (see entry 45), and the World Resources Institute (see entry 50). U.S. CAN produces *Hotline*, a free, occasional news digest. The international membership directory, which lists contacts by issue, is also free of charge. Since U.S. CAN is primarily made up of individuals who work for national organizations, the U.S. CAN coordinator is the best initial point of contact.

To stay up to date on the latest news from the international climate negotiations, read *ECO*, the Climate Action Network's electronic newsletter. Written by leading independent scientists and political analysts, *ECO* provides behind-the-scenes analysis of what is going on at current negotiations. To subscribe to *ECO*, send an e-mail message to Lelani Arris at **larris@igc.apc.org**.

ECO is also available in the *climate.news* conference on EcoNet (see entry 58) and at the Institute for Global Communications (see entry 57) ftp site (choose *pub*, then *ECO*).

Bulletin Boards

243 Clean Air Act Amendments Bulletin Board System (CAAA)

Maintained by the Environmental Protection Agency's Office of Air Quality Planning and Standards.

Bulletin Board: Available on the Technology Transfer Network (TTN) (see entry 245). At the main menu, choose *Gateway to TTN Technical Areas (Bulletin Boards)*, then *Clean Air Act (Rules/Policy/Guidance)*.
For technical support by phone, call the system operator at 919/541-5653.

Internet: TTN (see above) is available on the Internet.

The Clean Air Act Amendments Bulletin Board System (CAAA) is the best place for up-to-date information on the Clean Air Act (CAA) amendments of 1990. Regulators, the regulated community, and members of the general public can easily obtain information that will help them understand, implement, and comply with the requirements of the law. Users can search or download the full text of the CAA; read summaries of all eleven Titles; find out about recently signed Rules; browse policy and guidance memos; and learn about additional contacts and resources from CAA updates and news bulletins. There are also many nontechnical clean air documents available for browsing and downloading, including a chronology of major milestones, a directory of information services, a glossary, and a practical guide for small businesses. Questions can be left in the public message area.

244 Pollution Prevention Database (P²)

Maintained by the Environmental Protection Agency's Office of Air Quality Planning and Standards.

Bulletin Board: Available on the Technology Transfer Network (TTN) (see entry 245). At the main menu, choose *Gateway to TTN Technical Areas (Bulletin Boards)*, then *COMPLIance Information on Stationary Sources of Air Pollution*, then *Pollution Prevention/P²*.

For technical support by phone, call the system operator at 703/308-8723.

Internet: TTN (see above) is available on the Internet.

The *Pollution Prevention Database (P²)* provides electronic access to current documents on air pollution prevention issues and developments. *P²* first became available in November 1993 through the COMPLI bulletin board system on the Technology Transfer Network (see entry 245). *P²* files are organized within seven menu areas—case studies, regulatory actions, summary bulletins, other pollution resources, general documents, training and education, and contact lists—with an eighth area reserved for information requests. For each document in the summary bulletin section there is both an abstract file with a contact name and phone number and a full-text file that can be downloaded. *P²* contains information on a broad range of issues related to air pollution prevention, such as secondhand smoke, acid rain, global climate change, ozone depletion, the North American Free Trade Agreement (NAFTA), technology, competitiveness, energy efficiency, hazardous waste, and sustainable development. Anyone interested in air pollution prevention—be they regulator, policymaker, engineer, manager, lawyer, student, or activist—will find this easy-to-navigate database a great place to begin an information search.

245 Technology Transfer Network (TTN)

Maintained by the Environmental Protection Agency's Office of Air Quality Planning and Standards.

Bulletin Board: To connect to TTN by modem, dial 919/541-5742.

For technical support by phone, call the TTN Voice Help Line at 919/541-5384.

Internet: To access TTN, telnet to **ttnbbs.rtpnc.epa.gov**.

A comprehensive source of technical air pollution information, the Technology Transfer Network (TTN) is a network of electronic bulletin boards developed and operated by the Environmental Protection Agency's (EPA) Office of Air Quality Planning and Standards (OAQPS) to facilitate the exchange of air pollution control information and technology, primarily between EPA regional offices, state and local agencies, and industry. Other professionals and the general public, however, will also find an abundance of valuable information, and anyone can access the system at no charge by connecting directly via modem or through the Internet. Each bulletin board focuses on a different aspect of air quality and may contain databases, contact lists, relevant regulatory information, bibliographies, newsletters, studies, and reports. Information available on TTN includes Title summaries of the 1990 Clean Air Act Amendments (see entry 243, Clean Air Act Amendments Bulletin Board System); tools for estimating air pollutant emissions; emissions control strategies that have been applied to various sources by agencies and companies; asbestos inspection contractors and the reports they have filed, as well as pollution prevention information; air pollution control strategies; documentation on hazardous air pollutants; fuel economy information; and descriptions of courses offered by the Air Pollution Training Institute. The best way to get a handle on the depth and breadth of the information available on TTN is to experiment online; the menu-driven interface and clear instructions make what could be a complicated system easy to use. For additional assistance in locating many of the documents cited on these bulletin board systems, contact OAQPS's Air Information Center (AIC) at 919/541-2777. In addition to providing copies of OAQPS documents and related regulatory documents, AIC offers free literature searches for state and local air pollution agency employees and environmental groups.

Other Bulletin Boards

◆ The Ozone Action Information Clearinghouse (see entry 435, Pollution Prevention Information Exchange)

Directories

246 Directory of Information Resources Related to Health, Exposure, and Risk Assessment of Air Pollutants

Environmental Protection Agency, Air Risk Information Support Center, 1992. 83p. Free (paper).

The *Directory of Information Resources Related to Health, Exposure, and Risk Assessment of Air Pollutants* is an excellent directory for professionals and state and local agencies that need help obtaining, reviewing, or interpreting technical air pollution information. The directory is divided into two main sections, the first of which describes clearinghouses, hotlines, organizations, and non–Environmental Protection Agency (EPA) government agencies; the second section describes EPA offices. Each entry provides detailed descriptions of activities and services. Also useful is the section that briefly describes relevant databases and other reference materials: reports, summary documents, and bibliographies. This directory is the best place to start when developing, implementing, or analyzing air pollutant programs.

247 The Indoor Air Quality Directory

2nd ed. IAQ Publications, 1994. Annual. 378p. $125.00 (paper).

The *Indoor Air Quality Directory* is the first comprehensive directory in the air-quality field. The first four sections describe companies that work on air-quality issues; they are grouped under the following headings: air-quality services (architects and laboratories); manufacturers and distributors (air monitors and sealants); support services (attorneys and consultants); and training (workshops and courses). Entries include address, phone number, key personnel, number of employees, markets and areas served, services, products, expertise, and contaminants evaluated. The directory's final four sections list hundreds of periodicals, reports, and books that are relevant to those involved in air-quality issues, as well as state and federal agencies, professional associations, environmental organizations, legal institutions, and health

groups. The directory includes name, company, product, service, and state indices, and a glossary.

Reference Handbooks

248 The Atmosphere Crisis: The Greenhouse Effect and Ozone Depletion

SirS Critical Issues series. Social Issues Resource Series (SirS), 1989–. 20 new articles are added each year. $85.00 per volume of 100 articles.

CD-ROM: Available as part of the *SirS Researcher CD-ROM* from Social Issues Resource Series.

Because it includes reprints of articles, annotated bibliographies on dozens more, and a selected bibliography of books and pamphlets, *The Atmosphere Crisis* is considered the best primer on global atmospheric issues for a lay audience. The binder currently contains more than 150 reprinted articles, many by leading researchers. Approximately 10 percent come from general magazines, 50 percent from science and environment periodicals, 30 percent from newspapers, and a small percentage from government and university publications. The full text of articles cited in the bibliographies is available on the included microfiche. *The Atmosphere Crisis* also has a table of contents and a detailed subject index.

249 Dictionary of Global Climate Change

Compiled by W. J. Maunder as a contribution of the Stockholm Environment Institute to the Second World Climate Conference. Chapman & Hall, 1992. 256p. $45.00 (hardcover).

The *Dictionary of Global Climate Change* is the official dictionary of the Second World Climate Conference. The dictionary allows professionals from many fields—science, technology, law, economics, public policy—to communicate clearly when discussing climate change issues. Definitions range in length from one sentence to more than a page, and cover terms, concepts, people, organizations, and treaties. Subject coverage is broad enough to include adiabatic process, acid rain, global warming potential, and stratospheric and tropospheric ozone, as well as ultraviolet radiation and zooplankton. This dictionary is highly recommended for its insightful definitions and comprehensive coverage.

The *Carbon Dioxide and Climate Glossary*—free from the Carbon Dioxide Information Analysis Center (see entry 231)—is also useful, though it contains only definitions of terms and has slightly different coverage, as the title indicates.

250 Global Change Information Pack: Global Climate Change

2nd ed. National Agricultural Library, DC Reference Center, 1992; distributed by the National Agricultural Library, Office of Reference. Updated irregularly. Free.

The *Global Change Information Pack* is an excellent set of introductory materials for the layperson interested in climate change, particularly in the area of global warming. The pack provides a concise summary of the issues and reprints of several journal articles on the subject of global climate change; also included are lists and descriptions of additional articles, books, journals, bibliographies, abstracts and indices, and organizations. Due to budget constraints and the high cost of printing, future editions may only be available in electronic format via the Internet; call the National Agricultural Library's (NAL) DC Reference Center (202/720-3434) for details.

The DC Reference Center also produces bibliographies in the NAL Quick Bibliography Series (see entry 183, National Agricultural Library), including the well-annotated *Global Warming and the Greenhouse Effect: January 1986–January 1992*, and other materials on global climate change.

Introductory Reading

251 The Acid Rain Debate: Science and Special Interest in Policy Formation

Bruce Forster. Natural Resources and Environmental Policy series. Iowa State University Press, 1993. 170p. $27.95 (hardcover).

The Acid Rain Debate offers clear insight into the complex social, economic, and political forces largely responsible for inconsistent acid rain policy. Author Bruce Forster, dean of the College of

Business at the University of Wyoming, thoroughly reviews the full spectrum of relevant scientific information in an unbiased fashion, and argues that although the use of this data has enlightened the policy process, it has often been used selectively. Each of the book's eleven chapters is accompanied by an extensive reference list. Chapters cover sources of acid rain; agricultural, forest, and aquatic impacts; health impacts; control options and strategies; and the exaggeration of control costs. Anyone—from hydrologists to legislative aides—interested in acid rain will be able to gather valuable information from this case study on the use and misuse of science in the policy process.

252 Climate Change: The IPCC Scientific Assessments

Edited by J. T. Houghton, G. J. Jenkins, and J. J. Ephraums. Cambridge University Press, 1991. 365p. $75.00 (hardcover), $35.00 (paper).

253 Climate Change: The IPCC Impacts Assessment

Edited by W. J. Tegart, G. W. Sheldon, and D. C. Griffiths. Australian Government Publishing Service, 1991. 277p. $25.00 (paper).

254 Climate Change: The IPCC Response Strategies

Intergovernmental Panel on Climate Change. Island Press, 1991. 272p. $60.00 (hardcover), $39.95 (paper).

Together, these three publications—*Climate Change: The IPCC Scientific Assessments*, *Climate Change: The IPCC Impacts Assessment*, and *Climate Change: The IPCC Response Strategies*—provide the most authoritative and comprehensive analysis of climate change issues. The Intergovernmental Panel on Climate Change (IPCC) was convened in 1988 by the World Meteorological Organization and the United Nations Environment Programme (see entry 10). IPCC formed three working groups, each of which solicited input from several hundred scientists and other specialists from more than two dozen countries. The findings of Group I *(The IPCC Scientific Assessments)* reaffirm the consensus opinion among the broad majority of climatologists about the causes and meteorological effects of global climate change. In 1992 IPCC released an update to Group I's scientific assessment, called *Climate Change 1992* (Cambridge University Press), which does not alter the major conclusions; additional updates are expected on an irregular basis. Group II *(The IPCC Impacts Assessment)* assesses potential environmental and socioeconomic impacts; coverage includes agriculture, water resources, human settlement and health, and coastal zones. Group III *(The IPCC Response Strategies)* provides the factual basis for policy options, not policy recommendations; the group III report has come under a great deal of criticism for not basing its decisions on the findings of the other groups. All three IPCC reports have excellent executive summaries, but lack indices.

Greenpeace (see entry 32) has issued a 550-page compilation of essays entitled *Global Warming: The Greenpeace Report* (Jeremy Leggett. Oxford University Press, 1990) that critiques all three IPCC reports, though it primarily focuses on Group III's failure to recommend stringent measures to slow and reverse global warming. The Greenpeace publication also argues that the IPCC reports consistently understate the effects of climate change and the risks of extreme change.

255 Global Warming and Biological Diversity

Edited by Robert L. Peters and Thomas E. Lovejoy. Yale University Press, 1992. 407p. $45.00 (hardcover).

256 The Rising Tide: Global Warming and World Sea Levels

Lynne T. Edgerton. Sponsored by the Natural Resources Defense Council. Island Press, 1991. 140p. $29.95 (hardcover), $17.95 (paper).

The authors of *Global Warming and Biological Diversity* and *The Rising Tide: Global Warming and World Sea Levels* operate on the assumption that global climate change is occurring and that the changes will continue to have dramatic effects on ecosystems and people in the future. In addition, they try to persuade policymakers to act now to minimize damage. *Global Warming and Biological Diversity* is a compilation of moderately technical papers, all of them presented, by respected scientists, at a 1988 conference on

the interrelationship between these two issues. Following overviews of global warming policy and modeling, as well as descriptions of the effects of past climate changes on biota, this book explores the effects of global warming on biodiversity in general and on particular ecosystems such as the tropical forests, Arctic tundra, and North American forests. *The Rising Tide* is a smaller book that provides brief background information on the history and policy related to global warming; documents trends in sea-level rise and its effects; presents case studies of coastal damage; and outlines specific coastal policy measures that federal and state coastal administrators can adopt to protect their communities and ecosystems from rising seas. Both books are excellent resources for information about the current and potential effects of global warming on specific ecosystems.

257 Global Warming: Are We Entering the Greenhouse Century?

Stephen H. Schneider. Sierra Club Books, 1989; distributed by Random House. 317p. $18.95 (hardcover).

Global Warming presents an engaging introduction, for the lay reader, to the scientific complexities of the greenhouse effect, including policy options and consequences. Author Stephen H. Schneider, a leading climatologist and policy analyst, frames the issues in nonalarmist terms. Written from the premise that civilization is already twenty years into "the greenhouse century," the book focuses on the history of scientific debate on the issue and on the basis for current assessments and predictions. Although Schneider questions the notion that science has provided enough evidence to warrant many proposed remedies, he is careful to note that some precautionary measures must be taken. His analysis of the controversies and uncertainties regarding climate modeling is better than most. *Global Warming* is well referenced for a popular book.

For a sampling of what other well-known experts think about global climate change, consult *The Challenge of Global Warming* (Dean Edwin Abrahamson. Island Press, 1989). This compilation of twenty-one essays provides a nontechnical synthesis of mainstream scientific interpretation of the causes and effects of climate change. And Francesca Lyman's *The*

Greenhouse Trap: What We're Doing to the Atmosphere and How We Can Slow Global Warming (Beacon Press, 1990) suggests steps individuals can take to help alleviate global warming.

258 Ozone Crisis: The 15-Year Evolution of a Sudden Global Emergency

Sharon Roan. John Wiley & Sons, 1989. 285p. $18.95 (hardcover), $9.95 (paper).

259 Ozone Diplomacy: New Directions in Safeguarding the Planet

Richard E. Benedick. Harvard University Press, 1991. 300p. $27.95 (hardcover), $10.95 (paper).

Ozone Crisis and *Ozone Diplomacy* offer behind-the-scenes views of the science and politics surrounding stratospheric-ozone depletion. *Ozone Crisis*, written in an absorbing, journalistic style, provides an insightful account of the recognition of stratospheric-ozone depletion as an important global environmental issue. It explores the initial discovery that chlorofluorocarbons (CFCs) might be destroying the ozone layer; it then goes on to outline the subsequent government and corporate foot-dragging, public indifference, and environmentalists' reaction to the warnings. *Ozone Crisis* does not look seriously at the science of ozone depletion, but rather provides detailed accounts of the personal interactions between key figures in this environmental debate. *Ozone Diplomacy* evaluates the negotiating process of the Montreal Protocol, including insiders' maneuverings, and explores the various factors that contributed to the negotiators' eventual success and the lessons available for future diplomatic negotiations. Appendices include the texts of the Vienna Convention for the Protection of the Ozone Layer, the Montreal Protocol on Substances that Deplete the Ozone Layer, and the London Revisions for the Montreal Protocol.

For another interesting, but more science-based, account of stratospheric-ozone depletion, read John Gribbon's *The Hole in the Sky* (Bantam Books, 1988).

260 Policy Implications of Greenhouse Warming: Mitigation, Adaptation, and the Science Base

Panel on Policy Implications of Greenhouse Warming. National Academy Press, 1992. 944p. $89.95 (hardcover).

Geared toward policymakers, the exhaustive *Policy Implications of Greenhouse Warming* provides specific U.S. policy recommendations while it also addresses the need for an international response to global warming. The panel that authored this work concluded that although considerable uncertainties remain concerning the impact of global warming, the potential risks—economic and otherwise—warrant immediate and long-term action to reduce the buildup of greenhouse gases. Although the main objective of the report is to lay the groundwork for informed decision making based on mitigation and adaptation options, this report also provides insightful analysis of the current scientific understanding of climate change and its effects. A smaller volume, 144 pages in length, with the same title and publisher ($14.95), summarizes this more technical work.

Dead Heat: The Race Against the Greenhouse Effect, by Michael Oppenheimer and Robert Boyle (Basic Books, 1990), presents recommendations for the technological and political strategies needed to lessen the negative effects of global warming in a journalistic style more suitable for the lay reader.

Abstracts and Indices

261 Global Climate Change Digest: A Guide to Current Information on Greenhouse Gases and Ozone Depletion

Edited by Dr. Robert W. Pratt. Center for Environmental Information, 1988–. Monthly.

The *Global Climate Change Digest* is the best available abstract of general and technical world literature in the global climate change field. Each twenty-page issue is divided by type of information source: professional journal articles; reports and government documents; books and book reviews; conference proceedings; and popular periodical articles. The *Digest* is further divided into subject categories such as energy policy and law; economics; engineering and technology; impacts of climate change; and atmospheric science. In addition to concise annotations, readers will find research and policy news, a calendar of worldwide conferences and other events, sources of educational materials, and information on major research initiatives and opportunities. Selective and current, every researcher and policymaker concerned about ozone depletion and global warming should have access to this outstanding abstract.

Another abstract, the *Greenhouse Gases Bulletin* (International Energy Agency's Greenhouse Gas Research and Development Programme, 1991–. Biannual) abstracts books, articles, technical reports, and conference proceedings related to the field of greenhouse gases research.

Other Abstracts and Indices

◆ *Energy Research Abstracts* (see entry 345)

Periodicals

262 Energy, Economics and Climate Change (EECC)

Cutter Information. 1990–. Monthly. 16p. $547.00/year.

Database Vendor: Available as part of the *PTS Newsletter Database* on DIALOG, and as *Energy, Economics & Climate Change* on LEXIS/NEXIS and NewsNet.

263 Global Environmental Change Report (GECR)

Cutter Information. 1988–. Bimonthly. 8p. $257.00/year for universities, $457.00/year for all others.

Database Vendor: Available as part of the *PTS Newsletter Database* on DIALOG, and as the *Global Environmental Change Report* on LEXIS/NEXIS and NewsNet.

Both *Energy, Economics and Climate Change* and the *Global Environmental Change Report* are outstanding resources for economists, analysts, and policymakers wishing to stay abreast of develop-

ments on global climate change and related issues. *Energy, Economics and Climate Change* provides in-depth analysis of the latest economic studies on climate change and explores the impacts of actual policy initiatives on the worldwide energy industry. National and regional issues, climate impacts, new studies, and taxes and subsidies are regularly covered. Each article is followed by additional reading suggestions. *Global Environmental Change Report*, on the other hand, relies exclusively on shorter news briefs to inform readers about policy trends, scientific research, and industrial developments concerning a broader range of issues: global warming, stratospheric-ozone depletion, deforestation, and acid rain. For each of these newsletters, the subscription price includes regular bibliographic updates of current literature, a document delivery service for most works cited, and hotline access to editors—if questions cannot be answered, a referral will be made to another source.

264 Network Newsletter

National Center for Atmospheric Research, Environmental and Societal Impacts Group, 1986–. Quarterly. 16p. Free.

Anyone interested in or involved with climate-related impact assessment should regularly read the free quarterly *Network Newsletter*. Coverage includes all global climate change–related issues: the greenhouse effect, ozone depletion, deforestation, and carbon dioxide buildup in the atmosphere. This newsletter is best consulted for its insightful updates on organizations, new projects, and relevant newsletters and journals, but it also includes descriptions of upcoming meetings, summaries of past meetings, educational and career opportunity listings, and citations of recently released books and reports. The newsletter's production process is simple: readers, worldwide, send in submissions and the editors compile the information on pink copy paper bound with a single staple. The *Network Newsletter* provides readers with a reliable, easy way to remain on top of international climate change projects. An electronic version is expected in the future; it will probably be posted on the National Center for Atmospheric Research's (see entry 233) gopher site.

265 No Sweat News: Journal of Grassroots Action to Protect the Atmosphere

The Atmosphere Alliance. 1992–. Quarterly. 24p. $20.00/year.

EcoNet: A sample copy is available in the *climate.news* conference.

The editors of the tabloid-style *No Sweat News* are passionate about protecting the Earth from the negative effects of climate change, including stratospheric-ozone depletion, and refuting what they believe to be an abundance of scientific misinformation. The activist *News* summarizes and analyzes current research and government policies; reports on important news; updates readers on the activities of Atmosphere Alliance (see entry 236) members; uncovers the hidden agendas of reporters, politicians, organizations, governments, and companies; and recommends positive action for both individuals and governments. Many of the periodical's articles and news shorts include referrals to relevant organizations or experts. Every citizen interested in the potential effects of global warming and ozone depletion should have a subscription to this complete source of information.

Other Periodicals

◆ *Clean Air Network Online Today* (see entry 172, Environmental Information Networks)

◆ *Global Warming Network Online Today* (see entry 172, Environmental Information Networks)

◆ *Ozone Depletion Network Online Today* (see entry 172, Environmental Information Networks)

CHAPTER FOUR

Biodiversity

What This Chapter Covers

This chapter covers biological diversity and conservation efforts, including endangered species and entire ecosystems such as forests, tropical rainforests, and deserts. Land-use issues related to extracting natural resources such as timber and minerals can also be found here.

For More Information

- ◆ See **General** for resources on all environmental issues, including those related to biodiversity.
- ◆ See **Water** for resources on aquatic ecosystems such as lakes and oceans as well as marine biodiversity conservation.

Government Clearinghouses

266 Fish and Wildlife Reference Service (FWRS)
Department of Interior
Fish and Wildlife Service
5430 Grosvenor Lane, Suite 110
Bethesda, MD 20814

Phone: 800/582-3421; 301/492-6403. Fax: 301/564-4059

Paul Wilson, Project Manager

The Fish and Wildlife Reference Service (FWRS) is the premier source for biologists wishing to obtain unpublished literature on fish and wildlife research topics. Documents that FWRS receives—mostly technical research and final reports from state and federal agencies—are indexed in a database and stored in the document collection, which is available on diskette for $62.50. Many citations are also listed in the free FWRS quarterly newsletter, and photocopies of the full text of all documents will be mailed upon request. In general, services are free to state and federal employees; others must pay for copies, postage, and shipping, as well as $30 per literature search. *Endangered Species Recovery Plans* should be ordered here; other Fish and Wildlife Service (FWS) publications—including the official list of *Endangered and Threatened Wildlife and Plants*—should be ordered from the FWS Publications Unit (703/358–1711). FWRS can also provide referrals to state agencies and FWS offices, projects, and personnel.

Other Government Clearinghouses

◆ The National Park Service Office of Public Inquiries (see entry 620)

Organizations

For extensive descriptions of conservation organizations consult the *Conservation Directory* (see entry 65).

267 American Forests
P.O. Box 2000
Washington, DC 20013

Phone: 202/667-3300. Fax: 202/667-7751

Neil Sampson, Executive Vice President

Formerly known as the American Forestry Association, American Forests is one of the oldest—and one of the largest—conservation organizations in the United States. The group's efforts focus on educating the public about the benefits of trees and forests; American Forests operates a number of projects, such as the Global ReLeaf tree-planting program, Cool Communities, The Forest Policy Center, and the National Big-Trees Register. Periodicals include its flagship publication, *American Forests*; a separate action-oriented bimonthly titled *Urban Forests*; and the four-page biweekly *Resource Hotline: Issues, Events and People in Resource Policy*. Representative American Forests book titles include: *Famous and Historic Trees*; *Shading Our Cities: A Resource Guide for Urban and Community Forests*; and *Human Benefits from Protecting Biological Diversity: The Use of Pacific Yew and Taxol in Cancer Treatment*.

268 The Antarctica Project
P.O. Box 76920
Washington, DC 20013

Phone: 202/544-0236. Fax: 202/544-8483.
E-mail: antarctica@igc.apc.org

Beth Marks, Director

The Antarctica Project is the only environmental organization in the world that works exclusively to protect Antarctica. It cofounded and serves as the northern hemisphere secretariat for the Antarctic and Southern Ocean Coalition, a group of two hundred organizations in forty-nine countries that serves as the principal voice in the environmental community on issues involving Antarctica and the southern oceans. The group was instrumental in achieving the 1991 signing of the Environmental Protocol to the Antarctic Treaty, which bans mining and oil drilling south of 60 degrees latitude. In addition to working to implement the treaty, The Antarctica Project works to promote conservation measures for Antarctic fisheries; for the creation of a whale sanctuary in the Southern Ocean; and on other regional environmental issues. The Antarctica Project distributes many publications; most are of interest to members of the policy community, but many are also appropriate for educators, students, and the general public.

For information about Antarctica on the Internet, see the International Centre for Antarctica Information and Research site; on the World Wide Web, the URL is **http://icair.iac.org.nz/**.

269 Biodiversity Action Network (BIONET)

424 C Street, NE
Washington, DC 20002

Phone: 202/547-8902. Fax: 202/544-8483.
E-mail: bionet@igc.apc.org

Sheldon Cohen, Coordinator

The Biodiversity Action Network (BIONET) coordinates and supports the actions of its members to strengthen biodiversity laws and policies in accordance with the guidelines of the Convention on Biological Diversity. The Center for International Environmental Law (202/332–4840) launched BIONET in 1993 with the support of several other prominent organizations, including Conservation International, Defenders of Wildlife (see entry 272), the Environmental and Energy Study Institute (see entry 23), Sierra Club (see entry 45), and the World Resource Institute (see entry 50); the network now consists of more than one hundred organizations. BIONET provides its members and others in the environmental community—including policymakers, activists, and students—with fact sheets, news alerts, a quarterly newsletter called *Biodiversity Action*, and referrals to experts around the world. BIONET is a reliable source of legislative- and policy-related documents, including copies of the latest testimony from Capitol Hill, United Nations Environment Programme (see entry 10) reports, and press releases.

270 Biodiversity Resource Center

California Academy of Sciences
Golden Gate Park
San Francisco, CA 94118

Phone: 415/750-7361. Fax: 415/750-7106.
E-mail: amalley@calacademy.org

The Biodiversity Resource Center distributes public education materials and bibliographies free of charge. Most users visit the center in person while at the California Academy of Sciences library, and most callers are Californians. However, center staffers will handle information requests—including bibliographic searches of CD-ROM databases—from anyone. The one- to five-page bibliographies cover a variety of topics; sample titles include *Endangered Species, Biodiversity, Environmental Mailing Lists Available on the Internet,* and *Environmental Curriculum Guides.*

271 Center for Plant Conservation (CPC)

Missouri Botanical Garden
P.O. Box 299
St. Louis, MO 63166

Phone: 314/577-9450. Fax: 314/577-9465

Brien A. Meilleur, President

The Center for Plant Conservation (CPC) coordinates a network of twenty botanical gardens and arboretums that collect and maintain the National Collection of Endangered Plants. Those conducting research will find the CPC's $15 *Plant Conservation Directory* useful. For each state, the directory includes contact information for CPC members, federal and state officials, botanists, and others in private organizations, as well as rare-plant laws and lists of rare and endangered plants. CPC also works to develop and maintain data sets on native U.S. endangered plants. The *Plant Conservation* newsletter reports on CPC activities.

272 Defenders of Wildlife

1101 14th Street, NW, Suite 1400
Washington, DC 20005

Phone: 202/682-9400. Fax: 202/682-1331

Rodger Schlickeisen, President

Known as one of the more progressive mainstream environmental organizations, Defenders of Wildlife advocates, lobbies, and litigates to protect wildlife and its necessary habitats. Defenders of Wildlife focuses especially on endangered species. The organization publishes *Defenders* magazine, aimed at a popular audience, and an eight-page quarterly, *Wildlife Advocate,* that provides organizational news and updates on legislative and advocacy campaigns.

Defenders also coordinates the National Watchable Wildlife Program, which guides citizens to up to 150 sites in each state where they can view wildlife. Viewing guides for seventeen states are available from Defenders, as is *Nature Watch*, a manual to help resource agency personnel and private landowners promote wildlife viewing.

273 Earth First! (EF!)
P.O. Box 1415
Eugene, OR 97440

Phone: 503/741-9191. Fax: 503/741-9192.
E-mail: earthfirst@igc.apc.org

Earth First! (EF!) activists are united by their belief in nonviolent, uncompromising direct action in defense of the Earth. The Earth First! movement—it does not consider itself an organization—was founded "in response to a lethargic, compromising, and increasingly corporate environmental community." EF! sees itself as an expression of the philosophy of deep ecology, which is biocentric in focus rather than anthropocentric. Although EF! activists are most known for their "monkey-wrenching"—destroying the machinery of those who are destroying the Earth—and civil disobedience, they also use other tactics like public education, letter writing, testifying at hearings, and litigation. Earth First!ers are chiefly involved in protecting biodiversity and wilderness areas, but are also concerned about related issues such as overpopulation and animal rights. Most EF! groups operate at the local level; *Earth First! The Radical Environmental Journal* (see entry 308) is the best way to find their phone numbers and addresses and to stay on top of the news they create. Earth First! also offers primers on the Earth First! movement and on specific environmental issues.

274 Mineral Policy Center (MPC)
1612 K Street, NW, Suite 808
Washington, DC 20006

Phone: 202/887-1872. Fax: 202/887-1875

Philip M. Hocker, President

The Mineral Policy Center (MPC) is an essential resource for information on the environmental impact of mining. As the only national organization focusing on this issue, MPC offers a complete range of services for both laypeople and professionals. MPC provides technical, legal, and political strategy assistance to citizens' groups; the group also acts as a clearinghouse, distributing publications and audiovisual materials and answering questions. Sample publications include: a collection of articles on cyanide heap leaching; "report cards" on mining sites; reports such as *Burden of Gilt*, which calls for the cleanup of hardrock abandoned mines; and *Clementine: The Journal of Responsible Mineral Development*, a news-oriented periodical published occasionally. An additional publication, the *1994 Mining Conservation Directory*, provides contact information and descriptions for 341 conservation organizations working on damage from mining operations. MPC also lobbies to reform mining laws at the federal and state levels.

For statistical and other government information on minerals and mining, call the Bureau of Mines Minerals Information Office (Washington, D.C., 202/208–5520) or the U.S. Geological Survey Minerals Information Offices (Washington, D.C., 202/208-5512; Tucson, Ariz., 602/670-5544; Denver, Col., 303/236-5704; Reno, Nev., 702/784-5552; Spokane, Wash., 509/353–2649).

275 The Nature Conservancy (TNC)
1815 North Lynn Street
Arlington, VA 22209

Phone: 703/841-5300. Fax: 703/247-3725

John Sawhill, President and CEO

The Nature Conservancy (TNC) purchases and manages land in order to protect biological diversity. This well-funded nonprofit manages the largest private conservation system in the world—more than thirteen hundred nature sanctuaries. TNC stores information about its preserves' ecosystems and wildlife on databases. Since the organization is very decentralized, those looking for information on the topic of local biodiversity should work with the nearest state or regional TNC chapter. The glossy bimonthly *Nature Conservancy Magazine* includes human-interest stories on nature and environmental issues and updates members on organizational activities.

276 Rainforest Action Network (RAN)

450 Sansome, Suite 700
San Francisco, CA 94111

Phone: 415/398-4404. Fax: 415/398-2732.
E-mail: rainforest@igc.apc.org

Randall Hayes, Executive Director

EcoNet: RAN maintains several conferences, including *ran.news*, *ran.ragforum*, and *rainfor.timber*.

The Rainforest Action Network (RAN) is dedicated to saving rainforests and to protecting the human rights of those who live in the forests. RAN has developed an extensive media campaign to keep the issue of rainforest destruction and protection in the world spotlight. RAN is distinguished from other organizations working on rainforest issues by its emphasis on grassroots education and action. It now supports more than 150 Rainforest Action Groups (RAGs) that organize and train activists at the local level to respond quickly and directly to forces that threaten the rainforests. RAGs and other organizations and individuals can receive comprehensive information about rainforests from RAN, including numerous publications like fact sheets, letter-writing materials, and RAN's monthly *Action Alerts* newsletter and quarterly *World Rainforest Report*. RAN also produces resource guides and directories, including *Amazonia: Voices from the Rainforests* and *Southeast Asia Rainforests: A Resource Guide and Directory*. Both guides include directories of more than 250 international organizations working to protect rainforests. In these directories, the entries for each organization provide brief descriptions of the group's objectives and programs, a list of the group's available resources, and contact information. *Amazonia* also includes many photographs, maps, and sidebars, which provide facts, figures, and stories, while *Southeast Asia Rainforests* supplies country-by-country overviews of the major threats to Southeast Asia's forests as well as statistics of yearly rates of deforestation, size of remaining forests, volume of timber exports, and size of timber industry. RAN is an outstanding resource for learning the basics about rainforests or for remaining current on the latest actions and developments worldwide.

277 Rainforest Alliance (RA)

65 Bleeker Street
New York, NY 10012

Phone: 212/677-1900. Fax: 212/677-2187.
E-mail: canopy@igc.apc.org

Daniel R. Katz, Executive Director

The Rainforest Alliance (RA) develops and promotes economically viable and socially desirable alternatives to tropical deforestation. RA—a network of conservationists, professional organizations, scientists, and members of the business community—works closely with the business community and indigenous peoples to develop practices and set standards that will preserve the remaining rainforests. For instance, RA helps to set environmentally sustainable standards for banana companies in Central America, and, through its Smart Wood Certification Program, awards certificates to well-managed sources of tropical wood. In addition to distributing numerous fact sheets, a nationwide directory of speakers, and a quarterly newsletter, *The Canopy*, RA supports field research, debt-for-nature swaps, and the Conservation Media Center in Costa Rica, which writes and distributes conservation stories to more than eight hundred media outlets in the U.S. and Latin America.

278 Save America's Forests

4 Library Court, SE
Washington, DC 20003

Phone: 202/544-9219

Carl Ross and Mark Winstein, Co-directors

Save America's Forests links grassroots forest activists from around the country. More than four hundred member groups and businesses have joined this nonprofit to support its push for strong, comprehensive national laws that protect forest ecosystems, improve the financial security of forest-dependent communities, and create a sustainable forest products industry. Member groups can receive technical and strategic assistance. Publications include *Forest Action Alerts* and *D.C. Update*, which provides news and commentary on federal legislative issues and highlights grassroots actions.

Those interested in sustainable forestry should also be familiar with two other organizations: The Native Forest Network and the Institute for Sustainable Forestry. The Native Forest Network (406/585-9211 or 406/587-3389) provides support services similar to Save America's Forests, but works on international forest issues. The Institute for Sustainable Forestry (707/923-4719) is committed to creating new forest management paradigms, and certifies forest operations in the Redwood region of California.

279 The Wilderness Society

900 17th Street, NW
Washington, DC 20006

Phone: 202/833-2300. Phone (publications): 202/429-2652

Jon Roush, President

The Wilderness Society serves as an environmental watchdog for lands managed by the federal government. In addition to its glossy magazine, *Wilderness*, and fact sheets on a variety of topics, the society publishes other popular and technical reports, books, and handbooks, such as *Ten Most Endangered National Parks*; *Keeping It Wild: A Citizen's Guide to Wilderness Management*; *How to Appeal Forest Service Decisions: A Citizen Handbook on the 1989 Appeals Regulations*; and *Federal Forests and the Economic Base of the Pacific Northwest*. It also sponsored *These American Lands: Parks, Wilderness, and the Public Lands* (Dyan Zaslowsky and T. H. Watkins. Island Press, 1994), an excellent overview of public land issues.

A separate conservation organization, the National Parks and Conservation Association (NPCA) (800/628-7275 or 202/223-6722), is devoted to defending, expanding, and conserving the nation's national parks. NPCA publishes the bimonthly *National Parks* magazine and *Our Endangered Parks: What You Can Do to Protect Our National Heritage* (Foghorn Press, 1994), both for a popular audience.

280 The World Conservation Union (IUCN)

IUCN-U.S.
1400 16th Street, NW
Washington, DC 20036

Phone: 202/797-5454. Fax: 202/797-5461.
E-mail: iucnus@igc.apc.org

Allen Putney, Acting Executive Director

The World Conservation Union provides leadership and technical assistance to its members—sovereign states, government agencies, and nongovernmental organizations—in order to protect the planet's biological diversity. Formerly known as the International Union for Conservation of Nature and Natural Resources, the IUCN acronym is still officially used. IUCN devises conservation strategies; advises on environmental assessment, law, and education; analyzes interaction between human populations and resources; and provides practical techniques for conservation and sustainable living.

The office listed above, which conducts IUCN's affairs in North America, and the international headquarters in Switzerland (011 41 22 999 0001, fax: 011 41 22 999 0002) are, in general, not the best places for people needing information. IUCN's World Conservation Monitoring Centre (WCMC), located in Cambridge, England (011 223 277314, fax: 011 223 277136), is somewhat more accessible to the public. It houses many conservation-related databases and provides fee-based searches; unfortunately, turnaround time can be a bit slow.

Rather than contacting the organization, those gathering information on biodiversity issues should consult IUCN's publications, many of which are standard texts in the field. The authoritative reference handbook, *Global Biodiversity: Status of the Earth's Living Resources* (see entry 293), is a summary of WCMC's data. Other IUCN publications include the official *Red List of Threatened Animals*; various *Red Data Books* that describe the status of endangered species; authoritative surveys such as *Protected Areas of the World: A Review of National Systems*; and atlases produced for a popular audience, including *Deserts: The Encroaching Wilderness* (Tony Allen and Andrew Warren. Oxford Press, 1993), *The Random House Atlas of the Oceans* (Danny Elder and John Pernetta. Random House, 1991), and *Wetlands in Danger* (Patrick J. Dugan. Oxford University Press, 1993). For a complete IUCN publications catalog, contact Island Press (800/828-1302), which distributes many IUCN publications in the United States.

281 World Forestry Institute
World Forestry Center
4033 SW Canyon Road
Portland, OR 97221

Phone: 503/228-0803. Fax: 503/228-3624

Eric Landis, Director

The World Forestry Institute serves as a fee-based nonprofit clearinghouse for international forestry and forest products information. Using *CAB Abstracts* (see entry 222), *AGRICOLA* (see entry 221, *Bibliography of Agriculture*), and *AGRIS* (see entry 220, *Agrindex*), and tapping into a network of experts when necessary, the institute customizes searches to clients' specifications. Past searches include a published review of current literature on the natural regeneration of mahogany in Bolivia (for an academic research institution) and a report on timber commerce and its effect on the economy of Coos Bay, Oregon (for the Army Corps of Engineers). Though costs vary, searches cost a minimum of $200. The institute is an ideal resource for companies or large nonprofits that need independent forestry experts to compile bibliographies, analyze data, or write reports.

282 World Wildlife Fund (WWF)
1250 24th Street, NW
Washington, DC 20037

Phone: 202/293-4800. Phone (publications): 410/516-6951. Fax: 202/293-9211

Kathryn S. Fuller, President

EcoNet: The World Wildlife Fund for Nature maintains the *wwf.news* conference.

The World Wildlife Fund is the largest private organization working to protect endangered wildlife and wildlands. The above office is the U.S. affiliate of the international World Wildlife Fund for Nature (WWF), a family of WWF organizations in fifty countries. WWF conducts and supports hundreds of vastly different projects—conservation programs, scientific research, technical assistance and training, environmental education—that combine to preserve habitats and rescue endangered species. WWF is known particularly for its programs that preserve rainforests and monitor international wildlife trade. The group often collaborates with governments and other conservation and environmental organizations on all natural resource and environmental issues—particularly on matters relating to public policy. For example, the U.S. WWF office convened both the National Commission on the Environment, which produced the report *Choosing a Sustainable Future* (Island Press, 1993), and the National Wetlands Policy Forum, which produced *Statewide Wetlands Strategies: A Guide to Protecting and Managing the Resource* (see entry 488). Members receive *FOCUS*, an organizational newsletter, and occasional *Wildlife Alerts*. Request a publications catalog for all WWF books and reports, including *The Gardener's Guide to Plant Conservation*, *Rethinking the Materials We Use: A New Focus for Pollution Policy*, *International Wildlife Trade: A CITES Sourcebook*, and *A Guide to Financial Resource Development*.

Other Organizations

◆ The National Audubon Society (see entry 38)
◆ The National Wildlife Federation (see entry 39)
◆ Sierra Club (see entry 45)

Internet Sites

To learn about additional Internet gophers, consult the *International Biodiversity Information Available on the Internet Gopher System* (see entry 104, *A Guide to Environmental Resources on the Internet*).

283 CONSLINK: The Conservation Network

Maintained by the Smithsonian Institution's Conservation and Research Center.

EcoNet: The CONSLINK listserv on BITNET is available as the *bitl.conslink* conference.

Internet: To subscribe to the CONSLINK listserv, send an e-mail message to **listserv@sivm.si.edu** with the words **subscribe conslink <firstname lastname>** in the body of the message.

For more information about retrieving individual files by e-mail from the CONSLINK bulletin board, send an e-mail message to **listserv@sivm.si.edu** with the words **get conslink info** in the body of the message.

CONSLINK is also archived on the Smithsonian Natural History gopher. Gopher to **nmnhgoph.si.edu**; choose *Smithsonian Biological Conservation Programs and Data*, then *CONSLINK—The Conservation Network*.

For technical support, contact Michael Steuwe by phone at 703/635-6542 or by e-mail at **nzpem001@sivm.si.edu**.

CONSLINK: The Conservation Network provides a wealth of information on all topics related to biological conservation. It is both a bulletin board and a conference. All files on the bulletin board are posted to the conference. The bulletin board, however, does not allow users to browse and download files; instead, users send requests for files by e-mail. Among the files that reside on the CONSLINK bulletin board are regular editions of several newsletters (e.g., *The Conservation Digest Newsletter*, *Biodiversity Conservation Strategy Update* [see entry 302, *Global Biodiversity Strategy*], the *Biological Conservation Newsletter* [see entry 306]), a directory of biological field stations in tropical countries; and a guide to biodiversity Internet gophers.

The Smithsonian Natural History gopher, in addition to providing convenient access to the CONSLINK bulletin board, is a valuable source of biodiversity information. For example, it includes searchable archives of the bibliographic portion of the *Biological Conservation Newsletter*, supplies regular updates on the proposed National Biodiversity Information Center, and provides access to many biodiversity-related Internet gopher sites.

Directories

284 Parks Directory of the United States: A Guide to 4,700 National and State Parks, Recreational Areas, Historic Sites, Battlefields, Monuments, Forests, Preserves, Memorials, Seashores, and Other Designated Recreation Areas in the United States Administered by National and State Park Agencies

Edited by Darren L. Smith. 2nd ed. Omnigraphics, 1994. 831p. $145.00 (hardcover).

The *Parks Directory of the United States* is not a commercial travel guide intended for browsing, but it is useful as a library reference. In addition to mailing addresses and telephone numbers, each short description includes at-a-glance information on acreage, facilities, opportunities for recreational activities, and unique or outstanding characteristics. The hundred-plus national parks are listed alphabetically; the thousand-plus state parks are organized by state and then listed alphabetically. The section on national parks also includes historical information and entrance-fee requirements. This second edition includes an additional thousand sites (national forests, major urban parks, national wildlife refuges, national scenic and historic trails) over the original 1992 edition, and also some maps. A brief section at the book's end provides contact information for park and conservation–related organizations and government agencies, as well as for state travel and tourism offices. The directory includes alphabetical and type-of-park indices.

For the general public, there are many travel guides to our nation's vast parks system. One particularly good one is Laura and William Riley's *Guide to the National Wildlife Refuges* (Macmillan/Collier, 1992), available in most bookstores.

Other Directories

◆ The *Conservation Directory* (see entry 65)

Bibliographies

285 Books of the Big Outside

Dave Foreman. Ned Ludd Books. Quarterly. 72p. Free (paper).

Ned Ludd Books sells many of the latest and best conservation books; *Books of the Big Outside* describes what they have to offer. Author Dave Foreman—a founder of Earth First! (see entry 273) and one of the conservation movement's most independent thinkers—describes, reviews, and comments on more than four hundred items in this catalog of books. The blurbs are personal and biased, but they do convey the essence of each work. The focus is on wilderness, biodiversity, and environmental thought, though many related topics—e.g., natural history, justice, fiction, biography—are included. Readers can be assured of plenty of diverse listings for maps, music, videos, and field guides—as well as for an abundance of academic and pleasure books. Buying from the catalog will help ensure its continued publication.

For another excellent catalog of environmental books, see the *Island Press Environmental Sourcebook: Books for Better Conservation and Management* (see entry 110).

286 Changing Wilderness Values 1930–1990: An Annotated Bibliography

Edited by Joan S. Elbers. Bibliographies and Indexes in American History series. Greenwood Press, 1991. 138p. $42.95 (paper).

Changing Wilderness Values 1930–1990 is an essential guide for lay and professional researchers interested in American attitudes toward wildlife and wilderness from a conservation perspective. Most of the bibliography's 324 entries are books published after 1970, although a few articles from conservation magazines are included. Most of the works reviewed are personal, political, and scientific primary sources that seek to convince people of the value of wilderness. However, biographies of conservationists, histories of wilderness and wilderness movements, philosophical discourses on environmental ethics, natural history writing, fiction, and research on public attitudes toward wilderness are also covered. The descriptions, each of them fifty to two hundred words in length, are extremely well written, and the author and topical indices are detailed, making this a first-rate resource for beginning research.

Reference Handbooks

287 Animal Rights: A Beginner's Guide: A Handbook of Issues, Organizations, Actions, and Resources

Amy Blount Achor. WriteWare, 1992. 455p. $14.95 (paper).

Animal Rights: A Beginner's Guide is a valuable all-in-one reference for gathering information on animal rights issues. The book's first half intro-

duces the issues: companion animals; vegetarianism; factory farms; research, education, and testing; wildlife; and animals used in the entertainment industry. These chapters include advice for activists and references to resources that are described in the directory—the latter half of the book. Annotations for hundreds of national and state organizations range in length from one to ten sentences—enough information for the reader to get a sense of each organization's mission and scope. This guide also includes a diverse directory of products and services—everything from information referral organizations and computer networks to companies that provide leather alternatives—and a short annotated bibliography for further reading.

A related resource is Charles Magel's *Keyguide to Information Sources in Animal Rights* (McFarland & Company, 1989), a selective, well-annotated bibliography of 335 books and articles.

288 The Big Outside: A Descriptive Inventory of the Big Wilderness Areas of the United States

Dave Foreman and Howie Wolke. Revised ed. Harmony Books, 1992. 500p. $16.00 (paper).

The Big Outside records the condition of major roadless areas in the lower forty-eight states. Authors Dave Foreman and Howie Wolke, founders of Earth First! (see entry 273), describe the terrain and biodiversity of almost four hundred areas, each of them greater than 100,000 acres (more than 50,000 acres east of the Rocky Mountains). But what makes this reference book outstanding are the status reports for each site: Each report explains the importance of the area, describes threats to that area such as logging and tourism, and concludes with conservation recommendations. Also noteworthy are the insightful, one-sentence descriptions of conservation groups and publications, which readers will find useful in researching specific issues or geographic areas. The first edition of *The Big Outside* came out in 1989; expect revised editions every few years.

289 The Conservation Atlas of Tropical Forests: Africa

Edited by Jeffrey A. Sayer, Caroline S. Harcourt, and N. Mark Collins. Sponsored by the World Conservation Union. Simon & Schuster, 1992. 288p. $100.00 (hardcover).

290 The Conservation Atlas of Tropical Forests: Americas

Sponsored by the World Conservation Union. Simon & Schuster, 1995. 300p. $90.00 (hardcover).

291 The Conservation Atlas of Tropical Forests: Asia and The Pacific

Edited by N. Mark Collins, Jeffrey A. Sayer, and Timothy C. Whitmore. Sponsored by the World Conservation Union. Simon & Schuster, 1991. 256p. $95.00 (hardcover).

The Conservation Atlas of Tropical Forests: Africa, The Conservation Atlas of Tropical Forests: Americas, and *The Conservation Atlas of Tropical Forests: Asia and The Pacific* comprise an outstanding reference series on the state of tropical forests around the world. Each atlas begins with an introduction to regional issues, followed by chapters on each country within the region. Country sections describe the diversity of forests, current resource management strategies, the extent and impact of deforestation, and areas set aside for preservation and conservation. Color maps make it easy to see the location of various types of rain- and monsoon forests and both existing and proposed conservation areas. In addition to the maps, the text is supplemented by numerous charts and tables, and is well referenced. A precursor to this series, N. Mark Collins' *The Last Rainforests* (Simon & Schuster, 1990), frames much of the same information for a popular audience.

292 The Forest and the Trees: A Guide to Excellent Forestry

Gordon Robinson. Island Press, 1988. 257p. $24.95 (hardcover), $17.95 (paper).

The Forest and the Trees explains sustainable forestry to a lay audience. After outlining the history of forestry and the timber industry in the United States, Gordon Robinson, Sierra Club's (see entry 45) first professional forester, explains the fundamentals of multiple-use, uneven-aged forestry. He then teaches readers how to critically evaluate tree farming practices and logging plans. The last half of the book includes useful annotations for four hundred forestry research publications. *The Forest and the Trees* is widely acknowledged as the best sustainable forestry primer.

293 Global Biodiversity: Status of the Earth's Living Resources

Compiled by the World Conservation Monitoring Centre of the World Conservation Union. Chapman & Hall, 1992. 614p. $59.95 (hardcover).

For anyone with questions about biodiversity, *Global Biodiversity* is an excellent source of information. This comprehensive reference is the first systematic attempt to summarize the status, distribution, management, and utilization of biological wealth. *Global Biodiversity* is divided into three parts: a detailed inventory of genetic, species, and ecosystem diversity that comprises over half of this large book; a review of the uses and values of biodiversity; and national policies, international treaties, and conservation practices related to biological diversity. Throughout the book, the information summarized in tables and charts is often particularly useful; most pages have at least one chart, table, graph, or map. Although this first edition is not attractively presented, lacks indices, and contains some outdated information, it remains the most complete reference available on the subject. *Global Biodiversity* is an invaluable sourcebook that should be browsed for facts and figures, not read cover to cover.

294 The Official World Wildlife Fund Guide to Endangered Species of North America: Volumes 1 and 2

Edited by David W. Lowe, John R. Matthews, and Charles J. Mosely. Sponsored by World Wildlife Fund and The Nature Conservancy. Beacham Publishing, 1990. 1180p. $195.00 (hardcover).

295 The Official World Wildlife Fund Guide to Endangered Species of North America: Volume 3

Charles J. Mosely, Editor. Sponsored by World Wildlife Fund and The Nature Conservancy. Beacham Publishing, 1992. 457p. $85.00 (hardcover).

The Official World Wildlife Fund Guide to Endangered Species of North America is the best place to begin research on a particular U.S. endangered species. All three volumes comprise two-page descriptions of species listed on the Fish and Wildlife Service's list of Endangered and Threatened Wildlife and Plants (see entry 266, Fish and Wildlife Reference Service). The books are replete with black and white photographs, locator maps, and charts detailing living conditions and inhabited regions; entries describe a species, its behavior, habitat, historic range, and current distribution, as well as conservation and recovery programs. Entries also include brief bibliographies of published sources, and referrals to the appropriate government Office of Endangered Species. Within sections divided by species type—such as plants and crustaceans—entries appear in alphabetical order by scientific name. Coverage of the original two volumes is current to August 1989; the third volume includes species listed through December 1991. Unique to the third volume is a cumulative index to both scientific and common names and descriptions of information resources for photographs of endangered species.

The *Encyclopedia of U.S. Endangered Species* (ZCI Publishing, 1994. $35) is a CD-ROM that covers 700 species in more than 20,000 pages, including 3,500-plus photos, extensive overview information, and audiovisual presentations.

There are many other reference books that cover endangered species worldwide. Both the black-and-white, 1,230-page *Encyclopedia of Endangered Species* (Mary Emanoil. Gale Research, 1994. $95) and the color, 1,536-page *Endangered Wildlife of the World* (Marshall Cavendish, 1993. $399.95) are appropriate for high school and public libraries. The color, 1,100-page *Grolier World Encyclopedia of Endangered Species* (Grolier, 1993. $319) is targeted toward readers ages seven and up.

296 This Land Is Your Land: A Guide to North America's Endangered Ecosystems

Jon Naar and Alex J. Naar. HarperCollins Publishers, 1993. 400p. $15.00 (paper).

This Land Is Your Land should be the starting point for general information on ecology and conservation efforts. Written for a popular audience, it contains many "What You Can Do" sidebars that suggest ways in which citizens can facilitate environmental protection. After a short introduction that describes how ecosystems function, the bulk of the book focuses on particular natural environments, such as rivers, oceans, forests, and deserts. Selected case studies illustrate degradation and highlight conservation activities. Each chapter ends with a list of resources; appendices include a well-done directory of environmental organizations and a section on influencing legislation. Though lacking depth, *This Land Is Your Land* is a helpful introductory resource for budding conservationists.

Introductory Reading

For descriptions of new and recent books refer to *Books of the Big Outside* (see entry 285) and the *Island Press Environmental Sourcebook: Books for Better Conservation and Management* (see entry 110).

297 Ancient Forests of the Pacific Northwest

Elliot A. Norse. Sponsored by The Wilderness Society. Island Press, 1990. 327p. $34.95 (hardcover), $19.95 (paper).

Ancient Forests of the Pacific Northwest is a distinguished introduction to old-growth forest ecology. The first half of the book describes forest biological diversity and ecology, and discusses why saving the ancient forests is important. The remaining chapters examine threats to old-growth forests—from unsustainable timber operations to ozone depletion—and recommend ways to save them. Short essays by other scientists are interspersed throughout.

William Dietrich's *The Final Forest: The Battle for the Last Great Trees of the Pacific Northwest* (Simon & Schuster, 1992) provides a journalistic account of the politics of old-growth forest issues from the mind-sets of loggers, politicians, environmentalists, rangers, and others.

298 Beyond the Beauty Strip: Saving What's Left of Our Forests

Mitch Lansky. Tilbury House Publishers, 1992. 453p. $35.00 (hardcover), $19.95 (paper).

Beyond the Beauty Strip is an essential volume for forest activists. The term *beauty strip* in the title refers to that section of forest, visible along roads and rivers, that hides the clearcut land on the other side. This comprehensive study of industrial forestry and its effects in Maine can be applied to any second-growth forest. One by one, author Mitch Lansky (who has both run a forest activist organization and relied on forest products to earn a living) dispels myths advanced by the forestry industry. His criticism of industrial forestry is hard hitting and well referenced. Maps, charts, and jaw-dropping photos of clearcutting are included throughout.

299 Biodiversity

Edited by E. O. Wilson. National Academy Press, 1988. 521p. $24.50 (paper).

Biodiversity comprises papers from the 1986 National Forum on Biodiversity, the conference that pushed the current biodiversity crisis into the limelight. Divided into thirteen parts, *Biodiversity*'s fifty-seven essays survey the science of species and habitat diversity, offer political and technological solutions to ecological problems, and discuss economic and philosophical issues. The essays do not offer original insight, but they do provide clear restatements of the work of many of the world's foremost biologists, systematists, ecologists, and agricultural experts.

Other important, but more technical, collections of papers on biodiversity are *Conservation Biology: An Evolutionary-Ecological Perspective* (Sinauer, 1980), *Conservation Biology: The Science of Scarcity and Diversity* (Sinauer, 1986), *Conservation Biology: The Theory and Practice of Nature Conservation, Preservation, and Management* (Chapman & Hall, 1992), and *Conservation for the Twenty-First Century* (Oxford University Press, 1989).

300 The Diversity of Life

Edward O. Wilson. Questions of Science series. Harvard University Press, 1992. 424p. $29.95 (hardcover).

Written by preeminent entomologist and Pulitzer Prize–winning author Edward O. Wilson, *The Diversity of Life* is widely acclaimed as an eloquent introduction to species diversity. *The Diversity of Life* contains fifteen chapters that progressively build the reader's knowledge of the "whens, whys, and hows" of biological diversity. Three short, engaging chapters describe the resilience of plants and animals throughout time. The book's next five chapters provide a scientific overview of the evolutionary and ecological processes that affect biological diversity. The publication's last seven chapters examine the current human-created mass extinction—Wilson estimates that 27,000 species are lost each year—and, in practical terms, justify the conservation of biodiversity. Tables, charts, and pictures supplement *Diversity*'s text. The seventeen-page glossary not only defines biological terms, but includes the names of many of the foremost scientists mentioned in the text.

301 Ghost Bears: Exploring the Biodiversity Crisis

R. Edward Grumbine. Island Press, 1992. 290p. $25.00 (hardcover), $16.00 (paper).

Ghost Bears provides an excellent presentation—for a lay audience—of the science and significance of conservation biology. Author R. Edward Grumbine uses the grizzly bear of the Pacific Northwest as a springboard for discussing broader biodiversity issues: He views biocentrism as a viable path toward social transformation. The book's sections that analyze endangered species and forests in terms of policy, politics, and the law are particularly insightful. In addition, the past, present, and future of ecosystem management, particularly that of old-growth forests, are explored in detail. The combination of personal narrative and third-person history and analysis makes this read an enjoyable one.

302 Global Biodiversity Strategy: Guidelines for Action to Save, Study, and Use Earth's Biotic Wealth Sustainably and Equitably

Edited by Kathleen Courrier. World Resources Institute, The World Conservation Union, and United Nations Environment Programme, 1992. 244p. $19.95 (paper).

Global Biodiversity Strategy expresses the action-oriented hopes of the international conservation community for the coming years. The eighty-five policy-oriented proposals presented in this report were compiled by five hundred experts over three years. Examples of recommended actions include: "Modify national income accounts to make them reflect the economic loss that results when biological resources are degraded and biodiversity is lost" ; "Provide universal access to family planning services and increase funding to support their adoption" ; and "Integrate biodiversity concerns into education outside the classroom." Background information is given for each action, often with charts, tables, and diagrams. Written to influence the language of the Convention on Biological Diversity, *Global Biodiversity Strategy* puts forth a unified plan to conserve biodiversity, of which the Convention is a single component. For updates on implementation of the *Strategy*, see the *Biodiversity Conservation Strategy Update*, published by the World Resources Institute (see entry 50) and available electronically on CONSLINK (see entry 283).

Other Introductory Reading

- ◆ *Global Warming and Biological Diversity* (see entry 255)
- ◆ *These American Lands: Parks, Wilderness, and the Public Lands* (see entry 279, The Wilderness Society)

Abstracts and Indices

303 Biological Abstracts

BIOSIS, 1926–. Monthly.

CD-ROM: Available as *Biological Abstracts on Compact Disk* from SilverPlatter.

Database Vendor: Available as *BIOSIS Previews* on DIALOG, OCLC EPIC, and OCLC FirstSearch.

As the largest life sciences abstract available, *Biological Abstracts* is the essential resource for biology research. *Biological Abstracts* is widely available in libraries with good science collections, as is its companion volume, *Biological Abstracts/RRM (Reports, Reviews, Meetings)*. *BIOSIS Previews* is the electronic version of the combined records of *Biological Abstracts* and *Biological Abstracts/RRM*. *BIOSIS Previews* contains more than 8 million records dating to 1969; more than 500,000 new records—over half of which contain abstracts—are added each year. Subject coverage includes not only botany, zoology, and microbiology, but also information related to biochemistry, biotechnology, and medicine. Request the "How to Search BIOSIS Previews" pamphlet.

A smaller—120,000 new records a year—but similar biological abstract is the *Life Sciences Collection*, which is published by Cambridge Scientific Abstracts. The *Life Sciences Collection* is available on CD-ROM from SilverPlatter, and also available online on DIALOG.

304 Wildlife Worldwide

National Information Services Corporation, 1935–. Semiannual.

CD-ROM: Available from National Information Services Corporation.

Wildlife Worldwide is a comprehensive CD-ROM of more than 320,000 citations to published and unpublished literature on mammals, birds, reptiles, and amphibians. Though it includes citations from five other indices, most records are taken from the more widely available *Wildlife Review* (303/226-9401), a Fish and Wildlife Service (FWS) print index of published sources from thirteen hundred journals and periodicals. The National Information Services Corporation (NISC) offers two additional conservation CD-ROMs: *Fish and Fisheries Worldwide*, with roughly 150,000 citations, which includes FWS's *Fisheries Review*; and *Natural Resources Metabase*, covering more 120,000 abstracts and citations from federal databases that cover unpublished literature on natural resources, wetlands, ecosystems, and national parks. All NISC CD-ROMs have a user-friendly interface and can be searched in novice, advanced, or expert mode.

305 Zoological Record

BIOSIS and Zoological Society of London, 1865–. Annual.

CD-ROM: Available as *Zoological Record on Compact Disk* from SilverPlatter.

Database Vendor: Available as *Zoological Record Online* on DIALOG.

The *Zoological Record* indexes professional international zoological literature. Both the print and electronic versions of the *Record* include twenty-seven sections, divided by taxonomy, for example: protozoa, arachnida, and mammalia. The more frequently updated electronic versions—updated quarterly on CD-ROM and monthly online—date from 1978, with roughly seventy thousand citations from more than six thousand journals added each year. Potential or occasional users should request the free pamphlet "How to Search Zoological Record/Zoological Record Online" from BIOSIS. Regular users will want to have the $60 *Zoological Record Search Guide*, which includes the indexing vocabulary as well as indexing policies and search tips.

Other Abstracts and Indices

- ◆ *Biological Abstracts* (see entry 303)
- ◆ *Biological and Agricultural Index* (see entry 151)
- ◆ The *Biological Conservation Newsletter* (see entry 306)
- ◆ *Ecological Abstracts* (see entry 152)
- ◆ *Ecology Abstracts* (see entry 153)
- ◆ *Forestry Abstracts* (see entry 222, *CAB Abstracts*).

Periodicals

306 Biological Conservation Newsletter

Edited by Jane Villa-Lobos. Biological Conservation Newsletter, 1981–. Monthly. 4p. Free.

Internet: The *Biological Conservation Newsletter* can be received electronically from the CONSLINK (see entry 283) bulletin board. To receive the current issue, send an e-mail message to **listserv@sivm.si.edu** with the words **get conslink b-c-news** in the body of the message. To have issues delivered automatically as they are released, send a message to **listserv@sivm.si.edu** with the words **afd add conslink b-c-news** in the body of the message.

The *Biological Conservation Newsletter* is also archived and searchable on the Smithsonian Natural History gopher. Gopher to **nmnhgoph.si.edu**. Choose *Smithsonian Biological Conservation Programs and Data*, then *The Biological Conservation Newsletter and Bibliography*.

The *Biological Conservation Newsletter* serves as an excellent current awareness service for conservation biologists and other professionals. The newsletter contains a few short articles as well as information on new publications, fellowships and grants, job announcements, educational materials, and meetings. The bulk of the newsletter, however, consists of an extensive bibliography that cites all recent journal articles and monographs in the biological conservation field. This bibliographic portion of the newsletter serves as an outstanding index to literature in this field. The electronic format of the *Biological Conservation Newsletter* is the preferred method of distribution, but hard copies are also available from Jane Villa-Lobos, the editor (202/357-2027; fax 202/786-2563; or send an e-mail message to **mnhbo019@sivm.si.edu**), at the Department of Botany of the Smithsonian Institution's National Museum of Natural History.

307 Conservation Biology: The Journal of the Society for Conservation Biology

Sponsored by the Society for Conservation Biology. Blackwell Scientific Publications, 1987–. Bimonthly. 150p. $38.00/year for students, $100.00/year for individuals, $175.00/year for institutions.

Conservation Biology is an academic journal at the forefront of a relatively new scientific field. Although many articles—written by scientists from academia, government, and environmental organizations for their peers—are technical, several in each issue will be understandable to all interested individuals. The articles tend to focus on big-picture issues, addressing the economic, political, and philosophical aspects of conservation. News shorts and five in-depth book reviews are also included in each issue.

Another academic journal, *Biological Conservation* (Elsevier, sixteen times a year), has more technical articles and reprints of selected abstracts from *Ecological Abstracts* (see entry 152).

308 Earth First! The Radical Environmental Journal

Earth First! Journal, 1980–. 8 issues per year. 40p. $25.00/year.

Earth First! The Radical Environmental Journal is a great way to stay abreast of happenings in the no-compromise environmental movement. The *Journal* is the official newspaper of Earth First! (see entry 273), a voice for the diverse opinions Earth First!ers hold. It provides news, reviews, opinions, activist alerts, philosophy, analysis, and plenty of criticism of mainstream environmentalists. The language contributors use and ideologies they espouse is meant to provoke debate. Each *Journal* issue contains a directory of local Earth First! groups and updates on their activities.

309 Endangered Species Update

School of Natural Resources and Environment at the University of Michigan, 1983–. 10 issues per year. 8–32p. $23.00/year, $18.00/year for students and senior citizens.

The *Endangered Species Update* was started after the *Endangered Species Technical Bulletin*, a Fish and Wildlife Service newsletter, restricted its distribution to select government employees. (To maintain widespread distribution of the *Endangered Species Technical Bulletin*, *Endangered Species Update* reprints it [e.g., the September *Technical Bulletin* is inserted in the November *Update*].) The *Technical Bulletin* includes reports on the status of listed endangered species, discusses proposed species listings, and provides regional news. The *Update* adds at least one feature article, as well as a

book review, opinion page, and a "Bulletin Board" for news announcements. Special issues are published occasionally. Both parts of this newsletter are essential: the *Technical Bulletin* to follow Endangered Species Program activities and the *Update* for news and insight into endangered species research, management, and policy issues.

310 Wild Earth

Cenozoic Society, 1991–. Quarterly. 100p. $15.00/year for low-income individuals, $25.00/year for all others.

Wild Earth offers essential information for those following North American conservation issues, including politics, strategy, and ideology. The magazine broke away from *Earth First! The Radical Environmental Journal* (see entry 308) in 1990; in comparison to the *Journal*, *Wild Earth* contains more scientific articles on plants and animals, their behavior, the threats they face, and proposals for protection. The Wildlands Project (602/884-0875), a strategy to develop and implement a continental system of wildlands reserves, biological corridors, and buffers, is also covered regularly. *Wild Earth*'s holistic view of biodiversity conservation allows for articles about civil disobedience, environmental ethics, and population issues. Each issue includes more than twenty two- to three-page articles that are well referenced and that often include activist contact information. The magazine's last few pages, which include announcements, numerous book reviews, and summaries of articles in other publications, make this an outstanding source for keeping abreast of new projects and publications.

311 Wild Forest Review

Wild Forest Review, 1994–. 11 issues per year. 30p. $25.00/year.

Wild Forest Review is essential reading for those in the forest protection movement who need to make informed policy, organizing, or strategy decisions. Produced by committed environmental activists for other activists, *Wild Forest* serves as an open forum for airing a wide spectrum of views from the forest protection movement and offers readers an insider's perspective of the issues, groups, and personalities driving the movement. By exposing the flawed strategies and execution of forest protection efforts by state and federal regulatory agencies, *Wild Forest* has become a reliable government watchdog.

In addition, it regularly includes "Field Guides" to federal laws, investigative reports, and a "Tools for Activists" column that shares media relations tips, organizing advice, and strategies for approaching timber sale appeals.

Energy

What This Chapter Covers

This chapter centers around energy conservation, especially energy efficiency in buildings, industry, and transportation, and renewable-energy sources such as solar, wind, and geothermal. It also focuses on the environmental impact of fossil fuels (coal, oil, and natural gas). Nuclear energy issues and alternative transportation fuels are also covered.

For More Information

- See **General** for resources on all environmental issues, including those related to energy.
- See **Air** for resources on the effects of conventional energy use, such as air pollution and global climate change.
- See **Health and Toxics** and **Waste** for resources on radioactive and other hazardous wastes.
- See **Architecture** for resources on energy-efficient home design.
- See **Shopping** for resources that provide energy advice for consumers.

Government Clearinghouses

312   Electric Ideas Clearinghouse Hotline
Washington State Energy Office
P.O. Box 43171
Olympia, WA 98504

Phone (Pacific Northwest): 800/872-3568;
206/586-8588. Phone (other western states):
800/797-7584. Phone (remainder of U.S. and
international): 206/956-2237. Fax (Pacific
Northwest): 800/872-3882; 206/586-8303

Billie-Gwen Russell, Coordinator, Hotline Services

Bulletin board: The Electric Ideas Clearinghouse
Hotline maintains the Energy Ideas
Clearinghouse Electronic Bulletin Board Service
(see entry 328).

The Electric Ideas Clearinghouse Hotline is the
premier clearinghouse for commercial and industrial energy use and conservation for utility representatives and other energy professionals.
Because the Bonneville Power Administration
completely funds the clearinghouse's library
services, these services (e.g., online literature
searches, distribution of copies of articles and
reports, research of products and vendors) are
available only to those calling from Washington,
Oregon, Idaho, and Montana. However, callers
from all states may ask the clearinghouse for
help in locating other resources and libraries, or
for referrals to other hotlines more appropriate
for their use. The affiliated Energy Ideas Clearinghouse Electronic Bulletin Board Service (see
entry 328) is an excellent source of free information for everyone.

313   Energy Efficiency and Renewable Energy Clearinghouse (EREC)
Department of Energy
P.O. Box 3048
Merrifield, VA 22116

Phone: 800/363–3732. TDD: 800/273-2957.
Fax: 703/903-9750.
E-mail: energyinfo@delphi.com

Ann Dixon, Project Manager

Bulletin Board: To connect to the Energy
Efficiency and Renewable Energy Clearinghouse
BBS (EREC BBS) by modem, dial 800/273-2955.

In January 1994, the Department of Energy
(DOE) consolidated the Conservation and Renewable Energy Inquiry and Referral Service (CARE-
IRS) and the National Appropriate Technology
Assistance Service (NATAS) to create the Energy
Efficiency and Renewable Energy Clearinghouse
(EREC), which quickly became the best place to
begin any information search related to energy
use in small buildings. EREC's staff can send documents, make referrals, and provide technical
and business assistance on any topic related to
energy efficiency (e.g., caulking and weather-
stripping, insulation, energy-efficient landscaping, passive solar design) and renewable-energy
technologies (e.g., photovoltaics, biomass and
municipal solid waste-to-energy conversion, electric vehicles, alcohol fuels). The clearinghouse
has more than 150 detailed four- to eight-page
fact sheets (*Converting a Home to Solar Heat*;
Buying a Wood Burning Appliance) and other
publications (*Is the Wind a Practical Source of
Energy for You?*; *Tips for Energy Savers*), as well
as more than five hundred computer-generated
information briefs, including extensive lists of
trade and professional associations, research centers, and special-interest groups as well as citations to publications. Documents can also be
ordered from the EREC bulletin board system.
On-staff technical specialists provide assistance
in the design and comparison of energy systems
and help callers to fix both simple and complex
energy-related problems; financial specialists
advise entrepreneurs and inventors on business
planning, marketing, and financing. All products
and services of this user-friendly information
source are free of charge.

314   National Alternative Fuels Hotline
Department of Energy
P.O. Box 12316
Arlington, VA 22209

Phone: 800/423-1363; 703/528-3500.
Fax: 703/528-1953

Internet: The Alternative Fuels Data Center
has space on the National Renewable Energy
Laboratory (see entry 316) gopher and World
Wide Web sites. At either site, choose *Infor-*

mation Sources, then *NREL Information Systems*, then *Alternative Fuels Data Center (AFDC)*.

The National Alternative Fuels Hotline is a good place to call for information on alternative fuels for transportation (e.g., methanol, ethanol, natural gas) and alternative-fueled vehicles. The hotline disseminates technical information from the National Renewable Energy Laboratory's (see entry 316) Alternative Fuels Data Center (AFDC) on such topics as fleet emissions and performance characteristics. For a lay audience, this hotline provides background information on specialized topics (e.g., *Facts About CNG and LPG Conversion*), a guide to alternative fuel information sources, and a glossary. It also distributes the *AFDC Update*, an outreach newsletter also available on the Internet.

A separate Department of Energy hotline, the Clean Cities Hotline (800/224-8437), provides information on federal legislation dealing with alternative fuels and vehicles, the availability of alternative fuels and vehicles, and related state programs and legislation, as well as news about the Clean Cities program, which municipalities can voluntarily join in order to accelerate and expand the use of alternative-fueled vehicles.

315 National Energy Information Center (NEIC)
Department of Energy
Energy Information Administration
1000 Independence Avenue, SW
Forrestal Building, Room 1F-048
Washington, DC 20585

Phone: 202/586-8800. TDD: 202/586-1181.
E-mail: infoctr@eia.doe.gov

Bulletin Board: To connect to the Energy Information Administration's Electronic Publishing System (EPUB) by modem, dial 202/586-2557.

Internet: EPUB is available via FedWorld's GateWay (see entry 61). Choose *16* for *EPUB (DOE)*.

The National Energy Information Center (NEIC) is the best place to begin a search for energy-related statistical information. NEIC disseminates documents for the Energy Information Administration (EIA), the branch of the Department of Energy that collects and analyzes data on energy sources, reserves, production, consumption, dis-

tribution, and imports and exports. NEIC will not conduct tailored research, but the group will provide data that EIA has already compiled and will make referrals to additional sources of information. Major EIA publications include the *Monthly Energy Review*, the definitive source for U.S. production and consumption statistics, and the *Annual Energy Outlook*, which projects energy supply, demand, and price. Many EIA statistical publications on specialized topics are also available, such as the monthly *International Petroleum Statistics Report* and *Solar Collector Manufacturing Activity*, published annually. For a complete list of EIA publications, request the free *EIA Publications Directory*. Among the outstanding free publications offered are the *Energy Information Directory* (see entry 329), *Energy Education Resources: Kindergarten Through 12th Grade*, and *Energy Facts*, updated annually, a quick-reference guide to major energy statistics. EIA's bulletin board, the Electronic Publishing System, provides access to selected energy data from many of EIA's statistical reports.

A major source of energy statistics not published by the EIA is the *Energy Statistics Yearbook* (United Nations, 1984–. Annual), which provides country-by-country aggregate energy statistics.

316 National Renewable Energy Laboratory (NREL)
1617 Cole Boulevard
Golden, CO 80401

Phone: 303/275-3000. Phone (Document Distribution Service): 303/275-4363. Phone (Technical Inquiry Service): 303/275-4099.
Fax: 303/275-4053

Duane Sunderman, Director

Internet: To access NREL sites, gopher to **nrelinfo.nrel.gov**; or, on the World Wide Web, the URL is **http://nrelinfo.nrel.gov/**.

The National Renewable Energy Laboratory (NREL) is the major government research center working on all renewable-energy technologies, energy-efficiency technologies for buildings and industry, and alternative transportation fuels. It is operated for the Department of Energy (DOE) by the Midwest Research Institute. NREL's Technical Inquiry Service provides assistance with very technical questions, and its Document Distribution Service sends out technical documents. (For publicly available information, produced by NREL concerning renewable-energy technologies, contact the Energy Efficiency and Renewable Energy Clearinghouse [see entry 313] first.) NREL's Internet sites are good sources of information about sustainable-energy issues and NREL's research. In addition to background information, the sites contain a searchable database of NREL documents published since 1992, information from NREL's National Alternative Fuels Hotline (see entry 314), an online version of the *National Renewable Energy Laboratory Guide to Research Facilities*, and an outstanding directory—the *New Energy Information Locator* (see entry 331)—of governmental and nongovernmental electronic information sources on energy efficiency and renewable energy that are not available on the Internet.

Organizations

To locate local organizations, consult the *National Directory of Safe Energy Organizations* (see entry 332, *The Renewable Source*).

317 Alliance to Save Energy (ASE)
1725 K Street, NW, Suite 509
Washington, DC 20006

Phone: 202/857-0666. Fax: 202/331-9588

David Nemtzo, Executive Director

The Alliance to Save Energy (ASE)—highly respected as a mediating force between diverging interest groups in the energy-efficiency field—places a high priority on educating industry, policymakers, consumers, and the media about energy policy and energy-efficient technologies. To achieve these objectives, this nonprofit coalition—comprising utilities, businesses with interests in the energy field, and trade associations—formulates policies and program initiatives to improve the energy efficiency of residential, commercial, and federal buildings; provides technical assistance to industrial decision makers; participates in legislative task forces; helps organize the energy-efficiency

industry; works to facilitate product development; and evaluates and supports utility-sponsored consumer education programs. ASE produces a quarterly newsletter and many other publications, such as *Achieving Greater Energy Efficiency in Buildings: The Role of DOE's Office of Building Technologies*; *Energy Education on the Move: A National Energy Education Survey and Case Studies of Outstanding Programs*; and *Energy Efficiency Resource Directory: A Guide to Utility Programs*. ASE has also developed an IBM-compatible software program, called *ENVEST: Energy Efficiency Investment Software*, that performs economic and financial analyses of energy conservation and cogeneration projects.

318 American Council for an Energy-Efficient Economy (ACE[3])
1001 Connecticut Avenue, NW, Suite 801
Washington, DC 20036

Phone: 202/429-8873. Fax: 202/429-2248

Howard Geller, Executive Director

The leading nonprofit research organization on energy efficiency, the American Council for an Energy-Efficient Economy (ACE[3]) is best known for conducting in-depth technical and policy assessments and for publishing highly respected books and reports. ACE[3] also advises governments and utilities, works with businesses and other organizations, and organizes conferences. Sample ACE[3] titles include *Energy Efficiency in Industry and Agriculture: Lessons from North Carolina*; *Energy Strategies for a Sustainable Transportation System*; *An Introduction to DSM: The Business of Energy Conservation for Electric Utilities*; *The Most Energy-Efficient Appliances*; and *Structuring an Energy Tax So That Energy Bills Do Not Increase*. The organization also provides information for consumers in the authoritative *Consumer Guide to Home Energy Savings* (see entry 514). ACE[3] will furnish a complete publications catalog upon request.

319 American Solar Energy Society (ASES)
2400 Central Avenue, Suite G-1
Boulder, CO 80301

Phone: 303/443-3130. Fax: 303/443-3212

Larry Sherwood, Director

An association of scientists, architects, and other professionals who share an interest in advancing the use of solar energy, the American Solar Energy Society (ASES) provides support for twenty U.S. regional chapters and also serves as the U.S. branch of the International Solar Energy Society. The association sponsors the National Solar Energy Conference, coordinates public outreach activities, and publishes *Solar Today* (see entry 349) magazine as well as conference proceedings and other technical reports. ASES members and nonmembers can join the Solar Action Network (SAN), a project of ASES, to receive action alerts on legislative and policy issues affecting solar energy. The association's catalog includes technical publications such as the annual *Advances in Solar Energy*, as well as other, less technical documents like *The Independent Home: Living Well with Power from the Sun, Wind and Water*; *Passive Solar Energy: The Homeowner's Guide to Natural Heating and Cooling*; and the *Procurement Guide for Renewable Energy Systems*.

320 American Wind Energy Association (AWEA)

122 C Street, NW, 4th Floor
Washington, DC 20001

Phone: 202/383-2500. Fax: 202/383-2505.
E-mail: awea@mcimail.com

Randall Swisher, Executive Director

EcoNet: AWEA posts its newsletters, *Windletter* and the *Wind Energy Weekly*, in the *awea.windnews* conference.

Internet: For detailed information about AWEA offerings on the Internet, send an e-mail message to **wind-info@igc.apc.org**.
AWEA has space on Solstice, the Center for Renewable Energy and Sustainable Technology (see entry 321) site. From the gopher main menu, choose *Renewable*, then *Wind*, then *American Wind Energy Association*. From the World Wide Web home page, choose *American Wind Energy Association*.

The American Wind Energy Association (AWEA) is a trade association and individual membership organization that works to further the development of wind energy as a reliable energy alternative. AWEA addresses legislative issues of interest to the industry, works to expand wind-energy-related exports, and sponsors the annual WINDPOWER conference and trade show. AWEA publishes its own newsletters, fact sheets, reports, and books and also distributes relevant works from other publishers, including *Wind Turbine Technology: Fundamental Concepts of Wind Turbine Engineering* (American Society of Mechanical Engineers, 1994), the *Wind Energy Resource Atlas* (Pacific Northwest Laboratories, 1987, reprinted 1991), and *Wind Power for Home and Business: Renewable Energy for the 1990's and Beyond* (see entry 516). AWEA has two informative newsletters, *Windletter*, published monthly, and the *Wind Energy Weekly*, which are available both in print and electronically in numerous online locations, including EcoNet (see entry 58) and Solstice (see entry 321, Center for Renewable Energy and Sustainable Technology). AWEA offers additional wind energy information on the Solstice Internet site, including its publications catalog and membership directory. AWEA is the best place to contact for information on wind energy.

321 Center for Renewable Energy and Sustainable Technology (CREST)

Solar Energy Research and Education Foundation
777 North Capitol Street, NE, Suite 805
Washington, DC 20002

Phone: 202/289-5370. Fax: 202/289-5354.
E-mail: info@crest.org

Internet: CREST's Internet sites are called Solstice. To access Solstice, ftp to **solstice.crest.org**; gopher to **solstice.crest.org**; or, on the World Wide Web, the URL is **http://solstice.crest.org/**.

An education and training facility established to demonstrate today's renewable-energy and energy-efficiency technology, the Center for Renewable Energy and Sustainable Technology (CREST) encourages their use through hands-on interaction and education. Solstice, CREST's Internet site, serves as a clearinghouse for nongovernmental information on renewable energy and energy efficiency. Solstice contains *The CREST Guide to Alternative Energy Information on the Internet* (see entry 333) and other directories and publications by and about leading organizations, such as general information about the Rocky Mountain Institute (see entry 44); the Solar Energy Industries Association (see entry

325) membership directory; *Energywise Options for State and Local Governments* (Center for Policy Alternatives, 1993); and the International Institute for Energy Conservation's *Technical Information Directory*. CREST also produces CD-ROM multimedia education and training software (e.g., *Renewable Energy, Passive Solar Building Design*) and has an on-site demonstration facility. CREST is an excellent resource for government decision makers, utilities, educators, students, nongovernmental organizations, architects, engineers, and librarians.

322 Critical Mass Energy Project (CMEP)
Public Citizen
215 Pennsylvania Avenue, SE
Washington, DC 20003

Phone: 202/546-4996. Fax: 202/547-7392.
E-mail: cmep@essential.org

Bill Magavern, Project Director

The Critical Mass Energy Project (CMEP) is a leading voice on all sustainable-energy issues, especially in the movement to decrease reliance on nuclear power. CMEP works closely with grassroots activists and other environmental organizations to disseminate reports, lobby Congress, and act as a watchdog of key regulatory agencies. Recent investigative reports include *Hear No Evil, See No Evil, Speak No Evil: What the NRC Won't Tell You about America's Nuclear Reactors* and *The Dark at the End of the Tunnel: Federal Clean-Up Standards for Nuclear Power Plants*. Critical Mass also publishes *The Green Buyer's Car Guide: Environmental Ratings of 1994 Cars and Light Trucks* (see entry 604) and several directories, including *The Renewable Source: A National Directory of Resources, Contacts, and Companies* (see entry 332), the *National Directory of Safe Energy Organizations* (see entry 332, *Renewable Source*), and the National Directory of U.S. Energy Periodicals. Activists will want to receive CMEP's legislative alerts; to subscribe, send an e-mail message to **cmep@essential.org** asking to be placed on the mailing list.

Public Citizen, the consumer advocacy organization founded by Ralph Nader, administers many other projects besides CMEP that monitor government accountability, including the Health Research Group and the Litigation Group. Public Citizen's Congress Watch plays a leadership role in the Citizen's Trade Campaign, a national grassroots coalition that opposed the North American Free Trade Agreement (NAFTA) and the General Agreement on Tariffs and Trade (GATT). Another Nader program, the Government Purchasing Project (202/387-8030), publishes *Energy Ideas*, a quarterly newsletter that helps government purchasers save energy; it is available electronically on the *energy.forum* conference on EcoNet (see entry 58) and on the CICNet gopher (gopher to **gopher.cic.net**; choose *Electronic Serials*, then *Alphabetical List*, then *E*, then *Energy Ideas*).

323 Nuclear Information and Resource Service (NIRS)
1424 16th Street, NW, Suite 601
Washington, DC 20036

Phone: 202/328-0002. Fax: 202/462-2183

Michael Mariotte, Executive Director

Bulletin Board: NIRS maintains a bulletin board system called NirsNet. To connect by modem, dial 800/764-6477.

A leading voice against nuclear power and an active watchdog organization, the Nuclear Information and Resource Service (NIRS) serves as the "Washington office" for many grassroots nuclear activists and whistleblowers, media representatives, independent researchers, and educators. NIRS monitors commercial nuclear plants and waste sites, gives expert testimony, initiates and supports litigation, and provides technical assistance to other activists. The staff excels at explaining technical nuclear issues in lay language. Among NIRS publications are *The Nuclear Monitor* (see entry 347), *The Energy Audit Manual: How to Audit Campus, City and Other Buildings*, and a variety of information packets on nuclear power and nuclear waste, renewable-energy sources, and energy efficiency. Callers can receive referrals to dozens of local and regional antinuclear organizations and newsletters. NirsNet, a free electronic bulletin board system maintained by NIRS, includes Nuclear Regulatory Commission (NRC) policy documents, *The Nuclear Monitor, Rachel's Environment & Health Weekly* (see entry 402), action alerts, and relevant sections of the *Federal Register* and the *Code of Federal Regulations (CFR)*.

The Committee for Nuclear Responsibility (415/664-1933) is another well-established organization that can provide detailed information about all aspects of nuclear radiation.

324 Safe Energy Communication Council (SECC)
1717 Massachusetts Avenue, NW, Suite 805
Washington, DC 20036

Phone: 202/483-8491. Fax: 202/234-9194

Scott Denman, Director

The Safe Energy Communication Council (SECC) educates the media and the public about energy efficiency, renewable energy, and the economic and environmental liabilities of nuclear power. SECC was formed, in part, to counter the media arm of the nuclear power industry, the Nuclear Energy Institute (202/739-8000), formerly the U.S. Council for Energy Awareness. A nonprofit coalition of ten environmental (e.g., Environmental Action, the Nuclear Information and Resource Service, Sierra Club) and public-interest media (e.g., Media Access Project, Telecommunications Research and Action Center) organizations, SECC supplies newspapers and periodicals with commentaries and camera-ready graphics on energy and related issues, and serves as a referral center for journalists. SECC also provides citizens' groups with training in media skills and assists with organizing strategies and specific media campaigns. Publications include the *Media Skills Manual* and the *MYTHBusters* series of point–counterpoint reports on nuclear waste disposal, foreign oil dependence, the greenhouse effect, renewable energy, energy efficiency, nuclear reactor safety, and low-level radioactive waste.

325 Solar Energy Industries Association (SEIA)
122 C Street, NW
4th Floor
Washington, DC 20001

Phone: 202/383-2600. Fax: 202/383-2670

Scott Sklar, Executive Director

Internet: SEIA's membership directory is available on Solstice, the Center for Renewable Energy and Sustainable Technology's (see entry 321) Internet site. From the gopher main menu, choose *Energy Organizations*, then *Renewables and Alternatives*, then *General Renewable and Alternative Energy info*, then *SEIA*, then *The SEIA Membership Directory*. From the World Wide Web home page, choose *Solar Energy Industries Association Member Database*.

The Solar Energy Industries Association (SEIA) represents the interests of solar manufacturers, distributors, dealers, installers, and component suppliers. It is a good source for statistical information and manufacturing standards. The *Renewable Energy Publications Catalogue* includes items produced by SEIA and its affiliates: the Solar Rating and Certification Company, the National Wood Energy Association, the U.S. Export Council on Renewable Energy, and the Council for Renewable Energy Education. Sample titles include the *Consumer Guide to Solar Energy* (see entry 515), the *Directory of the U.S. Solar Thermal Industry*, *Networking: Renewable Energy in the States*, the *State Biomass Statistical Directory*, and the *Solar Industry Journal* (see entry 348), a quarterly magazine. The organization works closely with other trade associations and environmental organizations to promote renewable-energy sources.

326 SUN DAY Campaign
315 Circle Avenue, #2
Takoma Park, MD 20912

Phone: 301/270-2258. Fax: 301/891-2866

Ken Bossong, Director

The SUN DAY Campaign is a national research and advocacy network working to encourage and promote activities in support of renewable energy, improved energy efficiency, and alternatives to nuclear power and fossil fuels. The network comprises more than 650 national and local environmental, business, government, utility, religious, academic, and labor organizations and focuses on coordinating public awareness activities that celebrate existing sustainable-energy policies, products, and programs; these activities are planned in conjunction with Earth Day events in April and throughout the year, especially in October, which is National Energy Awareness Month. SUN DAY publishes two newsletters: the monthly *SUN DAY Update*, and the bimonthly *Sustainable Energy Resources Newsletter*, which provides news about sustainable-energy organizations and announcements of new publications. The organization also coordinates the Sustainable Energy Budget Coalition, which publishes the *Sustainable Energy Budget for the U.S. Department of Energy* (see entry 341). In addition, SUN DAY regularly produces several separate directories pertaining to sustainable-energy issues, including listings of government agencies, businesses, utilities, periodicals, trade associations, academics, and congressional energy aides; these directories are comprehensive, annotated, indexed, and available in print, on PC-compatible diskette, or on mailing labels.

Other Organizations

- The Energy Conservation Coalition (see entry 22, Environmental Action)
- The Real Goods Trading Company (see entry 504)
- The Rocky Mountain Institute (see entry 44)
- The Surface Transportation Policy Project (see entry 410)
- The Union of Concerned Scientists (see entry 47)

Internet Sites

For additional Internet sites, consult *The CREST Guide to Alternative Energy Information on the Internet* (see entry 333).

327 Energy Efficiency and Renewable Energy Network (EREN)

A joint project of three Department of Energy laboratories: National Renewable Energy Laboratory, the Oak Ridge National Laboratory, and the Argonne National Laboratory.

Internet: To access on the World Wide Web, the URL is **http://www.eren.doe.gov/**.

The premier site on the Internet for sustainable-energy issues, the Energy Efficiency and Renewable Energy Network (EREN) is a joint project of three national laboratories: the National Renewable Energy Laboratory (see entry 316), the Oak Ridge National Laboratory, and the Argonne National Laboratory. EREN was developed to help federal and state government employees obtain information on sustainable-energy issues, but the network is useful for anyone who needs

information on these topics. Among the resources that reside on EREN are the excellent *New Energy Information Locator* (see entry 331), which describes non-Internet electronic reference sources, and recent, selected entries of the *Energy Science and Technology Database* (see entry 345, Energy Research Abstracts). This Internet site is only available through a World Wide Web client; it is entirely searchable by WAIS, which makes finding specific information easy. EREN is the most convenient way to access sustainable-energy sites available on the Internet, such as the Center for Renewable Energy and Sustainable Technology's (see entry 321) Solstice site, which specializes in sustainable-energy information from trade associations and non-profit organizations, and the Energy Ideas Clearinghouse Electronic Bulletin Board Service (see entry 328).

Other Internet Sites

- The Center for Renewable Energy and Sustainable Technology (see entry 321)
- The National Renewable Energy Laboratory (see entry 316)

Bulletin Boards

328 Energy Ideas Clearinghouse Electronic Bulletin Board Service (EICBBS)

Maintained by the Washington State Energy Office.

Bulletin Board: To connect to EICBBS by modem, dial 800/762-3319 from Pacific Northwest states; 800/797-7584 from other western states; or 206/956-2212 from anywhere else.
    For technical support by phone, call the system operator at 206/956-2237.

Internet: To access EICBBS, telnet to **eicbbs.wseo.wa.gov**.

The Energy Ideas Clearinghouse Electronic Bulletin Board Service (EICBBS), maintained by the Washington State Energy Office, features information on commercial and industrial energy efficiency, but it also includes information on environmental and renewable-energy topics. In addition to e-mail privileges and more than fifty online discussion groups, the bulletin board contains a jobs database, a database of training events and materials, a listing of energy codes and legislation, and descriptions of energy-related programs and organizations. There are more than eight hundred downloadable files; names of file directories include "Energy Auditing Software/Information," "Climate Change Action Plan," "Energy/Environment Newsletters/Bulletins," and "Solar Thermal and Photovoltaic Systems." Included are the full text of such periodicals as *Home Power: The Hands-on-Journal of Home-made Power* (see entry 526) and the *Wind Energy Weekly* (see entry 320, American Wind Energy Association). The "Miscellaneous Energy Related Files and Utilities" file directory includes many bibliographies and guides to information sources. The Electric Ideas Clearinghouse Hotline (see entry 312), also operated by the Washington State Energy Office, serves as the system operator. EICBBS is an excellent repository of information on all sustainable-energy issues.

Other Bulletin Boards

◆ NirsNet (see entry 323, Nuclear Information and Resource Service)

◆ The Electronic Publishing System (see entry 315, National Energy Information Center)

◆ The Energy Efficiency and Renewable Energy Clearinghouse BBS (see entry 313)

◆ The Home Power BBS (see entry 526, *Home Power* magazine)

Directories

329 Energy Information Directory

Department of Energy, Energy Information Administration, 1994; distributed by the National Energy Information Center. Annual. 111p. Free (paper).

The *Energy Information Directory* is an annotated directory of government offices and trade associations in all energy-related areas. Roughly two-thirds of the five hundred entries are offices within the Department of Energy (DOE) (e.g., Office of Alcohol Fuels, Office of the Deputy

Assistant Secretary for Naval Petroleum and Oil Shale Reserves, Office of Civilian Reactor Development), though the publication also includes entries for fifty other federal offices and more than seventy trade associations. Each entry provides name, address, phone number, contact person, and a paragraph summary of the responsibilities of each office or association. In addition, contact information is provided for each state's governor, energy office, geologist, oil and gas agency, and Public Utility Commission. The directory was developed to help the staff of the National Energy Information Center (see entry 315) make referrals; it does not include those DOE offices that do not deal directly with the public. This directory is an invaluable resource for anyone trying to obtain information from the Department of Energy.

330 Energy Update: A Guide to Current Reference Literature

R. David Weber. Energy Information Press, 1991. 455p. $42.50 (hardcover).

Energy Update describes more than one thousand reference works on energy conservation, solar energy, alternative energy sources, electric power, nuclear power, fossil fuels, coal, and petroleum and natural gas. *Energy Update* profiles dictionaries and encyclopedias; handbooks and manuals; directories; statistical sources; indices, abstracts, and bibliographies; and databases. The lengthy, well-researched annotations relay the purpose, scope, arrangement, history, and special features of each publication, as well as all bibliographic information. This work covers resources published from the early 1980s through the beginning of 1990. Foreign-language items or those that deal exclusively with material outside the United States have been excluded. Entries are cross referenced; there are author, title, subject, and document number indices. This book, which updates the author's three-volume *Energy Information Guide* (ABC-CLIO, 1982–1984), is a valuable tool for those needing a comprehensive resource guide to technical energy information sources.

331 New Energy Information Locator (NEIL)

National Renewable Energy Laboratory, Information Services. Updated regularly.

Internet: Available on the National Renewable Energy Laboratory's (NREL) (see entry 316) gopher and World Wide Web sites. At either site, choose *Information Sources*, then *NREL Information Systems*, then *New Energy Information Locator (NEIL)*.

The *New Energy Information Locator (NEIL)* is an outstanding electronic database of electronic sources of information on renewable energy and energy efficiency that are not available on the Internet. *NEIL* describes databases (e.g., the *Renewable Electric Project Information System*, the *Industrial Assessment Center Database*, the *Natural Gas Vehicle Safety Database*), bulletin boards (e.g., Home Power BBS [see entry 526, *Home Power* magazine], National Photovoltaic Environmental, Health and Safety Information BBS), and information on diskette, including directories, mailing lists, product lists, and service lists (e.g., the *Official Guide to Demand Side Management Programs and Research*, the *Energy Conservation Products Retail Directory*, *U.S. Vendors of Geothermal Goods and Services*, the *Energy Efficient Building Association Master Mailing List*, the *PV People Phone and Address List*). The following information is provided for each entry: product name, producer and contact information, format, type of information, subjects, dates of coverage, geographic coverage, number of entries, updates, language, content/ description, method of delivery or access, vendor name and telephone number, and cost. *NEIL* is an excellent way to find out about both well-known and obscure non-Internet electronic energy reference sources.

332 The Renewable Source: A National Directory of Resources, Contacts, and Companies

Matthew Freedman. 4th ed. Public Citizen Publications, 1994. Annual. 234p. $40.00 (spiral bound).

Diskette: Available from Public Citizen Publications for $80.00.

For individuals looking for renewable-energy source experts in the United States, *The Renewable Source* is a good place to begin a search. The fourth edition provides contact information for 2,200 individuals and organizations. Entries are organized by state, then category: activist, business, government, research, trade, or utility. The business, research, and trade categories are further subdivided by technology, such as electric vehicles or wind energy technologies. Entries are indexed by organization name, contact person, category, and technology. Public Citizen's Critical Mass Energy Project (see entry 322) also publishes the *National Directory of Safe Energy Organizations* (8th ed. 1994. Annual. $30), which provides contact information for 1,200 antinuclear and other grassroots energy organizations. The SUN DAY Campaign (see entry 326) also produces several separate sustainable-energy directories (e.g., government agencies, businesses, utilities, periodicals, trade associations, academics, congressional energy aides). SUN DAY's directories are available in print, on diskettes, and on mailing labels, like the Public Citizen directories.

Another directory, *Energywise Options for State and Local Governments* (Center for Policy Alternatives, 1993) describes the best state and local programs on energy efficiency, transportation, waste reduction, and renewable energy; the directory is available electronically on the Solstice Internet site (see entry 321, Center for Renewable Energy and Sustainable Technology).

Other Directories

- ◆ The *Directory of U.S. Energy Periodicals* (see entry 322, Critical Mass Energy Project)
- ◆ *The Real Goods Solar Living Sourcebook* (see entry 509)
- ◆ The *SEIA Membership Directory* (see entry 325, Solar Energy Industries Association)

Bibliographies

333 The CREST Guide to Alternative Energy Information on the Internet

Electronic document. Compiled by Christopher Gronbeck and Andrew Waegel. Center for Renewable Energy and Sustainable Technology, 1994. Updated irregularly. Free.

Internet: Available on Solstice, the Center for Renewable Energy and Sustainable Technology's (CREST) (see entry 321) ftp, gopher, and World Wide Web sites.

At the ftp site, choose *pub*, then *online*, then *internet*, then *aeguide*.

From the gopher main menu, choose *Online Info and Resources*, then *Internet*, then *The CREST guide to Energy Info on the Internet*.

The hypertext version is available on the World Wide Web site. From the home page, choose *CREST's Guide to the Internet's Alternative Energy Resources*. The URL for this document is **http://solstice.crest.org/online/ aeguide/aehome.html**.

Since energy issues are often neglected on Internet gophers and in other Internet bibliographies, *The CREST Guide to Alternative Energy Information on the Internet*, compiled by the Center for Renewable Energy and Sustainable Technology (see entry 321) is essential. The August 1994 edition included eight World Wide Web sites, five gopher sites, three telnet sites, five ftp sites, five Usenet newsgroups, five electronic-mailing lists, and five e-mail addresses for renewable-energy experts. Most of these resources—for example, the *sci.energy.hydrogen* Usenet newsgroup, the Photovoltaic Design Assistance Center, the Electric Vehicle discussion mailing list, and the Energy Efficient Housing in Canada World Wide Web server—are devoted exclusively to energy issues, though some others—e.g., FedWorld (see entry 61), EcoGopher (see entry 54, EcoSystems)—cover a much broader range of topics. All access information and an insightful description of the resource's contents are included. The version on the World Wide Web is in hypertext, allowing users to access the resources directly from this bibliography.

Reference Handbooks

334 Chambers Nuclear Energy and Radiation Dictionary

Edited by P. M. B. Walker. W & R Chambers, 1992. 260p. $40.00 (hardcover).

335 Nuclear Choices: A Citizen's Guide to Nuclear Technology

Richard Wolfson. MIT Press, revised edition, 1993; original edition, 1991. 467p. $24.95 (paper).

Both the *Chambers Nuclear Energy and Radiation Dictionary* and *Nuclear Choices* are reference books that help nonspecialists understand nuclear technology. While the second half of the *Chambers Dictionary* provides definitions for some three thousand terms, the first half of the book provides a good overview of the general principles of nuclear physics, fusion and fission, nuclear safety and waste disposal, nuclear bombs, and radiation and its effects. This section is written much like a concise, technical encyclopedia. Definitions in the dictionary section range in length from one to three sentences, and complement the first half of the book. *Nuclear Choices* is similar to the first half of the *Chambers Dictionary*, but is meant especially for lay readers. The book is divided into three equal parts: the physics of the nucleus, the problems of extracting nuclear energy from the nucleus (e.g., safety, radiation, waste disposal), and the function, effects, and problems associated with nuclear weapons. Neither book argues for one side of the issue over another, but rather explains the technology to enable readers to decide for themselves.

Those who want to read explicit arguments for and against nuclear power should consult *Nuclear Power, Both Sides: The Best Arguments For and Against the Most Controversial Technology* (Michio Kaku and Jennifer Trainer. W. W. Norton & Company, 1982).

336 Energy and American Society: A Reference Handbook

Edited by E. Willard Miller and Ruby M. Miller. Contemporary World Issues series. ABC-CLIO, 1993. 418p. $39.50 (hardcover).

337 Nuclear Energy Policy: A Reference Handbook

Edited by Earl R. Kruschke and Byron M. Jackson. Contemporary World Issues series. ABC-CLIO, 1990. 246p. $37.00 (hardcover).

High school students and interested laypersons will find both *Energy and American Society* and *Nuclear Energy Policy* helpful. These one-stop reference books provide a hodgepodge of information background, including the history, current status, and future of technologies; chronologies of significant events; a directory of organizations; annotated bibliographies of reference materials, books, and audiovisual materials; and citations to articles and government documents. *Energy and American Society* includes a summary of major laws and regulations, while *Nuclear Energy Policy* includes biographies of key individuals. Like other volumes in ABC-CLIO's Contemporary World Issues series (e.g., *Environmental Hazards: Toxic Waste, Hazardous Material: A Reference Handbook* [see entry 440], and *Water Quality and Availability: A Reference Handbook* [see entry 484]), the bibliographic sections in these volumes are neither selective nor comprehensive, but they can be useful for beginning research, especially term papers.

338 Nuclear Power Plants Worldwide

Edited by Peter D. Dresser. 1st ed. Gale Research, 1993. Triennial. 556p. $129.00 (hardcover).

Diskette: Available from Gale Research.

Nuclear Power Plants Worldwide is a nontechnical guide to every commercial nuclear plant in thirty-nine countries. In addition to those plants currently operating, this directory also covers those that are planned, on order, under construction, canceled, indefinitely deferred, shut down, or decommissioned. Chapters are organized by country; each begins with a section describing the history and status of the country's nuclear program, including a chart that shows the country's power mix. Each plant profile is extremely detailed, providing complete contact information; basic facts for each reactor (e.g., status, megawatts, reactor system supplier); key dates; annual operating costs; and lengthy descriptions of the plant's history, including accidents and fines. Bibliographies follow each entry. Supple-

mentary sections add significantly to this reference book: they include a short essay on how a nuclear plant works; nine maps; a glossary; an index; charts that show Nuclear Regulatory Commission report cards for select U.S. plants; and a unique technical problems index, where users can see, for example, a list of all plants that have had major releases of radioactive steam from their generator tubes.

339 Renewable Energy: A Concise Guide to Energy Alternatives

Jennifer Carless. Walker & Company, 1993. 168p. $19.95 (hardcover).

340 Renewable Energy: Sources for Fuels and Electricity

Edited by Laurie Burnham, Thomas B. Johansson, Henry Kelley, Amulya K. N. Reddy, and Robert H. Williams. Sponsored by the United Nations. Island Press, 1992. 1,160p. $85.00 (hardcover), $45.00 (paper).

Both *Renewable Energy: A Concise Guide to Energy Alternatives* and *Renewable Energy: Sources for Fuels and Electricity* cover all aspects of renewable-energy technologies, including history, current applications, economic constraints, environmental impacts, and future of all technologies, from alternative fuels to wave power. *Sources for Fuels and Electricity*, commissioned by the United Nations Solar Energy Group for Environment and Development in support of the 1992 UNCED (United Nations Conference on Environment and Development) in Rio, is the definitive text in the field. Written by more than sixty scientists, it is far more detailed, more sophisticated in its analysis, and has more tables, charts, and maps than the *Concise Guide*, which is a primer. The *Concise Guide*'s quick-reference format makes it easy for all audiences to understand the status of the technologies presented.

Two other primers on renewable-energy technologies are also highly recommended for all audiences: *The Almanac of Renewable Energy* (Richard Golob and Eric Brus. Henry Holt and Company, 1993. 348p. $50), which includes a lengthy appendix of more than fifty tables, and *Cool Energy: Renewable Energy Solutions to Environmental Problems* (Michael Brower.

MIT Press, 1992. 219p. $12.95), which reads more like a policy report.

341 Sustainable Energy Budget for the U.S. Department of Energy: Fiscal Year 1995

2nd ed. Sustainable Energy Budget Coalition, 1993. Annual. 76p. $10.00 (paper).

Sustainable Energy Budget for the U.S. Department of Energy: Fiscal Year 1995 provides specific budget recommendations—and the reasoning behind them—for federal renewable-energy, energy-efficiency, nuclear energy, and fossil fuel programs. The report was written jointly by key advocates from environmental organizations and endorsed by some one hundred public-interest organizations. Each section provides contact information for individuals who can provide more information. The work is not a comprehensive budget for the Department of Energy; weapons, environmental restoration, and portions of the energy research programs are not included. Compared to Fiscal Year 1994 actual spending, the report recommends increases of $800 million in energy-efficiency and renewable-energy programs to achieve a budget of almost $1.8 billion, and decreases of more than $1.2 billion for nuclear power and fossil fuel programs to achieve a budget of almost $900 million. These recommendations would not only redirect priorities, but also provide a net savings of over $400 million in Fiscal Year 1995. The report is available from the SUN DAY Campaign (see entry 326), which is the coordinating organization of the Sustainable Energy Budget Coalition, a coalition of thirty environmental organizations, businesses, utilities, and state governments; it is also available from the other members of the coalition, including most environmental organizations that specialize in energy issues. This second edition updates and combines two November 1992 publications: *A Sustainable Energy Budget* and *A Sustainable Energy Blueprint*; future annual updates are planned. This is an interesting and important document produced by leading advocates for sustainable energy.

Other Reference Handbooks

- ◆ The *Consumer Guide to Home Energy Savings* (see entry 514)

- ◆ The *Consumer Guide to Solar Energy: Easy and Inexpensive Applications for Solar Energy* (see entry 515)
- ◆ The *Energy-Efficient Home* (see entry 514, *Consumer Guide to Home Energy Savings*)
- ◆ The *Independent Home: Living Well with Power from the Sun, Wind and Water* (see entry 504, Real Goods Trading Company)
- ◆ The *Solar 1 CD-ROM* (see entry 526, *Home Power*)
- ◆ *Wind Power for Home and Business: Renewable Energy for the 1990s and Beyond* (see entry 516)

Introductory Reading

342 Energy Efficiency and Human Activity: Past Trends, Future Prospects

Lee Shipper and Stephen Meyers, with Richard Howarth and Ruth Steiner. Sponsored by the Stockholm Environment Institute. Cambridge University Press, 1992. 385p. $49.95 (hardcover).

Energy Efficiency and Human Activity sets forth a unique, empirical analysis of energy efficiency. These authors, colleagues at Lawrence Berkeley Laboratories, avoid sweeping generalizations and pay particular attention to how energy use is linked to what people do and how they do it. In examining changes in world energy use over the past twenty years, the authors take an in-depth look at specific developments in the manufacturing, transportation, residential, and service sectors, and the demographic, social, and other trends that caused them. They then project future scenarios in each sector within three country groups: industrialized, former East Bloc, and developing. The book's last chapters provide a realistic and comprehensive overview of future policy options, stressing the importance of the full range of factors that shape energy efficiency. An appendix provides information on data sources for industrialized countries.

343 The Energy-Environment Connection

Edited by Jack M. Hollander. Island Press, 1992. 414p. $48.00 (hardcover), $25.00 (paper).

The Energy-Environment Connection is a collection of essays by leading scientists and policy analysts on the environmental impacts of energy use and other relationships between energy and the environment. The book's largest section, Part I, contains chapters that discuss the impacts of fossil fuels—e.g., air pollution, acid rain, global climate change, oil spills. There are also chapters on the impacts of nuclear power and biomass energy. Chapters in other parts discuss the benefits of energy efficiency in buildings, transportation, and manufacturing; ethical issues; and a vision of a sustainable-energy future. This is a good place to begin reading about environmental issues related to energy derived from conventional sources.

Two other significant titles appropriate for a general audience provide more detailed coverage on the environmental impacts of energy use: *Energy and the Environment in the 21st Century* (Jefferson W. Tester, David O. Wood, and Nancy A. Ferrari. MIT Press, 1991. 1,006p. $60), a collection of more than eighty papers presented at a 1990 conference, and *Energy Technologies and the Environment: Environment Information Handbook* (Department of Energy, Office of Environmental Analysis, 1988. 461p).

Abstracts and Indices

344   Alternative Energy Digests

Environmental Studies Institute of the International Academy at Santa Barbara, 1990–. Monthly.

Database Vendor: Available as part of the *PTS Newsletter Database* on DIALOG, and as *Alternative Energy Digests* on LEXIS/NEXIS.

Alternative Energy Digests summarizes recent literature on all sustainable-energy issues, including policy and technological advances. The abstracts—in both print and electronic versions—summarize articles appearing in popular and technical periodicals, news releases, government reports, books, and other published material. This abstract also contains announcements of reference books, computer software, videos, electronic information sources, and other items of interest. Though brief, these abstracts offer a good way to stay on top of the field. *Digests'* pub-

lisher, the Environmental Studies Institute at the International Academy at Santa Barbara, also publishes *Energy Review*, which combines information found in both *Alternative Energy Digests* and its sister publication, *Waste Information Digests* (see entry 452); *Energy Review* is also available in both a print version and an electronic online version, on DIALOG and LEXIS/NEXIS.

345   Energy Research Abstracts

Department of Energy, Office of Science and Technology Information, 1974–; distributed by the Government Printing Office. Biweekly.

CD-ROM: Available as *Energy Science and Technology* from DIALOG.

Database Vendor: Available as *Energy Science and Technology* on DIALOG.

Internet: Portions are available on the Department of Energy's (DOE) Energy Efficiency and Renewable Energy Network (see entry 327). Choose *Energy Information Resources*, then *Alphabetical Listing of All Sites*, then *Energy Science and Technology Database (EDB)*.

Energy Research Abstracts abstracts the scientific and technical literature produced by Department of Energy (DOE) research and development projects as well as selected worldwide research literature on subjects of interest to DOE. It contains citations to and abstracts of research results, journal articles, conference papers, books, and patent information. Roughly 7,000 new entries are added biweekly, half of which come from non-American sources. More than 300,000 of the 2.75 million records pertain to renewable-energy sources or energy conservation; some of these records are searchable on DOE's Energy Efficiency and Renewable Energy Network (see entry 327) on the Internet. Online, the abstract is known as the *Energy Science and Technology* database. Abstracts taken from *Energy Science and Technology* are published biweekly in seventeen separate periodicals in the Current Awareness series, including *Buildings Energy Technology, Geothermal Energy, Industrial Energy Technology, Photovoltaic Energy, Solar Thermal Energy Technology, Transportation Energy Research*, and *Wind Energy Technology*; these Current Awareness serials are sold through the National Technical Information Service (see entry 8). They are available free to DOE employees and contractors from the Office of Scientific and Technical Information (615/576-8401), which also distributes a free user's guide to the *Energy Science and Technology* database.

346 Synerjy: A Directory of Renewable Energy

Synerjy, 1974–. Semiannual. 52p. $20.00/year for individuals, $45.00/year for institutions (paper).

Diskette: Available from Synerjy.

Synerjy is an excellent source of citations to literature on alternatives to fossil fuels and nuclear energy. Sections (solar energy, biomass fuels, hydrogen fuels, geothermal energy, water power, wind power, electric energy utilization, energy transfer and storage) are divided by type of information source (books, patents, government publications, periodical articles). The largest categories, government publications and periodical articles, are further divided by subtopics such as fuel cells and refuse-driven fuels. Publication entries include date, title, page numbers or number of pages, report number, and price. Each section also includes manufacturers, current research, and facilities; these entries include an address and a few words describing the product sold, area of research, or nature of the facility. In addition, there is a comprehensive bibliographic list of periodicals that frequently contain renewable-energy articles and announcements of upcoming conferences. The Summer/Fall issue is cumulative for one year. *Synerjy* is a low-cost alternative to commercial online databases. Its publisher also offers inexpensive directories of renewable-energy product manufacturers and distributors: solar, biomass, and small-scale electric. All Synerjy directories are available on IBM-compatible diskettes.

Other Abstracts and Indices

- ◆ *Environment Abstracts* (see entry 155)

Periodicals

347 The Nuclear Monitor

Nuclear Information and Resource Service, 1985–. Bimonthly, except in July and August when the *Monitor* is published monthly. 8p. $35.00/year for environmental activists, $50.00/year for public libraries, $250.00/year for businesses and associations.

Bulletin Board: Articles in *The Nuclear Monitor* can be downloaded from NirsNet, a bulletin board of the Nuclear Information and Resource Service (NIRS) (see entry 323). From the main menu, choose *File System*, then *List Files*, then *Nuclear Monitor*.

An indispensable newsletter for antinuclear activists, *The Nuclear Monitor* covers Capitol Hill, the Nuclear Regulatory Commission and other executive branch agencies, and legislative and activist developments at the state and local levels. Each issue contains several news shorts and two or three longer articles. Representative articles include "OTA Slams Breeder Reactor Program; Key Votes Expected Soon; Is DOE Backtracking Again?" and "Proposed Decommissioning Rule Would Allow Partial Clean-up." Consult this newsletter for current nuclear regulatory watchdog information.

348 Solar Industry Journal

Solar Energy Industries Association, 1989–. Quarterly. 65p. $25.00/year.

349 Solar Today

American Solar Energy Society, 1987–. Bimonthly. 54p. $29.00/year.

Solar Industry Journal and *Solar Today* are extremely similar magazines that all audiences can read to keep abreast of the solar energy field. Both provide industry news, new product announcements, advertisements, research updates, a calendar of events, and news of their respective associations and their regional chapters. Feature articles in both review pending policies and legislation, profile facilities, examine current technologies, and report on trends in solar and related fields. Representative articles include "New Technology Developments from

Solar Hydrogen," "Using Solar Energy at the Sacramento Municipal Utility District," "Energy Policies for a Clean and Prosperous Future," and "The Value of Distributed PV Systems in Today's Electric Utilities." The slight difference in coverage in the two magazines reflects the nature of the associations that publish them: *Solar Industry Journal* is published by a trade association (see entry 325, Solar Energy Industries Association); *Solar Today* is published by a professional association (see entry 319, American Solar Energy Society). Reading both magazines regularly is a good way to stay on top of solar energy news.

Other Periodicals

◆ *Alternative Energy Network Online Today* (see entry 172, Environmental Information Networks)

◆ *Energy, Economics and Climate Change* (see entry 262)

◆ *Energy Ideas* (see entry 322, Critical Mass Energy Project)

◆ *Home Energy Magazine* (see entry 525)

◆ *Home Power* (see entry 526)

◆ The *Sustainable Energy Resources Newsletter* (see entry 326, SUN DAY Campaign)

CHAPTER SIX

Environmental Justice

What This Chapter Covers

This chapter covers environmental discrimination issues based on race or class, such as the disproportionate siting of hazardous waste sites in African-American communities, the disproportionate lead exposure in low-income urban areas, and the effects of pesticides on Latino farm workers.

For More Information

◆ See **General** for resources on all environmental issues, including those related to environmental justice.
◆ See **Health and Toxics** and **Waste** for resources on environmental justice advocates.

Government Clearinghouses

350 **Environmental Justice Hotline**
Environmental Protection Agency
401 M Street, SW, Mail Code 3103
Washington, DC 20460

Phone: 800/962-6215. Fax: 202/260-0852

The Environmental Justice Hotline was established to receive calls from people of color and/or from low-income populations who are treated unfairly under environmental laws. The hotline distributes documents free of charge and can make referrals to other federal agencies. Among the documents the hotline distributes are summaries of the initiatives of the Environmental Protection Agency's (EPA) Office of Environmental Justice; relevant copies of legislation and executive orders; EPA reports *(Environmental Equity: Reducing Risk For All Communities)*, and photocopies of articles. Request the bibliography, which lists items available from the hotline and describes important nongovernmental sources of information on environmental justice.

Organizations

For descriptions of additional environmental justice organizations, consult the *People of Color Environmental Groups* (see entry 353) directory.

351 **Commission for Racial Justice**
United Church of Christ
475 Riverside Drive, Room 1950
New York, NY 10115

Phone: 212/870-2077. Fax: 212/870-2162

Charles Lee, Research Director

The Commission for Racial Justice is an organizational leader in the fight for environmental justice. Charles Lee, research director of the United Church of Christ's Commission for Racial Justice, authored a landmark study in the field, *Toxic Wastes and Race in the United States: A National Report on the Racial and Socio-Economic Characteristics of Communities with Hazardous Waste Sites*, in 1987. He also coordinated the First National People of Color Environmental Leadership Summit, a watershed event in the environ-

mental justice movement. Both *Toxic Wastes and Race in the United States* ($20.00) and the *Proceedings of the First National People of Color Environmental Leadership Summit* (1992. $22.50) are available directly from the Commission for Racial Justice. *Toxic Wastes and Race Revisited* (Co-sponsored by the Center for Policy Alternatives, the National Association for the Advancement of Colored People, and the United Church of Christ Commission for Racial Justice, 1994. $20.00), which updates the 1987 report, is available from the Center for Policy Alternatives. For video highlights of the First National People of Color Environmental Leadership Summit ($30.00, plus shipping and handling), contact United Church Resources at the New York office of the United Church of Christ.

Other Organizations

◆ The Alliance to End Childhood Lead Poisoning (see entry 326, National Lead Information Center)

◆ The Citizen's Clearinghouse for Hazardous Wastes (see entry 423)

◆ The Environmental Research Foundation (see entry 370)

◆ The Environmental Support Center (see entry 27)

Internet Sites

352 **The EcoJustice Network**

A project of EcoNet.

EcoNet: The EcoJustice Network maintains the *env.justice* conference.

Internet: Available on the Institute for Global Communications (see entry 57) gopher. Choose *EcoNet–Environment*, then *Environmental Racism & Environmental Justice.*

For an electronic brochure about the network, send an e-mail message to **ecojustice-info@econet.apc.org**. For technical support by phone, contact the Institute for Global Communications at 415/442-0220.

The EcoJustice Network provides a centralized Internet location for information about environmental justice issues. Network browsers will find news, descriptions of environmental justice organizations, papers and studies, summaries of books, and a calendar of events. Among the resources available from the EcoJustice Network gopher are "Fighting Environmental Racism: A Selected, Annotated Bibliography," an article from the first edition of the *Electronic Green Journal* (see entry 169); back issues of *Rachel's Environment & Health Weekly* (see entry 402); the National Institute of Environmental Health Services Internet gopher (see entry 360, Enviro-Health); and the Right-to-Know Network (RTK NET) (see entry 378), which has a specific conference on environmental justice (choose *Environmental Justice Conference* from the main RTK NET menu) and makes available many databases of interest to those working on environmental justice issues. The outstanding *People of Color Environmental Groups* (see entry 353) directory is also available. Also, the EcoJustice Network maintains the *env.justice* conference on EcoNet (see entry 58). This EcoNet conference is also available as an Internet mailing list (to subscribe, send an e-mail message to **majordomo@econet.apc.org** with the words **subscribe ecojustice** in the body of the message); archives of the list are available on the EcoJustice Network gopher.

Bulletin Boards

◆ The Right-To-Know Network (see entry 378)

Directories

353 People of Color Environmental Groups

Compiled by Robert Bullard. 2nd ed. Charles Stewart Mott Foundation, 1994. Biannual. 194p. Free (spiral bound).

EcoNet: For a searchable version, choose *Online Databases*, *Directories*, then *People of Color Environmental Groups Directory*. The full text is available in the *env.color* conference.

Internet: Available on the EcoJustice Network (see entry 352).

The *People of Color Environmental Groups* directory is the best way to learn about and get con-

tact information for environmental, civil rights, and legal groups working on environmental and economic justice issues. The 1994–1995 edition includes 306 people of color groups in the United States (e.g., the Gulf Coast Tenants Organization, the Southwest Network for Environmental and Economic Justice, the South Bronx Clean Air Coalition), 49 in Canada (e.g., Mohawks of the Bay of Quinte), and 41 in Mexico (e.g., Movimento Ecologista Mexicano). Each entry provides the organization's mission, issues covered, and activities as well as other pertinent information such as number of paid staff and volunteers, membership base, and geographic focus. This second edition also includes 91 environmental justice resource groups and 34 legal resource groups, listing resources offered (e.g., media campaigns, health surveys, report preparation), issues covered, constituency served, and best known work. The directory also includes essays on environmental justice, reprints of important documents in the field, and an extensive annotated bibliography. To order the free print version, leave a voice-mail message on the Charles Stewart Mott Foundation publications line (810/766-1766).

Bibliographies

354 Environmental Justice: Annotated Bibliography

Laura J. Fitton, John Choe, and Richard Regan. Center for Policy Alternatives, 1993. 20p. $10.00 (paper).

Environmental Justice is an extensive annotated bibliography on environmental justice issues. It is organized by type of information source: books, reports, conference proceedings, videos, directories, periodicals, recent news articles, and federal and state legislation. Each resource has a one- to three-sentence annotation. The Center for Policy Alternatives (see entry 15) released the first addendum to the bibliography in August 1994; regular addendums are expected. There are several less extensive environmental justice bibliographies available.

Two notable bibliographies on environmental justice, which appeared as articles in the first edition of the *Electronic Green Journal* (see entry 169), are available free of charge on the Internet: *Environmental Equity: Broadening the Scope of*

Environmental Collections and *Fighting Environmental Racism: A Selected Annotated Bibliography*. The Environmental Protection Agency's Environmental Justice Hotline (see entry 350) also offers a free bibliography, which is available only in hard copy.

In addition, many books on the topic of environmental justice (e.g., *Toxic Struggles: The Theory and Practice of Environmental Justice* [see entry 357], *Confronting Environmental Racism: Voices from the Grassroots* [see entry 355]) summarize major literature and provide extensive bibliographies.

Other Bibliographies

◆ The Environmental Justice Hotline (see entry 350) offers a free bibliography

Introductory Reading

355 Confronting Environmental Racism: Voices from the Grassroots

Edited by Robert Bullard. South End Press, 1993. 259p. $40.00 (hardcover), $16.00 (paper).

356 Race and the Incidence of Environmental Hazards: A Time for Discourse

Edited by Bunyan Bryant and Paul Mohai. Westview Press, 1992. 251p. $33.00 (paper).

357 Toxic Struggles: The Theory and Practice of Environmental Justice

Edited by Richard Hofrichter. New Society Publishers, 1993. 206p. $16.95 (paper).

358 Unequal Protection: Environmental Justice and Communities of Color

Edited by Robert Bullard. Sierra Club Books, 1994; distributed by Random House. 400p. $25.00 (hardcover).

Each of these four collections of essays provides a good introduction to environmental justice issues. A wide range of topics—e.g., waste facility siting, childhood lead poisoning, migrant farmworker pesticide exposure—are covered in each book by a wide variety of authors: academ-ics, journalists, and activists. All four books are extremely similar in tone, providing a mix of academic essays, case studies, and personal statements. Introductions and conclusions weave themes together, making each work an excellent primer on the issues. In addition, through their content and bibliographic information, they also serve as guides to primary literature in the field, such as *Dumping in Dixie: Race, Class, and Environmental Quality* (Robert Bullard. Westview Press, 1990) and *Toxic Wastes and Race in the United States* (United Church of Christ, 1987).

Periodicals

359 Race, Poverty, and the Environment

A joint project of the California Rural Legal Assistance Foundation and the Earth Island Institute Urban Habitat Program, 1990. Quarterly. 48p. Free for low-income persons and community groups; $15.00/year for individuals; $30.00/year for institutions.

Race, Poverty, and the Environment is an excellent newsletter on environmental justice issues. Articles are written by leaders in the movement and are appropriate for grassroots organizers and activists, policymakers, environmental professionals, and concerned citizens. Each issue includes many one- to three-page analytical articles as well as news from local groups around the country, a directory of organizations, and a bibliography of published material. Past issues have featured articles on Latinos and the environment; urban habitats; and population and immigration. (Send submissions and subscription checks to RPE c/o Earth Island Institute [see entry 19]).

For lawyers interested in environmental justice issues, the California Rural Legal Assistance Foundation's Center for Race, Poverty and the Environment publishes the *Environmental Poverty Law Working Group* newsletter.

Other Periodicals

◆ *Rachel's Environment & Health Weekly* (see entry 402)
◆ *Everyone's Backyard* (see entry 423, Citizen's Clearinghouse for Hazardous Wastes)

CHAPTER SEVEN

Health and Toxics

What This Chapter Covers

This chapter covers all aspects of toxic substances, such as lead, asbestos, and chemicals, with particular focus on their health effects. The resources in this chapter can help you determine if toxic substances threaten your community, and can help direct you to medical, legal, and technical assistance. This chapter also covers multiple chemical sensitivities as well as other environmental health threats like radon and electromagnetic fields.

For More Information

◆ See **General** for resources on all environmental issues, including those related to environmental health and toxic substances.

◆ See **Agriculture** for resources on pesticides and food safety.

◆ See **Waste** for resources on hazardous waste.

◆ See **Architecture** and **Shopping** for resources on the impact of toxics in the home and living without toxics.

Government Clearinghouses

360 Enviro-Health

National Institute of Environmental Health Sciences (NIEHS)
100 Capitola Drive, Suite 108
Durham, NC 27713

Phone: 800/643-4794. Fax: 919/361-9408

Internet: To access the NIEHS site, gopher to **gopher.niehs.nih.gov**; or, on the World Wide Web, the URL is **http://www.niehs.nih.gov/**.

Sponsored by the National Institute of Environmental Health Sciences (NIEHS), the toll-free Enviro-Health hotline answers questions from the public—concerned citizens, environmental justice groups, grassroots environmental organizations, educators, students, and journalists—about environmental health. The mission of NIEHS, a branch of the National Institutes of Health, is to reduce the burden of human illness and dysfunction from environmental exposure, and to understand how environmental factors interrelate with individual susceptibility and age to contribute to human health and human disease. Enviro-Health answers questions on all environmental health issues, including pesticide exposure, estrogenic chemicals in the environment, and electromagnetic fields, as well as questions about worker exposure to chemicals and chemical spills, hazardous waste sites, and environmental justice issues. Information specialists can provide NIEHS fact sheets (*Toxicity of Lead in Children*) and pamphlets (*Medicine for the Layman: Environment and Disease*), make referrals to other clearinghouses and information sources, and search online databases to answer callers' questions. The NIEHS site on the Internet is a good place to look for environmental health information. In addition to information about NIEHS, users can find abstracts of National Toxicology Program reports on toxic substances and selected articles from *Environmental Health Perspectives*, the monthly NIEHS journal. The site also provides access to the NIEHS library card catalog and to related places of interest on the Internet.

361 National Institute for Occupational Safety and Health (NIOSH)

Department of Health and Human Services
Centers for Disease Control
4676 Columbia Parkway
Cincinnati, OH 45226

Phone: 800/356-4674. Fax: 513/533-8573

The National Institute for Occupational Safety and Health (NIOSH) hotline provides callers with free information on every topic related to the health consequences of hazards in the workplace. Cited hazards include noise pollution, video display terminals, chemicals, indoor air quality, and "sick building syndrome." The NIOSH hotline's phone routing system enables calling workers and health professionals to select from a variety of options, including an automated service that sends information on occupational health and safety topics recently in the news. Callers can also choose to speak with information specialists. These experts refer technical questions to the appropriate NIOSH office or search NIOSH's *Registry of Toxic Effects of Chemical Substances* (see entry 387) database of chemical information and the *NIOSHTIC* occupational safety and health literature database; they can also send callers recent journal articles and NIOSH publications. To find out more about NIOSH publications and databases, press "1" once the phone routing system has been accessed, or contact the NIOSH Publications Office directly by phone at 513/533-8287 or by electronic mail at **pubstaft@niosdt1.em.cdc.gov**.

362 National Lead Information Center

Environmental Protection Agency
c/o National Safety Council
1019 19th Street, NW, Suite 401
Washington, DC 20036

Phone (hotline): 800/532-3394.
Phone (clearinghouse): 800/424-5323.
Fax: 202/659-1192.
E-mail: ehc@cais.com

Janet Phoenix, Manager, National Lead Information Center

The National Lead Information Center offers two separate services that provide general and detailed information on lead poisoning and prevention. The first service, an automated hotline, sends a basic information packet that includes the Environmental Protection Agency (EPA) brochure *Lead Poisoning And Your Children*; three fact sheets; and a two-page list of contacts in each state. For health professionals and callers who want more substantive information than the hotline can provide, the second service, the National Lead Information Center Clearinghouse, distributes documents from the EPA, the Centers for Disease Control, and the Department of Housing and Urban Development—the government agencies that provide funding for the center. Clearinghouse information specialists can also supply regulatory and policy information and can provide referrals to other sources.

For more detailed information on state lead contacts, use the *State Lead Poisoning Prevention Directory* (see entry 379). The Alliance to End Childhood Lead Poisoning (202/543–1147), an independent public-interest organization, also distributes a free lead-information packet. For emergency assistance, call your local poison control center.

363 National Radon Hotline
Environmental Protection Agency
c/o National Safety Council
1019 19th Street, NW
Washington, DC 20036

Phone: 800/767-7236

Funded by the Environmental Protection Agency (EPA) and operated by the National Safety Council, the National Radon Hotline is the first point of contact for consumers concerned about radon. A computer answering system takes callers' addresses and sends the EPA brochure *Reducing Radon Risks* and an order form for a $9.95 radon test kit. The brochure briefly describes why all homeowners should test for radon; outlines the differences between short- and long-term testing; and responds to common myths about radon. Homeowners who still have questions can call 800/557-2366 to speak with an employee of the National Safety Council; however, state radon offices are generally the best point of contact for detailed questions; their phone numbers are listed in *Reducing Radon Risks* and are also available from the Indoor Air Quality Information Clearinghouse (see entry 232). For a more comprehensive introduction to radon exposure, including how it enters buildings, the pros and

cons of various types of tests, and recommendations for reducing high radon levels, read *Radon: The Invisible Threat: What It Is, Where It Is, How to Keep Your House Safe* (Michael Lafavore. Rodale Press, 1987. Out of print, but available in public libraries), or *Radon: A Homeowner's Guide to Detection and Control* (Consumer Reports, 1987).

364 Toxic Substances Control Act Assistance Information Service (TSCA Hotline)
Environmental Protection Agency
401 M Street, SW, Mail Code 7408
Washington, DC 20460

Phone: 202/554-1404. TDD: 202/554-0551. Fax: 202/554-5603

The Toxic Substances Control Act Assistance Information Service (TSCA Hotline) is the best place to call for information on federal regulations concerning toxic substances. Technical as well as general information is available to everyone—consumers, managers, lawyers, or teachers. In addition to detailed regulatory information, the hotline maintains lists of laboratories that test samples for toxic substances; refers technical information requests to the appropriate Environmental Protection Agency (EPA) office; and provides information on chemicals commonly found in the home—ammonia, formaldehyde, PCBs, etc. The *Chemicals-in-Progress Bulletin* is an outstanding source of up-to-date information on the regulatory activities of the EPA's Office of Toxic Substances. Other free publications available from the hotline include *The Layman's Guide to TSCA*; *Summary of Regulations Under TSCA*; *A Guide for Chemical Importers and Exporters*; *Citizens Petition Guidelines*, as well as numerous asbestos publications, including *Environmental Hazards in Your School: A Resource Handbook* and *Asbestos Fact Book*. This hotline is an excellent first point of contact for any question regarding the Toxic Substances Control Act (TSCA) or EPA toxicological and asbestos programs.

Contact the TSCA Non-Confidential Information Center (202/260–7099) for docket information—*Federal Register* notices, proposed rules, and section 5, 8(d), and 8(e) filings.

For personalized attention on asbestos issues, call the Small Business Ombudsman Hotline (see entry 9).

365 Toxicology Information Response Center (TIRC)
Department of Energy
Oak Ridge National Laboratory
1060 Commerce Park
Oak Ridge, TN 37830

Phone: 615/576-1746. Fax: 615/574-9888

Kim Slusher, Executive Director

The Toxicology Information Response Center (TIRC) serves as the national and international clearinghouse for the collection, analysis, and dissemination of information on all chemical substances: food additives, industrial chemicals, heavy metals, pesticides, etc. Members of the general public, environmental groups, lawyers, doctors, researchers, and scientists all have unrestricted access to TIRC's unparalleled research services. Since these services are subsidized by government funding, they are provided at cost. The staff has access to more than three hundred computerized databases, including the National Library of Medicine's TOXNET (see entry 375) information system, which TIRC assists in maintaining. To compile comprehensive, personalized literature packages—annotated bibliographies, custom reports, topical overviews, statistical data—the multidisciplinary staff works closely with users to refine and clarify needs. Depending on the request and type of response required, turnaround time can be immediate, or it can take up to three weeks. For example, a relatively simple request for information about the toxic properties of Bromine was answered two hours later by a detailed twenty-five-page fax. Publication lists and fact sheets are also available.

Other Government Clearinghouses

◆ The RCRA/UST/EPCRA/Superfund Hotline (see entry 422)

Organizations

For additional descriptions of organizations working on environmental health issues, consult *Tackling Toxics in Everyday Products: A Directory of Organizations* (see entry 380).

366 Chemical Injury Information Network (CIIN)
P.O. Box 301
White Sulphur, MT 59645

Phone: 406/547-2255

Cynthia Wilson, Executive Director

The Chemical Injury Information Network (CIIN) is a nonprofit advocacy organization run by the chemically injured for the chemically injured. CIIN is a rapidly expanding national network that serves as a clearinghouse for toxic health issues. Staff members and volunteers have access to and are willing to share a tremendous amount of in-depth, accurate information about all aspects of chemical exposure. CIIN provides research assistance to doctors, lawyers, and chemical-exposure victims in the form of medical and government studies, reports, and articles; profiles chemicals; compiles lists of symptoms and possible chemical causes; makes referrals to experts; and provides access to computer online services like MEDLARS (see entry 375, TOXNET) and DIALOG. Most research services are fee based; contact CIIN for details. CIIN often collaborates with the Environmental Research Access Network (EARN) (701/859–6363), an activist research organization that offers comprehensive fee-based toxicological research services. In addition, CIIN offers numerous vital resource materials, including the indispensable quarterly newsletter *Our Toxic Times*, which provides network and national news updates, an EARN chemical profile, resource lists, and lots of other valuable information; a directory of multiple-chemical-sensitivity organizations and other resources; the *Non-Toxic Buying Guide*; and *Chemical Exposure and Human Health: A Reference to 314 Chemicals with a Guide to Symptoms and a Directory of Organizations* (see entry 383), written by CIIN's executive director Cynthia Wilson. Contact CIIN's national office for details on state and local network members.

367 Citizens Environmental Laboratory
1168 Commonwealth Avenue
Boston, MA 02134

Phone: 617/232-5833. Fax: 617/232-3837

Fred Youngs, Laboratory Director

The Citizens Environmental Laboratory serves as a nonprofit, full-service analytical lab for the grassroots environmental movement. The lab offers testing (drinking water, industrial emissions, landfill leachate) and provides analysis of contaminants (PCBs, pesticides) in air, soil, and water. Owned and operated by the Jobs and Environment Campaign, an outgrowth of the now-defunct National Toxics Campaign, the laboratory assists organizations in investigating the presence of contaminants, distributes sampling kits and sampling guidelines, and can be contracted to take sample tests. The lab also assists in evaluating sampling strategies, reviewing test results from other laboratories, and providing clear explanations of technical material. Contact the staff before sending samples and for lab fees (community groups and nonprofits receive considerable discounts).

368 EMF Clearinghouse

Information Ventures
1500 Locust Street, Suite 1513
Philadelphia, PA 19102

Phone: 215/732-9083. Fax: 215/732-3754.
E-mail: kleinste@eniac.seas.upenn.edu

Diskette: The *EMF Database* is available from Information Ventures.

CD-ROM: The *EMF Database* is available from Information Ventures.

Internet: EMF-Link is available on the World Wide Web. To access, the URL is **http://infoventures.com/**.

The EMF Clearinghouse abstracts research literature on the biological and health effects of electromagnetic radiation from all sources, including magnetic resonance imaging, power lines, video display terminals, and cellular phones. Abstracts are published quarterly in the *Biological Effects of Nonionizing Electromagnetic Radiation (BENER) Digest Update* ($300 per year). More than fifteen thousand abstracts of electromagnetic field (EMF) research literature published in the field since 1972 are archived and searchable on the *EMF Database* (updated quarterly, $3,500). While these products are priced beyond the reach of the general public, lay audiences may be interested in subscribing to the *EMF Health Report* ($48 per year), a bimonthly newsletter that provides information, in clear, nontechnical language, on the latest EMF research,

especially on its significance to human health. The public will also be interested in viewing Information Ventures' site on the Internet, EMF-Link. EMF-Link includes the text of many of the articles from the *EMF Health Report*; it also includes news, background information on electromagnetic fields, and some abstracts of both published research and research in progress.

Two government clearinghouses are available to members of the public seeking information about electromagnetic fields: Enviro-Health (see entry 360), which is sponsored by the National Institute for Environmental Health Sciences, and the Environmental Protection Agency–sponsored EMF Infoline (800/363–2383).

369 Environmental Health Network (EHN)

Great Bridge Station
P.O. Box 16267
Chesapeake, VA 23328

Phone: 804/424-1162. Fax: 804/424-1517

Linda Price King, Founder/Executive Director

When Linda King became a victim of toxic exposure, she felt victimized by the system that was supposed to help her. So she organized the Environmental Health Network (EHN) to offer free technical, organizing, and emotional support to individuals and communities exposed to toxic chemicals. EHN's staff helps those suffering from environmental illnesses understand how they can compile and use technical health data to force corporations and government agencies to act on their behalf. An extensive referral program taps into a screened network of medical, legal, and other professionals experienced in environmental illness cases. EHN also provides support services for attorneys in the form of case preparation, expert witnesses, and video depositions. The organization distributes several well-researched publications, including *Inconclusive By Design* ($15), an investigative report on fraudulent health studies, and *Profiles on Environmental Health* (available to EHN members only), a remarkable quarterly newsletter that covers a different toxic substance each issue—providing both scientific background and analysis and horrifying personal stories. If you are sick due to chemical exposure—or fighting for someone who is—EHN will do whatever it takes to find someone who can help.

370 Environmental Research Foundation (ERF)

P.O. Box 5036
Annapolis, MD 21403

Phone: 410/263-1584. Fax: 410/263-8944.
E-mail: erf@igc.apc.org

Peter Montague, Director

Bulletin Board: ERF maintains the Remote Access Chemical Hazards Electronic Library (RACHEL) (see entry 377).

The Environmental Research Foundation (ERF) is a reliable and trusted government and industry watchdog for grassroots environmental activists. ERF specializes in providing information about hazardous materials and technologies, especially the health effects associated with landfills, incinerators, and toxic heavy metals. The best way to take advantage of ERF's expertise is through its highly regarded newsletter—*Rachel's Environment & Health Weekly* (see entry 402)—and bulletin board system, the Remote Access Chemical Hazards Library (RACHEL) (see entry 377). Information packs and books on a variety of topics are also available; the newsletter, some of ERF's other publications, and abstracts to articles from a variety of periodicals are available free of charge on RACHEL.

371 Human Ecology Action League (HEAL)

P.O. Box 49126
Atlanta, GA 30359

Phone: 404/248-1898. Fax: 404/248-0162

Muriel Dando, President

The Human Ecology Action League (HEAL) is an outstanding source for publications related to chemical exposure prevention and to the health effects of chemicals. HEAL is primarily a support network—with many local chapters—for individuals who suffer from multiple chemical sensitivities. The organization also educates the general public about the potential dangers of chemicals and produces publications aimed at helping people adopt healthy lifestyles. These documents include fact sheets on a wide range of topics, including laundry products, selecting an attorney, and disability benefits; resource lists of nontoxic-home consultants, baby supplies, and air filters; and reports on food sensitivities, electromagnetics, dentistry, and "sick building syn-

drome," to name a few. HEAL's thirty-seven-page *Selected Bibliography on Chemicals and Health* ($28) provides citations to more than four hundred titles gleaned from widely recognized reports and journals; anyone who needs scientific or legal information on chemical sensitivity would find this publication useful. Most HEAL items cost less than five dollars; HEAL members pay half price. *The Human Ecologist*, a quarterly news digest that keeps readers up to date on environmental health happenings, is another benefit of membership.

372 National Center for Environmental Health Strategies (NCEHS)

1100 Rural Avenue
Voorhees, NJ 08043

Phone: 609/429-5358.
E-mail: wjrd37a@prodigy.com

Mary Lamielle, President and Director

The National Center for Environmental Health Strategies (NCEHS) promotes awareness of chemical sensitivity disorders and health problems caused by environmental pollutants. Except for a few volunteers, this highly effective organization is a one-woman show. Mary Lamielle's activism and dedication stem from her own bouts with chemical sensitivity. NCEHS provides support, networking, and referral services; lobbies for more protective laws and regulations; and gathers information and compiles statistics on indoor and outdoor air pollutants, pesticides, natural foods, less-toxic products, and disability resources. The organization publishes an exceptional quarterly newsletter, *The Delicate Balance* ($15), which covers the rights of those disabled by environmental pollutants, provides updates on policy and legislation, summarizes scientific research, reviews books and other resources, and supplies information on appropriate consumer products. The organization also maintains a speakers' bureau and registry of individuals who believe their health problems are related to environmental contaminants. First-time callers receive an extensive, free information packet with valuable resource lists and articles. Although NCEHS does serve as a well-informed clearinghouse on chemical sensitivity, its services are in high demand compared to the limited resources of its staff.

Two books that help chemically sensitive individuals cope on a daily basis are John Bower's *Healthy House Building* (see entry 519) and Debra Lynn Dadd's *The Nontoxic Home and Office* (see entry 614).

373 Toxics Assistance Program (TAP)
University of Texas, Division of Preventive Medicine
Department of Environmental Toxicology
2.102 Ewing Hall J-10
700 Strand Street
Galveston, TX 77555

Phone: 409/772-9110. Fax: 409/772-9108

Amanda Daniel, Coordinator

The Toxics Assistance Program (TAP) is where environmental health organizations and experts turn for guidance on toxic exposure, though calls from the general public are also encouraged. This nonprofit clearinghouse was established to ensure that people afflicted with environmental illnesses would have free professional guidance, from the first signs of trouble until the problem is resolved. Established by Marvin Legator—professor at the University of Texas and author of *Chemical Alert! A Community Action Handbook* (see entry 384)—TAP benefits from direct access to multidisciplinary expertise at the university. The program also has long-established ties to other universities, federal and state agencies, and health organizations. When callers request information or report a problem, TAP utilizes its extensive network, as well as numerous toxicological databases, to investigate industrial activity in a particular region, conduct in-depth research on chemicals, or make referrals to local government agencies and organizations. The staff is equally receptive to both quick questions about known health effects of a hazardous substance and complicated problems that may take months of research.

374 Working Group on Community Right-To-Know
218 Pennsylvania Avenue, SE
Washington, DC 20003

Phone: 202/546-9707. Fax: 202/546-2461

Paul Orum, Coordinator

Bulletin Board: The Working Group on Community Right-To-Know's newsletter, *Working Notes*, is posted on the Right-to-Know Network (RTK NET) (see entry 378). Choose *Newsletters*, then *Working Notes on Community Right-to-Know*.

The Working Group on Community Right-To-Know coordinates the community Right-to-Know activities of twenty national environmental and public-interest organizations and serves as a technical and nontechnical information clearinghouse for hundreds of activist groups. (The term Right-to-Know refers to reporting releases of toxic chemicals.) As a watchdog organization, the working group also monitors the industrial use and release of toxic chemicals, as well as the results of other federal reporting requirements. The staff can supply individuals with information regarding federal and state Right-to-Know laws and requirements. Referrals to experts, local organizations, and other sources of information are supplied when requests exceed the group's resource limits. *Working Notes*, a free newsletter available in print form and electronically on the Right-to-Know Network (RTK NET) (see entry 378), keeps readers up to date on all Right-to-Know activities. Numerous information packs are also available for 5¢ a page, including *What is the Emergency Planning and Community Right-To-Know Act (EPCRA)?*; *Chemical Accidents and Communities*; and *Citizen Suits Under EPCRA*.

Other Organizations

- The Citizen's Clearinghouse for Hazardous Wastes (see entry 423)
- Clean Water Action (see entry 465)

Internet Sites

- Extension Toxicology Network (see entry 196)

Commercial Online Services

375 TOXNET (Toxicology Data Network)

National Library of Medicine
Specialized Information Services Division
8600 Rockville Pike
Bethesda, MD 20894

Phone: 301/496-1131; 301/496-6531

Database Vendor: Contact the National Library of Medicine's Specialized Information Services Division for details on connecting to TOXNET.

TOXNET serves as the premier access point to online databases in the fields of environmental science and occupational health and safety, particularly toxicology. TOXNET is part of the National Library of Medicine's MEDLARS data network; TOXNET users have access to the bibliographic databases on MEDLARS, including CANCERLIT, MEDLINE, POPLINE, and TOXLINE (see entry 399). TOXNET is a collection of more than ten—primarily nonbibliographic—databases (e.g., *Registry of Toxic Effects of Chemical Substances* [see entry 387]; *Hazardous Substances Data Bank* [see entry 386]; *Chemical Carcinogenesis Research Information Center*; *Integrated Risk Information System*; *Developmental and Reproductive Toxicology*; *Toxic Release Inventory* [see entry 381]), which together provide comprehensive information on chemicals, including emergency handling procedures, human exposure, environmental fate, regulator and reporting requirements, and carcinogenicity. TOXNET's usefulness is not limited to a medical and scientific clientele; activists, environmental organizations, and those in the fields of political science, public administration, and business will also find the databases relevant and useful. Request a complete information packet for details on accessing the network, search-software options, and comprehensive descriptions of each database available on MEDLARS—including those on TOXNET. For those who do not want to search the databases themselves, an affiliated government program, the Toxicology Information Response Center (see entry 365), offers reasonably priced search services.

Bulletin Boards

376 Hazardous Materials Information Exchange (HMIX)

Managed by the Federal Emergency Management Agency's Preparedness Division and the Department of Transportation's Office of Hazardous Materials Initiatives & Training.

Bulletin Board: To connect to HMIX by modem, dial 708/972-3275. For technical support by phone, call the HMIX help line at 800/367-9592 from Illinois or 800/752-6367 from anywhere else.

The Hazardous Materials Information Exchange (HMIX) is an essential tool for public and private emergency response and contingency planning personnel. This bulletin board system contains information on training, resources, technical assistance, and regulations. Those not directly involved in these professions may also find this system valuable and easy to use. In addition to the numerous technical conferences that provide a forum for questions and answers, there are many downloadable files that have broad appeal. These include lists of government and commercial online databases and bulletin board systems; referrals to professional coalitions, federal agencies, research centers, and environmental organizations; abstracts of major laws and regulations; extensive lists of educational resources, newsletters, and journals; and specialized bibliographies. Those without a computer or who need assistance can call HMIX's toll-free help line.

377 Remote Access Chemical Hazards Electronic Library (RACHEL)

Maintained by the Environmental Research Foundation.

Bulletin Board: To connect to RACHEL by modem, dial 410/263-8903. For technical support by phone, call the Environmental Research Foundation at 410/263-1584.

The Remote Access Chemical Hazards Electronic Library (RACHEL) is an outstanding storehouse of information—produced by and for activists—about a wide range of problems associated with hazardous materials. The nine separate databases are easy to use; sophisticated searchers can use the full range of boolean commands. Abstracts of thousands of environmentally relevant articles—from many popular and technical sources—can be quickly searched in the largest and most unique part of the system. Users can also enter the name of a particular chemical and get toxic profiles from Coast Guard fact sheets and *New Jersey Department of Health Fact Sheets* (see entry 389). Other RACHEL databases contain information on specific waste-handling companies, incinerators and landfills, civil dockets of corporate Environmental Protection Agency violations, and general reference information about toxics and the environment. *Rachel's Environment & Health Weekly* (see entry 402) is also available. The staffers at the Environmental Research Foundation, which maintains RACHEL, can help users develop search strategies.

378 Right-To-Know Network (RTK NET)

A joint project of the Unison Institute and OMB Watch.

Bulletin Board: To connect to RTK NET by modem at 9600 baud, dial 202/234-3505. To connect at 2400 baud, dial 202/234-8570. For technical support by phone, call 202/234-8494.

Internet: To access, telnet to **rtknet.org** and type **public** at the user-ID.

The Right-To-Know Network (RTK NET) provides free access to the most important federal toxic pollution information. RTK NET was started in 1989 to support the Emergency Planning and Community Right-to-Know Act (EPCRA), which mandated a publicly accessible online database of toxic emissions data. With little training, users—including activists, students, researchers, members of the media, government officials, and industry representatives—can easily develop toxicity profiles of a specific community, company, or geographic region using the *Toxic Release Inventory* (see entry 381) data file. In addition, users can uncover health facts about chemicals, using the *New Jersey Department of Health Fact Sheets* (see entry 389); gather corporate water permit compliance information (PCS); and look up Superfund related information (CERCLIS and the National Priorities List), as well as investigate regulatory reporting require-

ments, census data, and civil law suits brought on behalf of the Environmental Protection Agency (EPA) using other EPA databases. The Facilities Index System is also available and lets users know which EPA databases contain information about a specific facility that has released toxic substances. RTK NET also provides full-text search capabilities of important documents and articles, including notices of meetings, government regulations, special reports, and policy position papers, and offers guidance on using the Freedom of Information Act. Users can also exchange electronic mail and participate in electronic conferences on health and environmental justice issues. RTK NET provides an extraordinary forum for receiving practical answers to difficult questions concerning the release and health effects of toxic substances. RTK NET staff members provide in-person and online database training and can prepare and run complex searches upon request.

Directories

379 State Lead Poisoning Prevention Directory

3rd ed. National Conference of State Legislatures, 1994. Annual. 95p. $12.00 (paper).

Heightened concern about lead poisoning has led to increased activity and diversification of responsibility within state governments, making it more difficult to reach the correct expert. For both professionals and laypeople, the *State Lead Poisoning Prevention Directory* simplifies this search process. Users will find government agency contacts in each state for nineteen types of lead poisoning prevention programs, including legal, medical, environmental, blood screening, inspection, and public outreach projects. Short summaries, highlighting the special activities of each program, make it easy to determine the best point of contact.

For a free, two-page list of state contacts in the area of lead poisoning, call the National Lead Information Center (see entry 362).

380 Tackling Toxics in Everyday Products: A Directory of Organizations

Nancy Lilienthal, Michele Ascione, and Adam Flint. INFORM, 1992. 179p. $19.95 (paper).

Tackling Toxics in Everyday Products allows concerned citizens, public officials, and physicians to familiarize themselves with the problems associated with everyday toxics—and then to locate contacts that focus on their particular area of concern. The first part of the directory provides an overview of the potential threats posed by toxics, focusing on the various problems caused by these chemicals, previous campaigns against them, and current status reports. The remainder of the book is a directory of 253 organizations—including consumer watchdog groups, health organizations, legal defense funds, support networks, and scientific organizations—all of which are active in the fight against toxic substances in the home and workplace. A broad range of issues and services are covered: environmental illness, indoor air pollution, pesticides, ecolabeling, testing, litigation, compensation, regulations, and much more. In addition to telephone number, address, and contact person, each entry includes a detailed self-description. The ability for the reader to use indices in several different ways—to locate an organization by its activities, the environmental and health issues on which it focuses, or chemicals in which it has expertise or concern—tremendously enhances the usefulness of the book. This directory serves as a great resource for finding local contacts for all environmental health issues.

381 Toxic Release Inventory (TRI)

Environmental Protection Agency, Office of Pollution, Prevention, and Toxics, 1987–. Annual.

For general information, referrals, searches and searching assistance, and user support for all public-access *TRI* products, contact Toxic Release Inventory User Support (TRI–US) at 202/260-1531. For *TRI* publications, contact the RCRA/UST/EPCRA/Superfund Hotline (see entry 422) at 800/535-0202.

Diskette: Available from the Government Printing Office (see entry 5) and the National Technical Information Service (see entry 8).

CD-ROM: Available from the Government Printing Office and the National Technical Information Service.

Database Vendor: Available on TOXNET (see entry 375).

Bulletin Board: Available on the Right-to-Know Network (RTK NET) (see entry 378). Choose *Databases*, then *TRI (EPA Toxic Release Inventory)*.

Internet: RTK NET (see Bulletin Board, above) is available on the Internet.

Based on the premise that citizens have a right to know about toxic chemicals in their communities, Congress enacted the Emergency Planning and Community Right-to-Know Act (EPCRA) in 1986. It mandated the creation of the *Toxic Release Inventory (TRI)*—an electronic database—to record the annual estimated release of toxic chemicals into the environment by industry. Using *TRI*, searchers can locate the offending facilities by name as well as by zip code, city, and county, and then determine the amount of each chemical released into the environment, stored on site or transported to off-site locations. Examples of typical questions TRI can answer include: Which facilities in the 10012 zip code reported releases in 1991? What chemicals have been released into the Hudson River? What chemicals did company XYZ release to the environment? The database does not include every toxic chemical of concern, nor does it cover all facilities; nevertheless, *TRI* is one of the most powerful tools environmental activists can use.

382 The Toxics Directory: References and Resources on the Health Effects of Toxic Substances

Edited by Hanafi Russel. 4th ed. California Environmental Protection Agency, Office of Environmental Health Hazard Assessment, 1993; distributed by the California Department of General Services. 144p. $9.70 (paper).

The Toxics Directory: References and Resources on the Health Effects of Toxic Substances is an invaluable resource for those searching for information on toxic substances. It is divided into six distinct sections. Section one describes organizations and programs that can provide information or assistance concerning the health effects of toxic substances. These programs range from local to national, with heavy emphasis on California-based resources. Four subsections list references, without descriptions, to both print (e.g., books, textbooks, reports, booklets, journal articles) and electronic resources. The references are not intended to be exhaustive, but rather highly selective; only the most important publications are included. Section two covers general and standard toxic resources, including chemical dictionaries, abstracting and indexing services, and environmental guides and directories; it also includes subsections that cover electronic databases and less technical, citizen-oriented literature. Section three lists resources by substances in which toxins are found (e.g. air, water, food). Section four covers specific toxic substances, such as arsenic, electromagnetic fields, and radon. Section five covers several broad topics related to toxic substances, including carcinogens, reproductive hazards, and risk assessment. The directory's final section lists information about county agencies and laboratories in California. There is a subject/title index.

The Toxics Directory is not widely available in libraries, but two older works that cover similar topics and resources are available in many public and university libraries: *Toxic and Hazardous Materials: A Sourcebook and Guide to Information Sources* (James K. Webster. Greenwood Press, 1987) and *Information Resources in Toxicology* (Philip Wexler. Elsevier Science Publishing, 1988).

Bibliographies

◆ The *Selected Bibliography on Chemicals and Health* (see entry 371, Human Ecology Action League)

Reference Handbooks

383 Chemical Exposure and Human Health: A Reference to 314 Chemicals with a Guide to Symptoms and a Directory of Organizations

Cynthia Wilson. McFarland & Company, 1993. 339p. $45.00 (hardcover).

Chemical Exposure and Human Health is an excellent quick-reference source on the health effects of toxics. It took three years and seven doctors to diagnose author Cynthia Wilson's—executive director of the Chemical Injury Information Network (see entry 366)—formaldehyde poisoning; according to Wilson, this book was written so that other victims of chemical exposure need not suffer as she did. The bulk of this book is made up of summaries of health and toxicological information (e.g., recommended exposure levels, symptoms, synergistic effects) for 314 chemicals; this information was gathered from government databases such as the *Hazardous Substances Data Bank* (see entry 386). What makes this book outstanding are the three chapters that cross-reference the chemicals. By using these chapters, doctors and victims of exposure can identify the active chemicals based on symptoms, diseases, and health condition (e.g., kidney tissue death, nightmares, spontaneous abortion); primary targets for chemically induced damage (e.g., blood, lungs, teeth); or source of chemical exposure (e.g., acrylics, fax machines, sewage out-gassing). The annotated directory of organizations (e.g., Yavapai Association for the Chemically Sensitive, the Des Moines Allergy Support Group) is extremely comprehensive.

384 Chemical Alert! A Community Action Handbook

Edited by Marvin S. Legator and Sabrina F. Strawn. University of Texas Press, 1993. 256p. $35.00 (hardcover), $14.95 (paper).

385 Fighting Toxics: A Manual for Protecting Your Family, Community, and Workplace

Gary Cohen and John O'Connor. Island Press, 1990. 360p. $35.00 (hardcover), $19.95 (paper).

Both *Chemical Alert!* and *Fighting Toxics* are instructional manuals targeted toward concerned citizens wishing to get involved in their own community's fight against toxic pollution. *Chemical Alert!* offers a detailed step-by-step guide that can be used to determine if local health risks exist. Environmental, medical, and legal professionals instruct communities in investigative techniques and in working with local professionals to produce valid, scientific case studies of environmental hazards in their own neighborhoods. Dozens of communities have successfully utilized these techniques, and now readers can contact the Toxics Assistance Program (see entry 373)—founded by *Chemical Alert!* author Marvin Legator—for technical support. *Fighting Toxics* picks up where *Chemical Alert!* leaves off, focusing on actions communities can take once they determine a problem exists. *Fighting Toxics* is a more traditional activist handbook, serving as a detailed blueprint on organizing neighborhoods, influencing corporations, getting helpful information, and mounting media campaigns. *Fighting Toxics* also includes a comprehensive guide to using the law to win local toxics campaigns: when you need a lawyer, when you should sue, and other legal aspects of running an environmental campaign. Both works conclude with extensive and helpful resource guides to related materials.

Those needing further information on communities and toxics should see *Toxic Nation: The Fight to Save Our Communities from Chemical Contamination* (see entry 392) for case studies of polluted communities. For additional practical information on monitoring toxic pollution, including tips for using the *Toxics Release Inventory* (see entry 381), see *Preventing Industrial Toxic Hazards: A Guide for Communities* (see entry 445).

386 Hazardous Substances Data Bank (HSDB)

Electronic document. Agency for Toxic Substances and Disease Registry, 1972–. Quarterly.

CD-ROM: Available as part of *CHEM-BANK* from SilverPlatter.

Database Vendor: Available on TOXNET (see entry 375).

387 Registry of Toxic Effects of Chemical Substances (RTECS)

Electronic document. National Institute for Occupational Safety and Health, 1971–. Quarterly.

CD-ROM: Available as part of *CHEM-BANK* from SilverPlatter.

Database Vendor: Available on Chemical Information Systems, DIALOG, and TOXNET (see entry 375).

Both the *Hazardous Substances Data Bank (HSDB)* and the *Registry of Toxic Effects of Chemical Substances (RTECS)* are authoritative, factual, peer-reviewed electronic databases that cover thousands of chemicals while focusing on the toxicology of potentially hazardous chemicals. *HSDB*, partially supported by the Department of Health and Human Services' Agency for Toxic Substances and Disease Registry, provides information about safe levels of human exposure, handling guidelines, detection methods, environmental fate data, and regulatory requirements for more than 4,300 chemicals. *HSDB*'s records are extremely detailed and can be dozens of pages long. *RTECS* is similar in nature to *HSDB*, but offers less extensive records on a greater number of chemicals—more than 100,000. *RTECS*, maintained by the National Institute for Occupational Safety and Health (see entry 361), covers both acute and chronic effects, including irritation, carcinogenicity, mutagenicity, and reproductive consequences.

Other related databases include: *Chemical Carcinogenesis Research Information System (CCRIS)*, which is updated by the National Cancer Institute and contains carcinogenicity-related test results that appear in primary journals, current awareness publications, and special reports; and the *Integrated Risk Information System (IRIS)*, which contains the official Environmental Protection Agency consensus opinion on the chronic health risks of more than five hundred chemicals; contact IRIS User Support (513/569–7254) for additional information about distribution, access, and use. All four of these databases—*HSDB*, *RTECS*, *CCRIS*, and *IRIS*—are available on TOXNET (see entry 375) and should be used together to obtain a complete picture of the known toxic effects of chemicals.

388 Hazardous Substances Resource Guide

Richard P. Pohanish and Stanley A. Greene. 1st ed. Gale Research, 1993. 509p. $175.00 (hardcover).

The *Hazardous Substances Resource Guide* provides laypeople with the tools they need for a basic understanding of toxic chemicals found in their homes, offices, and communities; it also identifies organizations and other reference materials that can provide additional information. The guide begins with a detailed, easy-to-follow introduction to a wide range of hazardous substances, including household cleaning products, arts and crafts materials, automotive fluids, radon, and personal care products. This information is followed by profiles of more than one thousand hazardous substances, listed alphabetically by most common chemical name. Each profile includes the chemical's unique CAS number, other commonly used names, a brief summary of uses, associated hazards, effects of long- and short-term exposure, and a first-aid guide. The book's final section provides contact information and brief descriptions for fifteen hundred sources of hazardous substance information, including hotlines, poison control centers, government and private organizations, and books, magazines, and online databases. A glossary and three indices arranged by chemical name, CAS number, and resource name are also included. This guide's all-in-one style will appeal to lay readers who want sophisticated—but not overly technical—information about chemicals.

389 New Jersey Department of Health Fact Sheets

New Jersey Department of Health. 1,054 fact sheets. The first 10 fact sheets are free, each additional sheet is 25¢; $275.00 for the complete set.

Bulletin Board: Available on the Right-to-Know Network (RTK NET) (see entry 378). Choose *Text Datasets*, then *New Jersey Fact Sheets (Chemical Effects and Treatment)*.

The fact sheets are also available on the Remote Access Chemical Hazards Electronic Library (see entry 377). Choose *Rachel Database*, then *Easy Search System*, then *N.J. Department of Health Fact Sheets on Chemicals*.

Internet: Available on EcoGopher (see entry 54, EcoSystems). Choose *The Library*, then *General*, then *EPA Chemical Substances Factsheets*. RTK NET (see Bulletin Board, above) is also available on the Internet.

These detailed summaries of the health hazards associated with exposure chemicals, including

the 324 that are part of the *Toxic Release Inventory (TRI)* (see entry 381), are commonly known as *New Jersey Fact Sheets*. *New Jersey Fact Sheets* are a specific brand of Material Safety Data Sheet, a generic term that refers to condensed information on hazardous substances that the Occupational Safety and Health Administration (OSHA) requires many employers to make available to their employees. Since each employer (e.g., governments, schools, businesses) can write their own Material Safety Data Sheets, contents vary from version to version. *New Jersey Fact Sheets* are widely used and known because they are now officially used by the Environmental Protection Agency (EPA), which sometimes refers to them as *Hazardous Substances Fact Sheets*. Most *New Jersey Fact Sheets* are five pages long and contain information about acute health effects, chronic health effects, cancer hazards, reproductive hazards, and medical testing. In addition, since the fact sheets were developed to help educate workers, they contain information on workplace controls and practices, protective equipment, and answers to commonly asked questions.

390 Toxics A to Z: A Guide to Everyday Pollution

Edited by John Harte, Cheryl Holdren, Richard Schneider, and Christine Shirley. University of California Press, 1991. 576p. $32.45 (hardcover), $20.00 (paper).

An excellent primer on toxic substances, *Toxics A to Z* is popular in presentation and readability, yet technical enough to be a comprehensive introductory guide. Part One, "All About Toxics," discusses general issues concerning toxic hazards. Essays introduce readers to a variety of information, from basic medical information and sources of toxics in air, water, food, and consumer products to management of the main types of toxics: metals, petrochemicals, pesticides, and radiation. Part Two, "A Guide to Commonly Encountered Toxics," provides information on more than one hundred toxics. Each entry is two to three pages in length and has the following sections: "Physical and Chemical Properties," "Exposure and Distribution," "Health Effects," "Protection and Prevention," "Environmental Effects," "Regulatory Status," "Technical Information," and "Further Reading." *Toxics A to Z* concludes with a glossary, an index, and a list of resources, including reference books and sources of testing equipment.

Other Reference Handbooks

- The *Common Synonyms Guide to TRI Chemicals* (see entry 422, RCRA/UST/EPCRA/Superfund Hotline)
- *A Consumer's Dictionary of Household, Yard and Office Chemicals* (see entry 602)
- The *Dictionary & Thesaurus of Environment, Health & Safety* (see entry 138)
- *Preventing Industrial Toxic Hazards: A Guide for Communities* (see entry 445)
- *Toxics Law Reporter* (see entry 118, *Environment Reporter*)
- The *VNR Dictionary of Environmental Health and Safety* (see entry 150)

Introductory Reading

391 Atomic Harvest: Hanford and the Lethal Toll of America's Nuclear Arsenal

Michael D' Antonio. Crown Publishing, 1993. 304p. $22.50 (hardcover).

392 Toxic Nation: The Fight to Save Our Communities from Chemical Contamination

Fred Setterberg and Lonny Shavelson. John Wiley & Sons, 1993. 320p. $22.95 (hardcover).

The threat of environmental pollution and the potential for using democratic action to control it are the shared central themes of both *Atomic Harvest* and *Toxic Nation*. In shocking detail, *Atomic Harvest* tells the continuing story of the dumping of 440 billion gallons of lethal chemicals and the release of massive amounts of radioactive material into the air, water, and land at the Department of Energy's Hanford, Wash., nuclear weapons production facility. It is just as horrifying to read about the pressures on everyone involved at the site to remain silent as it is to learn of the devastation to life and the environment. Equally riveting reading, *Toxic Nation*, the result of a three-year investigation, reports on the horrifying effects of toxic chemicals on the lives of dozens of rural communities.

Many other books also document personal accounts of toxics victims and their successful fights; two other recommended titles are: *No Safe Place: Toxic Waste, Leukemia, and Community Action* (Phil Brown. University of California Press, 1990) and *The Polluters* (Susan Varlamoff. St. Johns Publishing, 1993).

For detailed, how-to activist manuals regarding toxic substances, consult *Chemical Alert! A Community Action Handbook* (entry 384) and *Fighting Toxics: A Manual for Protecting Your Family, Community, and Workplace* (entry 385).

393 Chemical Deception: The Toxic Threat to Health and the Environment

Marc Lappé. Sierra Club Books, 1991. 384p. $27.00 (hardcover), $15.00 (paper).

Chemical Deception examines the dangers of toxic chemicals, arguing that hazards are often underemphasized by manufacturers and overlooked by regulators. This book was written for people interested in the specific effects and the subsequent implications of chemical exposure and in the role of chemical companies in perpetuating health risks. Author Marc Lappé aims to dispel a series of popular myths about chemicals, including the ideas that our body's defenses work to fight off toxics; that naturally occurring substances (as opposed to synthetic) cause the most cancer; that our tap water is safe; that the effects of toxics disappear as doses diminish; and that our environment is resilient. In *Chemical Deception*, Lappé, a professor and renowned health policy expert, clearly illustrates the complex links between human irresponsibility, environmental damage, and eventual human injury. The issues are not oversimplified and thus the text is often technical, though not beyond the grasp of the lay reader. This is a fascinating book that is remarkably well referenced for a popular work.

For a less passionate but more systematic approach to risk assessment, read *The Dose Makes the Poison: A Plain Language Guide to Toxicology* (see entry 395).

394 Chemical Exposures: Low Levels and High Stakes

Nicholas A. Ashford and Claudia S. Miller. Van Nostrand Reinhold, 1991. 214p. $22.95 (hardcover).

Chemical Exposures is the most comprehensive resource available on the growing problem of chemical sensitivity disorders. The book is an expanded version of a highly regarded study conducted for the New Jersey Department of Health. Designed as an overview of chemical sensitivity issues, *Chemical Exposures* is highly recommended for those unfamiliar with chemical sensitivity and for those afflicted with the illness, as well as for health professionals and skeptics. An appendix includes summaries of studies that chronicle the health disorders associated with chemical exposure. The twenty-page bibliography, with numerous citations of studies, is invaluable as a springboard for additional research.

Another highly regarded reference work on this topic is *Chemical Sensitivity: A Guide to Coping with Hypersensitivity Syndrome, Sick Building Syndrome and other Environmental Illnesses* (Bonnye Matthews. McFarland & Company, 1992). Written from the perspective of someone who suffers from chemical sensitivity, the book describes what it is like to be chemically sensitive, explains how to cope with the condition, and provides twelve pages of resources, including support groups and government offices.

395 The Dose Makes the Poison: A Plain Language Guide to Toxicology

M. Alice Ottoboni, Ph.D. 2nd ed. Van Nostrand Reinhold, 1991. 255p. $24.95 (hardcover).

The Dose Makes the Poison provides individuals who have little or no science background with the tools they will need to understand reports about the hazardous health effects of synthetic and natural chemicals. This is an easy-to-understand narrative about what chemicals are, how they can be harmful, and the numerous factors that influence their toxicity. Readers will develop a clear understanding of why some chemicals are dangerously toxic while others are not. Although author M. Alice Ottoboni does not convey an extreme pro- or anti-chemical slant, she does consistently defend the chemical industry. She concludes that once individuals understand the principles of toxicology, they will realize that chemicals are not harmful when used responsibly.

Two other books that cover the same subject in a similar manner and from a similar ideological perspective are *Calculated Risks: The Toxicity and Human Health Risks of Chemicals in Our Environment* (Joseph Rodricks. Cambridge University Press, 1992) and *Toxic Risks: Science, Regulations, and Perception* (Ronald Gots. Lewis Publishers, 1992).

396 Electric and Magnetic Fields from 60 Hertz Electric Power: What Do We Know About Possible Health Risks?

Carnegie Mellon University, Department of Engineering and Public Policy, 1989. 45p. $3.50 (paper).

397 Warning: The Electricity Around You May Be Hazardous to Your Health: How to Protect Yourself from Electromagnetic Fields

Ellen Sugarman. Fireside Books, 1992. 256p. $11.00 (paper).

Both *Electric and Magnetic Fields from 60 Hertz Electric Power* and *Warning: The Electricity Around You May Be Hazardous to Your Health* provide introductions, appropriate for consumers, to electromagnetic fields and their possible health risks. *Electric and Magnetic Fields from 60 Hertz Electric Power* is widely recognized as the most accurate and reliable summary of what is known—and not known—about the health effects of electromagnetic fields, and can be ordered by sending a check for $3.50 to Carnegie Mellon University, Department of Engineering and Public Policy, Pittsburgh, PA 15213. This report—like most of the information currently available—will become outdated in the late 1990s, when scientists obtain results from the large wave of ongoing research. Ellen Sugarman's book, *Warning*, takes a less conservative view of the problem, as the subtitle suggests; though critics assert it contains some factual errors, it is acknowledged as the best straightforward, comprehensive book-length introduction to the topic of electromagnetic fields (EMFs).

Warning summarizes current research, legal issues, and other background information, and presents ways in which homeowners can lessen their risks. An appendix summarizes many studies that support the claim that EMFs pose a health risk.

Stephen Prata's *EMF Handbook: Understanding and Controlling Electromagnetic Fields In Your Life* (Waite Group, 1993) is similar to *Warning*, but less detailed. Also appropriate for lay readers are two investigative studies by Paul Brodeur—*Currents of Death: Power Lines, Computer Terminals, and the Attempt to Cover Up Their Threat to Your Health* (Simon & Schuster, 1989) and *The Great Power-Line Cover-Up: How the Utilities and the Government Are Trying to Hide the Cancer Hazard Posed by Electromagnetic Fields* (Little, Brown and Company, 1993)—and a more technical introduction to the topic by pioneering researcher Dr. Robert O. Becker: *Cross Currents: The Promise of Electromedicine, The Perils of Electropollution* (Jeremy P. Tarcher, 1990). The EPA Public Information Center (see entry 3) also offers pamphlets on the topic: *EMF in Your Environment: Magnetic Field Measurements Of Everyday Electrical Devices* and *Questions and Answers About Electric and Magnetic Fields (EMFs)*.

398 Principles and Practice of Environmental Medicine

Edited by Alyce Bezman Tarcher. Plenum Publishing Company, 1992. 620p. $85.00 (hardcover).

Principles and Practice of Environmental Medicine furnishes the reader with a detailed overview of what environmental medicine is, what it is not, and how it differs from occupational health. Emphasis is placed on the basic framework needed to assess and treat environmental illness and on the knowledge and skills needed to incorporate environmental factors into clinical practice. As such, the work is aimed at medical students and physicians. Appendices include a thorough resource guide to the fields of environmental and occupational medicine. This work serves as a valuable desk reference for those in the field and a much-needed introductory work for others—especially the first chapter, which clearly summarizes the principles and scope of environmental medicine.

Abstracts and Indices

399 TOXLINE (Toxicology Information Online)

Electronic document. National Library of Medicine, Toxicology Information Program, 1966–. Monthly.

CD-ROM: Available from SilverPlatter.

Database Vendor: Available on DIALOG and MEDLARS.

TOXLINE is the most comprehensive and widely used collection of citations to published sources of information on all subjects related to toxic substances and associated health effects. Although *TOXLINE*—which is not available in print—is geared toward the medical community, it is a valuable resource for anyone looking for technical literature on toxics. Some specific topics covered include food additives, birth defects, water treatment, radioactive materials, and pesticides and herbicides, as well as occupational and household hazards. *TOXLINE* contains more than one million in-depth abstracts selected from eighteen bibliographic databases. A closely related database that offers the same coverage and that is also only available online, *Toxicology Literature from Special Sources (TOXLIT)*, includes citations taken from sources that charge a royalty for use. For a comprehensive search, use *TOXLIT* and *TOXLINE* together.

Toxicological Abstracts (Cambridge Scientific Abstracts, 1978–. Monthly), which contains only a fraction of the records found on *TOXLINE* and *TOXLIT*, covers toxicological studies of industrial and agricultural chemicals, pharmaceuticals, heavy metals, natural toxins, and many other substances.

Other Abstracts and Indices

◆ *NIOSHTIC* (see entry 361, National Institute for Occupational Safety and Health)

Periodicals

400 Informed Consent: The Magazine of Health, Prevention, and Environmental News

Informed Consent, 1993–. Bimonthly. 56p. $18.00/year.

Though it is written especially for those who are chemically sensitive, anyone with an interest in environmental health would benefit from reading *Informed Consent: The Magazine of Health, Prevention, and Environmental News*. Each issue includes up to ten feature articles. Articles from one issue included "The MSG Controversy", "Carpet Concerns. Part Three: New Carpet Label Receives Mixed Reviews," "Less-Toxic Ant Control," and "Right to Know in the Workplace: What Every Employer and Worker Needs to Know." Each issue includes a summary of recent environmental health legislation and litigation, news briefs, and product and publication announcements, as well as advertisements for products and resources of interest to those who are chemically sensitive. The managing editor of the magazine, Cindy Duehring, is the Director of Research for the Environmental Access Research Network (see entry 366, Chemical Injury Information Network). *Informed Consent* is an inexpensive way to stay on top of environmental health news.

A more frequent though more expensive periodical is the *Health and Environment Digest* (Freshwater Foundation, 1987–. Monthly. $90 per year for the government/public sector, $115 per year for the private sector), which includes more news, though the publication lacks the in-depth articles that *Informed Consent* contains.

401 Microwave News

Microwave News, 1981–. Bimonthly. 20p. $285.00/year.

An independent journal covering significant developments related to the health effects of electromagnetic fields, *Microwave News* is widely acknowledged as the most authoritative source of reliable and current information on all aspects of this topic, from electric blankets to power lines. Each issue contains news on research, regulations, litigation and legal decisions, laws, new books and reports, and conferences and meetings. Articles are objective and explain all technical jargon. Though *Microwave News* is priced above the reach of the average person, collections of reprints of articles on special topics (e.g., "EMFs in the 90s," "EMFs & Breast Cancer") are also available ($25). The *EMF Resource Directory* (1995. $35) also published by Microwave News, provides contact information for hundreds of researchers, utility representatives, consultants, government officials, and citizens' groups. Microwave News also publishes *Video Display Terminal News* (Bimonthly. $127 per year), which provides news and research on all computer-related health risks.

402 Rachel's Environment & Health Weekly

Environmental Research Foundation, 1987–. Weekly. 2p. $25.00/year for individuals and citizen groups, $15.00/year for students and senior citizens, $80.00/year for professionals and government agencies, $400.00/year for businesses.

Diskette: A complete archive is available from the Environmental Research Foundation (see entry 370) for $25.00.

EcoNet: For a searchable version, choose *Online Databases*, then *News Services*, then *RACHEL's Environment & Health Weekly (RACHEL)*. It is also available in the *toxics.rachel* conference.

Bulletin Board: Available as a downloadable file on the Remote Access Chemical Hazards Electronic Library (see entry 377). Choose *File Areas*, then *File Area 1*.

Internet: To subscribe to the free electronic version, send an e-mail message to **erf@igc.apc.org**.

Back issues are archived at Software Tool & Die's The World ftp site. To view, gopher to **ftp.std.com**, choose *Periodicals, Magazines, and Journals*, then *Rachel's Environment & Health Weekly*. It is also available by anonymous ftp from this site.

Rachel's Environment & Health Weekly is one of the most informative newsletters in the environmental arena. It takes an aggressive pro-environment grassroots stance, delivering to activists the information they need to reduce local use and release of toxic chemicals. *Rachel's Environment & Health Weekly*, formerly *Rachel's*

Hazardous Waste News, focuses on landfills and incinerators, dangerous wastes—including municipal solid wastes, hazardous chemical wastes, and radioactive wastes—and other relevant stories making headlines. Each issue tackles a single topic; sample titles include "Dioxin and PCBs Linked to Endometriosis"; "PR Firms for Hire to Undermine Democracy"; "What Causes Breast Cancer?"; "Cabinet Status Won't Help EPA: An Illustration of EPA's Lack of Independence"; and "Risk Assessment: Judge Breyer's Prescription for Risk." Many issues of *Rachel's* include footnotes and resources that can be used for additional research. Although *Rachel's* covers technical, often complex, subjects, it is written in succinct, clear language that anyone can understand, and should be read by everyone active or interested in protecting people's health and the environment.

Other Periodicals

◆ *Environmental Health Monthly* (see entry 423, Citizen's Clearinghouse for Hazardous Wastes)

◆ Environmental Health Perspectives (see entry 360, Enviro-Health).

◆ *The Human Ecologist* (see entry 371, Human Ecology Action League)

◆ *Our Toxic Times* (see entry 366, Chemical Injury Information Network)

◆ *Profiles on Environmental Health* (see entry 369, Environmental Health Network)

CHAPTER EIGHT

Sustainable Communities

What This Chapter Covers

This chapter covers the environmental aspects of sustainable communities: a shared vision that neighborhoods and cities should be more socially, economically, and environmentally livable. The notion of sustainable communities includes planting neighborhood trees, minimizing community waste, conserving water and energy, reducing urban smog, and creating efficient transportation options.

For More Information

◆ See **General** for resources on all environmental issues, including how these issues pertain to communities.

◆ See **Architecture** for resources on sustainable architecture.

Government Clearinghouses

403 International Council for Local Environmental Initiatives (ICLEI)
World Secretariat
City Hall, East Tower, 8th Floor
Toronto, Ontario M5H 2N2 Canada

Phone: 416/392-1462. Fax: 416/392-1478.
E-mail: iclei@web.apc.org

Jeb Brugman, Secretary General

As the international environmental agency of local governments, the International Council for Local Environmental Initiatives (ICLEI) supports municipalities in their efforts to reform local development and resource management practices, to adapt to environmental change, and to work as partners in international efforts to address global environmental problems. ICLEI was created at the 1990 World Congress of Local Governments for a Sustainable Future by the International Union of Local Authorities, the U.S.–based Center for Innovative Diplomacy, and the United Nations Environment Programme (see entry 10). More than 130 cities, including Berkeley, Curitiba, Gdansk, New York, Toronto, Stockholm, and Yokohama, have become members as of June 1994. ICLEI publications include *Profiting from Energy Efficiency: A Financing Handbook for Municipalities; Overcoming Barriers to Large-scale Diversion of Municipal Solid Waste*; two newsletters (*Initiatives* and *Local Agenda 21 Network News*); and a series of case studies that includes *Citizen Participation in the Siting of Waste Facilities* (Linz, Austria) and *Local Water Pollution Control, Industrial Pretreatment and Biological Indicators* (Muncie, Indiana, USA).

Other Government Clearinghouses:

◆ The Clean Cities Hotline (see entry 314, National Alternative Fuels Hotline)

Organizations

404 Center for Neighborhood Technology
2125 West North Avenue
Chicago, IL 60647

Phone: 312/278-4800. Fax: 312/278-3840

Scott Bernstein, President

The Center for Neighborhood Technology works to promote public policies, new resources, and accountable authority—all of which go to support sustainable, just, and vital urban communities. The center's Campaign for a Sustainable Chicago—focused in the areas of transportation and air quality, energy, materials reuse and recycling, and sustainable manufacturing—works, with citizen-based plans and a broad-based constituency, to build a vision for the city's sustainable development. While most of the group's community organizing and community-based development activities are centered in the Chicago area, the organization's award-winning, bimonthly magazine, *The Neighborhood Works*, which provides news on community approaches to housing, energy, environment, transportation, and economic development, is read around the nation. Other publications include *Beyond Recycling: Materials Reprocessing in Chicago's Economy, Transportation for Sustainable Communities*, and *Ecoclean: An Assessment of a Dry Cleaning Alternative*.

405 Community Sustainability Resource Institute (CSRI)
P.O. Box 11343
Takoma Park, MD 20913

Phone: 301/588-7227. Fax: 301/587-7691.
E-mail: csri@igc.apc.org

Susanna MacKenzie Euston, President/Executive Director

The Community Sustainability Resource Institute (CSRI) promotes and supports initiatives that advance community sustainability at the local, regional, and national levels. CSRI sponsors national and regional conferences and a Washington, D.C.–area speakers' series, and provides technical assistance and outreach to other organizations working to advance the cause of community sustainability. Each issue of CSRI's newsletter, the *Community Sustainability Exchange*, contains an extensive directory that profiles other organizations and projects across the country working to build sustainable communities. The *Exchange* is also an excellent source of reviews and announcements of relevant reports, conferences, and other resources. CSRI is actively engaged in developing working relationships with other organizations.

406 The Global Cities Project
Environmental Policy Center
2962 Fillmore Street
San Francisco, CA 94123

Phone: 415/775-0791. Fax: 415/775-4159

Walter McGuire, President

A national clearinghouse for local environmental programs and policies, The Global Cities Project continually identifies and collects detailed information on practical, cost-efficient sustainable-development policies and programs being implemented by local governments nationwide. The Project then provides that information to communities—local governments, businesses, and citizens—to help them implement their own programs. The eleven-volume *Building Sustainable Communities: An Environmental Guide for Local Government* (see entry 412) handbook series summarizes much of this information. Case studies ($10) and sample ordinances ($5) on specific topics (e.g., "Start a Yard Waste Collection Program," "Adopt Purchasing Policies That Favor Recycled Products") are also available separately. Through the new Sustainable Cities Initiative, project staff members develop and consult with task forces comprising local environmental policymakers, business leaders, and members of environmental community groups to help their cities address their own environmental challenges. After working with these groups for three years, The Global Cities Project will provide that group with a final report, called a *Sustainable Cities Plan*, that covers each topic the task forces have addressed (e.g., air quality, toxics reduction) and that compares the city's sustainable-development programs against its own goals and the results achieved by other cities. Each *Sustainable Cities Plan* includes a summary of the task force's policy priorities and discussions, as well as specific recommendations for the future. The Global Cities

Project is the first place local governments should look to for advice that will help in their efforts to turn their own cities into sustainable communities.

407 Institute for Local Self-Reliance (ILSR)
2425 18th Street, NW
Washington, DC 20009

Phone: 202/232-4108. Fax: 202/332-0463

Neil Seldman, President

The Institute for Local Self-Reliance (ILSR) helps nonprofits, municipalities, and businesses develop and implement programs that reduce per capita consumption of raw materials and shift dependence toward renewable resources. The ILSR staff performs research and provides formal and informal consulting. Specific issues of interest vary; in the past, this nonprofit has published a series of reports on trade issues and their impact on the environment, evaluated incinerator technologies, and established a state coalition of organizations that support an energy-efficient economy. Most ILSR publications, such as *Beyond 40 Percent: Record-Setting Recycling and Composting Programs*, *The Carbohydrate Economy: Making Chemical and Industrial Materials from Plant Matter*, and *Getting the Most from Our Materials: Making New Jersey The State of the Art*, document policies and use case studies to demonstrate the economic viability of sustainable practices.

408 Land Trust Alliance (LTA)
1319 F Street, NW, Suite 501
Washington, DC 20004

Phone: 202/638-4725. Fax: 202/638-4730

Jean Hocker, President

The Land Trust Alliance (LTA) serves to strengthen organizations that accept donations to purchase and preserve land. Although LTA does have an information center to serve the public and the media, the organization primarily provides program support and assistance to its member organizations like The Nature Conservancy (see entry 275), the Trust for Public Land, the Conservation Fund, and hundreds of smaller organizations. Members receive discounts on publications such as *Starting a Land Trust: A*

Guide to Forming a Land Conservation Organization, Conservation Options: A Landowner's Guide, The Standards and Practices Guidebook: An Operating Manual, and the *National Directory of Conservation Land Trusts*. LTA also publishes two periodicals: the *Exchange*, a quarterly professional journal with articles on recent issues and projects; and *LTA Landscapes*, a quarterly newsletter updating members on meetings, legislative news, and recent achievements. For information about land trusts, this is the best place to begin a search.

409 Rails-to-Trails Conservancy (RTC)
1400 16th Street, NW, Suite 300
Washington, DC 20036

Phone: 202/797-5400. Fax: 202/797-5411

David Burwell, President

The Rails-to-Trails Conservancy (RTC) works to convert abandoned rail corridors, and connecting open space, into a nationwide network of public trails. Through its national headquarters in Washington and six chapter offices, RTC notifies trail advocates and local governments of railroad abandonments; assists public and private agencies in the legalities of trail-corridor acquisition; provides technical assistance on trail design, development, and protection; and publicizes rails-to-trails issues throughout the country. Members receive *Trailblazer*, a quarterly newsletter. Among the organization's reference handbooks are *Trails for the Twenty-First Century: Planning, Design, and Management Manual for Multi-Use Trails, Secrets of Successful Rail-Trails: An Acquisition and Organizing Manual for Converting Rails into Trails*, and *500 Great Rail-Trails*, a directory of trails in forty-four states. All RTC publications are available from the group's shipping department (800/888-7747).

The Recreation Resource Assistance Division of the National Park Service and the American Hiking Society are compiling a *Trail Conservation Directory*, a national directory of trail conservation organizations, similar to the *River Conservation Directory* (see entry 480); for more information, contact the American Hiking Society (703/255-9304).

410 Surface Transportation Policy Project (STPP)
1400 16th Street, NW, Suite 300
Washington, DC 20036

Phone: 202/939-3470. Fax: 202/939-3475.
E-mail: stpp@igc.apc.org

Hank Dittmar, Executive Director

EcoNet: The Surface Transportation Policy Project's newsletter, *Progress*, is available in the *transport* conference.

The Surface Transportation Policy Project (STPP) is a network that works to ensure that transportation policy and investments help conserve energy, protect environmental and aesthetic quality, strengthen the economy, promote social equity, and make communities more livable. STPP's policy goals are supported by more than one hundred organizations and coalitions, including the Environmental Defense Fund (see entry 24), the National League of Cities, and The Campaign for New Transportation Priorities (202/408–8362), a smaller coalition that has a similar mission. STPP is a good source of case studies and other practical information for those who participate in state and local transportation planning. It published *At Road's End: Transportation and Land Use Choices for Communities* (Daniel Carlson with Lisa Warmser and Cy Ulberg. Island Press, 1994), which includes case studies and new models for transportation planning as well as strategies for resolving community disputes. STPP's free newsletter, *Progress*, is an excellent source of national transportation news and announcements of new publications. STPP is a good resource for professionals and individuals committed to sustainable transportation.

411 Urban Ecology
405 14th Street, Suite 701
Oakland, CA 94612

Phone: 510/251-6330.
E-mail: urbanecology@igc.apc.org

David Early, President

Urban Ecology promotes urban environments that are ecologically, socially, and economically sustainable. Urban Ecology works mainly in the San Francisco Bay Area, but also gives presentations and leads discussions in conferences and symposia on sustainable urban development worldwide. Membership includes a subscription to *The Urban Ecologist*, an outstanding quarterly newsletter that includes in-depth articles, announcements and reviews of information sources, and news updates on projects around the world, in the United States, and in the Bay Area. Past themes of *The Urban Ecologist* have included greenways, transportation, housing, and sustainable economics. The organization sells its own publications (e.g., *Report of the First International Ecological Cities Conference*, *A Sustainable City Plan for Berkeley*) and distributes others (e.g., *A Green City Program for the San Francisco Bay Area and Beyond*, the *Gaia Atlas of Cities*, *Reclaiming Our Cities and Towns: Better Living With Less Traffic*).

Other Organizations

- The Bio-Dynamic Farming and Gardening Association (see entry 186) for information on Community Supported Agriculture (CSA).
- Co-op America (see entry 16)
- Cool Communities (see entry 267, American Forests)
- CONCERN (see entry 17)
- The Global Action and Information Network (see entry 30)
- Global ReLeaf (see entry 267, American Forests)
- Renew America (see entry 42)
- The Rocky Mountain Institute (see entry 44)

Bibliographies

- *Community Supported Agriculture (CSA): An Annotated Bibliography and Resource Guide* (see entry 186, Bio-Dynamic Farming and Gardening Association)
- The *Efficient House Sourcebook* (see entry 513)

Reference Handbooks

412 Building Sustainable Communities: An Environmental Guide for Local Governments

The Global Cities Project, 1991. $40.00 per handbook, $380.00 for the full set of 11 volumes; government, nonprofit organizations, and students with a valid ID pay $20.00 per handbook, $175.00 for the full set (paper).

Building Sustainable Communities provides nuts-and-bolts information that municipalities and businesses can use to implement local environmental programs and policies. Titles in the eleven-volume series are *Water: Conservation and Reclamation*; *Solid Waste: Reduction, Reuse, and Recycling*; *Toxics: Management and Reduction*; *Transportation: Efficiency and Alternatives*; *Open Spaces: Preservation and Acquisition*; *Energy: Efficiency and Production*; *Urban Forestry* (sold out); *Water Quality: Protection and Remediation*; *Air Quality: Pollution Prevention and Mitigation*; *Land Use: Stewardship and the Planning Process*; and *Environmental Management*. Each volume describes twenty to forty different projects: examples in the *Water* volume include a drought response contingency plan; a conservation training program for landscape maintenance personnel; industrial and home water audits; a consumer's guide to water-saving fixtures and equipment; and a school-based water conservation educational program. Each project includes descriptions of project modifications for other municipalities; the full text of ordinances is often included. At the end of each volume there is a bibliography of publications, a directory of organizations, and short case studies of all local programs mentioned in the volume.

The Global Cities Project (see entry 406) also offers some individual case studies and sample ordinances separately and can provide consulting services through its Sustainable Cities Initiative.

413 Creating Successful Communities: A Guidebook to Growth Management Strategies

Michael A. Mantell, Stephen F. Harper, and Luther Propst. Sponsored by The Conservation

Foundation. Island Press, 1990. 230p. $39.95 (hardcover), $24.95 (paper).

Creating Successful Communities introduces proven techniques for sustainable land use and growth management in suburban and rural areas. Chapters describe common threats and methods of protection for agricultural land, rivers and wetlands, historic and cultural sites, aesthetic resources, and open spaces. Several two- to three-page case studies of successful efforts follow each chapter; a companion volume, the *Resource Guide for Creating Successful Communities*, includes the complete text of actual ordinances and bylaws. Other sections in *Creating Successful Communities* give guidance on starting and managing nonprofit corporations, provide overviews of both growth-management tools and techniques, and clarify the tax benefits of private land conservation. The annotated bibliographies of related publications and organizations that follow each chapter multiply this book's value for concerned citizens and public officials fighting to preserve and restore their communities.

Another book, *Saving the Neighborhood: You Can Fight Developers and Win* (Peggy Robin. Woodbine House, 1990), leads citizens through the development process, providing strategic and organizing advice.

Those interested in consulting or networking with conservation and planning experts should contact The National Growth Management Leadership Project (202/628–1270). The project is a national network of conservation and planning organizations that advocates for state and regional land-use planning as a policy tool to address land conservation, housing, transportation, and other key growth-management concerns.

414 Sustainable Cities: Concepts and Strategies for Eco-City Development

Edited by Bob Walter, Lois Arkin, and Richard Crenshaw. Eco-Home Media, 1992. 354p. $20.00 (paper).

Sustainable Cities is an excellent all-in-one handbook for those interested in sustainable cities. *Sustainable Cities* offers more than fifty short essays on different aspects of sustainable cities (for example, economics, urban agriculture, and transportation) which were adapted from talks given at a 1991 conference in Los Angeles on eco-cities. The papers were presented by those working to build sustainable communities in Southern California, but the strategies and models they describe are widely applicable to other geographic regions. The annotated resource directory at the end of the book is extensive. It describes hundreds of relevant organizations, experts, and publications.

415 Toward Sustainable Communities: A Resource Book for Municipal and Local Governments

Mark Roseland. National Round Table Series on Sustainable Development. National Round Table on the Environment and the Economy, 1992. 340p. Free (paper).

Toward Sustainable Communities is an outstanding resource guide that leads readers in applying the concept of sustainable development to their own communities. Chapters provide an overview of the sustainable communities movement, focus on specific environmental issues such as transportation planning and traffic management, land use and growth management, energy conservation and efficiency, solid and hazardous waste reduction and recycling, and investment and purchasing. Each chapter includes a short overview of the issues and an outline of tools that can be used; these are followed by the core of the book: case studies of previous initiatives, detailed descriptions of organizations and reference handbooks that provide how-to assistance, and a bibliography of other sources. The publisher, the National Round Table on the Environment and the Economy, is a project of the Canadian government that allows for discussion between leaders in government, industry, organizations, and universities. A similar bibliography, *A Select, Annotated Bibliography on Sustainable Cities* (Mary Ann Beavis and Jeffrey Patterson. Institute of Urban Studies, University of Winnipeg, 1992), includes many citations to periodical articles and planning proposals from Canadian cities.

Other Reference Handbooks

◆ *At Road's End: Transportation and Land Use Choices for Communities* (see entry 410, Surface Transportation Policy Project)

- The *Economic Renewal Guide* (see entry 44, Rocky Mountain Institute)
- *Shading Our Cities: A Resource Guide for Urban and Community Forests* (see entry 267, American Forests)
- *Trails for the Twenty-First Century: Planning, Design, and Management Manual* (see entry 409, Rails-to-Trails Conservancy)

Introductory Reading

416 Sustainable Communities: A New Design Synthesis for Cities, Suburbs and Towns

Edited by Sim Van der Ryn and Peter Calthorpe. Sierra Club Books, 1986; paperback reprint, 1991. 238p. $20.00 (paper).

Sustainable Communities is a collection of essays that explores the ways in which some American communities are making the transition to sustainability. Editors Sim Van der Ryn, an architect, and Peter Calthorpe, an urban planner, contribute introductory essays. Other essayists such as Paul Hawken, John Todd, and David Morris write on specific subjects like economics, design, architecture and biology, urban agriculture, and transportation. This large-format book includes many drawings and case studies.

Those interested in delving further into the idea of community sustainability may want to take a look at two other books. A good introductory read on sustainable communities is *Ecotopia: The Notebooks and Reports of William Weston* (Bantam Books, 1990. Originally published in 1975), Ernest Callenbach's vision of an ecological utopian community. In his new book, *The Next American Metropolis: Ecology, Community, and the American Dream* (Princeton Architectural Press, 1993), the aforementioned Peter Calthorpe puts forth detailed guidelines for the many parts and features of sustainable communities.

Other Introductory Reading

- *Green Architecture: Design for an Energy-Conscious Future* (see entry 521)

Periodicals

417 Earthword: The Journal of Environmental and Social Responsibility

Eos Institute, 1991–. Published irregularly. 64p. $20.00/4 issues. $30.00/4 issues includes Eos Institute newsletter, plus reduced rates on Eos Institute lectures and workshops.

Written for planners, architects, designers, and builders, *Earthword* covers all aspects of the sustainable urban environment. The magazine's past themes have included sustainable transportation systems, sustainable urban landscape, and sustainable and indigenous architecture. Articles provide a wide range of viewpoints from experts in the field. Each *Earthword* issue is literally packed with extensive resource boxes that direct readers to organizations, books, and other sources of information. *Earthword* is an outstanding magazine for those working to build sustainable communities.

The Eos Institute, *Earthword*'s publisher, was founded in 1990 to promote the better understanding of the destructive consequences of existing land-use and construction practices in the United States. The Eos Development Group, a project of the Eos Institute, plans, designs, finances, and builds ecological communities.

418 In Context: A Quarterly of Human Sustainable Culture

Context Institute, 1983–. Quarterly. 64p. $24.00/year.

In Context provides a forum for discussion of sustainable solutions to social and environmental problems. Articles provide a mix of philosophical essays and descriptions of practical, solution-oriented proposals and case studies of projects at the local level. Sustainable community development and green building are common themes; other editions have explored ways to transform current educational systems, investigated the intersection between the environment and development, and questioned "What Is Enough?" in the consumer lifestyle. Robert Gilman, editor of *In Context* and director of the Context Institute, co-authored the *Household EcoTeam Workbook* (see entry 590, Global Action Plan) and speaks often at conferences on green building, sustainable communities, and other issues related to global sustainability.

Many other publications related to sustainable communities are available from the Context Institute, including a 1991 survey of ecovillages and intentional communities throughout the world.

Other Periodicals

◆ *Community Sustainability Exchange* (see entry 405, Community Sustainability Resource Institute)

◆ *The Urban Ecologist* (see entry 411, Urban Ecology)

◆ *Urban Forests* (see entry 267, American Forests)

CHAPTER NINE

Waste

What This Chapter Covers

This chapter covers all aspects of solid and hazardous waste. This includes solid waste management alternatives such as pollution prevention, recycling, and incineration as well as hazardous waste site cleanup and nuclear waste issues.

For More Information

◆ See **General** for resources on all environmental issues, including those related to waste.

◆ See **Health and Toxics** for resources on toxic substances.

Government Clearinghouses

419 Civilian Radioactive Waste Information Center
Department of Energy
P.O. Box 44375
Washington, DC 20026

Phone: 800/225-6972; 202/488-5513.
Fax: 202/488-5512

Ginger King, Education and Information Director

Bulletin Board: The Department of Energy's Office of Civilian Radioactive Waste Management maintains the Infolink bulletin board. Contact the Information Center for local access numbers and instructions.

The Civilian Radioactive Waste Information Center supplies government information on storing, transporting, and disposing of spent nuclear fuel and high-level radioactive waste. The center exists to allay the public's fears about nuclear waste, largely by distributing fact sheets, curricula, and videos to educators and students. Center staffers can also answer questions, or refer callers to other resources, regarding technical issues. Sample publications include reprints of relevant legislation and regulations, *Transportation Cask Systems Development Backgrounders*, the *Site Characterization Progress Reports* on the Yucca Mountain site, and the *OCRWM Bulletin*, a quarterly newsletter. A complete catalog of Office of Civilian Radioactive Waste Management (OCRWM) publications is available on Infolink, the OCRWM's electronic bulletin board system. Infolink is most useful to Department of Energy contractors, but it is also a good way for independent researchers to keep up with OCRWM activities.

420 Hazardous Waste Ombudsman Program
Environmental Protection Agency
401 M Street, SW, Mail Code 5101
Washington, DC 20460

Phone: 800/262-7937; 202/260-9361.
Fax: 202/260-8929

Robert L. Martin, Director, Office of the Ombudsman

The Hazardous Waste Ombudsman Program resolves problems and complaints of citizens, businesses, environmental groups, and professionals concerning the Environmental Protection Agency's (EPA) hazardous waste management programs. For example, if the RCRA/UST/EPCRA/Superfund Hotline (see entry 422), the EPA public affairs office, personnel in the Office of Emergency and Remedial Response, or other normal channels of communication break down, this independent and impartial program will intercede. Ombudsmen cannot reverse, modify, or bypass program decisions, but they will help callers get the answers and decisions they need. Callers should contact the ombudsman in their own EPA region; local numbers are included in many EPA directories, including *Access EPA* (see entry 62), or from the number listed above.

421 Pollution Prevention Information Clearinghouse (PPIC)
Environmental Protection Agency
401 M Street, SW, Mail Code 3404
Washington, DC 20460

Phone: 202/260-1023. Fax: 202/260-0178.
E-mail: ppic@epamail.epa.gov

Bulletin Board: PPIC maintains the Pollution Prevention Information Exchange (PIES) (see entry 435).

Internet: PIES (see Bulletin Board, above) is available on the Internet.

The Pollution Prevention Information Clearinghouse (PPIC) distributes, free of charge, Environmental Protection Agency (EPA) documents and other fact sheets and articles on solid waste source reduction and recycling. Students and homeowners can receive tips—especially on recycling and energy conservation—on preventing pollution in their homes. Policymakers are able to request background information on industry initiatives as well as overviews of federal and state government regulations and programs. The business community can benefit from PPIC's practical information on minimizing waste and preventing pollution through documents such as the *Reference Guide to Pollution Prevention Resources* (see entry 437), *Profiting from Waste Reduction in Your Small Business*, and *A Practical Guide to Pollution Prevention Planning for the Iron and Steel Industries*. The clearinghouse may refer questions to more appropriate organizations, state pollution prevention offices, EPA contacts, or the Pollution Prevention Information Exchange (PIES) (see entry 435), PPIC's companion bulletin board system. Callers can be added to PPIC's mailing list to receive the free quarterly newsletter *Pollution Prevention News*.

422 RCRA/UST/EPCRA/Superfund Hotline
Environmental Protection Agency

Phone (RCRA/UST): 800/424-9346.
Phone (EPCRA/Superfund): 800/424-9346.
TDD: 800/412-3323.
Fax (EPCRA document requests): 703/412-3333

The RCRA/UST/EPCRA/Superfund Hotline will answer—or will tell you who can answer—any waste-related question, from land disposal restrictions and locations of hazardous waste facilities to recycling and waste imports and exports to leaking underground storage tanks and toxic emissions. The hotline is particularly useful for technical or regulatory questions. Many free publications are available from this resource, including several essential bibliographies (the *Bibliography of Materials on the Emergency Planning and Community Right-To-Know Act*, the *Catalogue of Hazardous and Solid Waste Publications* [see entry 439], the *Bibliography of Municipal Solid Waste Management Alternatives* [see entry 438], the *Guide to EPA Materials on Underground Storage Tanks*) and an important report, *Characterization of Municipal Solid Waste in the United States*. Many additional fact sheets and educational materials for students and homeowners are also available. Common questions and answers are published regularly; order the *RCRA/Superfund Monthly Hotline Reports* from the National Technical Information Service (see entry 8), or look for them as bulletins on the Cleanup Information Bulletin Board (see entry 433). Most documents are delivered within three to five weeks. Since the hotline is very busy, it is easiest to get through quickly on Mondays and Fridays. This hotline is the best place for keeping up with the fast-changing world of RCRA, CERCLA, and EPCRA regulations.

Organizations

423 Citizen's Clearinghouse for Hazardous Wastes (CCHW)
P.O Box 6806
Falls Church, VA 22040

Phone: 703/237-2249

Lois Marie Gibbs, Executive Director

The Citizen's Clearinghouse for Hazardous Wastes (CCHW) provides information, training, and strategies to help grassroots activists and groups organize to win the cleanup of hazardous waste landfills—and to stop the siting of new ones. This highly regarded organization is also a good source of information on environmental justice issues such as medical waste disposal, toxics, and recycling. CCHW's regional coordinators work directly with groups around the country, linking those with similar interests, referring them to experts, and teaching individuals to do their own analysis and research. CCHW sells almost one hundred original publications on organizing (e.g., *How to Deal with a Proposed Facility*, *How to Win In Public Hearings*, *User's Guide to Experts*), science (e.g., *Solid Waste Incineration: The Rush to Burn*, *Safety Plans: What You Need to Know*) and other topics (e.g., *WMX Technologies: Corporate Profile*), as well as a variety of fact packs (e.g., "SLAPP Back Fact Pack," "PCBs," "Monsanto Corporate Information"). CCHW staffers can also print out a list from an Environmental Protection Agency computer database of known and suspected toxic waste sites in each state ($2.50 each) and will perform research in their own library for a $5 fee. *Everyone's Backyard*, a quarterly newsletter, updates readers on recent actions taken by the organization and the local groups it aids. CCHW is absolutely the first place local communities should consult about toxic substances in their neighborhoods.

424 Clean Sites
1199 North Fairfax Street, Suite 400
Alexandria, VA 22314

Phone: 703/683-8522. Fax: 703/548-8773

Edwin Clark, Executive Director

Bulletin Board: Clean Sites and the Environmental Law Institute cosponsor the State Superfund Network. Contact Clean Sites for more information.

The nonprofit Clean Sites seeks common ground between all those with a stake in hazardous waste cleanup through practically and politically feasible alternative settlement approaches and both technical consulting and site management. Clean Sites also publishes several policy-oriented reports (such as *Main Street Meets Superfund*, which examines local government involvement in Superfund) and sponsors others (*Cleaning Up the Mess: Implementation Strategies in Superfund* [see entry 446]). The State Superfund Network, an electronic bulletin board operated by Clean Sites and cofunded by the Environmental Law Institute (see entry 26), contains a wealth of pertinent hazardous waste information, though access is generally limited to state Superfund program officials.

425 Environmental Industry Associations (EIA)
4301 Connecticut Avenue, NW, Suite 300
Washington, DC 20008

Phone: 202/244-4700. Fax: 202/966-4818

Michael Frischkorn, President

Comprising three associations—the Hazardous Waste Management Association (HWMA), the National Solid Waste Management Association (NSWMA), and the Waste Equipment Technology Association (WASTEC)—the Environmental Industry Associations (EIA) provides members with technical assistance and lobbies on their behalf. Although most EIA publications are meant for companies in the industry—e.g., manuals, lists of industry manufacturing standards, equipment buying guides—those doing research on waste issues will find many of their other publications useful. Reports, such as *Recycling in the States* and *Landfill Capacity in North America*, provide an abundance of easy-to-interpret statistical data. *Waste Product Profiles* is a series of fact sheets on recyclable wastes, such as HDPE plastic containers and newspapers. In addition to *Waste Age* (see entry 454) and *Recycling Times* (see entry 454, *Waste Age*), EIA also produces *Infectious Waste News*, a biweekly newsletter on biohazardous wastes, and *Environmental Industry News*, a monthly newsletter for EIA members.

426 Household Hazardous Waste Project (HHWP)
1031 E. Battlefield, Suite 214
Springfield, MO 65807

Phone: 417/889-5000. Fax: 417/889-5012.
E-mail: househol@ext.missouri.edu

Marie Steinwachs, Director

The Household Hazardous Waste Project (HHWP) trains both professionals and citizens and publishes educational materials on household hazardous product identification, safe use, storage, proper disposal, and selection of safer alternatives. Since it is a program of the University of Missouri Extension Office, those closest to Springfield will gain the most from HHWP's services, but people around the country can attend training courses or purchase publications. HHWP can provide general advice about disposing of a particular item, though it is always best to contact the appropriate local collection program or official (waste hauler, landfill owner, wastewater treatment officer, etc.). HHWP publications include the *Guide to Hazardous Products Around the Home* (178p. $9.95); an annotated bibliography of educational materials and curricula; a survey that lets students determine if household products are stored safely in their homes and to estimate the community's total accumulation of toxic products; and a variety of fact sheets for use in school or community education. Discounts are available for bulk purchases.

For more information on household hazardous waste collection programs, consult the Waste Watch Center (see entry 431).

427 Military Toxics Project (MTP)
P.O. Box 845
Sabattus, ME 04280

Phone: 207/375-8482. Fax: 207/375-8485

Cathy Hinds, Director

The Military Toxics Project (MTP) is a national network of grassroots groups working to clean up and prevent further pollution created by the worst polluter in the United States—the Department of Defense. MTP links activists working on base closure, chemical weapons, depleted uranium from nuclear bombs and power plants, conventional munitions, and rocket toxics. MTP provides on-site organizing assistance and training, sponsors workshops and conferences, and pushes for policy changes. Among the publications MTP sells are *Fighting Military Toxics: A Citizen's Organizing Manual* and *The U.S. Military's Toxic Legacy: America's Worst Environmental Enemy*. MTP also publishes an informative quarterly newsletter, *Touching Bases*. MTP is the best place for activists to turn for information on military toxics.

Seth Shulman's *The Threat at Home: Confronting the Toxic Legacy of the U.S. Military* (Beacon, 1992) is a lively, journalistic account of many of the issues on which MTP focuses.

428 National Office Paper Recycling Project
U.S. Conference of Mayors
1620 Eye Street, NW, 4th Floor
Washington, DC 20006

Phone: 202/223-3088. Fax-on-demand service: 202/223-3089

Chris Denniston, Director

A nonprofit partnership of twenty-two public (e.g., National Conference of State Legislatures, National League of Cities) and private (e.g., Browning-Ferris Industries, Weyerhaeuser Company) organizations, the National Office Paper Recycling Project is a good first place to call for anyone with an interest in recycling office paper. The project's Paper Recycling Challenge, which aims to triple office paper recycling by 1995, asks business to voluntarily collect waste paper and to purchase recycled paper products. Organizations that register for the Challenge receive a newsletter and assistance in meeting their goals for waste paper collection and recycled paper purchasing programs. Any office, not just Fortune 500 companies, can join the Challenge or call the Project for information—the *Office Paper Recycling Guide* (85¢ per copy; the first five copies are free) answers most basic questions. To register for the Challenge, or to find out more about the organization's publications, use the Project's fax-on-demand service; try faxing before calling the regular phone number.

429 National Recycling Coalition (NRC)
1101 30th Street, NW, Suite 305
Washington, DC 20007

Phone: 202/625-6406. Fax: 202/625-6409

Marsha Rhea, Executive Director

The National Recycling Coalition (NRC) works to maximize recycling efforts throughout the United States and to develop a national recycling policy. As a coalition of businesses of all types, government offices, environmental groups, and individuals, the NRC serves as a network in which everyone with an interest in recycling—from the largest waste hauler to the smallest grassroots organization—can have input. Among NRC's publications are an annotated bibliography on recycling market development, a report on the state of recycling, and a summary of recycling-related legislation recently introduced in Congress. The organization also publishes a bimonthly newsletter, *The NRC Connection*, and two quarterly newsletters: *Market Development NewsLink* and *Buy Recycled Newsline*, a publication of NRC's Buy Recycled Business Alliance.

430 The Solid Waste Association of North America (SWANA)
P.O. Box 7219
Silver Spring, MD 20910

Hotline: 800/677-9424. Phone: 301/585-2898. Fax: 301/585-0297

Nancy Thacher, Research Specialist

Bulletin Board: SWANA operates the Solid Waste Information Clearinghouse (SWICH) bulletin board system. Contact SWANA for more information.

The Solid Waste Association of North America (SWANA) is dedicated to advancing the practice of environmentally and economically sound municipal solid waste management. Over two thirds of SWANA's members are from the public sector. SWANA sponsors conferences, trains and certifies professionals, tracks legislation, and, through its Peer Match Program, brings together individuals seeking technical assistance and colleagues in the solid waste management field. The SWANA librarian acts as a "clearinghouse," managing the organization's hotline and operating its bulletin board system. The hotline, now funded by the National Renewable Energy Laboratory (see entry 316), distributes photocopies of current articles without charge and sells SWANA publications. Most calls are from the general public, though the librarian can answer some technical questions. The bulletin board system, the Solid Waste Information Clearinghouse (SWICH), includes a catalog of the SWANA library and a solid waste legislative tracking system (updated biweekly); contact SWANA to set up an account ($150 for one user-ID).

431 Waste Watch Center
16 Haverhill Street
Andover, MA 01810

Phone: 508/470-3044. Fax: 508/470-3384

Dana Duxbury, President

The Waste Watch Center is dedicated to promoting awareness of household hazardous waste issues. This nonprofit organization—affiliated with Dana Duxbury and Associates, an environmental consulting firm—receives partial funding from the Environmental Protection Agency. The Waste Watch Center plans and manages conferences and symposia and provides technical assistance to both community organizers and solid waste professionals. Sample publications include: *Curbside Used Oil Collection Programs in the U.S.*, *Dry-Cell (Household) Battery Contacts*, the *Bibliography on Household Hazardous Waste*, and a quarterly newsletter. This is the place to call when researching household hazardous waste issues, especially for local government officials starting or adding a component to household hazardous waste collection programs.

Individuals and communities can also contact the Household Hazardous Waste Project (see entry 426) for information and training related to solid waste management.

Other Organizations

- Clean Water Action (see entry 465)
- INFORM (see entry 34)
- The Institute for Local Self Reliance (see entry 407)
- The Nuclear Information and Resource Service (see entry 323)

Commercial Online Services

- RecycleLine (see entry 597, *Recycled Products Guide*)

Bulletin Boards

432 Alternative Treatment Technology Information Center (ATTIC)

Maintained by the Environmental Protection Agency.

Bulletin Board: To connect to the Alternative Treatment Technology Information Center (ATTIC) by modem, dial 703/908-2138. For support by phone, call the ATTIC hotline at 703/908-2137.

Internet: ATTIC is available through FedWorld's GateWay (see entry 61). Choose *74* for *ATTIC (EPA)*.

433 Cleanup Information Bulletin Board (CLU-IN)

Maintained by Environmental Protection Agency's Office of Solid Waste and Emergency Response.

Bulletin Board: To connect to the Cleanup Information Bulletin Board (CLU-IN) by modem, dial 301/589-8366. For support by phone, call the system operator at 301/589-8368.

Internet: CLU-IN is available via FedWorld's GateWay (see entry 61). Choose *7* for *CLU-IN (EPA)*.

Both the Alternative Treatment Technology Information Center (ATTIC) and Cleanup Information Bulletin Board (CLU-IN) are Environmental Protection Agency (EPA) bulletin board systems for government officials and contractors cleaning up hazardous waste sites. Both are free and open to the public. ATTIC is a valuable source of scientific information on cleanup technologies. It includes a database of abstracts on site remediation literature and a database of expert contacts; both are searchable by keyword. CLU-IN is the best source for current information on hazardous waste site cleanup regulated by federal laws: Resource Conservation and Recovery Act, Superfund, Underground Storage Tanks, and the Toxic Substances Control Act. Among the available bulletins are EPA newsletters, including *Tech Trends* and *Bioremediation in the Field*; the *National Priorities List* of Superfund sites; and relevant sections of the *Federal Register* and *Commerce Business Daily*. Files available for downloading include the *Hazardous Waste Superfund Database* (see entry 451) and other bibliographies and government documents. The voice help line offers a user's guide (also available online) and "A Guided Tour of CLU-IN," which walks users through a sample session keystroke by keystroke. The general public can join a number of conferences, called Special Interest Groups (SIGs), on CLU-IN.

434 National Materials Exchange Network

Operated by the Pacific Materials Exchange.

Bulletin Board: To connect to the National Materials Exchange Network by modem, dial 509/466-1019. For technical support by phone, call 509/325-0507.

The National Materials Exchange Network facilitates the exchange of used or virgin and solid/hazardous materials throughout the United States. The network seeks to minimize waste by increasing reuse and recycling. All users, from an apartment landlord to the largest corporation, can post materials available or wanted, and find a match free of charge twenty-four hours a day. The term "materials" includes not only waste byproducts, but also surplus, off-spec, overstock, obsolete, or damaged materials. This national bulletin board, operated by the Pacific Materials Exchange and funded in large part by the Environmental Protection Agency, forwards its postings to regional exchanges which then match compatible parties. Regional exchanges can also be contacted directly; addresses and phone numbers may be obtained online on this bulletin board, or from either the *Recycling Sourcebook* (see entry 436) or *The Recycler's Manual for Business, Government, and the Environmental Community* (see entry 443). Another materials exchange that works on the international level is the Global Recycling Network, available on the Internet (on the World Wide Web, the URL is **http://www.clinet.fi/grn/**).

435 Pollution Prevention Information Exchange (PIES)

Maintained by the Environmental Protection Agency's Office of Pollution Prevention and Toxics.

Bulletin Board: For information on connecting by modem, contact the Pollution Prevention Information Clearinghouse (PPIC) (see entry 421).

The electronic component of the Pollution Prevention Information Clearinghouse (PPIC) (see entry 421), the Pollution Prevention Information Exchange (PIES) is an excellent medium for those who want to reduce or eliminate industrial pollution and who need answers to technical and policy questions. In addition to messages and bulletins, there are mini-exchanges for regional programs and other special topics. PIES contains nine databases, including abstracts of case studies and other documents; summaries of state, federal, and corporate pollution prevention programs; and a directory of grants for pollution prevention efforts. Access is unrestricted and free. A four-page "Quick Reference Guide" and a more complete user's guide are available from PPIC. The network also provides full access to two United Nations Environment Programme (see entry 10) computer networks: the International Cleaner Production Clearinghouse, which was patterned after and shares information with PIES, and the OzonAction Information Clearinghouse, which conveys technical, programmatic, and policy information on reducing or eliminating the use of ozone-depleting substances.

Other Bulletin Boards

◆ The Solid Waste Information Clearinghouse (see entry 430, Solid Waste Association of North America)

Directories

436 Recycling Sourcebook

Edited by Thomas J. Cichonski and Karen Hill. 1st ed. Gale Research, 1992. Quadrennial. 563p. $80.00 (hardcover).

Diskette: Available from Gale Research.

The *Recycling Sourcebook* is the most comprehensive directory available of recycling information sources. The book's first half contains twenty-eight essays on recycling trends and practices, which makes it similar in content but of lesser quality than *The McGraw-Hill Recycling Handbook* (see entry 442). The second half of the book—a directory of more than four thousand resources—is a valuable starting point for research on solid waste management, waste minimization, and household hazardous wastes, as well as recycling. Users will find associations, government offices, funding sources, libraries and research centers, brokers and dealers of recycled materials, manufacturers of recycling equipment and recycled products, and recycling collection facilities—all arranged by type of information source. Also included are 390 books, 61 directories, 125 periodicals, 43 videos, and 22 online databases. Annotations average about two sentences each, but the descriptions can be as long as five sentences. Most of the information is taken from other directories published by Gale Research. The subject index lists entry numbers only. Even with its limitations, the *Recycling Sourcebook* remains an invaluable reference—the best of its kind. Debi Kimball's *Recycling in America* (Contemporary World Issues series. ABC-CLIO, 1992) is similar in content but less comprehensive; it does, however, include a summary of state recycling laws.

437 Reference Guide to Pollution Prevention Resources

Edited by Beth Anderson and Deborah Hanlon. Environmental Protection Agency, Office of Pollution Prevention and Toxics, 1993; distributed by the Pollution Prevention Information Clearinghouse. 131p. Free.

Anyone who needs information on pollution prevention should have the outstanding, comprehensive *Reference Guide to Pollution Prevention Resources* on his or her desk. The directory's descriptions of university-affiliated and state-sponsored programs highlight key features—technical assistance, training, or regulatory advice—and provide contact information. All relevant federal programs are described in detail. In addition, state air pollution control agencies and regional pollution prevention contacts are listed. Other sections describe clearinghouses and hot-

lines, videos, manuals, reports, and fact sheets; these alone make this directory worth having.

Other Directories

◆ The *Recycled Products Guide* (see entry 597)

Bibliographies

438 Bibliography of Municipal Solid Waste Management Alternatives

Environmental Protection Agency, Office of Solid Waste, 1989; available from the RCRA/UST/EPCRA/Superfund Hotline. 103p. Free (paper).

The *Bibliography of Municipal Solid Waste Management Alternatives* describes handbooks, books, and other documents published by the private sector, nonprofit organizations, and the Environmental Protection Agency. Intended as an introduction to solid waste management issues for local decision makers, this bibliography can be useful to anyone in need of information on solid waste topics like waste stream analysis; source reduction; collection, transfer, and processing; recycling; composting; incineration; and landfilling. The book also has sections on educational resources and household hazardous wastes. Each entry includes a two-sentence abstract and provides the length, price, and date of the document, as well as where it can be found. Though most references are from the late 1980s, the work still provides a good foundation for research because many of its essential references remain relevant. Look for updates of this document as well as other bibliographies in the *Catalogue of Hazardous and Solid Waste Publications* (see entry 439).

439 Catalogue of Hazardous and Solid Waste Publications

7th ed. Environmental Protection Agency, Office of Solid Waste and Emergency Response, 1994; available from the RCRA/UST/EPCRA/Superfund Hotline. Updated regularly. 248p. Free (paper).

Internet: Available in chapter-by-chapter format on the Environmental Protection Agency (EPA) (see entry 56) gopher. Choose *EPA Offices and Regions*, then *Office of Solid Waste and*

Emergency Response, then *Office of Solid Waste (RCRA)*, then *Catalogue of Hazardous and Solid Waste Publications*.

Absolutely essential for research in the areas of hazardous and solid waste, the *Catalogue of Hazardous and Solid Waste Publications* describes roughly six hundred frequently requested Office of Solid Waste publications, and covers a wide range of issues: from air emissions to leachate to recycling to siting hazardous waste facilities. The catalog includes fact sheets, reports, bibliographies, and curriculum guides; most are recent, but some date back to the 1970s. The detailed subject index includes the full titles of publications. Annotations average two sentences in length. The catalog also explains where and how to order the cited documents, and is usually updated each year. Documents pertaining to underground storage tanks and Superfund are not covered; for these issues consult other Environmental Protection Agency (EPA) document bibliographies: *Guide to EPA Materials on Underground Storage Tanks* and *Compendium of Superfund Program Publications*. All three of these documents are free of charge. The catalog and the *Guide to EPA Materials on Underground Storage Tanks* can be ordered on the RCRA/UST/EPCRA/Superfund Hotline (see entry 422). Order the *Compendium* and its supplements from the National Technical Information Service (see entry 8).

Reference Handbooks

440 Environmental Hazards: Toxic Waste and Hazardous Material: A Reference Handbook

E. Willard Miller and Ruby M. Miller. Contemporary World Issues series. ABC-CLIO, 1991. 286p. $39.50 (hardcover).

Environmental Hazards is a one-stop source for high school–age toxic waste researchers. The book's first section provides an overview of waste management issues. It discusses oil pollution, toxics—including pesticides and asbestos—and hazardous waste: sites, control, transportation, and effects. A brief chronology highlighting significant pollution-related events is followed by summaries of relevant federal laws and regulations. The last half of the book is a guide to information sources: a directory of public and private organizations, and an annotated bibliography of dictionaries, indices, bibliographies, handbooks, books, and audiovisual materials. Emphasis is heaviest on books, and on numerous nonannotated listings of articles and government documents.

441 Guide to the Management of Hazardous Waste: A Handbook for the Businessman and Concerned Citizen

J. William Haun. Fulcrum Publishing, 1991. 224p. $34.95 (paper).

Though it is geared toward small business owners, concerned citizens and public officials can also use the *Guide to the Management of Hazardous Waste* to gain a firm understanding of hazardous waste issues. The guide is divided into three equal parts. The first gives background information, including: compliance procedures; citizen involvement; recognizing hazardous waste; and primers on toxicology, risk assessment, and risk management. The second part describes hazardous waste management technology related to land disposal and groundwater protection, incineration, treatment, and minimization and recycling. The final section provides summaries of two relevant laws, the Resource Conservation and Recovery Act (RCRA) and the Comprehensive Environmental Response, Compensation, and Liability Act (CERCLA), and covers the chemistry of waste materials. This publication offers a straightforward alternative to highly technical handbooks.

442 The McGraw-Hill Recycling Handbook

Edited by Herbert F. Lund. McGraw-Hill, 1993. 1,152p. $87.50 (hardcover).

443 The Recycler's Manual for Business, Government, and the Environmental Community

David R. Powelson and Melinda A. Powelson. Van Nostrand Reinhold, 1992. 544p. $64.95 (hardcover).

444 Taking Out the Trash: A No-Nonsense Guide to Recycling

Jennifer Carless. Island Press, 1992. 249p. $35.00 (hardcover), $16.00 (paper).

The McGraw-Hill Recycling Handbook, The Recycler's Manual for Business, Government, and the Environmental Community and *Taking Out the Trash* are considered to be the most comprehensive reference texts on recycling. *The Recycling Handbook*, a compilation of thirty-five essays written by recognized recycling experts, is the standard reference guide for managers of recycling programs. Main topics include: analysis of the solid waste problem; a history of recycling; descriptions of recyclable commodities such as paper, plastic, and tires; the role of legislation; and advice on planning and implementing a recycling program. *The Recycler's Manual* covers very similar ground in half the pages. It provides extensive directories of waste exchanges, end users of recyclable materials, and state recycling programs, and also has a complete list of periodicals that cover recycling issues. Writing in both is technical but clear. *Taking Out the Trash* remains substantive while translating much of the same information into language and a format that will appeal to a lay audience. As reference books for recycling issues, all three are excellent, and all are more complete than the first half of the *Recycling Sourcebook* (see entry 436), which covers similar material.

445 Preventing Industrial Toxic Hazards: A Guide for Communities

Marian Wise and Lauren Kenworthy. 2nd ed. INFORM, 1993. 200p. $25.00 (paper).

Preventing Industrial Toxic Hazards offers practical guidance for evaluating the source-reduction efforts of local factories. After introducing the merits of source reduction and describing the steps companies can take to implement source-reduction programs, this guide gives activists a step-by-step process for studying local plants. A lengthy section includes an excellent primer on the *Toxic Release Inventory (TRI)* (see entry 381) and other essential government information sources, preparatory questions for interviewing plant officials, and comprehensive yet easy-to-

understand worksheets for the entire process. The guide also includes information on monitoring a state government's source-reduction program. This exceptional book is extremely easy to use, especially for those with a limited technical background. It includes annotated chapter bibliographies, state contacts for *TRI* and pollution prevention information, sample Environmental Protection Agency reporting forms, a glossary, and a table that provides an overview of the known health effects of *TRI* chemicals.

Introductory Reading

446 Cleaning Up the Mess: Implementation Strategies in Superfund

Thomas W. Church and Robert T. Nakamura. The Brookings Institution, 1993. 209p. $34.95 (hardcover), $14.95 (paper).

Cleaning Up the Mess analyzes the notorious process that precedes the cleanup of a Superfund site. The research for the book was funded by Clean Sites (see entry 424). Background and case studies are given for three strategies—prosecution, accommodation, and public works. These strategies are evaluated according to four, often competing, criteria: appropriateness of remedy, minimization of taxpayer expense, speed of remediation, and minimization of transaction costs. The book's final two chapters synthesize its findings, show the tradeoffs of each strategy, and discuss considerations for reform, both in practice and in the structure of the law. Written concisely and objectively, this work is targeted toward policymakers, but anyone struggling to understand and reform Superfund will find this an informative starting point.

447 Nuclear Imperatives and Public Trust: Dealing with Radioactive Waste

Luther J. Carter. Resources for the Future. 1987. 473p. $30.00 (hard-cover) $14.95 (paper).

Nuclear Imperatives and Public Trust provides a comprehensive overview of the political and technical issues surrounding high- and low-level nuclear waste disposal. This book analyzes the United States' approach to waste problems associated with nuclear weapons and power; five other Western countries are also covered. The book is comprehensive and objective; it dispels popular public misconceptions concerning the potential dangers of nuclear waste and avoids emotional overstatement. Those wishing to stay abreast of current political wrangling on the subject of nuclear waste should contact the Nuclear Information and Resource Service (see entry 323) or the Civilian Radioactive Waste Information Center (see entry 419).

448 Recycling and Incineration: Evaluating the Choices

Richard A. Denison and John Ruston. Sponsored by the Environmental Defense Fund. Island Press, 1990. 322p. $34.95 (hardcover), $19.95 (paper).

Recycling and Incineration is a practical, sophisticated primer written to help concerned citizens, government officials, and businesspeople choose waste disposal methods. The book succeeds in supplying local communities with the hard data they will need to demonstrate that recycling is a viable component of successful solid waste management. *Recycling and Incineration* compares landfilling, incineration, recycling, and waste reduction based on health, legal, economic, and scientific considerations. Anyone whose community is struggling with solid waste decisions should consult this handbook to attain a clear understanding of the benefits and drawbacks of different strategies.

449 Rubbish! The Archaeology of Garbage

William Rathje and Cullen Murphy. HarperCollins Publishers, 1992. 256p. $23.00 (hardcover).

As the leader of a project that has sorted and cataloged 250,000 pounds of garbage, authors William Rathje and Cullen Murphy use *Rubbish! The Archaeology of Garbage* to summarize their findings and preach their beliefs. Interesting details and anecdotes show what our garbage consists of and what that says about the American lifestyle. The book contradicts many common assumptions about solid waste issues by denying the biodegradability of most trash, sorting through the fact and fiction of disposable diapers and incineration, and questioning recycling

as a panacea. In this book, there is no solid waste crisis; rather, it is presented as a real but solvable problem that has become far too politicized. However, *Rubbish!* is not as argumentative as Judd Alexander's thought-provoking *In Defense of Garbage* (Praeger, 1993), which belittles the waste problem.

450 War On Waste: Can America Win Its Battle With Garbage?

Louis Blumberg and Robert Gottlieb. Island Press, 1989. 301p. $34.95 (hardcover), $19.95 (paper).

War On Waste serves as an introduction to solid waste management, with an emphasis placed on the limits of incineration. Introductory chapters document the recent rise of incineration and the policy and politics of solid waste management. The book's middle chapters explore the environmental hazards and economic drawbacks of incineration and summarize a case study of a Los Angeles incinerator—based on the report from which *War on Waste* evolved. *War on Waste*'s last three chapters explore the need for the development of alternative waste policies: recycling, reusing, and reducing. Though its bias against incineration is blatant, this book remains a good guide to solid waste issues. Chapters contain numerous tables and graphs and extensive references.

Abstracts and Indices

451 Hazardous Waste Superfund Database (HWSFD)

Electronic document. Environmental Protection Agency, Office of Information Resources Management. Updated regularly.

Bulletin Board: Available on the EPA Online Library System (OLS) (see entry 60). Choose *Hazardous Waste*.

A compressed copy of the database can be downloaded from the Cleanup Information Bulletin Board (CLU-IN) (see entry 433). For more information, read Bulletin 805 on CLU-IN.

Internet: OLS (see Bulletin Board, above) is available on the Internet.

The *Hazardous Waste Superfund Database (HWSFD)* is an electronic database that abstracts items in the Environmental Protection Agency's (EPA) Hazardous Waste Superfund Collection. The full collection is housed at the EPA Headquarters library, but many documents are either available at EPA regional libraries, or from the National Technical Information Service (NTIS) (see entry 8). This special collection focuses on hazardous waste, especially from a regulatory perspective, but it also contains a number of resources on related topics, such as solid waste and toxicology. Documents include commercial books and periodicals, EPA reports, directives from the EPA's Office of Solid Waste and Emergency Response, and Superfund Records of Decisions. Database entries are brief but descriptive. For a directory of EPA publications on Superfund, order the free *Compendium of Superfund Program Publications* and its supplements from NTIS.

452 Waste Information Digests

Environmental Studies Institute of the International Academy at Santa Barbara, 1990–. Monthly.

Database Vendor: Available as part of the *PTS Newsletter Database* on DIALOG, and as *Waste Information Digests* on LEXIS/NEXIS.

The only abstract newsletter devoted to waste issues, *Waste Information Digests* describes published materials on all solid and hazardous waste–related issues—from activated sludge to nuclear waste to wastewater treatment. All angles are covered: research and technological advances; policy and legislation; and enforcement and compliance. Readers are just as likely to see a summary of an article from *Environmental Action* or the *Wall Street Journal* as they are a description of a report from the United Nations or a book from a publisher of technical monographs. Each issue includes about twenty-five entries; annotations average 150 to 200 words. *Waste Information Digests* offers a great way to stay current on all waste issues. The International Academy, *Waste Information Digests'* publisher, also produces *Energy Review*, which combines information found in both *Waste Information*

Digests and its sister publication, *Alternative Energy Digests* (see entry 344).

Periodicals

453 Toxic Trade Update

Greenpeace, Toxic Trade Campaign. Quarterly. 36p. $10.00/year for students, $20.00/year for individuals and nonprofits, $50.00/year for businesses.

EcoNet: For a searchable version, choose *Online Databases*, then *News Services*, then *Greenpeace Toxic Trade Updates*.

Internet: Available on the Institute for Global Communications (see entry 57) gopher. From the main menu, choose *Publications & News Services on the IGC Networks*, then *Greenpeace Toxic Trade Updates*.

Toxic Trade Update tracks the latest developments in the international trade of toxic wastes, toxic products, and toxic technologies. Each issue includes updates on international legislative affairs, grassroots movements against toxic trade, and recent toxic trade schemes in all parts of the world. Issues also include activist alerts, announcements of new information sources, and the Greenpeace Greenwash Award for notoriously negligent companies. Published by Greenpeace's (see entry 32) Toxic Trade Campaign, a leading watchdog project, the *Update* is the best way to keep abreast of issues related to the international toxic waste trade. The Toxic Trade Campaign also offers the community action kit *How to Make Your Community a Waste Trade Free Zone: A Grassroots Approach to Environmental Justice* for $3.

454 Waste Age

Environmental Industry Associations. Monthly. 1969–. 140p. $75.00/year, $105.00/2 years.

Waste Age is the most comprehensive and readable waste industry magazine. Articles focus on the economic and industrial aspects of waste collection, landfills, recycling, and other solid waste issues. Most articles survey current issues, with the aid of informative charts and graphs, and provide a good perspective on industry trends. *Waste Age* includes news on products, companies, and people, as well as extensive advertisements. *Waste Age*'s *Recycling Times* is a biweekly newspaper on the recycling industry; it includes prices of recyclable wastes around the country.

Other Periodicals

◆ *Wastelines* (see entry 22, Environmental Action)

CHAPTER TEN

Water

What This Chapter Covers

This chapter focuses on groundwater and surface water quality as well as the conservation of freshwater and marine ecosystems such as rivers, wetlands, coasts, and oceans. Drinking water, wastewater, freshwater availability, and marine biodiversity conservation are also covered.

For More Information

- ◆ See **General** for resources on all environmental issues, including those related to water.
- ◆ See **Agriculture** for resources on pesticides and other agricultural nonpoint sources of pollution.
- ◆ See **Air** for resources on acid rain.
- ◆ See **Waste** for resources on water pollution, such as leaking underground storage tanks.

Government Clearinghouses

455 National Drinking Water Clearinghouse (NDWC)
West Virginia University
P.O. Box 6064
Morgantown, WV 26506

Phone: 800/624-8301. Fax: 304/293-3161

Bulletin Board: NDWC maintains the Drinking Water Information Exchange (DWIE-BBS). To connect by modem, dial 800/932-7459.

Internet: DWIE-BBS (see bulletin board, above) is available via FedWorld's GateWay (see entry 61). Choose *81* for *DWIE-BBS (EPA).*

456 National Small Flows Clearinghouse (NSWC)
West Virginia University
P.O. Box 6064
Morgantown, WV 26506

Phone: 800/624-8301. Fax: 304/293-3161

Bulletin Board: NSWC maintains the Wastewater Treatment Information Exchange (WTIE-BBS). To connect by modem, dial 800/544-1936 or 304/293-5969.

Internet: WTIE-BBS (see bulletin board, above) is available via FedWorld's GateWay (see entry 61). Choose *37* for *WTIE-BBS (EPA).*

Both the National Drinking Water Clearinghouse (NDWC) and the National Small Flows Clearinghouse (NSWC) are comprehensive sources of information for water systems personnel in small communities. NDWC is funded by the Department of Agriculture's Rural Development Administration; NSWC—which covers wastewater—is funded by the Environmental Protection Agency. Both are operated by the Energy and Water Research Center at West Virginia University. Information specialists at each clearinghouse can provide free technical assistance and referrals, as well as free or low-cost educational publications and products. There is an electronic bulletin board system for each. *On Tap* and *Small Flows*—free clearinghouse newsletters—are useful to water professionals in both small and large communities.

457 National Water Information Clearinghouse (NWIC)
Department of Interior
U.S. Geological Survey
423 National Center
Reston, VA 22902

Phone: 800/426-9000. Fax: 703/648-5704

Donald Bingham, Hydrologist

The National Water Information Clearinghouse (NWIC) provides free access to data and information stored by the U.S. Geological Survey (USGS) on surface and groundwater quantity and quality. NWIC can perform simple searches to retrieve the actual data, but the clearinghouse will also refer callers to state Water Resource Centers, regional USGS offices, or other organizations that can provide the necessary data. The new National Water Information System (NWIS-II) now integrates all USGS hydrologic data—groundwater, water quality, biological, water use—into a single system. For summaries of USGS data—the most authoritative of its kind—and background information to understand its context, use USGS National Water Summary reports; each large biannual edition covers a particular topic such as floods and droughts, surface water quality, or water supply. Although primarily a referral center to USGS and other federal data on water, NWIC can also provide *A User's Guide to Water Resources Information: District of Columbia, Maryland, Virginia* and public and classroom education materials: fact sheets, pamphlets, and posters on groundwater, acid rain, and other topics.

458 Office of Water Resource Center
Environmental Protection Agency
401 M Street, SW, Mail Code RC-4100
Washington, DC 20460

Phone: 202/260-7786

The Office of Water Resource Center distributes documents produced by the Environmental Protection Agency's (EPA) Office of Ground Water and Drinking Water, Office of Science and Technology, and Office of Wastewater Enforcement and Compliance. The *Ground Water Technical Assistance Directory, Ambient Water Quality Criteria* documents, *Designing a Water Conservation Program: An Annotated Bibliography of*

Source Materials, the *Office of Water Environmental and Program Information Systems Compendium* (see entry 479), and the *Guide to Federal Water Quality Programs and Information* (see entry 478) are among the many public education materials and technical documents the Resource Center distributes. Numerous publications concerning storm water are also available, as are several separate publications lists. When calling, leave the title and number of the document desired on the voice answering system; delivery may take three to four weeks. Publications in stock are free of charge; otherwise, they must be purchased from the National Technical Information Service (see entry 8), the ERIC Clearinghouse for Science, Mathematics, and Environmental Education (see entry 527), or the National Small Flows Clearinghouse (see entry 456). To order EPA wetlands publications, contact the Wetlands Information Hotline (see entry 461); for oceans and watersheds call the National Center for Environmental Publications and Information (see entry 7).

459 Safe Drinking Water Hotline
Environmental Protection Agency
401 M Street, SW, Mail Code 4604
Washington, DC 20460

Phone: 800/426-4791. Fax: 202/260-8072

The Safe Drinking Water Hotline responds to consumers' concerns about the quality of their drinking water and supplies information on federal drinking water regulations. Answers to questions will often be supplemented with Environmental Protection Agency (EPA) publications at no charge. Consumers can be referred to appropriate federal, state, and local contacts for specific information on local drinking water conditions, bottled water, home water treatment units, and groundwater protection; referrals are also made to state contacts that can supply phone numbers for EPA-certified drinking water testing laboratories. The hotline cannot discuss manufacturers or recommend products. State and local officials can receive clarification of drinking water regulations and explanations of EPA policies and guidelines. This hotline is an excellent source of information on all aspects of drinking water.

460 Water Quality Information Center (WQIC)
Department of Agriculture
National Agricultural Library
10301 Baltimore Boulevard, 4th Floor
Beltsville, MD 20705

Phone: 301/504-6077. Fax: 301/504-7098.
E-mail: wqic@nalusda.gov

Joseph R. Makuch, Coordinator

Bulletin Board: WQIC has a sub-board on the Agricultural Library Forum (ALF) (see entry 197). From the main menu, choose *Join Conferences*, then *Water Quality Information Network*.

Internet: ALF (see bulletin board, above) is available via FedWorld's GateWay (see entry 61). Choose *2* for *ALF (USDA)*.

In addition, WQIC has space on the National Agricultural Library (NAL) (see entry 183) gopher. From the NAL gopher, choose *NAL Information Centers*, then *Water Quality Information Center*.

The Water Quality Information Center (WQIC) collects, organizes, and disseminates scientific information pertaining to the effects of agriculture on surface and groundwater quality. Callers are primarily researchers, but state governmental officials and private environmental organizations frequently use the resources provided by WQIC. WQIC performs brief literature searches on *AGRICOLA* (see entry 221, *Bibliography of Agriculture*) and *Selected Water Resources Abstracts* (see entry 500), maintains its own vertical files, makes referrals to experts and other information sources, and distributes National Agricultural Library Quick Bibliographies. Sample bibliographies include *Simulation Models*, *GIS and Nonpoint-Source Pollution*, and *Regulating Water Quality: Policy, Standards and Laws*. The center also provides extensive literature searches, using DIALOG, on a cost-recovery basis, and serves as the system operator for the Water Information Network (WIN), a sub-board on the Agricultural Library Forum (see entry 197) bulletin board system (since WIN allows user to download WQIC publications and other useful information, as well as ask questions, it is often more efficient to consult WIN before contacting the Information Center).

461 Wetlands Information Hotline
Environmental Protection Agency
2200 Clarendon Boulevard, Suite 900
Arlington, VA 22201

Phone: 800/832-7828. Fax: 703/525-0201

A primary source of information on wetlands, the Wetlands Information Hotline provides data on the values and functions of wetlands, as well as options for their protection. The hotline serves as the contact point for the Environmental Protection Agency's (EPA) Wetlands Division and handles many inquiries regarding wetlands protection regulations and guidelines. Federal regulatory questions can be answered over the phone and supplemented with EPA documents; questions pertaining to state or local wetlands regulations will be directed to appropriate state offices. Items on the hotline's publications list include the *Our Wetlands Need You Now* brochure, *404 (b)(1) Guidelines*, the *Catalog of State Wetlands Protection Grants*, and classroom educational materials. Most publications are distributed free of charge.

For maps of wetlands and other Department of Interior wetland resources, call the U.S Geological Survey's Earth Science Information Center at 800/USA-MAPS (872-6277) or 703/648-6045.

Other Government Clearinghouses

◆ The Water Efficiency Clearinghouse (see entry 463, American Water Works Association)

Organizations

To learn about local river conservation organizations and experts, consult the *Directory of River Information Specialists* (see entry 469, River Network) and the *River Conservation Directory* (see entry 480).

462 American Rivers
801 Pennsylvania Avenue, SE, Suite 400
Washington, DC 20003

Phone: 202/547-6900. Fax: 202/543-6142.
E-mail: amrivers@igc.apc.org

Kevin Coyle, President

American Rivers works to protect rivers—particularly to expand the National Wild and Scenic Rivers System—through lobbying, litigation, and cooperative negotiation with government and industry. The group is also a leader in monitoring and establishing environmentally sound hydropower policies. Publications include *Grassroots River Protection: Saving Rivers under the National Wild and Scenic Rivers Act through Community-Based River Protection Strategies and State Actions*; *The American Rivers Guide to Wild and Scenic River Designation*; and a comprehensive list of U.S. rivers that have been identified as possessing some outstanding ecological, recreational, cultural, historic, or scenic value. Membership includes the quarterly newsletter *American Rivers*. There are regional American Rivers offices in Seattle (206/545-7133) and Phoenix (602/264-1823).

463 American Water Works Association (AWWA)
6666 West Quincy Avenue
Denver, CO 80235

Phone: 303/794-7711. Fax: 303/794-7310

John Mannion, Executive Director

The American Water Works Association (AWWA) supports public water supply system professionals. Members and nonmembers can gain information in a number of ways. The annual *Buyers' Guide* is three directories rolled into one: a directory of members (suppliers, manufacturers, contractors, consultants); a directory of product information; and a catalog of more than four hundred AWWA publications. AWWA periodicals include the monthly *Journal* and the biweekly newsletter *Waterweek*. *WATERNET*, an abstract database of drinking water literature, is sold on CD-ROM by AWWA, and is also available online on DIALOG; AWWA's Information Services Department (303/347-6170) can perform searches for a fee and supply the full text of cited articles. Finally, AWWA's Small System Operational Support Program (800/366-0107) provides free assistance to small water systems serving one thousand connections or less (see also the National Drinking Water Clearinghouse [see entry 455]). AWWA also operates the recently established—Environmental Protection Agency–

funded—Water Efficiency Clearinghouse (800/559-9855), which aids utilities and water management professionals.

464 Center for Marine Conservation (CMC)
1725 DeSales Street, NW, Suite 500
Washington, DC 20036
Phone: 202/429-5609. Fax: 202/872-0619

Roger McManus, President

The Center for Marine Conservation (CMC) is the leading advocate for the worldwide protection of all marine life and its habitats. CMC conducts policy-oriented and in-the-field scientific research, promotes public awareness through education, helps citizens get involved in public policy decisions, and works closely with other conservation organizations, government, and industry to develop strategies that will further its five primary objectives: to conserve marine biological diversity; protect critical marine habitats; prevent marine pollution; protect endangered species, particularly wildlife threatened by international trade; and manage fisheries for conservation. CMC produces numerous educational materials, including books (e.g., *Environmental Quality in the Gulf of Mexico: A Citizen Guide*), reports (e.g., *Sewage Treatment: America's Pipe Dream*), newsletters (e.g., *Marine Conservation News*, *Sanctuary Currents*), and fact sheets, plus slide shows, videos, and posters. The organization also cosponsored another important report: *Global Marine Biological Diversity* (see entry 485).

For marine-related legislative information, contact the Marine Fish Conservation Network (contact Bill Mott at 202/857-3274). The network was created in 1993 by the CMC and several other conservation organizations to work for changes in the Magnuson Fishery Conservation and Management Act.

The Cousteau Society (804/523-9335) and the American Oceans Campaign (310/576-6162) are two additional organizations that are good sources of marine conservation information.

465 Clean Water Action (CWA)
1320 18th Street, NW, Suite 300
Washington, DC 20036

Phone: 202/457-1286. Fax: 202/457-0287

David Zwick, Director

Clean Water Action (CWA) is one of the largest and most effective grassroots environmental organizations. CWA works in a variety of ways—public-interest lobbying, research, canvassing, coalition building, and organizing—to achieve strong water-quality protection laws and to promote their enforcement. Its chief priorities are to protect and preserve coastal and inland waters; promote better testing and treatment of drinking water; and protect groundwater from toxic chemicals. Because of its interest in water, Clean Water Action is a grassroots leader on many waste and toxics issues, including fighting incineration, promoting source reduction and recycling, and cleaning up hazardous waste sites. The national office in Washington, D.C., is one of twenty-eight CWA offices around the country. Contributors of $24 or more receive a year's subscription to *Clean Water Action News*.

466 Coast Alliance
235 Pennsylvania Avenue, SE
Washington, DC 20003

Phone: 202/546-9554. Fax: 202/546-9609

Beth Millemann, Executive Director

The Coast Alliance works to increase public awareness of coastal issues and to strengthen programs and policies that protect coastal ecosystems. The Coastal Alliance does not have organizational or individual members; *Alliance* refers to the many leading coastal protection advocates from national and regional environmental organizations who sit on the group's board of directors. The group also has networks of individuals to contact in each of its areas of focus: the Coastal Barrier Resources Program; the National Flood Insurance Program; the Coastal Zone Management Act; and contaminated sediments. The Coast Alliance offers various fact sheets, issue papers, and longer works, such as *And Two If By Sea: Fighting the Attack on America's Coasts*, a citizen's guide to coastal management, and the *Briefing Book*, presented to the 103rd Congress on coastal, ocean and Great Lakes issues.

467 International Rivers Network (IRN)
1847 Berkeley Way
Berkeley, CA 94703

Phone: 510/848-1155. Fax: 510/848-1008.
E-mail: irn@igc.apc.org

Owen Lammers, Executive Director

EcoNet: IRN posts information and its periodicals in several conferences—e.g., *BankCheck Quarterly* is in *dev.worldbank*, and *World River Review, IRN Action Alerts*, and the *IRN Newssheet* are in *env.dams* and *env.water*.

The International Rivers Network (IRN) works to stop the construction of destructive river development projects (hydroelectric, irrigation, water supply, flood control, channelization, or transportation projects) and to promote sound river management options. IRN conducts research, publishes reports, and provides technical, financial, and communications assistance at the request of its individual and nongovernmental organization members. It also publishes the *World Rivers Review*, a quarterly newsletter that provides updates on antidevelopment campaigns and alternative river management strategies, and the *BankCheck Quarterly*, which features articles on the environmental, social, and economic impacts of the projects and policies of the World Bank and the International Monetary Fund (IMF). These and other publications, such as *IRN Action Alerts* and the *IRN Newssheet*, which abstracts recent articles, are available on EcoNet (see entry 58) conferences. IRN strives to make whatever information it obtains available to any organization requesting it, at no cost where possible.

468 National Ground Water Association (NGWA)

6375 Riverside Drive
Dublin, OH 43017

Phone: 614/761-1711. Phone (information center): 614/761-3222. Fax (information center): 614/761-3446

David Carpenter, Director of Information Center

Bulletin Board: The National Ground Water Association's National Ground Water Information Center (NGWIC) maintains the Ground Water Network. For more information contact NGWIC.

The National Ground Water Association (NGWA) sponsors many conferences and workshops for groundwater professionals, and publishes the periodicals *Ground Water Monitoring Review*,

Well Water Journal, and *Journal of Ground Water*, as well as more than four hundred other publications. NGWA's National Ground Water Information Center (NGWIC) offers unparalleled fee-based information services for all groundwater issues. NGWIC supplies technical assistance, expert referrals, literature searches, and document retrieval. Researchers can also dial in directly to fourteen databases on the electronic Ground Water Network, the largest of which is *Ground Water On-line*, an index to more than seventy thousand literature citations. The network contains a wealth of other information, including groundwater industry standards and regulations and directories of products, manufacturers, consultants, and software. The thirty thousand printed titles, ten thousand microfiche documents, and sixty videotapes in the NGWIC library are available through Inter-Library Loan.

469 River Network

P.O. Box 8787
Portland, OR 97207

Phone: 800/423-6747; 503/241-3506.
Fax: 503/241-9256.
E-mail: rivernet@igc.apc.org

Phil Wallin, Executive Director

The River Network supports grassroots river conservationists at the state and regional levels by helping them to build effective organizations and then linking them together. This national nonprofit organization provides strategic and fundraising assistance; organizational development support; and research assistance on river issues, threats, and protection tools. It also works to acquire and conserve riverlands and riparian areas. Callers can request a search of the *Directory of River Information Specialists (DORIS)*, a database of more than six hundred activists and organizations that are willing to share strategies and provide advice; *DORIS* includes many smaller organizations not included in the *River Conservation Directory* (see entry 480). The River Network publishes many materials that support river conservation organizations, such as the excellent quarterly newsletter *River Voices; People Protecting Rivers: A Collection of Lessons from Grassroots Activists; C(3) or C(4): Choosing Your Tax Exempt Status;* and *River Wealth*, a collection of fundraising ideas. The organization also sponsored the definitive guidebook *How to Save a River* (see entry 486). Partnership dues are on a sliding scale. The River Network is an outstanding, comprehensive resource for the river conservation activist.

470 Save Our Streams Program (SOS)
Izaak Walton League of America
707 Conservation Lane
Gaithersburg, MD 20878

Phone: 800/284-4952; 301/548-0150.
Fax: 301/548–0146

Karen Firehock, Program Director

The Save Our Streams Program (SOS) supports concerned citizens involved in volunteer water-quality monitoring projects, especially in rivers and streams. Its *Monitors* database contains more than five thousand water protection programs; many of these contacts participate in the SOS program, but others are also included. Most database printouts—e.g., relevant state officials, groups monitoring a particular river—are available at no charge. SOS will send out a kit ($8) that includes background information on volunteer monitoring and the materials necessary to survey and record the data. A free bibliography on volunteer water monitoring is updated annually. Save Our Streams is only one of many programs that support volunteer monitors. Those looking to find a volunteer monitoring program in their area or who need support for an existing program will also want to look through the *National Directory of Citizen Volunteer Environmental Monitoring Programs* (see entry 502, *The Volunteer Monitor*), or contact one of the other large volunteer monitoring assistance programs directly: the River Watch Network (800/639-8108; 802/223-3840 in Vermont, 915/772-8650 in Texas); the Global Rivers Environmental Education Network (GREEN) (fax: 313/761-4951 in Michigan—GREEN also has ten conferences on EcoNet [see entry 58] through which students share information); or the Adopt-a-Stream Foundation (206/388-3487 in Washington state).

471 Terrene Institute
1717 K Street, NW, Suite 801
Washington, DC 20006

Phone: 202/833-8317. Fax: 202/296-4071

Judy Taggert, Executive Vice President

The Terrene Institute is a nonprofit research and educational organization that specializes in freshwater quality, management, restoration, and nonpoint source pollution prevention. The institute sponsors conferences and workshops and produces many outstanding publications, often in cooperation with the Environmental Protection Agency. In addition to publishing *Nonpoint Source News-Notes* (see entry 501) and operating the Nonpoint Source Electronic Bulletin Board (NPS BBS) (see entry 474), Terrene also maintains the *Watershed Information Resource System (WIRS)*—formerly the *Clean Lakes Clearinghouse*—a database of more than four thousand abstracts of articles on lake and watershed restoration, protection, and management. Call 800/726-LAKE (5253) to have the staff perform a search ($25, plus 10¢ per reference, plus postage and handling), or purchase the entire database on an IBM-compatible disk ($250). The Terrene Institute also produces many other publications, both for professionals (e.g., *A Strategy for Evaluating the Effectiveness and Longevity of In-Lake Treatment*; *Development and Water Quality: A Decisionmaker's Guide to Protecting the Urban Environment*) and active citizens (e.g., *Organizing Lake Users: A Practical Guide*; *Lake Smarts: The First Lake Maintenance Handbook: A Do-It-Yourself Guide to Solving Lake Problems*; *Clean Water in Your Watershed: A Citizen's Guide to Watershed Protection*) as well as educational materials for teachers and the public. Ask for a catalog.

472 Water Environment Federation (WEF)
601 Wythe Street
Alexandria, VA 22314

Phone: 703/684-2400. Phone (membership hotline): 800/666-0206. Fax: 703/684-2492

Quincalee Brown, Executive Director

The Water Environment Federation (WEF) is an association that supports some forty thousand professionals and one thousand companies in wastewater treatment and water pollution control. In 1992, WEF led a coalition of more than eighty organizations that produced *A National Water Agenda for the 21st Century: Water Quality 2000: Final Report*—which provides consensus policy recommendations. WEF publishes *Standard Methods of the Examination of Water and Wastewater* and other operations manuals, technical reports, conference proceedings, and educational materials. Among the many periodicals WEF produces are *Water Environment and Technology*, a glossy monthly magazine that is distributed to all members; *Water Environment Research*, a monthly research journal; and *Water Environment Regulation Watch*, a monthly newsletter. Request a publications catalog.

Internet Sites

473 Universities Water Information Network (UWIN)

A project of the United States Geological Survey and the Universities Council on Water Resources.

Bulletin Board: To connect to UWIN by modem, dial 618/453-3324; log in as **guest**, and enter the password as **uwin** to reach the main menu of the Internet gopher server.

For technical support by fax, fax to 618/453-2671. For support by e-mail, send an e-message to **faye@uwin.uwin.siu.edu**.

Internet: To access UWIN, telnet to **gopher.uwin.siu.edu**; gopher to **gopher.uwin.siu.edu**; or, on the World Wide Web, the URL is **http://www.uwin.siu.edu/**.

The Universities Water Information Network (UWIN) serves as a networking and information tool for the water-related academic community. Access is free and available to everyone. Operated by the Universities Council on Water Resources (UCOWR) (618/536–7571) with support from the U.S. Geological Survey, this online system features UCOWR's *Expertise Directory* (see entry 476) and the entire contents of *Selected Water Resource Abstracts* (see entry 500). Other useful UWIN items include a calendar of events and a list of state Water Resource Centers as well as most of the technical and educa-

tional publications offered by UCOWR. A companion service, WaterTalk (to access, follow the directions after connecting to the system), is a set of bulletin boards (hydrology, international water resources, groundwater quality, water policy) on which users can ask questions of other users.

Bulletin Boards

474 Nonpoint Source Electronic Bulletin Board (NPS BBS)

Maintained by the Environmental Protection Agency's Office of Wetlands, Oceans, and Watersheds.

Bulletin Board: To connect to the Nonpoint Source Electronic Bulletin Board (NPS BBS) by modem, dial 301/589-0205. For technical support by phone, call the system operator at 301/589-5318.

Internet: NPS BBS is available via Fed World's GateWay (see entry 61). Choose *79* for *NPS-BBS (EPA)*.

Sponsored by the Environmental Protection Agency (EPA) and intended for government personnel, the Nonpoint Source Information Exchange Bulletin Board System (NPS BBS) has a wealth of information on a broad range of nonpoint source water pollution topics that will also interest researchers, businesspeople, and concerned individuals. There are eight Special Interest Groups (SIGs)—*Agricultural Issues*; *Fish Consumption Bans and Advisories*; *Waterbody System Support*; *NPS Research*; *Watershed Restoration Network*; *Total Maximum Daily Loads*; *Volunteer Monitoring*; and *Coastal NPS*—each with its own bulletins, file libraries, and messages. Access is free and all SIGs are open to everyone. The system's main menu provides access to databases on which users can search the *Compendium of Educational Materials on Water Environment* (see entry 481) (called the *Educational Materials Database* on this bulletin board system) and issues of the *Nonpoint Source News-Notes* (see entry 501). The searching software is extremely easy to use; order the *U.S. EPA Nonpoint Source Information Exchange Computer Bulletin Board System User's Manual* from the

National Center for Environmental Publications and Information (see entry 7) free of charge.

Other Bulletin Boards

◆ The Drinking Water Information Exchange (see entry 455, National Drinking Water Clearinghouse)

◆ The Wastewater Treatment Information Exchange (see entry 456, National Small Flows Clearinghouse)

Directories

475   Coral Reef Network Directory

Edited by Jeanne Kirby. Greenpeace, 1995. $5.00 (paper).

The *Coral Reef Network Directory* is the first guide to nongovernmental organizations working worldwide for the conservation of coral reef ecosystems. Descriptions are provided for almost one hundred international, national, regional, and local organizations. Each brief profile includes a contact person, address, electronic-mail address, and phone, fax, and telex numbers as well as information about geographical focus, areas of expertise, current projects, and publications. An appendix lists other important resources, such as periodicals and scientific institutions.

Another useful information resource, Coral Forest (415/788-7333), the only organization in the U.S. working exclusively on worldwide coral reef protection, produces an informative quarterly newsletter, *Coral Forest*, that summarizes coral reef conservation and related issues concerning pollution and coastal development. Two additional U.S.–based organizations, Reef Relief (305/294-3100) and Project Reef Keeper (305/642-9443), both of which focus on reefs off the coast of Florida, are also good sources of technical data on coral reef ecosystems.

476   Expertise Directory

Electronic document.

Internet: Available on the Universities Water Information Network (UWIN) (see entry 473). From the UWIN gopher main menu, choose

Water Resources Expert Directory. From the UWIN World Wide Web home page, choose *UWIN Water Expertise Directory.*

477   Nonpoint Source Water Quality Contacts Directory

Conservation Technology Information Center, 1994. Annual. 20p. $2.00 (paper).

Both the *Expertise Directory* and the *Nonpoint Source Water Quality Contacts Directory* are good sources of contact information for water professionals. The *Expertise Directory*—available only in an electronic format on the Internet—is an excellent source of contact information for university faculty who specialize in all water-related topics; consultants, state government officials, and other experts are also included. (The professionals voluntarily provide their own information: six keywords, language proficiencies, and how they can be contacted.) This directory is searchable by three hundred keywords on such varied topics as acid rain, desalination, groundwater modeling, shipping, rainfall-runoff processes, reservoir management, port facilities, mining, reefs, and wastewater treatment. It is not available in print. The *Nonpoint Directory* lists the names, addresses, and phone and fax numbers for individuals at the Soil and Water Conservation, Water Quality, and Coastal Zone Management agencies in all fifty states; it also provides state contacts for the following federal programs: Farm*A*Syst, the USDA Soil Conservation Service, the Cooperative Extension Service, and the USDA Agricultural Stabilization and Conservation Service. Both directories are reliable, up-to-date sources of information.

478   Guide to Federal Water Quality Programs and Information

Prepared by the Interagency Work Group on Water Quality. Sponsored by the Environmental Protection Agency, Environmental Statistics and Information Division, 1993; distributed by the Government Printing Office. 194p. $13.00 (paper).

Diskette: Available from the Environmental Protection Agency, Environmental Statistics and Information Division.

The *Guide to Federal Water Quality Programs and Information* is a directory of federal programs that provide statistics related to water quality. Entries—over a page in length each—include detailed descriptions of each program, the data the program covers, collection methods and frequency, geographic coverage, lists of resource publications and databases, and contact names. Topic areas include programs that monitor land, water, and resource use; pollutant loading programs; ambient surface and groundwater-quality programs; and preservation, protection, and restoration programs. Appendices describe and provide contact information for analytical tools, clearinghouses, data centers, and directories. Both this guide and the *Office of Water Environmental and Program Information Systems Compendium* (see entry 479) are truly indispensable for finding out which federal offices track what water-related data. The guide is available from the Office of Water Resource Center (see entry 458) free while supplies last.

479 Office of Water Environmental and Program Information Systems Compendium

Environmental Protection Agency, Office of Water, 1992; distributed by the Office of Water Resource Center. 152p. Free (paper).

The *Office of Water Environmental and Program Information Systems Compendium* is an outstanding directory of information sources and programs that are helpful to governmental water program managers, primarily those within the Environmental Protection Agency's (EPA) Office of Water (OW). The volume's first section includes two-page descriptions of twenty OW electronic and paper databases. The second section has paragraph-long descriptions of roughly seventy-five other specialized tracking and environmental systems, bulletin boards, bibliographies, clearinghouses, and hotlines within OW. A third section includes page-long descriptions of thirty-five selected tracking systems, informational systems, abstracts, indices, clearinghouses, and analytical tools outside OW, including those sponsored by the U.S. Geological Survey, the Fish and Wildlife Reference Service (see entry 266), and the National Oceanic and Atmospheric Administration. Matrices make it easy to see at a glance what type of information each system contains as well as common uses for each system. See the *Guide to Federal Water Quality Programs and Information* (see entry 478) for more detailed descriptions of information sources outside the Office of Water.

480 River Conservation Directory

American Rivers, 1994; distributed by the Rivers, Trails and Conservation Assistance Program of the National Park Service and the Government Printing Office. Biannual. 180p. $12.00 (paper).

The *River Conservation Directory* provides names and addresses for more than 2,050 organizations and agencies involved in river conservation efforts. Organized by state, listings include kayak clubs, fishing associations, nature centers, watershed councils, boating industry associations, and many other organizations that share river conservation interests. The directory also contains federal agencies and national and regional organizations. Most entries supply only address, phone number, and contact name, although some list number of members and include a one- or two-sentence organizational description. Those looking for local contacts may also want to call the River Network (see entry 469) for a search of their *Directory of River Information Specialists*.

Other Directories

- ◆ The *Directory of River Information Specialists* (see entry 469, River Network)

Bibliographies

481 Compendium of Educational Materials on the Water Environment

Compiled by the Alliance for Environmental Education. Sponsored by the Environmental Protection Agency, Office of Wetlands, Oceans, and Watersheds. 1991. $12.95 (paper).

Diskette: Available from the Alliance for Environmental Education for $10.00.

EcoNet: For a searchable version, choose *Online Databases*, then *Bibliographies & Library Catalogs*, then *EPA Water Compendium*.

Bulletin Board: Available on the Nonpoint Source Electronic Bulletin Board (NPS BBS) (see entry 474). At the main menu, choose *Online Databases/Programs*, then *Educational Materials Database*.

Internet: NPS BBS (see Bulletin Board, above) is available via FedWorld's GateWay (see entry 61).

The *Compendium of Educational Materials on the Water Environment* references more than seven hundred manuals, reports, pamphlets, fact sheets, and other outreach materials that are used by state and local governments to support their nonpoint source water pollution programs. Items are published by the private sector and various government offices. Many of these documents are practical; sample titles include *Help Us Monitor Your Lake*, *A Citizen's Handbook for Wetland Protection*, and *Drinking Water: A Community Action Guide*. Although there is some overlap with *Bibliography: Cooperative Extension System Water Quality Educational Materials* (see entry 482, *National Water Quality Database*), both bibliographies are excellent and should be used together.

482 National Water Quality Database

Maintained by the Purdue Cooperative Extension Service.

Internet: To access the *National Water Quality Database*, telnet to **hermes.ecn.purdue.edu**; log in as **cerf**; enter the password as **purdue**. Choose *National Water Quality Database*.
   To view the documents by gopher, gopher to **hermes.ecn.purdue.edu**. Choose *Purdue Cooperative Extension Gopher Information Server*, then *Environment*, then *Water Quality*. Choose *Publications* for an alphabetical list, or choose *water-quality.src* to search these titles by WAIS from the gopher.
   Some documents are also available by e-mail. For more information, send an e-mail message to **almanac@ecn.purdue.edu** with the words **send guide** in the body of the message.

The *National Water Quality Database* is an outstanding searchable database of both nontechnical and technical materials related to water. Sponsored by the Cooperative Extension Service, this database provides descriptions and ordering information for publications, audiovisuals, and software produced by Extension Service offices around the country. Topic coverage includes wells, testing, conservation, pest management, waste management, nutrient management, and drinking water quality. Representative sample titles include *Questions to Ask When Purchasing Water Treatment Equipment*, *What to Do If Your Septic Tank Fails*, *The Hidden Treasure: Instructional Materials for Groundwater Resources*, and *Recycling Used Motor Oil in New Jersey*. This database allows users to search for references, read the full text of many documents and to order them online. Items in the database were originally taken from a print document called *Bibliography: Cooperative Extension System Water Quality Educational Materials* that is no longer published; the last version (February 1992, $10) of the print bibliography may still be available from Agricultural Communication Service's Media Distribution Center at Purdue (317/494–6794).

Reference Handbooks

483 Environmental Hazards: Marine Pollution: A Reference Handbook

Martha Gorman. Contemporary World Issues series. ABC-CLIO, 1993. 252p. $39.50 (hardcover).

484 Water Quality and Availability: A Reference Handbook

E. Willard Miller and Ruby M. Miller. Contemporary World Issues series. ABC-CLIO, 1992. 430p. $39.50 (hardcover).

Like other volumes in ABC-CLIO's Contemporary World Issues series (*Environmental Hazards: Toxic Waste* and *Hazardous Material: A Reference Handbook* [see entry 440], *Nuclear Energy Policy: A Reference Handbook* [see entry 337]), *Environmental Hazards: Marine Pollution* and *Water Quality and Availability* provide a good place for high school students and other laypeople to start water research. *Marine Pollution* starts with a short introduction to pollutants (sewage, marine debris, toxic chemicals, heavy metals, oil, radioactive materials), and provides a conglomeration of reference materials (chronology of major events, biographical sketches, excerpts of treaties and laws, statistical facts and figures, quotations by experts on the issues), and a directory of information sources. *Water Quality and Availability* covers aspects of water supply and availability, and water-quality protection to a lesser extent. Like *Marine Pollution*, it provides background on the issues (e.g., physical characteristics of water, hydrologic cycle, U.S. consumption of water, sources of water contamination), a chronology of water-related topics, and a summary of federal water legislation. The directory of information sources is much larger than *Marine Pollution*'s, comprising the latter two thirds of the book. Coverage of national and international organizations, government agencies, periodicals, and audiovisual materials is basic but adequate for the intended audience. The deepest coverage in *Marine Pollution* lies in the section on books, which includes annotations, and citations of articles and government documents. Both volumes are good starting points for water research from the 1960s through the 1980s.

485 Global Marine Biological Diversity: A Strategy for Building Conservation into Decision Making

Edited by Elliot A. Norse. Co-sponsored by the Center for Marine Conservation, World Conservation Union, World Wildlife Fund, United Nations Environment Programme, and the World Bank. Island Press, 1993. 383p. $27.50 (paper).

Global Marine Biological Diversity offers a comprehensive overview of marine biodiversity conservation. In lay language, this book describes the importance of marine biological diversity, similarities and differences between marine and terrestrial conservation, threats to marine life, impediments to marine conservation, conservation methods, and existing protection programs. Like its sister document, *Global Biodiversity Strategy* (see entry 302), this book was written by more than one hundred authors from more than forty nations. However, unlike *Global Biodiversity Strategy*, this document contains more background information than policy prescriptions; only the final twenty-five pages offer recommendations for strategy implementation. Other recommended introductions to this topic are *The Living Ocean: Understanding and Protecting Marine Biodiversity* (Boyce Thorne-Miller and John G. Catena. Island Press, 1991) and *Diversity*

of Oceanic Life: An Evaluative Review (Melvin N. A. Peterson, Ed. Center for Strategic and International Studies, 1992).

486 How to Save a River: A Handbook for Citizen Action

Edited by David M. Bolling. Sponsored by the River Network. Island Press, 1994. 266p. $35.00 (hardcover), $17.00 (paper).

Sponsored by the River Network (see entry 469), *How to Save a River* provides river conservation organizations with the information they need to conduct successful campaigns. *How to Save a River* provides detailed information on organizational development; fundraising; coalition building; campaign development, including building public support; media outreach; and development of credible alternatives to damaging projects. The book details case studies from successful river campaigns and suggests many sources for further information.

487 The Poisoned Well: New Strategies for Groundwater Protection

Edited by Eric P. Jorgensen. Sponsored by Sierra Club Legal Defense Fund. Island Press, 1989. 415p. $35.00 (hardcover), $19.95 (paper).

The Poisoned Well walks grassroots activists through legal strategies for groundwater protection. The book begins with a concise introduction to groundwater issues—groundwater systems, health effects of groundwater contamination, sources of contamination, methods of testing—and then offers general advice to activists on organizing a campaign and interacting with government agencies and the courts. The bulk of the book provides the groundwater activist with step-by-step advice to fight contamination from underground storage tanks, mining, landfill seepage, pesticides, and all other sources. Relevant federal laws and government programs are discussed for each source of contamination. The book's final section summarizes strategies for dealing with state and local governments. *The Poisoned Well* is well organized, well referenced, and easy to use.

488 Statewide Wetlands Strategies: A Guide to Protecting and Managing the Resource

Compiled by the World Wildlife Fund. Island Press, 1992. 268p. $60.00 (hardcover), $40.00 (paper).

Statewide Wetlands Strategies is a comprehensive wetlands conservation guide for state managers. The guide is based on the recommendations of the National Wetlands Policy Forum, a diverse group representing industry, government, farming, ranching, and environmental concerns. The work's largest section analyzes the strengths and weaknesses of federal, state, local, and private wetlands programs; this allows managers to select appropriate strategies that will result in no net loss of wetlands. Another section shows how to collect and use wetlands data and reviews wetland classification systems, maps, and databases, as well as methods for evaluating, ranking, and categorizing wetlands. The handbook also discusses the effective development and management of a wetlands conservation program with support from varied interests. Numerous practical appendices include an accounting system for measuring no net loss and an extensive directory of state and federal contacts.

489 The Water Encyclopedia

Edited by Frits van der Leeden, Fred L. Troise, and David Keith Todd. 2nd ed. Lewis Publishers, 1989. 808p. $149.95 (hardcover).

With more than six hundred tables, as well as maps, charts, lists, diagrams, and illustrations, *The Water Encyclopedia* is an at-a-glance data source for all water-related issues. Chapter headings include: "Climate and Precipitation," "Hydrological Elements," "Surface Water," "Ground Water," "Water Use," "Water Quality," "Environmental Problems," and "Water Resources Management." A typical table, "Acreage Irrigated with On-farm Pumped Water in the United States" is broken down by state and year; users can also find information on "Potential Water Savings of Household Fixtures" and "Maximum Depths of the Oceans." Although some data is old, all of it is clearly cited. The book's last two chapters outline water law and treaties and provide directories of federal and state agencies, commissions, universities, organizations, and associations. The volume is well indexed and easy to use. For other sources of water data, consult *Water in Crisis: A Guide to the World's Fresh Water Resources* (see entry 490) and the National Water Information Clearinghouse (see entry 457).

490 Water in Crisis: A Guide to the World's Fresh Water Resources

Edited by Peter H. Gleick. Sponsored by the Pacific Institute for Studies in Development, Environment, and Security and the Stockholm Environment Institute. Oxford University Press, 1993. 473p. $55.00 (hardcover), $29.95 (paper).

Water in Crisis is an excellent source of information and data on the availability and quality of fresh water. The book's first one hundred pages consist of essays that provide an overview of critical freshwater issues, including health, ecosystems, agriculture, energy, development, politics and international law, and global climate change. All of the essays are well written, and compare favorably to *Last Oasis* (see entry 492) and *Water: The International Crisis* (see entry 493). The two hundred–plus tables that constitute the main part of the book are similar in content to those found in *The Water Encyclopedia* (see entry 489); examples include "Six estimates of the annual average continental water balance," "River transport of suspended sediment load to the oceans, by climatic region," and "Cost of water production versus Gross National Product for selected countries." Compared to *The Water Encyclopedia*, *Water in Crisis* neglects marine resources, has more of an international than national focus, and lacks graphics other than tables. However, each table in *Water in Crisis* includes a description of what the data actually means, as well as a discussion of the data's strengths and weaknesses. This volume is highly recommended.

Other Reference Handbooks

◆ *Is Your Water Safe To Drink?* (see entry 613)

Introductory Reading

491 Cadillac Desert: The American West and Its Disappearing Water

Marc Reisner. Penguin Books, original edition, 1986; updated 1993. 582p. $14.00 (paper).

Cadillac Desert is an informative and entertaining history of efforts, over the past fifty years, to dam Western rivers and divert their flow to crops and cities. *Cadillac Desert* concentrates especially on the individual and institutional players in the politics of water resources development, particularly the Bureau of Reclamation and the Army Corps of Engineers. The strength of this widely acclaimed book lies in author Marc Reisner's journalistic ability to weave facts about the politics of each water project and anecdotes about key players in the western water industry with his own personal insight. Another book, *Overtapped Oasis* (Marc Reisner and Sarah Bates. Island Press, 1990), sets forth policies for reforming water resources development.

492 Last Oasis: Facing Water Scarcity

Sandra Postel. Worldwatch Environmental Alert series. Sponsored by Worldwatch Institute. W. W. Norton & Company, 1992. 239p. $19.95 (hardcover), $9.95 (paper).

493 Water: The International Crisis

Robin Clarke. MIT Press, 1993. 193p. $30.00 (hardcover), $15.95 (paper).

Both *Last Oasis* and *Water* are excellent overviews of global freshwater scarcity issues. Both books discuss the factors that affect and that are affected by limited water resources, such as climatic change, degradation of land, decrease in water quality, and international water disputes. Each book also makes several suggestions for more efficient water use, ranging from high-tech solutions like desalination and industrial recycling to more traditional techniques like runoff farming. Both books are easy to follow and contain extensive documentation on cited resources. *Water* is more of a description of the problem and a summary of trends, presented with an abundance of statistics, whereas *Last Oasis*

focuses on policy solutions that will prevent even greater scarcity in the future.

494 Entering the Watershed: A New Approach to Save America's River Ecosystems

Bob Doppelt, Mary Scurlock, Chris Frissell, and James Karr. Sponsored by the Pacific Rivers Council. Island Press, 1993. 510p. $55.00 (hardcover), $27.50 (paper).

495 Restoration of Aquatic Ecosystems: Science, Technology and Public Policy

Compiled by the National Research Council. National Academy Press, 1992. 552p. $39.95 (hardcover).

Entering the Watershed and *Restoration of Aquatic Ecosystems* are landmark policy reports on the restoration of surface water ecosystems. *Restoration* describes the status and functions of lake, river and stream, and wetland ecosystems; the effectiveness of restoration efforts; associated technology; and the research, policy, and institutional reorganization required to build a national strategy for aquatic restoration. In this volume, recommendations for that strategy include four elements: national restoration goals and assessment strategies for each ecoregion, principles for priority setting and decision making, policy and program redesign for federal and state agencies to emphasize restoration, and innovation in financing and use of land and water markets. *Entering the Watershed* covers similar content in support of a particular strategy to restore river ecosystems. It argues that attempting to save the worst areas first is backward. By preserving the high-quality, at-risk waters first, restoration efforts will have something positive and stable on which to build. Both reports are widely acclaimed for their detailed analyses of existing problems and solutions as well as their policy recommendations.

496 The State of the Marine Environment

Joint Group of Experts on the Scientific Aspects of Marine Pollution. Blackwell Scientific Publications, 1991. 146p. $32.95 (paper).

497 The Wasted Ocean

David K. Bulloch. Sponsored by the American Littoral Society. Lyons & Burford, 1989. 150p. $16.95 (hardcover), $9.95 (paper).

Both *The State of the Marine Environment* and *The Wasted Ocean* offer concise introductions to the subject of marine pollution. *The State of the Marine Environment*, written by a panel of experts that advises United Nations organizations on marine pollution, documents and assesses the effects of human activities (including population growth, accelerated development, chemical pollutants, and global climate change) upon the international seas. The book also contains a section on marine pollution control and prevention. The report is largely a summary of recent trends. *The Wasted Ocean*, written for concerned citizens, will be less intimidating for lay readers. Author David K. Bulloch, an industrial chemist, reviews the causes of increased toxins and chemicals in coastal environments, examines current U.S. conservation policies, and offers advice on fighting and preventing pollution. Appendices include a directory of appropriate state and federal government agencies and environmental organizations, as well as summaries of major federal legislation.

498 The Wild and Scenic Rivers of America

Tim Palmer. Island Press, 1993. 339p. $45.00 (hardcover), $22.95 (paper).

The Wild and Scenic Rivers of America is a comprehensive guide to the National Wild and Scenic Rivers System. Author Tim Palmer discusses the political forces that led to the creation of the Wild and Scenic Rivers Act in 1968, the process by which rivers are added to the system, problems with the existing program, and what needs to be done to protect the other 99.7 percent of American rivers that are not part of the system. This book also describes the characteristics of each of the protected rivers. For a history of the past eighty years of the American river conservation movement, read Palmer's *Endangered Rivers and the Conservation Movement* (University of California Press, 1986). For an overview of the values of preserving (and threats to the preservation of) the nation's river system, read Palmer's *Lifelines: The Case for River Conservation* (Island Press,

1994). All three books are well researched, with primary references, and include original analysis.

Other Introductory Reading

- ◆ *The Rising Tide: Global Warming and World Sea Levels* (see entry 256)

Abstracts and Indices

499 Aquatic Sciences and Fisheries Abstracts (ASFA)

Cambridge Scientific Abstracts. 1978–. Monthly.

CD-ROM: Available from SilverPlatter.

Database Vendor: Available on DIALOG, OCLC EPIC, and OCLC FirstSearch.

Aquatic Sciences and Fisheries Abstracts (ASFA) offers the most comprehensive coverage of international literature on the science, technology, and management of marine, freshwater, and brackish water environments. *ASFA* is produced in cooperation with four United Nations agencies, and is available in the following separate print versions: *Part 1: Biological Sciences and Living Resources*; *Part 2: Ocean Technology, Policy, and Non-Living Resources*; and *Part 3: Aquatic Pollution and Environmental Quality*. In electronic formats, these three parts are combined with two other print volumes: *ASFA Aquaculture Abstracts* and *ASFA Marine Biotechnology Abstracts*. One quarter of the 3,000 entries added each month and the more than 400,000 total entries found in the five parts pertain to freshwater. *Oceanic Abstracts* (Cambridge Scientific Abstracts, 1964–. Monthly), covers marine and brackish water environments more selectively; it is also available on CD-ROM from SilverPlatter and online on DIALOG.

500 Selected Water Resources Abstracts

U.S. Geological Survey, 1967–1993. Monthly.

CD-ROM: Available as *Water Resources Abstracts* from the National Information Services Corporation and SilverPlatter.

Database Vendor: Available as *Water Resources Abstracts* on DIALOG.

Internet: Available on the Universities Water Information Network (UWIN) (see entry 473). From the UWIN gopher main menu or the World Wide Web home page, choose *USGS WRSIC Research Abstracts.*

Selected Water Resources Abstracts is the major bibliographic database devoted to freshwater issues. This abstract is particularly strong in its coverage of water use, supply, condition, management, and characteristics. It cites articles related to science, engineering, and law. Abstracts describe national and international journal articles, reports, books, and conference proceedings. The database, which currently contains more than 250,000 records, is available on CD-ROM and online; it is also fully searchable at no cost on the Internet through the Universities Water Information Network (see entry 473). Publication ceased in October 1993, but is expected to begin again—perhaps by another company and under a different name. For details about the *Abstracts'* current status, contact the National Water Information Clearinghouse (see entry 457).

Other Abstracts and Indices

- *Biological Abstracts* (see entry 303)
- *Ground Water On-line* (see entry 468, National Ground Water Association)
- *WATERNET* (see entry 463, American Water Works Association)
- The *Watershed Information Resource System* (see entry 471, Terrene Institute)

Periodicals

501 Nonpoint Source News-Notes

Sponsored by the Environmental Protection Agency, Assessment and Watershed Protection Division of the Office of Wetlands, Oceans, and Water. Terrene Institute, 1989. Approximately 8 issues per year. 32p. Free.

Bulletin Board: Available on the Nonpoint Source Electronic Bulletin Board (see entry 474). To search articles, at the main menu choose *Online Databases/Programs*, then *NPS News-Notes Database.*

Complete issues can also be downloaded. For example, Issue 36 is "NEWS-36.ZIP".

Nonpoint Source News-Notes is packed with information on the condition of the water-related environment, the control of nonpoint source pollution, and the ecologically sensitive management and restoration of watersheds. The best way to keep up with these issues, this publication includes reviews of conferences, reports, books, manuals, and other publications; summaries of new policies, proposed legislation, and regulatory changes; announcements of new organizations and projects; news from states and localities; and a listing of conferences. Articles are lengthy for a news bulletin—half a page to three pages—and contact information follows every article. To subscribe, contact the Terrene Institute (see entry 471) at 202/833-8317; for editorial inquiries, call 202/260-3665 or fax 202/260-1517.

502 The Volunteer Monitor: The National Newsletter of Volunteer Water Quality Monitoring

Volunteer Monitor. Semiannual. 24p. Free.

Bulletin Board: Articles from *The Volunteer Monitor* are available as downloadable files on the Nonpoint Source Electronic Bulletin Board (NPS BBS) (see entry 474). From the main menu, choose *Join SIGs*, then *Volunteer Monitoring (VolMon) SIG*, then *File Directories*, then *Articles from the Volunteer Monitor Newsletter.*

Internet: NPS BBS (see Bulletin Board, above) is available via FedWorld's GateWay (see entry 61). Choose *79* for *NPS-BBS (EPA).*

The *Volunteer Monitor* offers an outstanding way to keep up with volunteer water monitoring efforts and strategies across the nation. It is filled with practical advice, contacts, and news. Each issue is co-edited by a different organization and is devoted to a particular theme, such as staying afloat financially or school-based monitoring. This newsletter is only one of a number of projects funded by the Environmental Protection Agency (EPA) to facilitate national-level communication among volunteer monitors. EPA also sponsors conferences; publishes a *National Directory of Citizen Volunteer Environmental Monitoring Programs*, conference proceedings, and how-to manuals; and runs a Special Interest Group (SIG) on the Nonpoint Source Electronic Bulletin Board (see entry 474). This SIG contains back issues of the *Volunteer Monitor* and a wealth of other information. To request EPA publications, write to Alice Mayio, Volunteer Monitoring Coordinator, Environmental Protection Agency, 401 M Street, SW, Mail Code 4503, Washington, DC 20460. To subscribe to the *Volunteer Monitor*, send your name and address to Volunteer Monitor.

There are many support organizations for volunteer monitors; see the Save Our Streams Program (see entry 470) for more information.

Other Periodicals

◆ The *National Wetlands Newsletter* (see entry 26, Environmental Law Institute)

PART TWO

Green Living

CHAPTER ELEVEN

Architecture

What This Chapter Covers

The resources in this chapter can help architects, builders, do-it-yourselfers, and property owners integrate environmental concerns into the design, construction, renovation, or maintenance of homes and other buildings. For example, the information sources explain how environmental issues are involved in building, aid in the selection of resource-efficient and environmentally sound building materials, furnishings, and appliances, and help professionals design structures in ways that do not adversely affect the environment.

For More Information

◆ See **Gardening** for resources on landscape architecture.
◆ See **Shopping** for resources on maintaining and living in your house.

Government Clearinghouses

- ◆ The Energy Efficiency and Renewable Energy Clearinghouse (see entry 313)
- ◆ The Indoor Air Quality Information Clearinghouse (see entry 232)

Organizations

503 Center for Resourceful Building Technology (CRBT)
P.O. Box 3866
Missoula, MT 59806

Phone: 406/549-7678. Fax: 406/549-4100

Steve Loken, Founder, and Rod Miner, Executive Director

The Center for Resourceful Building Technology (CRBT) promotes resource-efficient building, design, materials, and construction through demonstration building projects, by conducting research, and by sharing information on new technologies and materials with home builders, architects, and consumers. CRBT's initial demonstration project, the ReCRAFT 90 home, boasts carpeting made from recycled plastic milk bottles, paving bricks made from oil-contaminated soil, and other innovative materials and processes. CRBT's research and expertise is shared in their annual *Guide to Resource Efficient Building Elements (GREBE)*, a detailed directory of more than three hundred engineered wood products, products that use reconstituted paper and agricultural fibers, recycled-content materials, and other materials that are produced in a resource-efficient manner. CRBT also sells an excellent $3 bibliography, *Resource Efficiency Information Sources and Demonstration Projects*, and performs consulting for homeowners and residential builders through its National Design Assistance Center for Resourceful Building.

504 Real Goods Trading Company
966 Mazzoni Street
Ukiah, CA 95482

Phone (orders): 800/762-7325. Phone (subscriber service line): 707/468-9214. Fax (orders): 707/468-9486

John Schaeffer, President

The Real Goods Trading Company is a mail-order company that specializes in renewable energy and conservation appliances, as well as other environmentally friendly products. Its selection of materials and equipment is larger than that of most of its competitors. Membership includes the Real Goods regular catalog, a discount on an expanded catalog *(The Real Goods Solar Living Sourcebook: The Complete Guide to Renewable Energy Technologies & Sustainable Living* [see entry 509]), and two informative periodicals. The company also has a national referral network of professionals who can design an appropriate home energy system—everything from assessing needs to ordering parts and talking to a contractor—free if recommended parts and equipment are purchased from Real Goods. The company's Institute for Independent Living sponsors workshops that help people learn how to live without being connected to the electrical power grid. Chelsea Green publishes a number of books in Real Goods' Independent Living series, including *Wind Power for Home and Business: Renewable Energy for the 1990s and Beyond* (see entry 516), *The Independent Home: Living Well with Power from the Sun, Wind and Water* (Michael Potts. 1993), and *Eco-Renovation: The Ecological Home Improvement Guide* (see entry 517).

Another mail-order company that caters to green-building enthusiasts is Environmental Construction Outfitters (800/238-5008 or 212/334-9659; 44 Crosby Street, New York, NY 10012), which publishes an extensive catalog of resource-efficient and environmentally sound building materials, furnishings, and appliances; the group also offers consulting services.

Other Organizations

- ◆ The Rocky Mountain Institute (see entry 44)

Directories

505 Environmental By Design: A Sourcebook of Environmentally Conscious Choices for Homeowners, Builders and Designers

Kim LeClair and David Rousseau. Hartley & Marks, 1992. 261p. $19.95 (paper).

Environmental By Design offers detailed descriptions of more than 170 green-building materials. This first volume covers interior materials like carpeting, installation materials, floorings, finishes, and furniture. The directory's primary goal is to raise awareness of environmental concerns in materials selection. It accomplishes this by analyzing the environmental impact of building products throughout their life cycles—by looking at everything from the energy efficiency of manufacturing processes to a product's ability to be cleaned with a minimal amount of toxics, to durability and recyclability. Icons show which of fourteen life-cycle categories the product has passed. To be included in the book, products must pass at least two categories. Section introductions analyze the strengths and weaknesses of products commonly used in construction and interior design (fiberglass vs. polystyrene insulation, for example), while each product description includes specifications. *Environmental By Design* is appropriate for motivated homeowners; architects, designers, and builders may want to purchase a subscription to the more comprehensive and frequently updated professional looseleaf edition. To order, send $40 plus $5 handling (both U.S. dollars) for the initial three-ring binder to Environmental By Design, P.O. Box 34493, Station D, Vancouver, BC V6J 4W4, Canada.

506 Interior Concerns Resource Guide: A Guide to Sustainable and Healthy Products and Educational Information for Designing and Building

Edited by Victoria Schomer, ASID. 3rd ed. Interior Concerns Publications, 1994. Annual. 221p. $40.00 (spiral bound).

507 SAFE HOME DIGEST'S: Healthy Building Resource Guide

Nadia Henry. Lloyd Publishing. $33.00 for initial 100 pages and three-ring binder, $18.00 for each semiannual update.

508 The Sourcebook for Sustainable Design: A Guide to Environmentally Responsible Building Materials and Processes

Edited by Andrew St. John, AIA. 1st ed. Architects for Social Responsibility, 1992;

distributed by the Boston Society of Architects. 140p. $28.00 (spiral bound).

The *Interior Concerns Resource Guide*, *SAFE HOME DIGEST'S: Healthy Building Resource Guide*, and *The Sourcebook for Sustainable Design* provide extensive lists of suppliers of green-building products and information sources. All are recommended, but none is comprehensive; because of this, building professionals may want to choose the most recently updated one, or, better yet, consult all three. Chapters in all three books each contain short introductions (except for *SAFE HOME DIGEST'S: Healthy Building Resource Guide*); in all, entries are described in at least one sentence. Although all three are good places to find organizations, periodicals, names of consultants, and other information sources, *Interior Concerns* is the most comprehensive volume of the three; it also lists the largest number of suppliers. The bimonthly *Interior Concerns Newsletter* is included for an extra $25. *SAFE HOME DIGEST'S: Healthy Building Resource Guide* has fewer listings, but a wider range; it includes more consumer products as well as more health-related issue areas (e.g. recycled paper, nontoxic fabrics, electromagnetic field meters, publications). The *Sourcebook* is least appropriate for consumers; however, it has the most descriptive information for professionals.

Similar directories on more specialized aspects of green building are the $19.95 *Healthy Buildings Resource Guide* (Healthy Building Associates, 1993), which covers indoor air quality, and the widely acclaimed $20 *Guide to Resource Efficient Building Elements* (see entry 503, Center for Resourceful Building Technology).

509 The Real Goods Solar Living Sourcebook: The Complete Guide to Renewable Energy Technologies & Sustainable Living

John Schaeffer & the Real Goods Staff. 8th ed. Chelsea Green, 1994. 676p. $20.00 (paper).

The Real Goods Solar Living Sourcebook is much more than an extensive Real Goods Trading Company (see entry 504) mail-order catalog of products for energy-generating and resource-efficient homes. The essays by experts and background information on household conservation, plus the extensive descriptions of products, make this a complete guide to energy-conserving and renewable-energy technologies. The *Sourcebook* has everything needed by environmentally concerned homeowners and those in "independent homes" : PV systems, wind energy generators, electric vehicle conversion kits, super-efficient lighting systems, nontoxic cleaners, water purification devices, and recycled toilet paper, to name just a few of the products offered. There is also a resource section that includes books, videos and software, and a list of organizations.

510 Sustainable Building Sourcebook

Laurence Doxsey, Mary McLeod, and Doug Seiter. City of Austin Environmental and Conservation Services Department, Green Building Program, 1992. $25.00 (three-ring binder).

The *Sustainable Building Sourcebook* contains an enormous amount of practical information for building professionals. The Green Building Program was created by and is directly applicable to the City of Austin, Texas, but those in other cities can still apply much of the same information or modify it to fit their needs. The sourcebook is meant to be used in conjunction with the City of Austin's award-winning *Green Building Guide*, which teaches homeowners to itemize and score the entire environmental impact of their houses, including building materials, water and energy consumption, and waste generation. In this sourcebook, categories such as wall paneling, programmable thermostats, and electromagnetic field hazards are described and analyzed according to the maturity of the technology, availability of suppliers, relative cost, and implementation factors. Extensive guidelines and specifications for use and installation are supplied. In addition, lists of suppliers, consultants, and general information sources are included; this part compares favorably to the *Interior Concerns Resource Guide* (see entry 506).

511 Woods of the World

Electronic document. Tree Talk, 1994.

Diskette: Available from Tree Talk for $250.00; a condensed version is available for $150.00.

CD-ROM: Available from Tree Talk for $250.00.

Woods of the World is a multimedia database that provides a wealth of information on roughly eight hundred species of timber and wood composite materials. This database is ideal for anyone who works with wood, from the hobbyist to the professional; architects, designers, and contractors will find it particularly useful. Because information is computerized and interactive, users can easily tailor their searches to meet extremely specific needs. They can: browse the information by species; view a scanned image of the wood, showing its color and grain patterns; locate a specific species by searching for its scientific, trade, or common names; search for a particular color of wood; search for species appropriate for a particular end-use; identify trees native to, or grown in, a specific region; or search for woods harvested in a sustainable manner. In addition, detailed information about the environmental status of each species is also included. *Woods of the World* supplies a directory of sources for purchasing temperate and tropical wood products obtained from well-managed harvesting operations, a list of all known wood certification organizations, names and addresses of all companies with products found in the database, and a glossary of wood terms. A hard-copy version of *Woods of the World* is not available.

Additional wood-use resources include the *Wood User's Guide* (Rainforest Action Network, 1991. $10), which lists tropical and temperate wood alternatives, nonwood alternatives, and other supplies; the Rainforest Alliance's (see entry 277) Smart Wood Certification Program, which recognizes sustainably managed sources of tropical wood; and Scientific Certification Systems' (see entry 592) Forest Conservation Program, which gauges the relative performance of timber operations.

Other Directories

◆ *The Indoor Air Quality Directory* (see entry 247)

Bibliographies

512 Annotated Bibliography: A Selected Listing of Useful Resources

West River Communications, 1993. 8p. $6.00 (paper).

Annotated Bibliography: A Selected Listing of Useful Resources describes more than fifty handbooks, directories, and periodicals on all aspects of green building. It is divided into the following sections: sustainable building design and construction; resource-efficient materials; energy efficiency; passive solar energy; landscape design and water conservation; urban planning and sustainable communities; and indoor air quality. Each entry includes insightful one- to three-sentence descriptions and all necessary purchasing information. Contact the publishers of *Environmental Building News* (see entry 524) to order this bibliography; to stay on top of new resources as they come out, look to regular issues of *Environmental Building News*.

513 The Efficient House Sourcebook

Robert Sardinsky and the staff of the Rocky Mountain Institute. 6th ed. Rocky Mountain Institute, 1992. Updated regularly. 166p. $15.00 (paper).

The Efficient House Sourcebook is an outstanding guide that describes books, periodicals, catalogs, and organizations related to energy- and resource-efficient housing. This means everything from weatherizing to solar power to waste disposal to community housing—with plenty more in between. Some entries—such as *Building with Junk and Other Good Stuff* and *Manifold Destiny: The One! The Only! Guide to Cooking on Your Car Engine*—may seem eccentric to some, but most of them—such as the Energy Efficient Building Association's *The Super Insulated Retrofit Book: A Home Owner's Guide to Energy-Efficient Renovation*, and *Making Space: Design For Compact Living*—are immensely practical for all. Reviews are lively and extremely insightful, and entries for publications include excerpts from the sources. This sourcebook also includes a state-by-state directory of energy contacts. Professionals and do-it-yourselfers interested in conventional and unconven-

tional building—from design to planning to shopping to financing—should turn here first.

Other Bibliographies

◆ *Resource Efficiency Information Sources and Demonstration Projects* (see entry 503, Center for Resourceful Building Technology)

Reference Handbooks

514 Consumer Guide to Home Energy Savings

Edited by Alex Wilson and John Morrill. 4th ed. American Council for an Energy-Efficient Economy, 1995. Annual. 250p. $7.95 (paper).

The *Consumer Guide to Home Energy Savings* is a must for anyone interested in protecting the environment and saving money by reducing the amount of energy used at home. The *Consumer Guide* is the energy equivalent of *Consumer Reports*: The guide is crammed with listings and ratings of hundreds of the most energy-efficient products—lightbulbs, refrigerators, furnaces, air conditioners, washing machines, etc.—by brand name and model number. The book guides consumers through the selection process and provides tips on equipment use. *The Energy-Efficient Home* (Rocky Mountain Institute, 1994) helps consumers evaluate and improve their homes' energy efficiency. The Energy Efficiency and Renewable Energy Clearinghouse (see entry 313) is an excellent resource for homeowners to call for free information.

515 Consumer Guide to Solar Energy: Easy and Inexpensive Applications for Solar Energy

Scott Sklar and Ken Sheinkopf. Bonus Books, 1991. 181p. $10.00 (paper).

516 Wind Power for Home and Business: Renewable Energy for the 1990's and Beyond

Paul Gipe. Chelsea Green, 1993. 384p. $35.00 (paper).

The *Consumer Guide to Solar Energy* is a good source for consumers who want to understand how solar energy can be used in everyday life. It provides a solid introduction to solar water heating and solar electricity and introduces many applications for each: home cooling and heating, water purification, cooking, and even heating swimming pools. The last chapter includes descriptions of selected publications and organizations. Author Scott Sklar is executive director of the Solar Energy Industries Association (see entry 325).

Wind Power for Home and Business, much more detailed than the *Consumer Guide to Solar Energy*, is the most complete reference on wind power. It not only provides background information on how wind energy works and tips on how to tap this source of power, but also includes wind region maps for all fifty states and tables that estimate the annual electricity production from all sizes of wind turbines under various wind conditions. The author, Paul Gipe, is an expert on wind energy technology and is the West Coast representative of the American Wind Energy Association (see entry 320).

517 Eco-Renovation: The Ecological Home Improvement Guide

Edward Harland. Chelsea Green and the Real Goods Trading Company, 1994. 263p. $16.95 (paper).

Eco-Renovation is a perfect book for do-it-yourself homeowners who wish to make their existing homes as ecologically friendly as possible. Author Edward Harland, an architect who specializes in the ecological renovation of houses, provides a concise overview of the major ecological problems facing homeowners and then offers practical solutions and suggestions for ecological renovation projects. Readers will learn how to convert and maximize existing living space, reduce heating and utility bills, protect themselves from toxic substances, and select building materials that are resource efficient and environmentally safe. *Eco-Renovation* clearly explains and demonstrates the importance of each of these areas and offers "priorities for action" based on the ecological principles of recycling, self-sufficiency, renewability, conservation, and efficiency. Numerous illustrations and tables reinforce and clarify much of the advice provided in the text. The book concludes with a checklist for a home ecological assessment, as well as lists of companies, organizations, books,

and periodicals that can help readers locate appropriate products and obtain further information and advice.

518 Environmental Resource Guide (ERG)

American Institute of Architects (AIA), Committee on the Environment, 1992–. Quarterly. $125.00 for AIA members, $150.00 for nonprofits, and $350.00 for corporations.

The *Environmental Resource Guide (ERG)* is a green building looseleaf subscription service. Partially funded by a grant from the Environmental Protection Agency, the guide is noted for its collection of life cycle analyses of building materials, such as aluminum, carpet, and particle board. It also includes a variety of other sections: reprints of recent articles, reports by task groups of the Committee on the Environment (COTE) of the American Institute of Architects (AIA), case studies, and bibliographies. *ERG* has come under criticism for relying too heavily on conventional practices and materials, but overall it is an excellent resource for architects.

AIA also offers a video of *Case Studies in Environmental Design* for $57 and the following videos of lectures and panel discussions for $47 each: *Energy and Resource Efficiencies*, *Healthy Buildings and Materials*, and *Sustainable Communities*.

519 Healthy House Building: A Design and Construction Guide

John Bower. The Healthy House Institute, 1993. 381p. $21.95 (paper).

Healthy House Building is an excellent resource for the designer, builder, or dedicated homeowner who wants to build a healthy home. Though the focus here is on preventing indoor air pollution through choices in construction practices and building materials, other topics, such as energy efficiency and water quality, are also considered. For each stage of house construction—from finding a site to picking paints, varnishes, and caulks—author John Bower reviews conventional building practices and materials, identifies their potential health effects, examines the pros and cons of both conventional and nontoxic and less-toxic alternative methods, and describes techniques he used while building his own model healthy house. Other chapters include advice on selecting a designer and contractor and locating and purchasing healthy materials, as well as reprints of the floor plans for Bower's model house. Names of recommended product manufacturers are highlighted throughout. This volume updates and expands Bower's widely respected *The Healthy House: How to Buy One, How to Cure a "Sick" One, How to Build One* (Lyle Stuart, 1989). Also available from Bower's Healthy House Institute (812/332–5073) are a companion videotape and shorter reports. Personal consulting—$50.00 per hour—is also available.

520 Your Home, Your Health, and Well-Being

David Rousseau, W. J. Rea, M.D., and Jean Enwright. Ten Speed Press, 1988. 300p. $14.95 (paper).

Your Home, Your Health, and Well-Being offers a practical introduction to indoor air pollution as it relates to house design. Light, color, temperature, humidity, and sound are also considered. An architectural designer and builder, author David Rousseau gears most of his information toward his peers, though the average homeowner will also be able to follow the explanations. Included are introductions to indoor air pollutants (including how to control them); design considerations for each room; tips for choosing the right systems for ventilation, heating and cooling, home maintenance, and water treatment; drawings for construction; and information and resources for contamination testing. Rousseau's *Environmental By Design* (see entry 505) updates this book's section on selecting materials. Chapters by W. J. Rea and Jean Enwright provide expert and personal introductions to chemical sensitivity. Concise writing, clear layout and graphics, and quality information make this guide exceptional.

Other Reference Handbooks

- ◆ *The Independent Home: Living Well with Power from the Sun, Wind and Water* (see entry 504, Real Goods Trading Company)
- ◆ *The Most Energy-Efficient Appliances* (see entry 318, American Council for an Energy-Efficient Economy)

Introductory Reading

521 Green Architecture: Design for an Energy-Conscious Future

Brenda Vale and Robert Vale. Bulfinch Press, 1991. 192p. $40.00 (hardcover).

Green Architecture introduces environmental concerns that affect buildings, including houses. The authors propose that green buildings should conserve energy, use the local climate and natural energy sources whenever possible, minimize new resources, respect the needs of those using the building, and respect the site by integrating it with the natural surroundings. For each of these topics, many case studies, complete with plans and pictures, are provided. In addition, the book begins with an overview of environmental issues relevant to buildings and ends with a call for developing a green attitude toward cities and all architecture.

522 The Natural House Book: Creating a Healthy, Harmonious, and Ecologically-Sound Home Environment

David Pearson. Simon & Schuster, 1989. 287p. $29.95 (hardcover), $17.95 (paper).

The Natural House Book is a holistic introduction to all aspects of environmental home building. The book's first chapters set forth a definition for a "natural house" —it should be healthy for the body, peaceful for the spirit, and harmonious with the environment—and identify pollutants that make a house dangerous. Author David Pearson discusses systems (air, water, scent, sound, light, and color) and building materials; he also includes sections on kitchens, bathrooms, and other living areas, such as nurseries and meditation spaces. Appendices summarize practical tips that are integrated throughout the text and provide resources for further reading and contact information for organizations and companies. The concise text and numerous color photos and illustrations make this book the best source for homeowners who want to learn about and visualize what constitutes an environmentally friendly home.

523 The Naturally Elegant Home: Environmental Style

Janet Martinelli with Robert Kourik. Little, Brown & Company, 1992. 232p. $45.00 (hardcover).

The Naturally Elegant Home demonstrates that environmentally sound houses need not be bare-bones or ugly, but can use techniques—in the tradition of Frank Lloyd Wright—that respect and enhance nature, such as windows that frame views and sunspaces that bring the outside in and the inside out. Author Janet Martinelli provides nuts-and-bolts advice on passive solar design, sustainable building materials, adapting a house to suit the local climate, and integrating water conservation, recycling and natural food production into everyday life. A chapter on landscaping—it includes sections on edible landscaping and landscapes that conserve energy, water, and soil—is of particular interest. Full-color photos of sample houses and references to information sources and suppliers are included throughout.

Periodicals

524 Environmental Building News: A Bimonthly Newsletter on Environmentally Sustainable Design and Construction

West River Communications. 1992–. Bimonthly. 20p. $60.00/year for individuals and organizations with fewer than 25 people, $95.00/year for other organizations and corporations.

Environmental Building News is highly recommended for anyone seriously interested in green buildings. Produced by leaders in the field, each issue includes product and material reviews, news on the latest projects and developments in the field, construction advice, and an in-depth feature on a topic such as minimizing construction and demolition waste, CFCs in insulation materials, or old-growth timber. Articles end with contact information. The events calendar and the thorough book reviews alone make a subscription worthwhile. *Environmental Building News* is absolutely the best way for building professionals to stay current with green-building news and resources.

525 Home Energy Magazine

Energy Auditor & Retrofitter. 1984–. Bimonthly. 48p. $49.00/year.

Written for energy conservation professionals but usable by the weekend do-it-yourselfer, the straightforward *Home Energy Magazine* contains well-researched articles about lighting, weatherization, new technologies, energy-efficient products, and ways to identify energy waste in homes. Articles provide in-depth, hands-on information and often include step-by-step illustrations and reference lists. The unique "Conservation Clips" section contains brief summaries of recent reports and articles. Another regular department reviews books, periodicals, and manuals. Ask the publisher for a copy of the complete subject index to find past articles.

Energy Design Update (Cutter Information. Monthly. $297/year) is a newsletter that keeps builders, designers, utility executives, and manufacturers up to date on news in the field of energy-efficient residential construction.

526 Home Power: The Hands-on Journal of Home-made Power

Home Power, 1987–. Bimonthly. 116p. $15.00/year.

CD-ROM: The *Solar 1 CD-ROM* is available from the Redwood Alliance for $29.00 for individuals and $229.00 for utilities.

Bulletin Board: Back issues of *Home Power* and related information are available on the Home Power BBS. To connect by modem, dial 707/822-8640. For technical support by phone, call the Redwood Alliance at 707/822-7884.

Home Power is the premier information source for enthusiasts who wish to live "off the grid," i.e., without being connected to the electrical power system. This publication provides a balance between technical and general interest articles on all aspects of home power—selecting appropriate appliances and utilizing new technologies, as well as designing and maintaining solar, wind, and water power systems. Many articles are accompanied by graphs, charts, diagrams, resource lists, and step-by-step instructions. Each issue contains a cumulative subject index of articles and book reviews. While this is not a clearing-house, the magazine's staff members are dedicated, friendly, knowledgeable, and willing to answer questions over the phone (provided they have time). The Home Power BBS has back issues of the magazine; there is no charge for access or downloading. The *Solar 1 CD-ROM* (net proceeds from the sales help keep the Home Power BBS operating) includes thousands of renewable energy reports, answers to frequently asked questions, tables, newsletters, graphics, resource guides, and other files on sustainability and the environment. The CD-ROM also supplies articles and graphics from the first thirty-five issues of *Home Power*.

Other Periodicals

◆ *Earthword* (see entry 417)

◆ *In Context* (see entry 418)

◆ The *Interior Concerns Newsletter* (see entry 506, *Interior Concerns Resource Guide*)

CHAPTER TWELVE

Education

What This Chapter Covers

The resources in this chapter can help teachers integrate environmental themes into their elementary and secondary school classrooms. For instance, many of the resources assist in the acquisition of curricula, lesson plans, and classroom materials. Additional sources of information can help students learn about undergraduate and graduate programs related to the environment.

For More Information

◆ See **General** for resources on environmental advocacy organizations, most of which produce and distribute classroom education materials.

◆ See **Employment** for resources on the educational requirements of environmental careers.

◆ See **Travel** and **Employment** for resources on volunteer opportunities in the environmental field.

Government Clearinghouses

**527 ERIC Clearinghouse for Science,
Mathematics, and Environmental
Education (ERIC/CSMEE)**
Ohio State University
1929 Kenny Road
Columbus, OH 43210

Phone: 614/292-6717. Fax: 614/292-0263.
E-mail: ericse@osu.edu

David L. Haury, Director

CD-ROM: The ERIC database is available as *ERIC*
from DIALOG, as *ERIC on CD-ROM* from the
National Information Services Corporation, and
as *ERIC on SilverPlatter* from SilverPlatter.

Database Vendor: The ERIC database is available
as *ERIC* on DIALOG, OCLC EPIC, and OCLC
FirstSearch.

Internet: To access the ERIC Clearinghouse for
Science, Mathematics, and Environmental
Education (ERIC/CSMEE) gopher site, gopher to
gopher.ericse.ohio-state.edu.

The ERIC Clearinghouse for Science, Mathematics, and Environmental Education (ERIC/CSMEE)
is of most use to researchers and scholars. ERIC/
CSMEE is one of sixteen clearinghouses in the
Educational Resources Information Center (ERIC)
system, which indexes and abstracts documents,
journal articles, papers, conference proceedings,
literature reviews, and curricula materials for
the world's largest education-related database,
known as *ERIC*. ERIC/CSMEE is responsible for col-
lecting and adding records to *ERIC* that pertain
to environmental education—currently 6,000 of
the 700,000 total records. Although the majority
of the abstracts discuss research in environmental education and many citations date from the
1970s, it is possible to find curricula and more current documents pertaining to classroom and
experiential education appropriate for all age
levels. ERIC/CSMEE performs searches for a fee,
locates hard-to-find documents, refers calls to
other information sources, and publishes documents concerning issues and materials in environmental education. Recent publications include
*Using the ERIC Database to Support Curricular
Change in Environmental Education, Activities
to Teach Mathematics in the Context of Envi-*

ronmental Studies, and *Environmental Literacy: Its Roots, Evolution, and Directions in the
1990's.* The full text of shorter publications
and other information is available on the ERIC/
CSMEE Internet gopher site. ERIC/CSMEE also
distributes some Environmental Protection
Agency documents at low cost; ask for the
free catalog.

Those interested in the academic aspects of
environmental education may also want to consult the *Journal of Environmental Education* (Heldref Publications, quarterly).

Organizations

528 Alliance for Environmental Education (AEE)
9309 Center Street, Suite 101
Manassas, VA 22110

Phone: 703/330-5667. Fax: 703/330-3268.
E-mail: alliance@igc.apc.org

Duane A. Cox, President

EcoNet: The Alliance maintains several
conferences, including *aee.calendar,
aee.curriculum, aee.directory, aee.news,* and
aee.questions.

The Alliance for Environmental Education (AEE)
provides a forum for the exchange of information about environmental literacy. AEE is a coalition of some three hundred professional
associations, businesses, government agencies,
and education and environmental organizations,
including most of the large distributors of environmental educational materials. In partnership
with the Tennessee Valley Authority and the Environmental Protection Agency, AEE created a
national network of interactive environmental
education and training centers that serve schools
as well as the public. Members communicate
through EcoNet (see entry 58), where the Alliance sponsors several conferences, including one
(*aee.news*) that contains back issues of *The Network Exchange,* the organizational newsletter.
AEE works on a variety of other projects,
including an annual conference, and produces
publications such as *Education for the Earth: A
Guide to Top Environmental Studies Programs*
(see entry 533) and the *Compendium of Educa-*

tional Materials on the Water Environment (see entry 481). The Alliance is a major force in environmental education.

529 Center for Environmental Education (CEE)
991 Alma Real Drive, Suite 300
Pacific Palisades, CA 90272

Phone: 310/454-4585. Fax: 310/454-9925.
E-mail: cee@earthspirit.org

Coreen Walsh, Executive Director

The Center for Environmental Education (CEE) works locally and nationally to eliminate duplication of environmental curricula and to maximize the funds spent on environmental education. The group's lending library houses more than nine hundred teacher-reviewed kindergarten–twelfth grade environmental education curricula titles and more than five thousand other relevant items. This nonprofit organization can also recommend environmental education materials and make referrals to other curricula specialists. *Blueprint for a Green School* (Scholastic, 1995), CEE's major publication, introduces all environmental issues impacting schools and suggests activities and resources for further action. *Blueprint* is geared toward principals, librarians, and in-service educators, while a shorter, adapted version, *Parents Guide to an Environmentally Safe School*, is less technical. CEE's semiannual newsletter, *Grapevine,* includes many news shorts of interest to environmental educators and students, including announcements of new classroom materials.

530 National Consortium for Environmental Education and Training (NCEET)
University of Michigan
School of Natural Resources and Environment
430 East University Avenue
Dana Building
Ann Arbor, MI 48109

Phone: 313/998-6726. Fax: 313/998-6580.
E-mail: nceet-info@nceet.snre.umich.edu

Paul Nowak, Director

Internet: NCEET maintains EE-Link (see entry 532).

The National Consortium for Environmental Education and Training (NCEET) coordinates a national effort to improve the efficiency and effectiveness of environmental education, especially in kindergarten–twelfth grade settings. NCEET was started in 1992 by a grant from the Environmental Protection Agency's (EPA) Office of Environmental Education (202/260-4484). NCEET's EE Toolbox is a collection of publications for educators who conduct environmental education teacher training programs, including nine components of the *Workshop Resource Manual*, which aids those who facilitate teacher training workshops, a *National Survey of EE Teacher Inservice Education* ($6.95), and the highly recommended *Getting Started: A Guide to Bringing Environmental Education Into Your Classroom* ($9.95; bulk purchase discounts available). Most of the items in the Toolbox, as well as many other items of interest to environment educators, are available electronically through EE-Link (see entry 532), NCEET's Internet site.

531 North American Association for Environmental Education
P.O. Box 400
Troy, OH 45373

Phone: 513/676-2514

Edward McCrea, Executive Director

The North American Association for Environmental Education is the professional association for individuals active in and concerned with environmental education. It provides support for those in nonformal education (e.g. nature centers, museums, zoos) and elementary and secondary education and university faculty and students, as well as those offering educational programs focusing on the conservation of natural resources. Most efforts revolve around the group's annual conference. Association members receive the bimonthly newsletter *Environmental Communicator* and discounts on other publications, such as conference proceedings, reports (*Funding Your Environmental Education Program: Strategies and Options*), and collections of papers (*Computer-Aided Environmental Education, Essential Learning in Environmental Education*). A list of colleges and universities with environmental education programs is available from the association for $4.

Other Organizations

- ◆ The Center for Environmental Citizenship (see entry 13)
- ◆ Cool It! (see entry 39, National Wildlife Federation)
- ◆ The Student Environmental Action Coalition (see entry 46)

Internet Sites

532 EE-Link

Maintained by the National Consortium for Environmental Education and Training.

Bulletin Board: To connect to EE-Link by modem, dial 313/763-6520 at 1200 baud, dial 313/998-1302 at 2400 baud, dial 313/998-1303 at 9600 baud, v.32, or dial 313/998-1304 at 19200 baud, v.32 bis. Choose *UM-EELink*, then, at the prompt, type your e-mail address. This brings users to the main gopher menu on the Internet.

Internet: To access EE-Link, telnet to **nceet.snre.umich.edu** and log in as **eelink**; gopher to **nceet.snre.umich.edu**; or, on the World Wide Web, the URL is **http://www.nceet.snre.umich.edu/**.

EE-Link is a must-see resource that provides a centralized location on the Internet for environmental educators. Sponsored by the National Consortium for Environmental Education and Training (NCEET) (see entry 530), EE-Link offers electronic versions of many of the items in NCEET's EE Toolbox (e.g., *Getting Started: A Guide to Bringing Environmental Education Into Your Classroom*). EE-Link also contains a wealth of other materials: guides to sources of curricula and other teaching materials; the full text of some curricula; a guide to other environmental education clearinghouses; articles on environmental education; grant information; directories of upcoming conferences, meetings, and courses; and directories of environmental education organizations, people, and projects. EE-Link also provides access to many other educational and environmental sources of information on the Internet.

Other Internet Sites

- ◆ Campus EarthNet (see entry 13, Center for Environmental Citizenship)

Bulletin Boards

- ◆ The Classroom Earth BBS (see entry 53, Consortium for International Earth Science Information Network)

Directories

533 Education for the Earth: A Guide to Top Environmental Studies Programs

Sponsored by Alliance for Environmental Education. Peterson's Guides, 1993. 175p. $10.95 (paper).

Education for the Earth describes more than one hundred undergraduate environmental programs. Each program description lists information about faculty size, student/faculty ratio, number of degrees conferred, and contacts, as well as information about the school, such as costs and entrance-level difficulty. Program descriptions—each a page in length—include special features and information about the career paths of graduates. Environmental science and natural resource management programs dominate, but environmental engineering and design, environmental health, and environmental studies programs are also included. Programs were selected for inclusion only if they have existed for at least four years, if they have at least thirty students enrolled, and if more than half the students found jobs or began a masters-level program within six months of graduation. *Education for the Earth* begins with five short essays expressing views on future job trends and opportunities, including the education and training needed for an environmental career, and ends with a glossary of technical terms, a bibliography of additional resources, and geographical and alphabetical indices.

For a guide to alternative undergraduate programs in social change—environmental awareness, peace, social justice, women's studies—at seventy-one institutions (e.g., Armand Hammer

United World College, Audubon Expedition Institute, Colorado State University, Institute for Social Ecology, School for Field Studies, Tufts University), consult Miriam Weinstein's *Making a Difference College Guide: Education for a Better World Guide* (Sage Press, 1993).

534 Wilderness U.: Opportunities for Outdoor Education in the U.S. and Abroad

Bill McMillon. Chicago Review Press, 1992. 280p. $12.95 (paper).

Wilderness U. is a directory of nature study programs, most of which are in the United States. Programs are geared toward students looking to spend a semester or a summer outdoors, although nonstudents looking for a seminar or a lengthier tour are also well accommodated. The programs are sponsored by colleges and universities, nature centers, museums, and other non-profit and commercial organizations. The second half of the book includes reprints of narratives that describe outdoor education experiences. There are subject and regional indices, as well as an index that lists programs offering college credit. Author Bill McMillon has also written other related directories, including *Volunteer Vacations: Short-Term Adventures That Will Benefit You and Others* (4th ed. Chicago Review Press, 1993) and *Nature Nearby: An Outdoor Guide to 20 of America's Cities* (Wiley, 1990). For short descriptions of more than seventy organizations involved with outdoor experiential education, request the free *Outdoor Education Directory* from the ERIC Clearinghouse on Rural Education and Small Schools (800/624–9120).

Bibliographies

535 Business and the Environment: A Resource Guide

Edited by Allison A. Pennell, Patricia E. Choi, and Lawrence Molinaro, Jr. Sponsored by the Management Institute for Environment and Business. Island Press, 1992. 364p. $55.00 (hardcover).

Business and the Environment is an excellent sourcebook for those who wish to incorporate environmental issues into business education,

theory, or practice. It contains two distinct parts: a guide to published literature and a directory of faculty with a professional interest in environmental issues. Both sections are divided into the following broad subject categories: accounting and finance; business, government, and society; management; marketing; production and operations management; and strategic management. These sections are then further divided into smaller categories—e.g., social accounting, Total Quality Management (TQM)—making this book easy to browse. The first part describes hundreds of journal articles, books, and reports, as well as 112 case studies and 28 videos. The overwhelming majority of entries were published in 1990 and 1991. Each entry includes a three- to five-sentence abstract, a list of keywords (e.g., *design for disassembly, Eastern Europe, life cycle cost analysis, mergers and acquisitions, organizational behavior, source reduction, political pressures, Procter and Gamble*) and all necessary information for locating a given publication. The book's second part describes 185 faculty members, mostly from business schools. Each profile includes affiliation, relevant publications, courses taught, research activity, education, and employment history. The *Resource Guide* includes author, keyword, and subject indices for resource listings, and both name and university indices for faculty members. Contact the Management Institute for Environment and Business (MEB) (1220 16th Street, NW, Washington, DC 20036; phone: 202/833-6556; fax: 202/833-6228) for course modules (i.e., full text of items abstracted here, plus a syllabus) and more current information.

536 E for Environment: An Annotated Bibliography of Children's Books with Environmental Themes

Edited by Patti K. Sinclair. R. R. Bowker, 1992. 292p. $39.95 (hardcover).

E for Environment describes 517 recommended fiction and nonfiction books with environmental themes targeted at children in preschool through age 14. Editor Patti K. Sinclair is a librarian and a former editor of *Children's Magazine Guide*. The books are divided into five categories: introductions to nature, ecosystems, environmental issues, human interaction with the environment, and hands-on experiments and activities. Sample titles include *The Lorax* (Dr. Suess. Random House, 1971) and *The Ozone Layer* (Jane Duden. Crestwood, 1990). Annotations average 150 words and include appropriate age level and awards received. Most publication dates fall between 1982 and 1991, though some older works are cited. *E for Environment* also offers a briefly annotated list of 43 environmental classics for adults. This book is an excellent resource for librarians, teachers, and parents.

Other Bibliographies

- The *Compendium of Educational Materials on the Water Environment* (see entry 481)
- The Curricula and Compendia Project (see entry 532, EE-Link)
- *Energy Education Resources: Kindergarten Through 12th Grade* (see entry 315, National Energy Information Center)

Reference Handbooks

537 Environmental Education Teacher Resource Handbook: A Practical Guide for K–12 Environmental Education

Edited by Richard J. Wilke. Teacher Resource Handbook series. In cooperation with National Science Teachers Association. Kraus International Publications, 1993. 448p. $19.95 (paper).

The *Environmental Education Teacher Resource Handbook* is a one-stop reference book for classroom environmental educators. This handbook is a great everyday reference on curriculum materials and other important information, and an excellent resource for teachers seeking to design or revise environmental education curricula. Each clearly written essay is authored by a different expert and includes a complete bibliography. Topics include: history and background on environmental education curricula; a practical guide to creating or revising environmental education curricula; discussion of measurement, testing, assessment, and evaluation in environmental education; and a guide to planning special projects. Among the useful reference materials in other chapters are: an annotated directory of curriculum guides and supplementary materials; a directory of curriculum material producers; a

directory of funding sources for programs that are studying or developing curricula; summaries and analyses of state environmental education guidelines, including bibliographic information for each state's environmental education curriculum documents; an annotated bibliography of children's trade books; bibliographic information for textbooks in different states; and citations to reviews of curriculum guides, lesson plans, project books, computer software, videos, and filmstrips that were published in educational journals, magazines, and newsletters between July 1991 and June 1993. As the first attempt to gather all of this information in one place, the project succeeds admirably. All environmental educators should use this book.

Other Reference Handbooks

- *Campus Ecology: A Guide to Assessing Environmental Quality & Creating Strategies for Change* (see entry 46, Student Environmental Action Coalition)
- *Getting Started: A Guide to Bringing Environmental Education Into Your Classroom* (see entry 530, National Consortium for Environmental Education and Training)

Introductory Reading

538 Ecological Literacy: Education and the Transition to a Postmodern World

David W. Orr. SUNY Series in Constructive Postmodern Thought. State University of New York Press, 1992. 210p. $49.50 (hardcover), $16.95 (paper).

The most renowned of many academic books critiquing current educational systems from an environmental perspective, *Ecological Literacy* is a collection of fifteen essays that David Orr—currently a professor of Environmental Studies at Oberlin College—wrote in the 1980s while at the Meadowcreek Project, an interdisciplinary environmental education program he cofounded. The first essays attempt to define the scope and depth of the crisis of sustainability; latter essays reflect on the relationship between sustainability and the educational process, especially in higher education. For Orr, environmental literacy should be based on the following foundations: all education is environmental education; environmental issues cannot be fully understood by a single discipline or department; education occurs in part as a dialogue with a place and has the characteristics of good conversation; educational methods are as important as content; and experience in the natural world is essential. *Ecological Literacy* is a bit academic, but readable and good food-for-thought for all those interested in environmental education and strategies for reforming the current educational system.

Abstracts and Indices

◆ *ERIC* (see entry 527, ERIC Clearinghouse for Science, Mathematics, and Environmental Education)

Periodicals

539 Green Teacher

Green Teacher, 1991–. 5 issues per school year. 50p. $27.00/year.

Green Teacher introduces ideas and practical strategies that primary and secondary school teachers can use to integrate environmental and other global concerns into the classroom. Teachers contribute articles that describe the methods they find effective; many ready-to-use activities are also shared. Each issue has a theme; past articles have included "Playground on a Budget: The Art of Creative Reuse," "Getting into Hot Water: Energy Education," and "Twinning Schools on a Small Planet." Resource listings and in-depth reviews of curricula and other relevant materials

are also included in every issue. Produced in Canada, the magazine emphasizes Canadian educational materials, but the case studies and teaching strategies are broadly applicable to any classroom. This publication is a down-to-earth and practical resource for generating classroom ideas.

540 Taproot

The Coalition for Education in the Outdoors. 1987–. Quarterly. 40p. $25.00/year.

For those in the field of outdoor education, *Taproot* serves as an excellent tool for staying informed. The Coalition for Education in the Outdoors is a network of businesses (L. L. Bean), institutions (Cornell University's Department of Natural Resources), outdoor education centers (Pocono Environmental Education Center), government agencies (Missouri Department of Conservation), organizations (National Wildlife Federation) and associations (American Camping Association) that support education in, for, and about the outdoors. *Taproot*, the group's newsletter, enables members of the network and other outdoor educators to share information. It includes news articles and analysis of issues in the field, and is packed with book reviews; announcements of programs, curricula, catalogs, and products; news from affiliates and descriptions of outdoor education programs; announcements of professional opportunities and workshops; and a comprehensive conference calendar.

Other Periodicals

◆ The *Journal of Environmental Education* (see entry 527, ERIC Clearinghouse for Science, Mathematics, and Environmental Education)

CHAPTER THIRTEEN

Employment

What This Chapter Covers

The resources in this chapter can help students, recent graduates, and career-changers gather information about different types of environmental employment. Those actively seeking a job or internship will find directories of environmental employers, handbooks that offer job-search advice, and periodicals devoted to environmental job opening announcements and volunteer opportunities. Several additional resources can help environmental entrepreneurs develop ideas.

For More Information

- ◆ See **General** for additional directories of organizations, associations, and companies that employ environmental professionals.
- ◆ See **Education** for resources that can help you choose environmental education programs that prepare students for environmental careers.
- ◆ See **Travel** for resources on volunteer opportunities in which environmental career experience may be gained.

Organizations

541 The Environmental Careers Organization (ECO)
National Office
286 Congress Street
Boston, MA 02210

Phone: 617/426-4375. Fax: 617/423-0998

John R. Cook, Jr., Founder and President

The Environmental Careers Organization (ECO) is a nonprofit organization dedicated to protecting and improving the environment "through the promotion of careers and the development of professionals." ECO's Boston office serves only New England; contact other regional offices in San Francisco (415/362-5552), Tampa (813/886-4330), Cleveland (216/861-4545), or Seattle (206/625-1750). Each year, ECO places more than three hundred college students, recent graduates, and career changers in temporary, paid positions where they gain the practical experience necessary to find a permanent job. Application to the program is $15. ECO also sponsors conferences, job fairs, and local seminars and workshops. Persistent callers looking for job advice will be rewarded; others will be referred to ECO's major publication, *The New Complete Guide to Environmental Careers* (see entry 548). Another ECO publication of interest is the *Environmental Salary Survey Report*.

Reference Handbooks

542 Earth Work: Resource Guide to Nationwide Green Jobs

Edited by Joan Moody and Richard Wizansky. Sponsored by the Student Conservation Association. HarperCollins West, 1994. 200p. $25.00 (hardcover), $14.00 (paper).

Sponsored by the Student Conservation Association, publishers of *Earth Work* magazine (see entry 550), *Earth Work: Resource Guide to Nationwide Green Jobs* offers introductory information on selected topics related to environmental careers. The book's first chapter answers commonly asked questions, such as "Can I work in the environmental field and make a living at the same time?", "What kind of college degree is best?", and "What are the hottest environmental professions?" The next three chapters provide background information on networking for green jobs, graduate schools, and salaries, while the next four chapters offer insight into federal agencies that hire natural resource and environmental professionals, describe what it is like to work for nonprofit conservation groups, and summarize career opportunities in environmental management and several related fields, including environmental marketing, education, and engineering. The final chapter covers the role of minorities in the environmental community. Several career profiles of individuals are also included as sidebars. An appendix supplies the addresses of more than one thousand organizations that offer green jobs.

543 Ecopreneuring: The Complete Guide to Small Business Opportunities From the Environmental Revolution

Steven J. Bennett. John Wiley & Sons, 1991. 308p. $39.95 (hardcover), $19.95 (paper).

Ecopreneuring is for anyone interested in meeting the new demand for green products and services. Introductory chapters provide general advice for developing ideas, generating capital, cultivating customers, and managing a business. The remainder of the book describes entrepreneurial opportunities in environmental industries like recycling and energy conservation, and ideas for selling environmentally friendly products and services, such as safe foods, investment services, and travel services. These chapters provide some practical information on market size, growth potential, capital requirements, overhead and special equipment, insurance, regulation, competition, and marketing. *Ecopreneuring* does not spell out the details of starting a business, but because it recounts stories of successful entrepreneurs, it is helpful for generating ideas.

Another primer on environmental entrepreneuring is *The Green Entrepreneur: Business Opportunities That Can Save the Earth and Make You Money* (Gustav Berle. Liberty Hall Press, 1991).

**544 Environmental Career Directory:
A Practical, One-Stop Guide to Getting
a Job in Preserving the Environment**

Career Advisor series. 1st ed. Visible Ink Press,
1993. Triennial. 348p. $34.00 (hardcover), $17.95
(paper).

The *Environmental Career Directory* is geared
toward the high school or college student who is
looking for his or her first environmental job or
internship. The directory is divided into four distinct parts that correspond to steps in a typical
job search: identifying an area of interest;
reviewing the fundamentals of the search; tar-
geting specific companies; and researching prospects. Part One provides advice from experts in
eleven areas of specialization: forestry, horticulture, geosciences, wetland management, fisheries management, microbiology, industrial
hygiene, botanical gardens, natural resources
management, environmental education, and soil
and water conservation. Most essays cover relevant college courses and other experiences that
offer good career preparation, specific skills,
what companies look for in an applicant, the typical career path, and salary information. Part Two
presents a detailed step-by-step process for initiating any job search; it tells job seekers how to
evaluate personal strengths and weaknesses, set
goals, target companies and network, prepare a
resumé, and write letters. Part Three lists, with
paragraph-long descriptions and contact information, 225 consumer product manufacturers
and paper, metal, mining, energy, and chemical
companies that offer entry-level environmental
jobs and internships in the United States. These
listings are similar to the corporate listings found
in *Green at Work: Finding a Business Career That
Works for the Environment* (see entry 546) and
Peterson's Job Opportunities in the Environment
(see entry 547). The final part of the book is an
annotated resource list of job listings, career
guides, periodicals, professional associations,
and employment agencies.

**545 Environmental Careers: A Practical Guide to
Opportunities in the 90s**

David J. Warner. Lewis Publishers, 1992. 267p.
$39.95 (hardcover).

Environmental Careers provides quality at-a-
glance information to people who already have
an interest in pursuing an environmental career.
Information is detailed and practical, rather than
persuasive. The first half of the book offers more
than fifty two- to three-page descriptions of specific green career opportunities and includes
information about educational preparation,
types of potential employers, and contacts for
more information. (Author David J. Warner
defines "environmental professionals" loosely:
he includes professionals whose skills can be indi-
rectly applied to saving the earth, such as artists,
public relations specialists, and data-processing
specialists.) The second half of the book includes
chapters on various related topics: international
work; jobs in government, industry, consulting,
organizations, and academia; salaries; advice for
career changers; volunteer opportunities and
internships; ten environmental careers with the
most promising prospects for growth; and job-
search strategies.

**546 Green at Work: Finding a Business Career
That Works for the Environment**

Susan Cohn. Island Press, 1992. 280p. $30.00
(hardcover), $16.00 (paper).

**547 Peterson's Job Opportunities in the
Environment 1995**

2nd ed. Peterson's Guides, 1994. Annual. 296p.
$18.95 (paper).

Green at Work and *Peterson's Job Opportunities
in the Environment* are perfect sourcebooks for
anyone thinking about a future with environmental service companies or corporations that
include environmental considerations in their
management practices. Both works focus on companies involved in environment-related industries such as energy production, health services,
manufacturing, business services, chemicals and
allied products, electronics, and environmental
quality and conservation. The bulk of *Green at
Work* is a directory of more than two hundred
environmental service and Fortune 500 corporations likely to recruit at business schools. Each
entry provides a corporate environmental contact, a one-paragraph description of what the
company does, and another detailed paragraph
about the company's environmental programs

and projects. The remainder of the book provides a general summary of career opportunities in environment-related fields, strategies for planning and executing a job search, and a series of environmental career profiles in management, consulting, finance, and the nonprofit sector. *Green at Work* concludes with an extensive and extremely useful resource list of publications, organizations, and associations. *Job Opportunities* provides a more extensive list of companies—twelve hundred—but offers far less insightful information about each. The book's authors focus on basic statistical information—date of incorporation, annual sales, number of employees, number of managerial employees hired in a recent year, human resources contacts—but neglect the environmental significance of each company, providing only a one-sentence description of a company's principal activity. A unique and valuable feature of *Opportunities* is the index of hiring needs, which allows users to look up specific areas of expertise such as chemical engineering, accounting, or biology, and determine those companies that are in need of specific skills. While neither work includes many nonprofit environmental organizations, *Green at Work* is far more focused than *Job Opportunities* on those companies that are working to have a positive influence on the environment, rather than those that simply conduct business in an environment-related industry.

548 The New Complete Guide to Environmental Careers

Kevin Doyle, Project Director, and Bill Sharp, Principal Author. 2nd ed. Sponsored by the Environmental Careers Organization. Island Press, 1993. 364p. $29.95 (hardcover), $15.95 (paper).

The New Complete Guide to Environmental Careers captures the essence of working in an environmental career. Brief introductory chapters provide guidance for choosing an educational strategy, tips for making the most of volunteer programs and internships, and advice for breaking into the field. The core of the book discusses careers in education and communication, planning, solid and hazardous waste management, air- and water-quality management, land and water conservation, fishery and wildlife management, parks and outdoor recreation, and forestry. Each chapter discusses history and background, issues and trends, types of employers, salaries, and educational requirements, and sets forth lists of organizations to contact for more information. The eleven case studies of projects and thirty-four profiles of people in the field put a human face on the guide's career descriptions. This book is an outstanding guide for individuals who are interested in acquiring a deeper understanding of the career choices available in environment-related fields.

549 Opportunities in Environmental Careers

Odom Fanning. 5th ed. "Opportunities in" series. VGM Career Horizons, 1991. 146p. $13.95 (hardcover), $10.95 (paper).

Opportunities in Environmental Careers is a good starting point for high school students interested in an environmental career, especially in the sciences. For roughly twenty categories of environmental jobs, author Odom Fanning provides five to six pages of detailed information on particular job titles, educational requirements, salary averages, and employment outlook. The book also explores educational options, highlighting specific undergraduate environmental programs, and explains how to plan for a career. This book is part of a series (e.g., *Opportunities in Waste Management, Opportunities in Forestry*) that is widely available in public libraries and career centers. Other related titles published by VGM include *Careers for Animal Lovers and Other Zoological Types, Careers for Nature Lovers and Other Outdoor Types, Careers for Environmental Types and Others Who Respect the Earth,* and *Resumes for Environmental Careers.*

Other Reference Handbooks

◆ The *Environmental Salary Survey Report* (see entry 541, Environmental Careers Organization)

◆ *Resumes for Environmental Careers* (see entry 549, *Opportunities in Environmental Careers*)

Periodicals

550 Earth Work

Student Conservation Association, 1991–. 11 issues per year. 24p. $19.95/6 issues, $29.95/11 issues.

Earth Work is a magazine of conservation issues and opportunities. It features interviews with heads of natural resource agencies, salary surveys, and stories on a myriad of topics, from cultural diversity and women in the environmental movement to educational resources for those seeking natural resource careers. At least two thirds of each issue is devoted to the "Job Scan" section, which lists more than a hundred job openings with resource management agencies and environmental organizations, ranging from internship and entry-level positions to CEOs and directorships. Each job listing includes a detailed description of the position offered and qualifications, along with salary information and directions for applying. *Hotline* ($16.95 for 6 issues for *Earth Work* subscribers, $19.95 for 6 issues for nonsubscribers) is a mid-month supplement to the "Job Scan" section of *Earth Work*.

Earth Work's publisher, the Student Conservation Association (SCA), also offers numerous volunteer opportunities. SCA's Conservation Career Development Program (703/524-2441) encourages students, especially minority students, to explore environmental education and career opportunities and helps with job placement.

The biweekly *Environmental Careers World* (Environmental Career Center, $19.00 for 4 issues, $88.00 for 24 issues) is another useful career newsletter. In addition to the more than two hundred job openings listed in each issue, regular features include career news, employer interviews, career advice, and a career networking calendar.

551 Environmental Career Opportunities

Brubach Publishing, 1992–. Biweekly. 40p. $29.00/two months for individuals, $129.00/year for individuals, $189.00/year for corporations.

Environmental Career Opportunities posts more than two hundred nationwide environmental positions—more than any environmental career bulletin. Each issue is divided into six sections:

environmental advocacy, communication and fundraising; environmental policy, legislation and regulation; wildlife and plant conservation; environmental engineering, risk assessment, and impact analysis; scientific research and education; and environmental internships. Jobs located in Washington, D.C.—a special emphasis—are listed first in each section. *Environmental Career Opportunities* maintains a good mix of private, nonprofit, government, and academic jobs, as well as a good balance of entry- and upper-level positions.

552 Environmental Opportunities

Environmental Opportunities, 1982–. Monthly. 12p. $5.00/1 issue, $26.00/6 issues.

Environmental Opportunities describes environmental jobs available throughout the United States. Job categories include administration; agriculture; ecology/fisheries/wildlife; environmental education; horticulture; natural resources; nature centers; organizational; outdoor education; overseas; parks and recreation; research; teaching; and seasonal. A brief calendar of upcoming nationwide conferences is also provided. The numerous volunteer, internship, and outdoor teaching opportunities make this newsletter especially useful for those who do not have extensive career or educational experience.

553 In Business

JG Press, 1979–. Bimonthly. 50p. $29.00/year.

In Business offers news, trends, and other items of interest to owners of small environmental companies. The magazine regularly covers retailing, design, textiles, recycling, and every other type of environment-related business. It also highlights successful management, marketing, and financing strategies and describes new and useful business resources. Each issue has roughly twelve one- to three-page articles filled with references to companies and projects. Regular departments include green retailing, clean technologies, new business ideas, new products, networks and events, and public policy. This publication is excellent browsing material for people thinking of starting their own environmental business.

554 The Job Seeker

Job Seeker. Biweekly. 16p. $19.50/6 issues, $36.00/12 issues, and $60.00/24 issues for individuals; $22.50/6 issues, $44.00/12 issues, and $84.00/24 issues for organizations.

Roughly one hundred environmental career positions from across the nation are described in each issue of *The Job Seeker,* especially those that are technical and career oriented. Job descriptions are grouped in the following cate-gories: forestry, biology, fisheries, conservation, environmental action and policy, administration, environmental education, parks and recreation, internships, and soil and water conservation. *The Job Seeker* often includes job-searching features, such as "How to Prepare an SF-171 Application."

Other Periodicals

◆ *Environmental Careers World* (see entry 550, *Earth Work*)

CHAPTER FOURTEEN

Gardening

What This Chapter Covers

The resources in this chapter can help you make environmentally sensitive choices in planning your garden, landscaping your yard, and controlling pests both inside and outside your home.

For More Information

- ◆ See **Agriculture** for resources on sustainable agriculture and pesticides, and additional resources on pest control.
- ◆ See **Health and Toxics** for resources on the health effects of pesticides and other toxic substances.

Government Clearinghouses

- The Alternative Farming Systems Information Center (see entry 181)
- The National Pesticide Telecommunications Network (see entry 184)

Organizations

555 Rodale Press
33 East Minor Street
Main Building
Emmaus, PA 18098

Phone (distribution): 800/848-4735

Robert Teufel, President

A large publisher of gardening, health, and home maintenance books, Rodale Press publishes the most authoritative organic gardening handbooks available. These books are compiled by experts and benefit from research conducted by the Rodale Institute Research Center (610/683-6009), one of the world's leading research facilities for organic horticulture and sustainable agriculture. The gardening handbooks that are broadest in scope are *Rodale's All-New Encyclopedia of Organic Gardening,* for reference, and *Rodale's Chemical-Free Lawn and Garden,* for how-to instructions. Many specialized titles are available, including *Rodale's Garden Insect, Disease and Weed Identification Guide; The Organic Gardener's Handbook of Natural Insect and Disease Control;* and *Growing Fruits and Vegetables Organically.* Each handbook contains an extraordinary amount of information in an easy-to-use format. Gardeners on all levels are bound to find a title that suits their needs; browse the bookstore or public library, order a list of publications, or join Rodale's Organic Gardening Book Club. For advice on a monthly basis, subscribe to Rodale's *Organic Gardening* magazine (see entry 565).

Other Organizations

- agAccess (see entry 185)
- The Bio-Dynamic Farming and Gardening Association (see entry 186)
- The Bio-Integral Resource Center (see entry 187)

Reference Handbooks

556 Building a Healthy Lawn: A Safe and Natural Approach

Stuart Franklin. 2nd ed. Storey Communications, 1993. 168p. $9.95 (paper).

Building a Healthy Lawn operates from the premise that chemical fertilizers and pesticides are unnecessary. The book—written in clear, straightforward language—provides positive, practical steps anyone can use to achieve a low-cost, low-maintenance—yet lush—lawn. Seeding, soil building, thatching, mowing, pest control, and weed control are covered, as well as groundcovers and mulches.

Those who want a historical and cultural analysis of America's fascination with lawns, as well as an exploration of the environmental damage they wreak, should read *Redesigning the American Lawn: A Search for Environmental Harmony* (F. Herbert Bormann, Diana Balmori, Gorden T. Geballe. Yale University Press, 1993). For alternatives to grass lawns, see *Landscaping with Wildflowers* (see entry 563) and *Noah's Garden* (see entry 564).

557 Common-Sense Pest Control: Least-Toxic Solutions for Your Home, Garden, Pets and Community

William Olkowski, Sheila Daar, and Helga Olkowski. Sponsored by the Bio-Integral Resource Center. Taunton Press, 1991. 715p. $39.95 (hardcover).

558 Pest Control for Home and Garden: The Safest and Most Effective Methods for You and the Environment

Michael Hansen, Ph.D. Consumers Union, 1993. 372p. $22.95 (hardcover).

Both *Common-Sense Pest Control* and *Pest Control for Home and Garden* are complete, definitive guides to understanding and eliminating pests through least-toxic methods. In *Common-Sense Pest Control*, chief staffers of the Bio-Integral Resource Center (see entry 187) share their expertise in Integrated Pest Management (IPM). A mammoth reference, this book can be used to solve problems caused by pests in the house, garden, and community, or inside the human body. For every type of pest, text and graphics relay biological background on the organism, the damage it causes, and both indirect and direct control strategies. *Pest Control for Home and Garden* is less encyclopedic and more of a how-to guide for a lay audience. For each problem, it gives advice on when to take action, long- and short-term control strategies, and "last resorts"—which usually entail using chemicals. Also included are detailed ratings of pesticide products based on effectiveness and their toxicity to humans, animals, and the environment. Both books contain appendices of companies and products and both are likely to be found in public libraries.

Paperback reference guides that supply the same high-quality advice with less background material are *Gardening for a Greener Planet: A Chemical-Free Approach* (Jonathan Erickson. TAB Books, 1993. $13.95) and *Dan's Practical Guide to Least Toxic Home Pest Control* (Dan Stein. Hulogosi, 1991. $8.95).

559 The New Organic Grower: A Master's Manual of Tools and Techniques for the Home and Market Gardener

Eliot Coleman. Chelsea Green, 1989. 269p. $19.95 (paper).

560 Step by Step Organic Vegetable Gardening

Shepherd Ogden. Rev. ed. HarperCollins, 1992. 299p. $23.00 (hardcover).

The New Organic Grower and *Step by Step Organic Vegetable Gardening* are personal, easy-to-use guides to growing vegetables organically. Both give clear directions for all stages of gardening, from site selection to cultivation, and provide details on the most common vegetables. Between Shepherd Ogden and his grandfather, Big Sam, who wrote the popular 1971 edition,

Step by Step contains more than fifty years of gardening wisdom. It is one of the best introductions to the subject of organic gardening for the beginning gardener. Eliot Coleman, who has learned from experimenting with his garden for twenty years, geared his book, *The New Organic Grower*, especially toward five-acre gardens in colder climates; he also provides more information for those in the gardening business, including sections on hiring help and marketing. The annotated bibliography and the appendix of recommended tools and supplies are helpful. *The New Organic Grower* also has a chapter on extending the growing season year-round, which Coleman's second book, *The New Organic Grower's Four-Season Harvest* (Chelsea Green, 1992), fully develops.

561 The Organic Gardener's Home Reference: A Plant-by-Plant Guide to Growing Fresh, Healthy Food

Tanya Denckla. Compiled by Wooden Angel Publishing. Storey Communications, 1994; distributed by HarperCollins Publishers. 304p. $29.95 (hardcover), $22.95 (paper).

The idea for *The Organic Gardener's Home Reference*—a "centralized nuts-and-bolts reference for rapid answers"—originated when the author found herself flipping through many different books trying to find everything she needed to know about a specific aspect of gardening. This outstanding guide goes a long way toward solving this problem. For more than sixty edible plants, the left page, of a two-page spread, provides information on growing, common pests and diseases, harvesting, storage requirements, allies, companions, and enemies, while the page on the right describes different varieties of plants. Precise information—taste of each variety, first and last seed starting dates, planting depth, humidity for fresh storage, etc.—is easily found. Chapters on diseases and pests have charts that describe both the problem and organic remedies. A final chapter discusses allies (plants that repel insects or enhance growth or flavor) and companions (crops that can share space). Backmatter includes an extensive annotated bibliography and directories of suppliers and environmentally concerned state gardening associations. The full text of the proposed

National Organic Growing Standards is also included. Advice in this work assumes prior gardening knowledge.

Other Reference Handbooks

- ◆ *Growing Fruits and Vegetables Organically* (see entry 555, Rodale Press)
- ◆ *The Organic Gardener's Handbook of Natural Insect and Disease Control* (see entry 555, Rodale Press)
- ◆ *Rodale's All-New Encyclopedia of Organic Gardening* (see entry 555, Rodale Press)
- ◆ *Rodale's Chemical-Free Lawn and Garden* (see entry 555, Rodale Press)
- ◆ *Rodale's Garden Insect, Disease and Weed Identification Guide* (see entry 555, Rodale Press)

Introductory Reading

562 Environmental Gardening

Karen Arms. Halfmoon Publishing, 1992. 350p. $23.95 (paper).

Environmental Gardening provides an introduction to the interrelationship between gardening and ecology. A biologist and gardener, author Karen Arms discusses not just organic gardening but also the many ways in which gardens and landscapes affect the environment. She especially focuses on achieving harmony between horticulture and natural ecological systems (for example, she advocates using native plants and encourages attracting birds); she also discusses, however, such subjects as limiting the consumption of fresh water and fossil fuels, and gardeners' increased risk of skin cancer exacerbated by the thinning ozone layer. Though much of the book consists of sections on growing trees, shrubs, lawns, flowers, herbs, fruits, and vegetables, it contains more background information than how-to advice. This book has a little bit of everything, making it a good first read on the subject.

563 Landscaping With Wildflowers: An Environmental Approach to Gardening

Jim Wilson. Houghton Mifflin, 1992. 244p. $35.00 (hardcover), $18.95 (paper).

564 Noah's Garden: Restoring the Ecology of Our Back Yards

Sara Stein. Houghton Mifflin, 1993. 294p. $21.95 (hardcover).

Both of these books—*Landscaping With Wildflowers* and *Noah's Garden*—provide alternatives to the conventional lawn—alternatives that are well integrated with, rather than antagonistic toward, the natural environment. These personal accounts are not straightforward handbooks, but both books have enough practical advice to get gardeners started. *Landscaping with Wildflowers* includes many color photographs and dispenses advice on planning, planting, and maintaining meadows, prairies, and other landscapes. There is also a chapter on attracting butterflies and birds. The listings of native wildflowers for each region of the country, and the directories of wildflower societies and mail-order companies, are extremely helpful. *Noah's Garden* recounts the steps one gardener took to attract the native wildlife that no longer roamed her garden. Tidbits on ecology, biology, and natural history are woven throughout this well-written and inspirational story. *Noah's Garden* includes an annotated bibliography.

Periodicals

565 Organic Gardening

Rodale Press. 1942–. 9 issues per year. 100p. $25.00/year.

Organic Gardening is the most popular magazine for organic growing enthusiasts. It provides news updates, growing advice, and product comparisons in plain language for a national audience of gardeners and small farmers. Articles regularly feature all gardening information, including pest control, composting, fertilizers, and crop rotation for a variety of crops. The editors and other readers share tips on successful growing methods. Advertisements for gardening supplies are prominent. Many gardeners prefer reading issue by issue, rather than consulting Rodale Press reference books like *Rodale's All-New Encyclopedia of Organic Gardening* (see entry 555, Rodale Press).

CHAPTER FIFTEEN

Grants

What This Chapter Covers

The resources in this chapter can help you identify national, regional, and local foundations that provide grants for environmental projects; they can also help you learn about past grants awarded to specific environmental efforts.

Organizations

566 Environmental Data Research Institute
1655 Elmwood Avenue, Suite 225
Rochester, NY 14620

Phone: 716/473-3090. Fax: 716/473-0968

Edith C. Stein, President

The Environmental Data Research Institute is an independent nonprofit organization that compiles, analyzes, and disseminates information on environmental funding. The Institute's database tracks more than two thousand private environmental grantmakers and their grants; the large majority of this information is available in the group's directory, *Environmental Grantmaking Foundations* (see entry 569). The Environmental Data Research Institute performs custom database searches for $50 per hour; searches generally average $150 to $250 each. These searches inform grantseekers of their most likely funding sources.

567 Foundation Center
79 Fifth Avenue
New York, NY 10003

Phone (customer service): 800/424-9836. Phone: 212/620-4230

Database Vendor: The Foundation Center's Grants Database is available from DIALOG.

The Foundation Center is the best place to start a search for funding. The center was established by foundations to provide an authoritative source of information on private philanthropic giving; it provides service to grantseekers through its national library collections in New York City and Washington, D.C. (202/331-1400), its field offices in Atlanta (404/880-0094), Cleveland (216/861-1934), and San Francisco (415/397-0902), and its network of two hundred cooperating libraries in all fifty states. Through these libraries, grantseekers have free access to core Foundation Center publications plus a wide range of other relevant books, periodicals, and research documents. Its core publications include: the *Foundation Directory*, the *Guide to U.S. Foundations, Their Trustees, Officers, and Donors*, the *Foundation Grants Index*, the *Foundation Grants to Individuals*, and the *National Directory of Corporate Giving*. Much of the information found in these directories about grantmakers and the grants they distribute is available electronically in the *Grants Database*, available from DIALOG; contact the Foundation Center's New York office for online technical support services. The *National Guide to Funding for the Environment and Animal Welfare* (see entry 571) and *Grants for Environmental Protection and Animal Welfare* (see entry 570) are both outstanding Foundation Center guides for environmental grantseekers. Seminars and books that offer advice on researching and applying for grants are also available: Some highly regarded books include *Foundation Fundamentals*, which provides a complete overview of the grantseeking process; the *Guide to Proposal Writing*; *Managing for Profit in the Nonprofit World*; and *A Nonprofit Organization Operating Manual*. Libraries affiliated with the Foundation Center also have many other noncenter resources vital to environmental grantseekers, such as *GrantsLists* (see entry 572), *The Environmental Grantmakers Association Directory* (see entry 568), and *Environmental Grantmaking Foundations* (see entry 569). Whether one visits the libraries or purchases the publications, every grantseeker should take full advantage of the Foundation Center's resources and services.

Other Organizations

- ◆ The Environmental Support Center (see entry 27)
- ◆ The Institute for Conservation Leadership (see entry 35)

Directories

568 The Environmental Grantmakers Association Directory

5th ed. Environmental Grantmakers Association, 1994. Annual. 200p. $20.00 (paper).

The Environmental Grantmakers Association Directory offers an inexpensive way to learn about a select number of environmental grantmakers, though only members of the

Environmental Grantmakers Association are included. The association's membership now includes more than 160 grantmaking professionals—mostly from private foundations—with an interest in funding environmental projects. Each entry in the directory provides a rough sketch of the information grantseekers need most, including financial information from the past three years, areas of interest and emphasis, and grant limitations. No sample grants are listed. The publication includes topical indices arranged by issue, type of projects and programs supported, and geographical focus area.

569 Environmental Grantmaking Foundations

Edited by Edith C. Stein. 3rd ed. Environmental Data Research Institute, 1995. Annual. 800p. $75.00 (paper)

Environmental Grantmaking Foundations offers the most detailed coverage of more than four hundred environmental grantmakers. This book encompasses all environmental issues—coastal lands, wastewater treatment, population, development, etc. Each two-page entry includes: a history and philosophy of the foundation, sample grants, monetary range of environmental grants, percentage of total grants awarded that were environmental, and a summary of both emphases and limitations of activities, recipients, types of support, and geography. The book's five indices are comprehensive. Of all environmental funding directories, this one by the Environmental Data Research Institute (see entry 566) is the most complete, and the one that makes it easiest to decide which grants to pursue.

570 Grants for Environmental Protection and Animal Welfare

Edited by Ruth Kovacs. 4th ed. Grant Guides series. Foundation Center, 1994. Annual. 221p. $65.00 (paper).

Grants for Environmental Protection and Animal Welfare is a comprehensive list of past environmental grants of $10,000 or greater. The three thousand grant listings provide recipient name and location, date, and, in most cases, a one-sentence description of the funded project. Since grants are arranged by grantmaker and include a summary of grant limitations, this directory can be used to target prospective funding sources. The publication contains indices: grant recipient, geographical, and keyword. A brief statistical section shows researchers the total amount and distribution of environmental grant money awarded in several different categories—including total dollar amount by type of support and subject area.

571 National Guide to Funding for the Environment and Animal Welfare

Edited by Stan Olson, Ruth Kovacs, and Suzanne Haile. 2nd ed. Foundation Center, 1994. Annual. 322p. $85.00 (paper).

The *National Guide to Funding for the Environment and Animal Welfare* provides the broadest coverage of environmental grantmakers. Entries include more than one thousand private foundations and almost one hundred corporate giving programs that have demonstrated a commitment to animal welfare, conservation, ecology, environment, wildlife, and waste reduction. Each entry packs in the basic information grantseekers need: grantmaker addresses, financial data, giving priorities, contact names. This guide also includes more than 2,700 descriptions of specific grants recently awarded. Six comprehensive indices make it easy to search by name, location, type of support, subject area, etc. This guide also contains a two-page bibliography of articles related to environmental funding.

Periodicals

572 GrantsLists

Environmental Grantmakers Association, 1988–. Quarterly. 25p. $35.00/year.

GrantsLists offers the best way to stay on top of the latest environmental grants. The magazine covers news about environmental associations, including personnel changes, and describes more than seven hundred environmental grants awarded by Environmental Grantmakers Association (EGA) members. In *GrantsLists*, grants are arranged by grantmaker, but not every grantmaker is listed in every issue. *GrantsLists* has been posted on EcoNet (see entry 58) in the *ega.grants* conference in the past, and EGA plans to resume posting current issues there. EGA also publishes the *Environmental Grantmakers Association Directory* (see entry 568), which provides information about EGA members.

CHAPTER SIXTEEN

Investing

What This Chapter Covers

The resources in this chapter can help financial professionals develop investment portfolios based on the social and financial performance of companies. Individual investors can use this chapter to learn about socially responsible investing issues like animal testing, employee ownership, and pollution violations; evaluate socially responsible mutual funds and stocks; and choose a financial advisor who specializes in socially responsible investing.

Organizations

573 Coalition for Environmentally Responsible Economies (CERES)

711 Atlantic Avenue
Boston, MA 02111

Phone: 617/451-0927. Fax: 617/482-2028

Judy Kuszewski, Corporate Program Director

Commonly referred to as CERES, the nonprofit Coalition for Environmentally Responsible Economies (CERES) brings together environmental groups and the investment community to promote environmentally and financially sound economic activities and investment philosophies. To achieve these goals, this membership organization launched the CERES Principles project to help U.S. companies adopt environmentally sound practices. By endorsing the CERES Principles, originally called the Valdez Principles, a company commits to long-term improvement in its environmental performance. The ten principles address a wide range of topics, including protection of the biosphere; sustainable use of natural resources; energy conservation; and risk reduction. CERES also publishes a quarterly newsletter, *On Principle*, that keeps readers informed of progress with endorsements of the CERES Principles and includes news related to environmental and social investing.

Another group, the Global Environmental Management Initiative (202/296-7449), is a coalition of blue-chip U.S. companies that has devised its own set of broad environmental principles for companies.

574 Council on Economic Priorities (CEP)

30 Irving Place
New York, NY 10003

Phone: 800/729-4237; 212/420-1133. Fax: 212/420-0988

Alice Tepper Marlin, Executive Director

Bulletin Board: The executive summaries of some CEP reports are available on the Right-to-Know Network (RTK Net) (see entry 378). Choose *Text Datasets*, then *Corporate Profiles (Council on Economic Priorities)*.

A leading source of information on corporate social responsibility, the Council on Economic Priorities (CEP) is perhaps best known for producing *Shopping for a Better World* (see entry 616). This nonprofit, public-interest research organization provides a host of other valuable publications and services for organizations, companies, and individuals interested in the social and environmental impact, policies, and actions of corporations. SCREEN, CEP's primary research service for money managers, offers original social performance research on roughly seven hundred domestic and international companies in eleven issue areas. SCREEN subscriptions (contact CEP for details on pricing) include updated quarterly reports on the issue areas, use of the SCREEN database, and Corporate Environmental Data Clearinghouse reports. Each report (available separately for $250 each for the first two, with discounts available for larger purchases—nonprofit prices begin at $80 each) provides between fifteen and fifty pages of detailed information about the environmental impact of one corporation's activities. The reports analyze various aspects of the company's practices, including corporate compliance records, lobbying and political activities, energy efficiency, hazardous waste disposal policies, and the environmental consequences of the company's technologies and products. CEP membership includes *Shopping for a Better World* and the monthly newsletter *Research Report*, which is useful for staying abreast of corporate responsibility topics. CEP is receptive to individual callers and is an exceptional source of reliable information concerning both corporate responsibility and sound investment opportunities.

The Social Investment Organization, based in Ontario, Canada, provides similar services and dozens of publications geared toward a Canadian audience (416/360-6047).

575 DataCenter

464 19th Street
Oakland, CA 94612

Phone: 510/835-4692. Fax: 510/835-3017.
E-mail: datacenter@igc.apc.org

Fred Goff, Executive Director

DataCenter serves as a grassroots clearinghouse on corporate responsibility. DataCenter's extensive file collection—more than fifteen thousand company files—is particularly strong in the areas of human rights, censorship, corporate social responsibility, and environmental protection. The clippings in the environmental files cover virtually every area related to the environment, from electromagnetic fields and transportation of hazardous materials to deforestation and endangered species to environmental racism and green marketing. Patrons may utilize the walk-in library or opt for the center's customized research services. The library contains more than 450 mainstream and alternative periodicals, 400 file drawers of well-organized documents and articles, and 5,000 books, directories, and reports. Research services cost $75 per hour—with pro bono services available—and include focused searches of the DataCenter's library resources as well as the Internet and nine databases, including NEXIS and DIALOG. A personalized clipping service is also available; rates vary according to the number of periodicals monitored and frequency of delivery. The DataCenter is an outstanding source of comprehensive information on the actions and environmental records of U.S. and foreign corporations.

576 First Affirmative Financial Network (FAFN)
1040 South 8th Street, Suite 200
Colorado Springs, CO 80906

Phone: 800/728-3473; 719/636-1045. Fax: 719/636-1943

George Gay, Vice President

The First Affirmative Financial Network (FAFN) is a network of fifty-six socially responsible investment advisors in nineteen states, all of whom offer complete brokerage services. Although individual FAFN advisors work independently, each has access to FAFN's support services and numerous research reports, which include both original research and research supplied by several highly regarded research services. Using this research, FAFN can customize accounts to meet each investor's social and environmental concerns. Socially responsible insurance coverage is also available. Call for a free consultation. (Securities are offered through Walnut Street Securities (WSS), member NASD SIPC. First Affirmative is a financial services firm and is not an affiliate or subsidiary of WSS.)

577 Franklin Research and Development Corporation (FRDC)
711 Atlantic Avenue
Boston, MA 02111

Phone: 800/548-5684. Phone: 617/423-6655

Joan Bavaria, President

As an investment advisor company, Franklin Research Development Corporation (FRDC) conducts research for and provides advice to active individual investors and institutions that want socially responsible criteria applied to the management of their funds. Currently, Franklin Research maintains extensive social responsibility assessments on one thousand companies and tracks selected social issues for another thousand. Company evaluations focus on the following areas: the environment, renewable energy utilization, employee relations, animal rights, product quality, international human rights, and military procurement and conversion. Franklin researches corporations by reviewing their literature, interviewing corporate executives, and seeking verification from nonprofit research groups, government agencies, and stakeholder groups. The firm also publishes a monthly newsletter, *Franklin's Insight: Investing for a Better World* ($29.95 per year), which rates and recommends responsible investments of all kinds, from community loan funds to stocks and bonds, and provides practical information on evaluating the social performance of corporations. The company works closely with the Coalition for Environmentally Responsible Economies (CERES) (see entry 573)—founded by Franklin president Joan Bavaria—to lobby corporations to submit standardized environmental annual reports.

578 Investor Responsibility Research Center (IRRC)
1350 Connecticut Avenue, NW, Suite 700
Washington , DC 20036

Phone: 202/833-0700. Fax: 202/833-3555

Margaret Carroll, Executive Director

The Investor Responsibility Research Center (IRRC) is a highly respected independent nonprofit corporation that conducts research and publishes impartial reports on corporate social and environmental responsibility. Its work is funded by the more than four hundred institutional investors, investment managers, and corporations that subscribe to its services. IRRC's Environmental Information Service, which has a sliding-scale pricing structure based on the scope of services selected, has two primary components: the *Corporate Environmental Profiles Directory*, and the *Investor's Environmental Report* newsletter. The directory summarizes the environmental records, potential environmental liabilities, and environmental management programs of companies on *Standard & Poor's 500*. Information for these profiles is gathered from Environmental Protection Agency and other federal agency databases, corporate public securities filings, and IRRC's annual management practice survey, as well as from searches of more than one hundred major newspapers and trade publications. Each two-page corporate profile includes: environmental capital expenditures, hazardous waste cleanup responsibilities, toxic chemical releases, reported spills, compliance data (e.g., number of penalties, total value of penalties), secondary industries of parent company, environmental policy components, environmental staff, environmental auditing programs, environmental achievements, current environmental projects, and summaries of recent articles. The *Investor's Environmental Report*—which may be purchased separately for $150.00 per year—is a bimonthly newsletter that, although targeted toward institutional investors and corporate executives, will also appeal to less technical readers because of its concise, easy-to-understand style. This newsletter regularly includes in-depth features that thoroughly analyze the full range of environmental corporate responsibility and investing issues, including major legislative and judicial actions affecting business, environmental trends that will have an impact on business and investors, and performance of environmental mutual funds—with emphasis on environmental industry sector funds. Several special reports—which may be purchased separately for $25 to $100 each—re also included as part of the service.

579 Kinder, Lydenberg, Domini & Co. (KLD)
129 Mount Auburn Street
Cambridge, MA 02138

Phone: 617/547-7479. Fax: 617/354-5353

Peter Kinder, President

Kinder, Lydenberg, Domini & Co. (KLD) provides research services for money managers on the financial, social, and environmental performance of corporations. KLD concentrates its research on the largest American companies, evaluating each company based on a full range of social screens, including the environment; the environmental screens weed out the most flagrant environmental abusers listed in *Standard & Poor's 500*. Companies that satisfy each of the screens are included in the *Domini 400 Social Index*—the Domini Social Index Trust is a mutual fund comprising these same companies. KLD disseminates its research in several formats: a monthly performance list for companies on the *Domini 400 Social Index*, one- to three-page company profiles, an online database providing details on the social records of more than 750 companies, and individually tailored research. The principals of KLD also write books that appeal to an audience broader than just money managers, including *Investing for Good: Making Money While Being Socially Responsible* (see entry 583).

580 Progressive Asset Management (PAM)
1814 Franklin Street, Suite 710
Oakland, CA 94612

Phone: 800/786-2998; 510/834-3722. Fax: 510/836-1621

Peter Camejo, Chief Executive Officer

A leader in environmentally conscious investing, Progressive Asset Management (PAM) is the oldest and largest full-service socially responsible brokerage firm in the United States. Through PAM, individuals can receive financial planning, insurance, and brokerage services for all major investment vehicles. Brokers, institutional investors, and high-net-worth individuals can receive portfolio management services that include original, personally tailored research conducted by PAM investment professionals. Call for a free consultation.

581 Social Investment Forum (SIF)
121 Mount Vernon Street
Boston, MA 02108

Phone: 617/723-7171. Fax: 202/331-8166

Carla Mortensen, Executive Director

The Social Investment Forum (SIF) is the sole professional association for the social investment industry. SIF was established in 1981 to encourage and support the growth of socially responsible investing. As a consensus builder and neutral figure in the industry, the group does not answer questions concerning the nature of specific funds or financial professionals. However, it does produce *The Social Investment Services Guide* ($85 to nonmembers), which offers descriptions of nearly half of SIF's 1,400 individual and institutional members. Membership includes the *Guide* and the quarterly *Forum Newsletter*, which features book reviews, stock picks, announcements of new funds, and a performance chart of selected socially screened funds. The Washington, D.C., office (202/833-5522) focuses on serving its membership on a day-to-day basis, while the Boston headquarters focuses on analyzing long-term trends that will affect investment opportunities and the investment industry.

Other Organizations

- ◆ Clean Yield Asset Management (see entry 587, *Clean Yield*)

Directories

582 Good Money's Social Funds Guide

1st ed. Good Money Publications, 1993. Biannual, with annual updates. 121p. $29.95 (paper).

Good Money's Social Funds Guide offers the most comprehensive analysis and commentary available on more than forty socially screened mutual, money market, and bond funds, including twelve environmental funds. The guide's clear, graphical layout—which features an abundance of tables, graphs, and pie charts—allows both individual investors and investment professionals to understand and locate needed information easily. For each fund, the *Social Funds Guide* provides all the pertinent basic infor-

mation, such as phone numbers, portfolio manager, fees, purchasing options, and investment minimums; financial performance comparisons to funds within the same category (e.g., growth, income), within other categories, and to *Standard & Poor's 500* as a whole; and the names of the largest holdings in the portfolio by industry category (e.g., industrial, environmental, financial). In addition, Good Money Publications screened the portfolios of all funds included in the guide, providing summaries of each fund's history and critiques of its screening criteria; each portfolio manager was then given the opportunity to comment on these evaluations. The insight provided by the portfolio managers' in-depth explanations of each fund's social criteria and approach to investment selection is a unique and useful feature. Another interesting feature of this indispensable guide compares nonscreened environmental funds to screened environmental funds.

Good Money Publications also publishes the *Good Money: The Newsletter for Socially Concerned Investors* (see entry 589) newsletter and other investing guides, such as the thirty-eight-page *Energy, Environment & Animal Rights Investment Strategy Guide*.

Other Directories

- ◆ The *Corporate Environmental Profiles Directory* (see entry 578, Investor Responsibility Research Center)
- ◆ The *Social Investment Services Guide* (see entry 581, Social Investment Forum)

Reference Handbooks

583 Investing for Good: Making Money While Being Socially Responsible

Peter D. Kinder, Steven D. Lydenberg, and Amy L. Domini. 1st ed. HarperCollins Publishers, 1993. 320p. $23.00 (hardcover).

584 Social Investment Almanac

Edited by Peter Kinder, Steven D. Lydenberg, and Amy L. Domini. Henry Holt and Company, 1992. 904p. $50.00 (hardcover).

Both *Investing for Good* and the *Social Investment Almanac* provide thorough overviews of socially conscious investing. Compiled by the principals of the investment research firm Kinder, Lydenberg, Domini & Co. (KLD) (see entry 579), the *Social Investment Almanac* serves as a desk reference for investment professionals, while *Investing for Good* is a primer for nonspecialists. The almanac is a compilation of forty essays by fifty-one prominent professionals that covers all aspects of socially conscious investing: shareholder activism, corporate accountability research, social portfolio management, community development investing, consumer and employment issues, international investing, and green consumerism. Other features include an explanation of the origins of social investing and an appendix identifying major areas of strength and weakness of the companies in the *Domini 400 Social Index*, a financial index developed by KLD. *Investing for Good* begins by walking readers through the history and basic principles of socially conscious investing, exploring questions of performance and thoroughly explaining the concept of social screens, both positive and negative. The remainder of the book considers, in detail, the primary categories of social investing: weapons manufacturing, community involvement, employee relations, treatment of minorities, product quality and customer relations, and environmental awareness. The chapter on the environment discusses how federal regulations, the *Toxic Release Inventory (TRI)* (see entry 381), genetic engineering, energy production, water use, and many other environment-related topics affect socially conscious investing decisions. Both of these works include detailed glossaries and directories of hundreds of brokers, consulting firms, institutional investors, venture capital firms, mutual funds, and other social investment service providers.

585 Investing from the Heart: The Guide to Socially Responsible Investments and Money Management

Jack A. Brill and Alan Reder. Crown Publishing, 1993. 414p. $20.00 (hardcover), $12.00 (paper).

Investing from the Heart is an ideal starting point for beginning investors concerned with social responsibility. Author Jack A. Brill's financial consulting experience and Alan Reder's con-

versational writing style make it enjoyable to learn about money management and financial planning. *Investing from the Heart* outlines entry-level financial management options, from socially responsible credit cards to low-minimum-deposit mutual funds; describes social issues investors may want to use as screening criteria; and lists companies that excel or lag behind in particular issue areas, including many environmental concerns like solar and geothermal energy, water supply, and toxic pollution. What sets this guide apart from other introductions to socially responsible investing are its sections on financial planning and money management. It provides all the necessary tips, worksheets, and guidelines to allow anyone to begin investing according to his or her own social conscience.

586 Socially Responsible Financial Planning Handbook

Co-op America, 1993. Updated irregularly. 30p. $5.00 (paper).

A practical guide for novices, the *Socially Responsible Financial Planning Handbook* introduces the basic concepts of financial planning in a socially responsible light. Each edition contains financial planning worksheets, a table of socially screened mutual funds—with all the pertinent financial information, including fees, initial investment, total assets of fund, one-, three-, and five-year returns, etc.—and a resource guide of financial managers, research services, and publications. Representative articles from past editions include "Your Personal Financial Plan," "Rating Your Bank," "Retirement Planning—Start Today!," and "Environmental Investing." A valuable and up-to-date resource for individuals who want to implement a socially conscious investing strategy. The handbook is available free to members of Co-op America (see entry 16).

Periodicals

587 The Clean Yield

Clean Yield Publications, 1985–. Monthly. 8p. $95.00/year for individuals and nonprofits, $125.00/year for businesses.

The Clean Yield helps active individual investors and investment professionals select stocks that meet strict social, environmental, and economic criteria. Each issue contains detailed one-page profiles of two publicly traded companies that include such information as financial strength rating, earnings information, twelve-month price target, and suggested buy price, as well as facts about the company's environmental and community relations records, executive cash compensation, international operations, labor and affirmative action records, and military contracts. Brief updates on eight stocks that are part of the Clean Yield Model Portfolio are also included in each issue. The model portfolio does not include the stocks of companies that have environmental pollution violations or labor conflicts, nor those that have involvement with weapons manufacturing, nuclear power generation, tobacco production, or liquor production. The last page of each issue provides recent financial information for each model portfolio stock, including buy and sell recommendations. Regular columns take a technical look at the current stock market climate, report on developments in the socially responsible movement, and provide educational information on investment techniques. Investors who wish to invest a minimum of $250,000 can use Clean Yield Asset Management as a portfolio management service; contact Clean Yield Publications (800/944-9616, 802/533-7178) for more information.

588   Environmental Business Journal (EBJ)

Environmental Business International, 1988–. Monthly. 16p. $395.00/year.

The *Environmental Business Journal (EBJ)* is a leading source of business news and financial information on the environmental industry. Each issue of EBJ focuses on a specific theme, providing readers with a thorough analysis of a particular management issue or market segment. Previous issues have covered air pollution control, investment and public capital, venture financing, alternative energy, the bioremediation market, environmental investing, defining the environmental industry, the state of technology, and international markets. Each issue also includes a valuable "Stock Reporter" section that provides an overview of stock market trends; compares the EBJ Index—which includes several

hundred companies—to the Dow Jones Industrial Average, *Standard & Poor's 500*, and other indices; lists the financial information of each stock on the EBJ Index; and highlights the top gainers and biggest losers over the past month. *EBJ*'s publisher, Environmental Business International, also offers other periodicals (*Global Environmental Business Journal* and *EBJ's Environmental Consulting Manager*) and comprehensive reports (e.g., *Environmental Industry Overview, The Water/Wastewater Market*), as well as consulting services.

The *ERG Guide to Environmental Stocks* (Environmental Resources Group, $99 per year), is a monthly independent six-page newsletter that rates more than two hundred environmental industry stocks. It also includes news briefs and company updates, and tracks the performance of stocks on the ERG index. Both the *Environmental Business Journal* and the *ERG Guide to Environmental Stocks* are good choices for investors who wish to buy stocks in companies that are driven by, or have a vested interest in, environmental regulation and awareness.

589   Good Money: The Newsletter for Socially Concerned Investors

Good Money Publications, 1982–. Bimonthly. 12p. $75.00/year.

Geared toward the nonexpert, individual investor, *Good Money* reports on those companies in which social and environmentally responsible mutual funds invest, as well as on the mutual funds themselves. Two stock averages besides the Dow Jones Industrial Average (DJIA) are tracked in *Good Money*, the Good Money Industrial Average (GMIA) and the Good Money Utility Average (GMUA). The GMIA contains stocks of the best-of-industry companies for the same industry categories found on the DJIA, while the GMUA is screened for no-nuclear connections and for companies developing or using alternative and renewable energy resources. Charts and graphs regularly compare the performance of GMIA and GMUA stocks to those stocks that fall short of the acceptance criteria: for example, "Tobacco Stocks Versus the GMIA," "Major Polluters Versus GMIA," and "Nuclear Utilities with Poor Operating Records Versus Nonnuclear Utilities with Good Records." Regular feature articles focus on developments in the socially responsible investing industry, successful investing strategies, and updates on companies that were recently considered socially responsible, but now have problems that need to be looked at more closely. Subscriptions to *Good Money* include a subscription to *Netback*, a bimonthly reader forum and networking newsletter of the socially responsible investing community.

Good Money Publications also publishes guides, books, and reports, and provides consulting, custom research, and portfolio audit services.

Other Periodicals

◆ *Investing for a Better World* (see entry 577, Franklin Research and Development Corporation)

◆ The *Forum Newsletter* (see entry 581, Social Investment Forum)

◆ The *Investor's Environmental Report* (see entry 578, Investor Responsibility Research Center)

CHAPTER SEVENTEEN

Shopping

What This Chapter Covers

The resources in this chapter can help you make environmentally responsible choices in everyday decisions, and enable you to audit your personal impact on the earth. In addition to assisting with the evaluation of consumer products, from cleansers to office equipment to clothing, the resources in this chapter provide advice on other aspects of green living like water conservation in the home or office, green commuting, and living without toxics.

For More Information

- ◆ See **Architecture** for resources on designing, constructing, renovating, or maintaining homes and other buildings in an environmentally sensitive manner.
- ◆ See **Gardening** for resources on gardening, lawn care, and pest control inside and outside the home.
- ◆ See **Investing** for resources on the environmental records of companies that manufacture consumer products.

Government Clearinghouses

- ◆ The Energy Efficiency and Renewable Energy Clearinghouse (see entry 313)
- ◆ The Indoor Air Quality Clearinghouse (see entry 232)
- ◆ The National Lead Information Center (see entry 362)
- ◆ The National Pesticide Telecommunications Network (see entry 184)
- ◆ The National Radon Hotline (see entry 363)
- ◆ The Pollution Prevention Information Clearinghouse (see entry 421)
- ◆ The Safe Drinking Water Hotline (see entry 459)
- ◆ The Toxic Substances Control Act Assistance Information Service (see entry 364)

Organizations

590   Global Action Plan (GAP)
P.O. Box 428
Woodstock, NY 12498

Phone: 914/679-4830. Fax: 914/679-4834.
E-mail: dgershon@igc.apc.org

David Gershon, President

Global Action Plan (GAP) helps individuals change their behavior and empowers them to live environmentally sustainable lifestyles through its Household EcoTeam Program. GAP's *Household EcoTeam Workbook* allows households to assess their current environmental impact, and gives practical advice on moving closer to sustainability. In 1993, the average household participating in the Household Eco-Team Program sent 42 percent less garbage to landfills, used 25 percent less water, cut carbon dioxide output by 16 percent, used 16 percent less transportation fuel—and saved over $400 to boot. GAP membership includes a copy of the *Workbook*, a team start-up kit, and a coach, who guides the household teams through the group's six-month program.

591   Green Seal
1730 Rhode Island Avenue, NW, Suite 1050
Washington, DC 20036

Phone: 202/331-7337. Fax: 202/331-7533

Norman Dean, President and CEO

Green Seal sets design and manufacturing standards for product categories, such as paper towels, based on their environmental impact. Standards are developed after conducting a life cycle analysis: assessing a product from production through disposal. To illustrate: paint must not contain more than a certain level of volatile organic compounds, must not discharge any pollutant in its manufacturing process, and its packaging must not contain any toxics; in addition, it must meet certain performance requirements. Standards have been completed for dishwashers, household cleaners, newsprint, reusable utility bags, and others. A nonprofit organization started by the environmental community, Green Seal sets preliminary standards and then asks for public comment before final standards are approved. Manufacturers who comply with the standards can apply to have the Green Seal logo on their products. Underwriters Laboratories (UL) conducts product testing and factory inspection for Green Seal.

592   Scientific Certification Systems (SCS)
One Kaiser Plaza, Suite 901
The Ordway Building
Oakland, CA 94612

Hotline: 800/326-3228. Phone: 510/832-1415.
Fax: 510/832-0359

Stanley Rhodes, President and CEO

Scientific Certification Systems (SCS) certifies green claims and documents the environmental burdens (i.e., resources used, energy consumed, air and water pollutants released, waste generated) of products. The independent, scientific analysis is paid for by the company that requests SCS's services. (Products that have been certified for a particular claim, such as biodegradability or percentage of recycled content, show a green cross and globe.) Consumers can also benefit from SCS research in a number of other ways. The hotline answers questions about SCS certification, environmental claims, and consumer choices that make the most difference for the environment. Another SCS program inventories the environmental burdens throughout the life cycle of the product; this Environmental Report Card appears as a graph on the product label. For $5, SCS will calculate personal environmental report cards based on household transportation, energy use, food consumption, and use of other consumer goods. SCS also tests farmers' produce for pesticide residues, and can score forest management practices.

Other Organizations

◆ The Buy Recycled Business Alliance (see entry 429, National Recycling Coalition)

◆ Co-op America (see entry 16)

◆ The Household Hazardous Waste Project (see entry 426)

◆ The Human Ecology Action League (see entry 371)

◆ The National Center for Environmental Health Strategies (see entry 372)

◆ The Real Goods Trading Company (see entry 504)

Directories

593 Co-op America's National Green Pages: The Yellow Pages for People and the Planet

3rd ed. Co-op America, 1994. Annual. 110p. $5.95 (paper).

594 The Eco-Networker Directory: A Community Resource Guide to Green Products, Services, Groups, Musicians, and Others Working for a Better Planet

2nd ed. Imagination Station Communications, 1993. 64p. $7.95 (paper).

Both *Co-op America's National Green Pages* and *The Eco-Networker Directory* are outstanding places for consumers to find hundreds of environmental products and services. Both are meant to serve as alternative Yellow Pages, serving not only the environmental community but also those interested in social responsibility and the New Age. Subjects covered include a hodge-podge of categories, including T-shirts, travel

and investment services, bedding, hemp products, vegetarianism, telephone services, pet care products, environmental organizations, and computer and legal services. Neither directory is comprehensive; for the same product categories, they often list entirely different sets of companies. Entries include one- to two-sentence descriptions, as well as addresses and phone and fax numbers. *Co-op America's National Green Pages*, which is the fall issue of *Co-op America Quarterly*, also serves as a membership directory for Co-op America's Business Network (see entry 16, Co-op America) and contains more companies that provide services for environmental businesses. *The Eco-Networker Directory*, affiliated with the *Earthbeat* radio show, has a particularly lengthy section on environmental musicians; it is also available on America Online.

595 The Consumer's Guide to Planet Earth: A Media Resource Guide to Environmental and Health-Oriented Products and Services

9th ed. Schultz Communications, 1994. Semiannual. 44p. $7.00 (paper).

The Consumer's Guide to Planet Earth is a unique way to find green products and services. The guide is essentially a cooperative press release that describes companies and their products; it is mailed free to media professionals, who can use it to write articles. Consumers can also purchase copies, and can use the guide to find sources of gardening, automotive, energy conservation, organic food, personal care, and many other products. Compared to *Co-op America's National Green Pages* (see entry 593) and *The Eco-Networker Directory* (see entry 594), *The Consumer's Guide* has fewer resources (about one hundred total) listed, though each has a much lengthier description (one to two paragraphs).

For detailed descriptions of many catalogs that feature eco-friendly merchandise, consult Cheryl Gorder's *Green Earth Resource Guide: A Comprehensive Guide About Environmentally-Friendly Services and Products* (Blue Bird, 1991); there are no plans for a revised edition at this time.

596 Green Groceries: A Mail-Order Guide to Organic Foods

Jeanne Heifetz. HarperPerennial, 1992. 330p. $16 (paper).

Green Groceries is a comprehensive directory of more than 275 companies that sell organic herbs, bread, fresh fruits and vegetables, meat, tea, cheese—you name it. Each entry (in addition to providing contact information and types of foods offered) lists whether it is possible to visit the farm directly, if a catalog is available, minimum order, and methods of ordering, payment, and shipping. Company descriptions, sometimes more than a page in length, introduce readers to the people and philosophies behind the farms. *Green Groceries* also includes bulk distributors for buying clubs, regional wholesalers, certification organizations, and distributors of organic seeds and plants. There are cross references at each chapter's end, as well as alphabetical and state-by-state indices; this large book is very easy to navigate—the next best thing to buying organic food locally.

Two other directories of organic producers and distributors are not meant explicitly for consumers, but they are helpful to those who purchase in large quantities: *National Organic Directory: A Guide to Organic Information and Resources* (see entry 202) and *The Humane Consumer and Producer Guide: Buying and Producing Farm Products for a Humane Sustainable Agriculture* (see entry 201).

597 Recycled Products Guide (RPG)

Recycling Data Management, 1994. Annual. 450p. $175.00 (hardcover).

Diskette: Available from Recycling Data Management for $500.00.

Database Vendor: Available on RecycleLine. Contact Recycling Data Management for subscription information.

The *Recycled Products Guide (RPG)* is the most comprehensive directory available of products made from recycled materials. For more than five hundred types of products—from insulation and newsprint to fly swatters and baseballs—manufacturers' names, addresses, phone and fax numbers are listed. For each of the three thousand products, the percentage of minimum recycled content is listed, along with either the percentage of postconsumer or recovered material. The executive summary lists company information alphabetically. Listings are free of charge to manufacturers who certify their product's recycled

content. *RPG* includes geographical and brand-name indices, indices by type of recycled material used, and a directory of appropriate government offices. *RPG* subscribers include the Los Angeles Public Library, Ben and Jerry's, and the State of Tennessee. The directory is also available online on RecycleLine, a commercial online service devoted to information on recycling. A subscription ($275) includes the current *RPG*, the executive summary ($49 separately), updates, a monthly newsletter ($75 separately), and RecycleLine access, including three free hours.

Other Directories

- The *Non-Toxic Buying Guide* (see entry 366, Chemical Injury Information Network)
- *Tackling Toxics in Everyday Products: A Directory of Organizations* (see entry 380)
- *Water-Efficient Technologies: A Catalog for the Residential/Light Commercial Sector* (see entry 44, Rocky Mountain Institute)

Reference Handbooks

598 Clean and Green: The Complete Guide to Nontoxic and Environmentally Safe Housekeeping

Annie Berthold-Bond. Ceres Press, 1990. 162p. $8.95 (paper).

599 Clean Your House Safely and Effectively Without Harmful Chemicals: Using "From the Cupboard" Ingredients

Randall Earl Dunford. Magni Company. 1993. 160p. $12.95 (paper).

Both *Clean and Green* and *Clean Your House Safely and Effectively Without Harmful Chemicals* offer excellent, nontoxic alternatives to age-old cleaning methods. Though brief, both contain multiple recipes for all imaginable household cleaning chores, such as removing stains, polishing and waxing, clearing drains, and doing laundry. Recipes are simple and most call for common ingredients—vinegar, baking soda, lemon juice, etc. *Clean and Green*, written by the editor of *Green Alternatives for Health and the Environment* (see entry 619) magazine, has an introductory section on the harm toxic cleansers cause to health and the environment and a final chapter on safe commercial products. In between are 485 recipes. On the other hand, *Clean Your House Safely* focuses on cleaning advice and instructions; its more than 150 recipes are found throughout the text in easy-to-read boxes.

600 The Complete Book of Home Environmental Hazards

Roberta Altman. Facts on File, 1990. 304p. $24.95 (hardcover), $12.95 (paper).

601 Healthy Homes in a Toxic World: Preventing, Identifying and Eliminating Hidden Health Hazards in Your Home

Maury M. Breecher, M. P. H. and Shirley Linde, Ph.D. John Wiley & Sons, 1992. 256p. $29.95 (hardcover), $14.95 (paper).

The Complete Book of Home Environmental Hazards and *Healthy Homes in a Toxic World* are two excellent reference books that enable consumers to educate themselves on the toxic hazards lurking within their houses. Concepts are explained clearly, and subheadings make it easy to locate information. Lead, radon, asbestos, pesticides, drinking water, and many other topics are covered in detail. In *The Complete Book of Home Environmental Hazards*, author Roberta Altman includes chapters on environmental hazards outside the home, such as hazardous waste sites and nuclear weapons production plants, while authors Maury Breecher and Shirley Linde choose in *Healthy Homes* to include allergens and electromagnetic fields. Both books contain contact information for numerous state offices and references to other useful resources.

Similar books can be found at the public library; other recommended titles include Janice Marchak's *Oh No! Not My Electric Blanket, Too? A Guide to a Healthier Home* (Jetmarc Group, 1991), which uses a question-and-answer format to present similar information, and Linda Mason Hunter's *The Healthy Home: An Attic-to-Basement Guide to Toxin-Free Living* (Rodale Press, 1989), which includes large sections on home security and creating a healthy emotional atmosphere. (Since each book stresses different issues and some information is still being debated, it is necessary to consult several of these works for a complete understanding of healthy home issues.)

602 A Consumer's Dictionary of Household, Yard and Office Chemicals

Ruth Winter. Crown Publishing, 1992. 329p. $12.00 (paper).

Consumers can use *A Consumer's Dictionary of Household, Yard and Office Chemicals* to find out whether common chemical ingredients are harmful or harmless, and what their effects are. Chemical names (carbon monoxide, dodecylammonium methenarsonate) and categories of chemicals (aerosols, phosphates), product names (Mr. Clean Liquid Household Cleaner, Downy Fabric Softener), and categories of products (dog flea foam shampoo, lens cleaner) are listed from A to Z. Entries are well cross referenced; by the end of a search—starting at Purex Fabric Softener, for example, and turning to bleach and then to silicates—the user will be able to grasp the potential harm of everyday products. A short introduction provides an overview of the toxic effects of chemicals and preventive measures readers can take. Also by the author and in the same format are *A Consumer's Dictionary of Food Additives* (4th ed. Crown Publishing, 1994) and *A Consumer's Dictionary of Cosmetic Ingredients* (4th ed. Crown Publishing, 1994). All are perfect for those without a background in chemistry who want an alternative to intimidating technical handbooks.

603 EarthScore: Your Personal Environmental Audit & Guide

Donald W. Lotter. Morning Sun Press, 1993. 105p. $8.95 (paper).

EarthScore helps people understand the impact their daily lives can have on the environment. It asks readers 107 questions about their behavior in 14 environmental categories (e.g., transportation; consumerism: durable goods; consumerism: paper and forest products; family planning) and lets readers tally their results. For example, the question "My water heater is _____" offers the following responses: solar (1 point), gas and insulated (3 points), gas and uninsulated (6 points), electric and insulated (9 points), electric and uninsulated (12 points). A fold-out chart allows readers to determine their impact ratings (e.g., Eco-Hero, Eco–Average Citizen, Eco-Slowpoke) and action ratings (e.g., Awesome, Good, I could do better!). Each chapter includes selected sources of additional information. *EarthScore* is based on the author's personal environmental auditing software called Enviro-Account, available on an IBM-compatible or Macintosh disk. To order EnviroAccount, send a check for $49.95 to EnviroAccount Software, 605 Sunset Court, Davis, CA 95616, or order by phone at 800/554-0317 or 916/756-9156.

604 The Green Buyer's Car Guide: Environmental Ratings of 1994 Cars and Light Trucks

Christopher Dyson with Bill Magavern, Jigar Shah, and Todd Stephens. Public Citizen Publications, 1994. 52p. $5.00 (paper).

Prepared by the staff of Public Citizen's Critical Mass Energy Project (see entry 322), this report examines and compares the environmental impact of every car and light truck model sold in the United States. Each vehicle (three hundred models sold in California and six hundred models sold in the rest of the country) is given a rating based on smog and carbon monoxide emissions, global warming and oil spill impact, ozone-layer-depleting CFC impact, and recycling (points are given for each part of the vehicle that either contains recycled materials or that can actually be recycled). Each rating, on a scale from 1 to 100, is then weighted to provide an overall environmental impact rating (emissions 35 percent, fuel economy 35 percent, CFCs 20 percent, recycling 10 percent). The guide lists the ratings in a tabular format, arranged by type of vehicle (e.g., two-seaters, midsize cars, four-wheel-drive special purpose vehicles). Tips for environmentally responsible driving and car maintenance are also included. The data for the guide's ratings was obtained from automakers and the Environmental Protection Agency. This guide is a condensed version of *The Green Buyer's Car Book* (Public Citizen Publications, 1994. 200p. $75), which includes the actual data, not just the ratings, and much more background information.

605 The Green Commuter

Joel Makower. Compiled by Tilden Press. National Press Books, 1992. 176p. $9.95 (paper).

The Green Commuter educates consumers so that they can make environmentally responsible transportation choices. An overview assesses the environmental impacts of cars—everything from water pollution to land use—while the majority of the book provides practical advice on buying, driving, maintaining, and disposing of cars with the environment in mind. Two final chapters describe alternatives to the automobile (walking, bicycling, telecommuting, public transportation, etc.) and discuss the future of green transportation, including alternative fuels and electric vehicles. Appendices include directories of organizations, government agencies, major manufacturers, and local transit authorities for major cities.

An extensive array of car care tips can also be found in *The Planets Mechanic's Guide to Environmental Car Care* (Jeff Shumway. B&B Publishing, 1993). Drivers looking for more advice on reducing air pollution should seek out Robert Sikorsky's 110-page *Car Tips for Clean Air: How to Drive and Maintain Your Car to Cut Pollution and Save Money* (Perigee Books, 1991).

606 The Green Consumer

Joel Makower, John Elkington, and Julia Hailes. Rev. ed. A Tilden Press Book. Penguin Books, 1993. 339p. $11.00 (paper).

The Green Consumer is currently the best book available on all aspects of green consuming. The book chiefly provides advice on choosing foods, gifts, clothing, cleaning products, appliances, and other products, discussing characteristics to avoid and alternatives that make a difference. *The Green Consumer* is not a directory of companies and it does not rate products, but it does have enough detailed product descriptions to allow consumers to make earthwise purchases. It goes beyond *Nontoxic, Natural, and Earthwise* (see entry 615) by discussing other environment-related consumer issues, such as commuting, traveling, and investing. It also includes a general introduction to environmental issues, a section on activism, and an excellent directory of environmental organizations. *The Green Consumer* is well organized and easy to understand.

Two other comparable books exist, though both are dated: *The Green Lifestyle Handbook: 1001 Ways to Heal the Earth* (Jeremy Rifkin. Henry Holt, 1990) presents essays by experts and has lists of products, and *Ecologue: The Environmental Catalogue and Consumer's Guide for a Safe Earth* (Prentice Hall, 1990), edited by Bruce Anderson, has lengthy descriptions of more than five hundred products.

607 The Green PC: Making Choices That Make a Difference

Steven Anzovin. 2nd ed. Windcrest Books, 1994. 248p. $19.95 (paper).

In *The Green PC*, Steven Anzovin, a columnist for *Compute!* magazine, explores every possible way in which computers affect the environment. According to Anzovin, green computing means using resources efficiently, minimizing waste, and using computers as a communication and education tool. Concise chapters provide information on the following topics: maximizing use of current hardware, buying a green computer, reducing energy consumption, reducing paper consumption, recycling computer products, telecommuting, the health effects of working with computers, polluting in the manufacturing process, environmental educational software, sources of electronic environmental information, and environmental advocacy using computers. Each chapter ends with an extensive resource list of publications, organizations, and companies. *The Green PC* contains everything a computer user needs to begin learning about environmentally responsible computing.

608 Green Supermarket Shopping Guide

John F. Wasik. Warner Books, 1993. 348p. $5.99 (paper).

The *Green Supermarket Shopping Guide* provides background information and product ratings for everything that can be bought in a grocery store. This includes: a variety of foods, beverages, baby products, paper products, personal care products, pet supplies, over-the-counter medicines, and other items such as lightbulbs and batteries. Author John F. Wasik provides purchasing advice for these products and notes some particularly good—and bad—

brands. Ratings for more than two thousand nationally available products indicate whether a product's packaging is recycled; whether the amount of material used for product packaging has been reduced; the product's potential as recycled material; and whether the product has been certified by Scientific Certification Systems (see entry 592). The environmental performance of the product's manufacturer is rated on a twenty-point scale. The book also has numerous other sections: background information on green claims, environmental labeling, and product packaging; a survey of the environmental efforts of 102 supermarkets; details on how anyone can rate a company's environmental performance; and resources for further information. Wasik's New Consumer Institute (708/526-0522) publishes the *Conscious Company Consumer* newsletter and provides consulting in the area of green marketing. The *Green Consumer Supermarket Guide* (Penguin, 1991), by Joel Makower, covers similar ground more concisely, but his guide has a simpler product rating system and contains fewer product listings.

609 Healthy Homes, Healthy Kids: Protecting Your Children from Everyday Hazards

Joyce M. Schoemaker, Ph.D. and Charity Y. Vitale, Ph.D. Island Press, 1991. 221p. $19.95 (hardcover), $12.95 (paper).

Healthy Homes, Healthy Kids interprets scientific, medical, and government data on the health effects of toxics in the home and provides methods of prevention. The book is similar to *The Complete Book of Home Environmental Hazards* (see entry 600), except that portions of each chapter show why children may be especially vulnerable to the described threats. Topics include lead, radon, asbestos, art materials, yard chemicals, bites from pests, indoor and outdoor air pollution, protection from the sun, food and water safety, electromagnetic fields, safe household products, and disposal of household hazardous wastes. It is easy to find and understand all of the information presented. The resources listed at the end of each chapter are extremely useful for finding test kits and other products, hotlines and organizations, and published materials. A similar book is *Raising Children Toxic Free: How to Keep Your Child Safe From Lead, Asbestos, Pesticides, and Other Environmental Hazards* (Herbert L.

Needleman and Philip J. Landrigan. Farrar, Straus and Giroux, 1994).

610 Home Ecology: Simple and Practical Ways to Green Your Home

Karen Christiansen. Fulcrum Publishing, 1990. 334p. $15.95 (paper).

An invitation to begin the transition toward a sustainable lifestyle, *Home Ecology* is replete with down-to-earth practical advice. Author Karen Christiansen touches on everything that is part of the green lifestyle: gardening, pet care, recycling, transportation, nontoxic living, energy consumption, indoor air pollution, home design, radiation, child care—even time management. Extensive lists of publications from the 1980s follow each chapter. This book is a good mix of background on the issues ("The Ozone Layer," "Problems with Power") and philosophical insights ("Eating Together," "Cultivating a Green Thumb"), making this a holistic and useful green lifestyle primer.

611 How to Get Water Smart: Products and Practices for Saving Water in the Nineties

Buzz Buzzelli, Peggy Good, Janice S. McCormick, and John R. McCormick. Terra Firma, 1991. 128p. $9.95 (paper).

612 Saving Water in the Home and Garden

Jonathan Erickson. TAB Books, 1993. 150p. $12.95 (paper).

How to Get Water Smart and *Saving Water in the Home and Garden* offer much practical advice without preaching to the reader. People who want to save money on their water bills or who simply believe in conserving fresh water, as well as those living through droughts, can learn common and unconventional ways to reduce their water consumption with little effort. *Water Smart* provides water-saving tips for the bathroom, kitchen, laundry room, yard, garden, pool, car, and garage. Each tip includes the contact name and phone number for purchasing a product or getting more information, as well as a generous estimate of how much water is actually saved. *Saving Water* covers similar issues, but it goes into more depth and has more how-

to diagrams for repairing leaks and installing water-saving technologies.

613 Is Your Water Safe to Drink?

Raymond Gabler. Consumers Union, 1988. 390p. Out of print.

Is Your Water Safe to Drink? allows consumers to understand drinking water–quality issues and the fight to make their water safer. Author Raymond Gabler clearly explains the potential contaminants in tap water—microbial, inorganic, and organic, as well as chlorination—and describes the health threats they pose. The second half of the book covers individual and community responses to potential hazards, including determining and improving home water quality, bottled water, community action, and water shortages. Other books that also present this information well are *Drinking Water Hazards: How to Know If There Are Toxic Chemicals In Your Water and What to Do If There Are* (John Stewart. Envirographics, 1990) and *But Not a Drop to Drink! The Lifesaving Guide to Good Water* (Steve Coffel. Rawson, 1989). For homeowners who do not need background information, *The Drinking Water Book: A Complete Guide to Safe Drinking Water* (Colin Ingram. Ten Speed Press, 1991) is highly recommended for its in-depth coverage of water-sample analysis and evaluations of bottled water and water purifiers. All are very user-friendly handbooks that allow homeowners to identify and correct problems.

For government assistance with drinking water–quality issues, contact the Safe Drinking Water Hotline (see entry 459).

For water saving tips, see *How to Get Water Smart: Products and Practices for Saving Water in the Nineties* (see entry 611) and *Saving Water in the Home and Garden* (see entry 612).

614 The Nontoxic Home and Office: Protecting Yourself and Your Family From Everyday Toxics and Health Hazards

Debra Lynn Dadd. Jeremy Tarcher, 1992; distributed by St. Martin's Press. 220p. $10.95 (paper).

The Nontoxic Home and Office is a comprehensive guide to understanding and avoiding the most common and dangerous toxics. Since becoming chemically sensitive in 1980, author Debra Lynn Dadd has devoted her life to researching these issues. Other books usually stress either toxics in the house (see *The Complete Book of Home Environmental Hazards* [see entry 600]) or toxics in household products (see *Nontoxic, Natural and Earthwise* [see entry 615]), but this one integrates all elements of nontoxic living—everything from tap water and unsafe food to radon and lead to dishwater detergent and flame-resistant fabrics. Descriptions of the health effects of each hazard are followed by homemade recipes containing natural ingredients, strategies for choosing alternative products, and other prevention techniques. The twenty-five pages devoted to the nontoxic office—covering everything from plain paper fax machines to correction fluid to artificial light—were not included in the original edition, *The Nontoxic Home* (Jeremy Tarcher, 1986). This new edition is easy to use and read. For brand names of nontoxic products consult the author's *Nontoxic, Natural and Earthwise* (see entry 615).

615 Nontoxic, Natural and Earthwise: How to Protect Yourself and Your Family From Harmful Products and Live in Harmony With the Earth

Debra Lynn Dadd. Jeremy Tarcher, 1990; distributed by St. Martin's Press. 360p. $12.95 (paper).

Nontoxic, Natural and Earthwise helps consumers assess the environmental strengths and weaknesses of products and lists many items from which consumers can choose. Like the *Green Supermarket Shopping Guide* (see entry 608), *Nontoxic, Natural, and Earthwise* contains all items generally found in supermarkets, but the book also includes sections on automobiles, gardening, yard care, furnishings, appliances, and building materials. It has more text describing the health and environmental effects of products, and has extensive product listings—more than two thousand products and more than six hundred mail-order companies. It also provides more than four hundred homemade alternatives. Two similar guides to and directories of consumer products, *Shopping for a Better Environment* (Laurence Tasaday with Katherine Stevenson. Meadowbrook Press, 1991) and *The*

Green Pages: Your Everyday Shopping Guide to Environmentally Safe Products (The Bennett Information Group. Random House, 1990), are out of print. As attempts to catalog all available environmentally friendly products, all three of these books are somewhat dated; consumers may also want to look at *Sustaining the Earth: Choosing Consumer Products That Are Safe for You, Your Family, and the Earth* (see entry 617) for current information.

616 Shopping for a Better World

Compiled by the Council on Economic Priorities. 5th ed. Sierra Club Books, 1994; distributed by Random House. Annual. 400p. $14.00 (paper).

For years, the best-selling *Shopping for a Better World* has allowed consumers to evaluate corporate responsibility and then "vote" with their purchases at the checkout counter. *Shopping for a Better World* has expanded its coverage beyond the supermarket shelf to include durable goods such as automobiles, home appliances, and computers. The book continues to grade almost two hundred companies (from "A" to "F") in eight major areas of social responsibility (environmental stewardship, opportunities for women, opportunities for minorities, workplace issues, family benefits, community outreach, charitable giving, corporate disclosure) and on fifteen "extra" social issues ranging from animal testing to benefits for same-sex partners. More than two thousand brand-name products appear in easy-to-read charts that award the social performance grades for the products' manufacturers. An introduction clearly explains the criteria used for evaluating the corporations and highlights the twenty most (e.g., General Mills, Rhino Records) and eight least (e.g., ConAgra, MCI Communications) responsible corporations. For a shopping guide more focused on rating products based on environmental criteria, see the *Green Supermarket Shopping Guide* (see entry 608).

617 Sustaining the Earth: Choosing Consumer Products That Are Safe for You, Your Family, and the Earth

Debra Dadd-Redalia. Hearst Books, 1994. 352p. $15.00 (paper).

The primer *Sustaining the Earth* gives background information on product assessment and guidelines for finding and choosing specific products based on their sustainability. The book's first two hundred pages provide general information for environmental consumers (chapter titles include "Reading Labels," "Product Life Cycles") and detailed explanations of the different characteristics that constitute sustainability (renewable and natural; organic, organically grown, biodynamically grown, wildcrafted; reduced, reusable, refillable, reclaimed, recycled, recyclable; sustainably harvested; energy-efficient, energy-saving, water-efficient, water-saving; nontoxic; no VOCs, CFC-free, ozone friendly, ozone safe; biodegradable, degradable, photodegradable, compostable; socially responsible). The remainder of the book provides guidelines for finding and choosing more than one hundred categories of products used in the home (e.g., art supplies, blankets and afghans, condiments, drain cleaners). Unlike *Nontoxic, Natural and Earthwise* (see entry 615), a previous title by the same author that lists many brand-name products and companies, this book uses product names only as examples and should not be used as a directory of products, but rather as a tool that educates consumers in choosing products now and in the future. Backmatter includes an annotated bibliography of periodicals and books, a directory of green retail stores, and a directory of more than one hundred mail-order catalogs.

Other Reference Handbooks

♦ The *Guide to Hazardous Products Around the Home* (see entry 426, Household Hazardous Waste Project)

Introductory Reading

618 How Much Is Enough?: The Consumer Society and the Future of the Earth

Alan Thein Durning. The Worldwatch Environmental Alert series. Sponsored by the Worldwatch Institute. W. W. Norton & Company, 1992. 200p. $19.95 (hardcover), $8.95 (paper).

How Much Is Enough? takes a thought-provoking look at consumerism: its myths, the role it plays in society, and the impacts it has, including environmental effects. Author Alan Thein Durning divides the world into three broad classes—consumers (annual income more than $7,500), the middle income (annual income $700 to $7,500), and the poor (annual income less than $700). He argues that the people at both extremes, each a fifth of the world's population, are contributing to consumption of natural resources at unsustainable levels; those in the middle live largely sustainable lives. This brief book focuses on the characteristics and behavior of each of these three classes, but it places most emphasis on the impact of the consumer class, especially the environmental costs of transportation, food production, consumption of raw materials, and waste generation. Durning ends with a plea both to reduce overconsumption of natural resources and to cultivate nonmaterial means of fulfillment.

Periodicals

619 Green Alternatives for Health and the Environment

Greenkeeping, 1991–. Bimonthly. 50p. $18.00/year.

Green Alternatives is a down-to-earth magazine that covers the full range of lifestyle choices that are healthy and safe for the environment. Clearly presented practical information allows consumers to minimize their health risks and to make wise purchasing decisions. Past articles have focused on testing indoor air quality, making nontoxic cleansers out of common ingredients, choosing recycled papers, buying safe food, selecting nontoxic paint, and limiting exposure to electromagnetic fields. Extensive resource lists of products, companies, and organizations follow most articles. Every environmentally concerned citizen should have access to the vital information found here.

CHAPTER EIGHTEEN

Travel

What This Chapter Covers

The resources in this chapter can help you understand what makes a trip environmentally responsible and can help you select vacations that reflect environmental interests and concerns. This includes not only nature travel, but also low-impact hiking and camping, volunteer vacations, and adventure travel.

Government Clearinghouses

620 National Park Service Office of Public Inquiries
Department of Interior
P.O. Box 37127
Washington, DC 20013

Phone: 202/208-4747

The National Park Service Office of Public Inquiries distributes general information about national parks and refers callers to other Park Service resources. Publications include a guide and map of America's national parks, as well as brochures for each park. Campers who wish to make park reservations should call Mistix at 800/365-2267. For those doing academic and scientific research about national parks, the National Park Service Technical Information Center (303/969-2130) has a database of 500,000 relevant documents and will perform searches free of charge.

Organizations

621 The Center for Responsible Tourism
P.O. Box 827
San Anselmo, CA 94979

Phone: 415/258-6594. Fax: 415/454-2493

The Center for Responsible Tourism is the North American link in a global network that addresses issues of justice, human rights, and cultural and environmental sustainability in tourism. This nonprofit organization aims to change the attitudes and practices of travelers and to persuade them to be part of the struggle for justice in tourism in developing countries. The center has a directory of alternatives to mass travel in the Third World. In addition, when a member of the all-volunteer staff is in the office, he or she can provide guidance over the phone; these staffers are particularly helpful with supplying names of responsible travel operations with whom they work and trust.

622 The Ecotourism Society
P.O. Box 755
North Bennington, VT 05257

Phone: 802/447-2121. Fax: 802/447-2122

Megan Epler Wood, Executive Director

Founded in 1990, the nonprofit Ecotourism Society, a professional association, sets standards and raises awareness about trips that protect the environment and benefit the local population. The group accomplishes these goals by conducting research, sponsoring conferences, highlighting successfully managed programs, and distributing publications. Although most Society members are tour operators, conservation professionals, park managers, and other professionals with an interest in the business of environmental travel, ten percent of the organization's members are active ecotourists. Questions from people planning a trip cannot be answered. Membership includes an eight-page quarterly newsletter and discounts on Society publications such as *Ecotourism: A Guide for Planners and Managers*.

Other Organizations

- The American Hiking Society (see entry 409, Rails-to-Trails Conservancy)
- Co-op America (see entry 16)
- The Rails-to-Trails Conservancy (see entry 409)

Directories

- The *Guide to the National Wildlife Refuges* (see entry 284, *Parks Directory of the United States*)
- The *Parks Directory of the United States* (see entry 284)
- *Wilderness U.: Opportunities for Outdoor Education in the U.S. and Abroad* (see entry 534)

Reference Handbooks

623 The Buzzworm Magazine Guide to Ecotravel

The Editors of Buzzworm Magazine. Buzzworm, 1993; distributed by Publishers Group West. 240p. $9.95 (paper).

The Buzzworm Magazine Guide to Ecotravel is a guide to one hundred packaged national and international environmental tours. Coverage of each trip includes a description, basic information (e.g., representative meal, cost, what not to bring), details about the sponsoring company, a map of the tour area, and an explanation of the trip's environmental significance. Two-page descriptions make it easy to compare trips. Offerings include a good mix of nature watching, volunteer vacations, and adventure travel. An annotated directory of 150 ecotravel tour operators is included in the appendix. *Buzzworm* magazine is no longer published, but this useful travel guide is still in print.

624 earthTrips: A Guide to Nature Travel on a Fragile Planet

Dwight Holing. Sponsored by Conservation International. Living Planet Press, 1992. 212p. $12.95 (paper).

earthTrips will help travelers generate ideas for nature trips. The introductory chapters are short but packed with informative advice; they are followed by a continent-by-continent guide to national parks, protected areas, and other scenic outdoor places. Descriptions are brief; there are no maps or information about specific tours. Interspersed throughout are "Conservation Alerts" and commentary of interest to hikers and photographers. *earthTrips* also includes informative descriptions of volunteer vacations, nature study programs, and tour operators and travel agencies, as well as an annotated bibliography of additional resources.

625 Ecotours and Nature Gateways: A Guide to Environmental Vacations Around the World

Carole Berglie and Alice M. Geffen. 1st ed. Clarkson N. Potter, 1993. 324p. $15.00 (paper).

Ecotours and Nature Gateways describes hundreds of packaged nature tours in all parts of the world. The book begins with an introduction to nature tourism and general travel advice. Then, for each of the 46 regions covered (e.g., Alaska and the Yukon Territory, 11 pages; the Galapagos, 7 pages; Southern Africa, 14 pages; Siberia, Central Asian Republics, and Mongolia, 3 pages), several trips are described, arranged by tour operator. Each tour description includes number of days, month traveled, relative price (price is calculated from the city where the tour departs), and a one- to three-sentence overview of the tour. One page of background information on each region is also provided. The final section of the book is a directory of tour operators that offer trips described in the book.

626 Environmental Vacations: Volunteer Projects to Save the Planet

Stephanie Ocko. 2nd ed. John Muir Publications, 1992; distributed by W. W. Norton & Company. 248p. $16.95 (paper).

Environmental Vacations is the ideal book for someone interested in learning about volunteer scientific expeditions. The book describes ways in which nonscientists can assist experts in such activities as monitoring the biodiversity of rainforests, observing animal behavior, or working in an experimental sustainable community in Arizona. *Environmental Vacations* also discusses project living conditions, providing many quotes from scientists and volunteers. Other chapters offer questions and answers about what to expect, perspectives of scientists, information on costs, traveling tips, and descriptions of groups that match volunteers and scientists.

627 Going off the Beaten Path: An Untraditional Travel Guide to the U.S.

Mary Dymond Davis. 2nd ed. Noble Press, 1991. 463p. $15.95 (paper).

Going off the Beaten Path is not a travel guide, but a directory of organizations and places that are significant to the American environmental movement. The book covers a hodgepodge of locations and activities, including outdoor recreation opportunities, places associated with famous environmentalists, resource-conserving buildings and structures, alternative energy sites, intentional communities, peace sites, natural areas, restoration projects, nature study camps, and vegetarian restaurants. The directory is not comprehensive, but it does provide descriptions of several locations around the country. It also offers enough tips, contacts, and background information for the reader to become more involved not only at the site, but in his or her own community as well. Annotated bibliographies of environmental information sources and outdoor supplies, as well as a geographical index, are also included.

628 The Green Travel Sourcebook: A Guide for the Physically Active, the Intellectually Curious, or the Socially Aware

Daniel Grotta and Sally Wiener Grotta. John Wiley & Sons, 1992. 312p. $14.95 (paper).

The Green Travel Sourcebook is a directory of national and international tour operators that offer green travel programs. The sourcebook's definition of green travel is not limited to environmental responsibility; the book also cites trips that immerse the traveler in nature or another culture: adventure travel, study opportunities, field research, homestays, trips to Third World countries, volunteer vacations, and green cruises. Tour operator descriptions average two pages in length and include program length, number of participants, total cost, cost per day, what the cost does and does not include, and comments from program participants. Other chapters help readers choose and prepare for their trips. *The Green Travel Sourcebook* includes a geographical index of tour locations. This is a highly recommended guide—the most talked about in the field.

629 Rainforests: A Guide to Research and Tourist Facilities at Selected Tropical Forest Sites in Central and South America

James L. Castner. Feline Press, 1990. 380p. Out of print.

Rainforests is suitable for the independent nature traveler as well as for researching biologists. This publication is really two complete rainforest books in one: a practical, personal travel guide and an annotated rainforest bibliography.

The travel guide covers Peru, Ecuador, French Guiana, Venezuela, Trinidad, Costa Rica, and Panama, giving travel advice for three dozen rainforest sites, lodges, and biological stations. Lists of books, maps, travel agencies, and conservation and scientific organizations are supplied for each country. Chapter Two is a one-hundred-page annotated bibliography of rainforest information sources ranging from pre-1950 travel books to flora and fauna guides to environmental organizations. Chapter Three is an annotated directory of organizations that sponsor research trips. Chapter Four describes sources of funding for biologists. Appendices include a listing of tour operators, tips for travelers, and an English–Spanish dictionary of relevant words, as well as select lists of rainforest experts and U.S. public zoos and botanical gardens.

630 Soft Paths: How to Enjoy the Wilderness Without Harming It

Bruce Hampton and David Cole. Sponsored by the National Outdoor Leadership School. Stackpole Books, 1988. 167p. $10.95 (paper).

Soft Paths describes practical ways in which hikers and campers can reduce their impact upon the wilderness. The first part of the book gives general guidance on selecting a campsite, using fires and stoves, and coping with sanitation and waste disposal. Latter chapters give special minimum-impact guidance for a variety of environments: deserts, rivers and lakes, coasts, tundra, snow and ice, and bear country. Though the book is brief, it contains information with which all hikers and campers should be familiar. Another introduction to minimum-impact camping is *Backwoods Ethics: Environmental Issues for Hikers and Campers* (Laura and Guy Waterman. Countryman Press, 1993).

Periodicals

631 EcoTraveler

Skies America Publishing, 1994–. Bimonthly. 80p. $12.00/6 issues, $20.00/12 issues.

EcoTraveler is a special-interest magazine devoted to ecotravel: "a marriage of adventure, discovery and environmental responsibility." It provides a good blend of interesting and informative news shorts and detailed descriptions of off-the-beaten-path travel opportunities. At least seven destinations are highlighted in each issue. They range from day trips to intense overseas adventures, including such activities as white water rafting, hiking, rock climbing, scuba diving, and sightseeing. Feature articles provide insight into a location's history, stories that capture other travelers' experiences, maps, beautiful color photographs, and directions. Although many of the travel destinations seem more exciting than environmentally responsible, *EcoTraveler* is still a fun, practical magazine that takes environmental protection more seriously than any other mainstream travel magazine.

Appendices

Federal Information Centers

Federal Information Centers have trained information specialists who can answer questions about the federal government or direct callers to the person in the federal government who can answer your questions. These toll-free numbers offer a good way to begin a search for government information on any topic.

Dial the phone number for your metropolitan area. If you are not in one of the areas listed, call 301/722-9000. TDD/TTY users may call 800/326-2996 from anywhere in the United States.

Alabama
Birmingham, Mobile
800/366-3998

Alaska
Anchorage
800/729-8003

Arizona
Phoenix
800/359-3997

Arkansas
Little Rock
800/366-2998

California
Los Angeles, San Diego,
Sacramento, San Francisco,
Santa Ana
800/726-4995

Colorado
Colorado Springs, Denver, Pueblo
800/359-3997

Connecticut
Hartford, New Haven
800/347-1997

Florida
Fort Lauderdale, Jacksonville,
Miami, Orlando, St. Petersburg,
Tampa, West Palm Beach
800/347-1997

Georgia
Atlanta
800/347-1997

Hawaii
Honolulu
800/733-5996

Illinois
Chicago
800/366-2998

Indiana
Gary
800/366-2998
Indianapolis
800/347-1997

Iowa
All locations
800/735-8004

Kansas
All locations
800/735-8004

Kentucky
Louisville
800/347-1997

Louisiana
New Orleans
800/366-2998

Maryland
Baltimore
800/347-1997

Massachusetts
Boston
800/347-1997

Michigan
Detroit, Grand Rapids
800/347-1997

Minnesota
Minneapolis
800/366-2998

Missouri
St. Louis
800/366-2998
All other locations
800/735-8004

Nebraska
Omaha
800/366-2998
All other locations
800/735-8004

New Jersey
Newark, Trenton
800/347-1997

New Mexico
Albuquerque
800/359-3997

New York
Albany, Buffalo, New York City,
Rochester, Syracuse
800/347-1997

North Carolina
Charlotte
800/347-1997

Ohio
Akron, Cincinnati, Cleveland,
Columbus, Dayton, Toledo
800/347-1997

Oklahoma
Oklahoma City, Tulsa
800/366-2998

Oregon
Portland
800/726-4995

Pennsylvania
Philadelphia, Pittsburgh
800/347-1997

Rhode Island
Providence
800/347-1997

Tennessee
Chattanooga
800/347-1997
Memphis, Nashville
800/366-2998

Texas
Austin, Dallas, Fort Worth,
Houston, San Antonio
800/366-2998

Utah
Salt Lake City
800/359-3997

Virginia
Norfolk, Richmond, Roanoke
800/347-1997

Washington
Seattle, Tacoma
800/726-4995

Wisconsin
Milwaukee
800/366-2998

Database Vendors

Database vendors are commercial online services that provide access to many different databases, especially scientific, business, and legal abstracts, and the full text of periodicals. Most database vendors charge an annual fee in addition to an hourly rate for connect time. These services are relatively expensive and are most widely utilized by university and company researchers. The address and phone number of each vendor is listed alphabetically by the name of the service rather than by the name of the company that provides the service.

Chemical Information Systems
810 Gleneagles Court, Suite 300
Towson, MD 21286
800/247-8737; 410/321-8440

DIALOG
DIALOG Information Services
3460 Hillview Avenue
P.O. Box 10010
Palo Alto, CA 94303
800/324-3564; 415/858-3785

LEXIS/NEXIS
9443 Springboro Pike
P.O. Box 933
Dayton, OH 45401
800/543-6862; 513/859-5398

MEDLARS
National Library of Medicine
Specialized Information Services
Division
8600 Rockville Pike
Bethesda, MD 20894
301/496-1131

NewsNet
945 Haverford Road
Bryn Mawr, PA 19010
800/952-0122; 610/527-8030

OCLC EPIC
Online Computer Library Center
6565 Frantz Road
Dublin, OH 43017
800/848-5878; 614/764-6000

OCLC FirstSearch
Online Computer Library Center
6565 Frantz Road
Dublin, OH 43017
800/848-5878; 614/764-6000

RecycleLine
Recycling Data Management
Box 577
Ogdensburg, NY 13669
800/267-0707; 315/471-0707

TOXNET
National Library of Medicine
Specialized Information Services
Division
8600 Rockville Pike
Bethesda, MD 20894
301/496-1131

WESTLAW
West Publishing
620 Opperman Drive
P.O. 64779
Saint Paul, MN 55164
800/328-9352; 612/687-7000

WILSONLINE
H. W. Wilson Company
950 University Avenue
Bronx, NY 10452
800/367-6770; 718/588-8400

APPENDIX C

Publishers

This appendix supplies addresses and phone numbers for publishers and distributors of publications, diskettes, and CD-ROMs mentioned in the book.

ABC-CLIO
P.O. Box 1911
Santa Barbara, CA 93116
800/422-2546; 805/968-1911

Academic Press
1250 6th Avenue
San Diego, CA 92101
800/321-5068; 619/231-0926

AgAccess
P.O. Box 2008
Davis, CA 95617
916/756-7177

Air & Waste Management Association
P.O. Box 2861
Pittsburgh, PA 15230
412/232-3444

Allen Press
P.O. Box 368
Lawrence, KS 66044
800/547-8889; 913/843-1234

Alliance for Environmental Education
P.O. Box 368
The Plains, VA 22171
703/330-5667

Alternative Farming Systems Information Center
Department of Agriculture
10301 Baltimore Boulevard, Room 304
Beltsville, MD 20705
301/504-6559

American Business Publications
1000 Connecticut Avenue, NW, Suite 802
Washington, DC 20036
202/833-3098

American Chemical Society
1155 16th Street, NW
Washington, DC 20036
800/227-5558; 202/872-4564

American Council for an Energy-Efficient Economy
2140 Shattuck Avenue, Suite 202
Berkeley, CA 94704
510/549-9914

American Farmland Trust
1920 N Street, Suite 400
Washington, DC 20036
800/886-5170; 202/659-5170

American Institute of Architects Press
1735 New York Avenue, NW
Washington, DC 20006
800/365-2724; 202/626-7300

American Institute of Graphic Arts
1059 3rd Avenue
New York, NY 10021
212/752-0813

American International Distribution
64 Depot Road
Colchester, VT 05446
800/488-2665; 800/366-6151; 802/878-0315

American Littoral Society
18 Hartshorne Drive
Sandy Hook
Highlands, NJ 07732
908/291-0055

American Political Network
3129 Mount Vernon Avenue
Alexandria, VA 22305
703/518-4600

American Society of Mechanical Engineers
345 East 47th Street
New York, NY 10017
800/843-2763; 212/705-7722

American Solar Energy Society
2400 Central Avenue, Suite G-1
Boulder, CO 80301
303/443-3130

Appropriate Technology Transfer for Rural Areas
P.O. Box 3657
Fayetteville, AR 72702
800/346-9140; 501/442-9824

Architects for Social Responsibility
See Boston Society of Architects

Ashgate Publishing
Old Post Road
Brookfield, VT 05036
802/276-3162

Atmosphere Alliance
P.O. Box 10346
Olympia, WA 98502
206/352-1763

Atrium Publications Group
11270 Clayton Creek Road
Lower Lake, CA 95457
800/275-2606; 707/995-3906

Australian Government Publishing Service
P.O. Box 7
Planetarium Station
New York, NY 10024
212/799-3854

B & B Publishing
P.O. Box 96
Walworth, WI 53814
800/386-3228; 414/275-9474

Baker & Taylor Books
2709 Water Ridge Parkway, Suite 500
5 Lakepointe Plaza
Charlotte, NC 28217
704/357-3500

Bantam Books
See Bantam Doubleday Dell Publishing Group

Bantam Doubleday Dell Publishing Group
1540 Broadway
New York, NY 10036
800/223-6834

Basic Books
10 East 53rd Street
New York, NY 10022
800/242-7737; 212/207-7057

Beacham Publishing
2100 S Street, NW
Washington, DC 20008
800/466-9644; 202/234-0877

Beacon Press
25 Beacon Street
Boston, MA 02108
617/742-2110

Belknap Press
See Harvard University Press

Biological Conservation Newsletter
Smithsonian Institution
Department of Botany, Mail Code MRC 166
National Museum of Natural History
Washington, DC 20560
202/357-2027

BIOSIS
2100 Arch Street
Philadelphia, PA 19103
800/523-4806; 215/587-4800

Blackwell Publishers
238 Main Street
Cambridge, MA 02142
617/547-7110

Blackwell Scientific Publications
238 Main Street
Cambridge, MA 02142
800/759-6102; 617/876-7000

Blue Bird Publishing
1739 East Broadway, Suite 306
Tempe, AZ 85282
602/968-4088

BNA Books
1250 23rd Street, NW
Washington, DC 20037
800/372-1033; 202/833-7470

Bonus Books
160 East Illinois Street
Chicago, IL 60611
800/225-3775; 312/467-0580

Bookpeople
7900 Edgewater Drive
Oakland, CA 94621
800/999-4650; 510/632-4700

Boston Society of Architects
52 Broad Street
Boston, MA 02109
617/951-1433, ext. 222

Brookings Institution
1775 Massachusetts Avenue, NW
Washington, DC 20036
800/275-1447; 202/797-6000

Brubach Corporation
P.O. Box 15629
Chevy Chase, MD 20825
301/986-5545

Bulfinch Press
34 Beacon Street
Boston, MA 02108
617/248-2473

Bureau of National Affairs
1231 25th Street, NW
Washington, DC 20037
800/862-4636; 202/833-7470

Business Publishers
951 Pershing Drive
Silver Spring, MD 20910
800/724-0122; 301/587-6300

Business Roundtable
1615 L Street, NW, Suite 1100
Washington, DC 20036
202/872-1260

Buzzworm
2305 Canyon Boulevard, Suite 206
Boulder, CO 80302
303/442-4875

California Department of General Services
Publications Section
P.O. Box 1015
North Highlands, CA 95660
916/574-2200

California Environmental Protection Agency
Office of Environmental Health Hazard Assessment
2151 Berkeley Way
Berkeley, CA 94704
510/540-3063

California Institute of Public Affairs
P.O. Box 189040
Sacramento, CA 95818
916/442-2472

Cambridge Scientific Abstracts
7200 Wisconsin Avenue, Suite 601
Bethesda, MD 20814
800/843-7751; 301/961-6750

Cambridge University Press
40 West 20th Street
New York, NY 10011
800/221-4512; 212/924-3900

Canadian Almanac and Directory Publishing Company
134 Adelaide Street East, Suite 207
Toronto, Ontario M5C 1K9
Canada
905/238-6074

Carnegie Mellon University
Department of Engineering and Public Policy
Pittsburgh, PA 15213

Carol Publishing
600 Madison Avenue
11th Floor
New York, NY 10022
212/486-2200

Cenozoic Society
P.O. Box 455
Richmond, VT 05477
802/434-4077

Center for Environmental Information
50 West Main Street
Rochester, NY 14614
716/262-2870

Center for Environmental Research Information
Publications Division
26 West Martin Luther King Drive
Cincinnati, OH 45268
513/569-7562

Center for Marine Conservation
1725 DeSales Street, NW, Suite 500
Washington, DC 20036
202/429-5609

Center for Policy Alternatives
1875 Connecticut Avenue, NW, Suite 710
Washington, DC 20009
202/387-6030

Center for Renewable Energy and Sustainable Technology
Solar Energy Research and Education Foundation
777 North Capitol Street, NE, Suite 805
Washington, DC 20002
202/289-5370

Center for Resourceful Building Technology
P.O. Box 3866
Missoula, MT 59806
406/549-7678

Center for Science in the Public Interest
1875 Connecticut Avenue, NW, Suite 300
Washington, DC 20009
202/332-9110

Center for Strategic and International Studies
1800 K Street, NW, Suite 400
Washington, DC 20006
202/775-3119

Ceres Press
Box 87
Woodstock, NY 12498
914/679-5573

Chapman & Hall
29 West 35th Street
New York, NY 10001
212/244-3336

Charles Stewart Mott Foundation
1200 Mott Foundation Building
Flint, MI 45802
810/766-1766

Chelsea Green
P.O. Box 428
205 Gates-Briggs Building
White River Junction, VT 05001
800/639-4099; 802/295-6300

Chemical Information Systems
810 Gleneagles Court, Suite 300
Towson, MD 21286
800/247-8737; 410/321-8440

Chicago Review Press
814 North Franklin Street
Chicago, IL 60610
800/888-4741; 312/337-0747

Citation Directories
1003 Central Avenue
P.O. Box 1036
Fort Dodge, IA 50501
800/848-9059; 515/955-1600

**City of Austin Environmental and
Conservation Services Department**
Green Building Program
Attention: Laurence Doxsey
206 East Ninth Street
Austin, TX 78701
512/499-7827

Clarkson N. Potter
See Random House

Clean Yield Publications
Box 1880
Greensboro Bend, VT 05842
800/944-9616; 802/533-7178

Co-op America
1612 K Street, NW, Suite 600
Washington, DC 20006
202/872-5307

Coalition for Education in the Outdoors
P.O. Box 2000
S. U. N.Y. Cortland
Cortland, NY 13045
607/753-4971

Columbia University Press
562 West 113th Street
New York, NY 10025
212/316-7129

**Community Alliance with Family
Farmers**
P.O. Box 363
Davis, CA 95617
800/852-3832; 916/756-8518

Community Environmental Council
930 Miramonte Drive
Santa Barbara, CA 93109
805/963-0583

Competitive Enterprise Institute
1001 Connecticut Avenue, NW, Suite
1250
Washington, DC 20036
202/331-1010

Congressional Information Service
4520 East-West Highway, Suite 800
Bethesda, MD 20814
800/638-8380; 301/654-1550

Conservation International
1015 18th Street, NW
Washington, DC 20036
202/429-5660

**Conservation Technology Information
Center**
1220 Potter Drive, Room 170
West Lafayette, IN 47906
317/494-9555

Consortium Book Sales & Distribution
1045 Westgate Drive
St. Paul, MN 55114
800/283-3572; 612/221-9035

Consumer Reports
101 Truman Avenue
Yonkers, NY 10703
800/272-0722; 914/378-2000

Context Institute
P.O. Box 11470
Bainbridge Island, WA 98110
206/842-0216

Council on Economic Priorities
30 Irving Place
New York, NY 10003
212/420-1133

Countryman Press
P.O. Box 175
Woodstock, VT 05091
802/457-1049

CRC Press
2000 Corporate Boulevard, NW
Boca Raton, FL 33431
800/272-7737; 407/994-0555

Crestwood
See Macmillan

Crown Publishing
See Random House

Cutter Information
37 Broadway
Arlington, MA 02174
800/964-5118; 617/648-8700

Department of Agriculture
National Agricultural Library
10301 Baltimore Avenue
Beltsville, MD 20705
301/504-5755

Department of Energy
Energy Information Administration
1000 Independence Avenue, SW
Washington, DC 20585
202/586-8800

Department of Energy
Office of Scientific and Technical
Information
P.O. Box 62
Oak Ridge, TN 37831
615/576-8401

DIALOG Information Services
3460 Hillview Avenue
P.O. Box 10010
Palo Alto, CA 94303
800/324-3564; 415/858-3785

Donley Technology
Box 335
Garrisonville, VA 22463
703/659-1954

Dovetale Publishers
2 Main Street
Gloucester, MA 01930
800/274-9909; 508/283-3200

Earth Action Network
P.O. Box 5098
Westport, CT 06881
203/854-5559

Earth First!
P.O. Box 1415
Eugene, OR 97440
503/741-9191

Earth Island Institute
300 Broadway, Suite 28
San Francisco, CA 94133
415/788-3666

Earth Times Foundation
Box 3363
Grand Central Station
New York, NY 10163
212/297-0488

Earth Works
1400 Shattuck Avenue
Box 25
Berkeley, CA 94709
510/841-5866

EarthPress
4882 Kellogg Circle
Boulder, CO 80303
800/748-1175

Eco-Home Media
4344 Russell Avenue
Los Angeles, CA 90027
213/662-5207

Educational Communications
P. O. Box 351419
Los Angeles, CA 90035
310/559-9160

Edward Elgar Publishing Company
Old Post Road
Brookfield, VT 05036
802/276-3162

Eight Bit Books
See Online

Electronic Newsstand
1225 19th Street, NW, Suite 650
Washington, DC 20036
800/403-NEWS; 202/466-8688

Elsevier Science Publishing
P.O. Box 882
Madison Square Station
New York, NY 10159
212/989-5800

Energy Auditor & Retrofitter
2124 Kittredge Street, Suite 95
Berkeley, CA 94704
510/524-5405

Energy Information Press
1100 Industrial Road, Suite 9
San Carlos, CA 94070
213/724-5740

EnviroAccount Software
605 Sunset Court
Davis, CA 95616
800/554-0317; 916/756-9156

Envirographics
P.O. Box 334
Hiram, OH 44234
216/527-5207

Environment Today
1165 Northchase Parkway, Suite 350
Marietta, GA 30067
404/988-9558

Environmental Action
6930 Carroll Avenue, Suite 600
Takoma Park, MD 20912
301/891-1100

Environmental and Energy Study Institute
122 C Street, NW, Suite 700
Washington, DC 20001
202/628-1400

Environmental Business International
P.O. Box 371769
San Diego, CA 92137
619/295-7685

Environmental By Design
P.O. Box 34493
Station D
Vancouver, BC V6J 4W4
Canada

Environmental Career Center
22 Research Drive
Hampton, VA 23666
804/865-0605

Environmental Careers Organization
National Office
286 Congress Street
Boston, MA 02210
617/426-4375

Environmental Data Research Institute
1655 Elmwood Avenue, Suite 225
Rochester, NY 14620
800/724-1857; 716/473-3090

Environmental Grantmakers Association
1290 Avenue of the Americas, Suite 3450
New York, NY 10104
212/373-4260

Environmental Industries Association
1120 Connecticut Avenue, NW
Washington, DC 20036
202/659-4513

Environmental Law Institute
1616 P Street, NW, Suite 200
Washington, DC 20036
800/433-5120; 202/939-3844

Environmental News Network
P.O. Box 1996
Sun Valley, ID 83353
208/726-4164

Environmental Opportunities
P.O. Box 788
Walpole, NH 03608
603/756-4553

Environmental Protection Agency
Air Risk Information Support Center
Research Triangle Park, NC 27711
919/541-0888

Environmental Protection Agency
Environmental Statistics and
Information Division
401 M Street, SW, Mail Code 2163
Washington, DC 20460
202/260-2680

Environmental Protection Agency
Office of Water Resource Center
401 M Street, SW, Mail Code RC-4100
Washington, DC 20460
202/260-7786

Environmental Protection Agency
Public Information Center
401 M Street, SW, Mail Code 3404
Washington, DC 20460
202/260-7751

Environmental Resources Group
P.O. Box 27341
Albuquerque, NM 87125
800/368-3781; 505/298-5344

Environmental Studies Institute of the International Academy at Santa Barbara
800 Garden Street, Suite D
Santa Barbara, CA 93101
800/530-2682; 805/965-5010

Eos Institute
580 Broadway, Suite 200
Laguna Beach, CA 92651
714/497-1896

Estrin Publishing
1900 Avenue of the Stars, Suite 670
Los Angeles, CA 90067
800/358-5897; 310/552-9988

Executive Enterprises Publications
See John Wiley & Sons

Facts on File
460 Park Avenue South
New York, NY 10016
800/322-8755; 212/683-2244

Farrar, Straus, and Giroux
19 Union Square West
New York, NY 10003
800/631-8571; 212/741-6900

Feline Press
P.O. Box 7219
Gainesville, FL 32605
904/371-6439

Fireside Books
See Simon & Schuster

First Editions
P.O. Box 2578
Sedona, AZ 86336
602/282-9574

Foghorn Press
555 DeHaro Street, Suite 220
San Francisco, CA 94107
800/842-7477; 415/241-9550

Food Products Press
See Haworth Press

Foundation Center
79 Fifth Avenue
New York, NY 10003
800/424-9836; 212/620-4230

Freshwater Foundation
Spring Hill Center
725 County Road 6
Wayzata, MN 55391
612/449-0592

Fulcrum Publishing
350 Indiana Street, Suite 350
Golden, CO 80401
800/992-2908; 303/277-1623

G. K. Hall & Company
See Macmillan

Gale Research
835 Penobscot Building
Detroit, MI 48226
800/877-4253; 313/961-2242

Garland Publishing
717 Fifth Avenue, Suite 2500
New York, NY 10022
800/627-6273; 212/751-7447

Global Tomorrow Coalition
1325 G Street, NW, Suite 1010
Washington, DC 20005
202/628-4016

Good Money Publications
Box 363
Worcester, VT 05682
800/535-3551; 802/223-3911

Gordon & Breach Science Publishers
820 Town Center Drive
Langhorne, PA 19047
800/545-8398

Government Institutes
4 Research Plaza, Suite 200
Rockville, MD 20850
301/921-2355

Government Printing Office
710 North Capitol Street, NW
Washington, DC 20402
202/783-3238

Green Teacher
95 Robert Street
Toronto, Ontario M5S 2K5
Canada
416/960-1244

GreenDisk
P.O. Box 32224
Washington, DC 20007
800/484-7616, ext. 3475

Greenkeeping
Box 87
Rhinebeck, NY 12572
914/876-6525

Greenpeace
1436 U Street, NW
Washington, DC 20009
202/462-1177

Greenwood Press
88 Post Road West
Westport, CT 06881
800/225-5800; 203/226-3571

GreenWorld Environmental
Publications
253 A 26th Street, Suite 306
Santa Monica, CA 90402
310/815-8867

H. W. Wilson Company
950 University Avenue
Bronx, NY 10452
800/367-6770; 718/588-8400

Halfmoon Publishing
P.O. Box 30279
Savannah, GA 31410
912/897-1300

Harmony Books
See Crown Publishing

HarperSanFrancisco
See HarperCollins Publishers

HarperCollins Publishers
10 East 53rd Street
New York, NY 10022
800/331-3761; 212/207-7000

HarperCollins West
See HarperCollins Publishers

HarperPerennial
See HarperCollins Publishers

Hartley & Marks
P.O. Box 147
Point Roberts, WA 98281
206/945-2017

Harvard University Press
79 Garden Street
Cambridge, MA 02138
800/448-2242; 617/495-2600

Haworth Press
10 Alice Street
Binghamton, NY 13904
800/342-9678

Healthy Building Associates
7190 South Fisk Road
Clinton, WA 98236
206/579-2962

Healthy House Institute
7471 North Shiloh Road
Unionville, IN 47468
812/332-5073

Hearst Books
See William Morrow & Company

Heldref Publications
1319 18th Street, NW
Washington, DC 20036
800/365-9753; 202/296-6267

Hemisphere Publishing
1900 Frost Road, Suite 101
Bristol, PA 19007
800/821-8312; 215/785-5800

Henry A. Wallace Institute for
Alternative Agriculture
9200 Edmonston Road, Suite 117
Greenbelt, MD 20770
301/441-8777

Henry Holt and Company
115 West 18th Street
New York, NY 10011
800/488-5233; 212/886-9200

Home Power
P.O. Box 275
Ashland, OR 97520
916/475-3179

Houghton Mifflin
222 Berkeley Street
Boston, MA 02116
800/225-3362; 617/725-5000

Hulogosi Communications
P.O. Box 1188
Eugene, OR 97440
503/343-0606

Humane Society of the United States
2100 L Street, NW
Washington, DC 20037
202/452-1100

Humanities Press International
165 First Avenue
Atlantic Highlands, NJ 07716
908/872-1441

IAQ Publications
4520 East-West Highway, Suite 610
Bethesda, MD 20814
301/913-0115

Imagination Station Communications
945 Bracero Road
Encinitas, CA 92024
619/632-0770

INFORM
381 Park Avenue South
New York, NY 10016
212/689-4040

Information Ventures
1500 Locust Street, Suite 1513
Philadelphia, PA 19102
215/732-9083

Informed Consent
P.O. Box 1984
Williston, ND 58802
701/774-7760

Institute for Agriculture and Trade
Policy
1313 5th Street, SE, Suite 303
Minneapolis, MN 55414
612/379-5980

Institute for Southern Studies
2009 Chapel Hill Road
Durham, NC 27707
919/419-8311

Interior Concerns Publications
P.O. Box 2386
Mill Valley, CA 94942
415/389-8049

International Alliance for Sustainable
Agriculture
1701 University Avenue, SE
Minneapolis, MN 55414
612/331-1099

International Energy Agency Greenhouse Gas R & D Programme
CRE
Stoke Orchard
Cheltenham, Gloucestershire GL52 4RZ
England, United Kingdom

International Institute for Sustainable Development
161 Portage Avenue East, 6th Floor
Winnipeg, Manitoba R3B 0Y4
Canada
204/958-7700

International Society for Ecological Economics
P.O. Box 1589
Solomons Island, MD 20688
410/326-0794

International Specialized Book Services
5804 Northeast Hassalo Street
Portland, OR 97213
800/944-6190; 503/287-3093

Investor Responsibility Research Center
1755 Massachusetts Avenue, NW, Suite 600
Washington, DC 20036
202/833-0700

Iowa State University Press
2121 South State Avenue
Ames, IA 50010
800/862-6657; 515/292-0155

Island Press
1718 Connecticut Avenue, NW, Suite 300
Washington, DC 20009
800/828-1302; 202/232-7933

Jeremy Tarcher
5858 Wilshire Boulevard, Suite 200
Los Angeles, CA 90036
213/935-9980

Jetmarc Group
P.O. Box 755
Latrobe, PA 15650
412/539-3788

JG Press
Box 351
Emmaus, PA 18049
610/967-4135

Job Seeker
Route 2, Box 16
Warrens, WI 54666
608/378-4290

John Muir Publications
P.O. Box 613
Santa Fe, NM 87504
800/888-7504; 505/982-4078

John Wiley & Sons
605 Third Avenue
New York, NY 10158
800/225-5945; 212/850-6000

Johns Hopkins University Press
2715 North Charles Street
Baltimore, MD 21218
800/537-5487; 410/516-6900

Kluwer Academic Publishers
101 Philip Drive
Assinippi Park
Norwell, MA 02061
617/871-6600

Knowledge Systems
7777 West Morris Street
Indianapolis, IN 46231
800/999-8517; 317/241-0749

Kraus International Publications
358 Saw Mill River Road
Millwood, NY 10546
800/223-8323; 914/762-2200

League of Conservation Voters
1707 L Street, NW, Suite 550
Washington, DC 20036
202/785-8683

Lewis Publishers
121 South Main Street
P.O. Box 519
Chelsea, MI 48118
313/475-8619; 800/272-7737

Liberty Hall Press
See McGraw-Hill

Libraries Unlimited
P.O. Box 6633
Englewood, CO 80155
800/237-6124; 303/770-1220

Little, Brown & Company
1271 Avenue of the Americas
Time & Life Building
New York, NY 10020
800/343-9204; 212/522-8700

Living Planet Press
2940 Newark Street, NW
Washington, DC 20008
202/686-6262

Lloyd Publishing
24 East Avenue, Suite 1300
New Canaan, CT 06840
203/966-2099

Longman Publishing Group
10 Bank Street
Longman Building
White Plains, NY 10606
800/447-2226; 914/993-5000

Lyle Stuart
See Carol Publishing

Lyons & Burford Publishers
31 West 21st Street
New York, NY 10010
212/620-9580

Macmillan
See Simon & Schuster

Magni Company
P.O. Box 849
McKinney, TX 75069
214/540-2050

Management Institute for Environment and Business
1220 16th Street, NW
Washington, DC 20036
202/833-6556

Marier Communications
620 Central Avenue North
Milaca, MN 56353
800/922-3736; 612/983-6892

Marshall Cavendish
2145 Jerusalem Avenue
North Bellmore, NY 11710
800/821-9881; 516/826-4200

McFarland & Company
Box 611
Jefferson, NC 28640
910/246-4460

McGrath Associates
256 Post Road East
Colonial Green
Westport, CT 06880
203/221-8335

McGraw-Hill
1221 Avenue of the Americas
New York, NY 10020
800/722-4726; 212/512-2000

Meadowbrook Press
18318 Minnetonka Boulevard
Deephaven, MN 55391
800/338-2232; 612/473-5400

Mercury House
201 Filbert Street, Suite 400
San Francisco, CA 94133
800/998-9129; 415/433-7042

Microwave News
P.O. Box 1799
Grand Central Station
New York, NY 10163
212/517-2800

MIT Press
55 Hayward Street
Cambridge, MA 02142
800/356-0343; 617/625-8481

Morning Sun Press
P.O. Box 413
Lafayette, CA 94549
510/932-1383

National Academy Press
2101 Constitution Avenue, NW
Box 285
Washington, DC 20055
800/624-6242

National Acid Precipitation Assessment Program
722 Jackson Place, NW
Washington, DC 20503
202/296-1002

National Agricultural Library
DC Reference Center
14th Street and Independence Avenue, SW, Room 1052 South
Washington, DC 20250
202/720-3434

National Agricultural Library
Office of Reference
10301 Baltimore Boulevard, Room 111
Beltsville, MD 20705
301/504-5204

National Audubon Society
700 Broadway
New York, NY 10003
212/979-3000

National Book Network
4720A Boston Way
Lanham, MD 20706
800/462-6420; 301/459-8696

National Cancer Institute
9030 Old Georgetown Road
Bethesda, MD 20892
800/422-6237; 301/496-7403

National Center for Atmospheric Research
Environmental and Societal Impacts Group
P.O. Box 3000
Boulder, CO 80307
303/497-8119

National Center for Environmental Publications and Information
11029 Kenwood Road
Cincinnati, OH 45242

National Coalition Against the Misuse of Pesticides
701 E Street, SE, Suite 200
Washington, DC 20003
202/543-5450

National Conference of State Legislatures
1560 Broadway, Suite 700
Denver, CO 80202
303/830-2200

National Energy Information Center
1000 Independence Avenue, SW, Room 1F-048
Washington, DC 20585
202/586-8800

National Information Services Corporation
3100 St. Paul Street, Suite 6
Wyman Towers
Baltimore, MD 21218
410/243-0797

National Library of Medicine
Specialized Information Services Division
8600 Rockville Pike
Bethesda, MD 20894
301/496-1131

National Outdoor Leadership School
P.O. Box AA
Lander, WY 82520
307/332-6973

National Press Books
7200 Wisconsin Avenue, Suite 212
Bethesda, MD 20814
800/275-8888; 301/657-1616

National Renewable Energy Laboratory
1617 Cole Boulevard
Golden, CO 80401
303/275-4363

National Round Table on the Environment and the Economy
1 Nicholas Street, Suite 1500
Ottawa, Ontario K1N 7B7
Canada
613/992-7189

National Science Teachers Association
3140 North Washington Boulevard
Arlington, VA 22201
703/243-7100

National Technical Information Service
5285 Port Royal Road
Springfield, VA 22161
703/487-4650

National Wildlife Federation
8925 Leesburg Pike
Vienna, VA 22184
800/432-6564; 703/790-4000

Natural Resources Defense Council
40 West 20th Street, 11th Floor
New York, NY 10011
212/727-2700

Nature Conservancy
1815 North Lynn Street
Arlington, VA 22209
703/247-3749

Ned Ludd Books
P.O. Box 5141
Tucson, AZ 85703
602/628-9610

New Environmentalist Magazine
Michael Manning, Publisher
e-mail: manning@access.digex.net

New Jersey Department of Health
Right to Know Program
CN 368
Trenton, NJ 08625
609/984-2202

New Society Publishers
4527 Springfield Avenue
Philadelphia, PA 19143
800/333-9093; 215/382-6543

Noble Press
213 West Institute Plaza, Suite 508
Chicago, IL 60610
800/486-7737; 312/642-1168

North Point Press
See Farrar, Straus, and Giroux

Northwest Coalition for Alternatives to Pesticides
P.O. Box 1393
Eugene, OR 97440
503/344-5044

Nuclear Information and Resource Service
1424 16th Street, NW, Suite 601
Washington, DC 20036
202/328-0002

Odonian Press
2500 Pantano Road, Suite 118
Tucson, AZ 85715
800/732-7867; 602/296-4056

Omnigraphics
Penobscot Building
Detroit, MI 48226
800/234-1340; 313/961-1340

Online
462 Danbury Road
Wilton, CT 06897
800/248-8466; 203/761-1466

Organization for Economic Cooperation and Development
Publications and Information Division
2001 L Street, NW, Suite 700
Washington, DC 20036
800/456-6323; 202/785-6323

Oryx Press
4041 North Central
Phoenix, AZ 85012
800/279-6799; 602/265-2651

Oxford University Press
200 Madison Avenue
New York, NY 10016
800/445-9714; 800/451-7556; 212/679-7300

Pacific Rivers Council
P.O. Box 309
Eugene, OR 97440
503/345-0119

Peachpit Press
2414 6th Street
Berkeley, CA 94710
800/283-9444; 510/548-4393

Penguin Books
See Viking Penguin

Pergamon Press
660 White Plains Road
Tarrytown, NY 10591
914/524-9200

Perigee Books
See Putnam Publishing Group

Pesticide Action Network
P.O. Box 610
San Francisco, CA 94101
415/541-9140

Peterson's Guides
P.O. Box 2123
Princeton, NJ 08543
800/338-3282; 609/243-9111

Pira International
Randalls Road
Leatherhead, Surrey KT22 7RU
England, United Kingdom
+44 0372 376161

Plenum Publishing
233 Spring Street
New York, NY 10013
800/221-9369; 212/620-8000

Point
P.O. Box 38
Sausalito, CA 94966
415/332-1716

Pollution Prevention Information Clearinghouse
Environmental Protection Agency
401 M Street, SW, Mail Code 3404
Washington, DC 20460
202/260-1023

Praeger Publishers
Box 5007
88 Post Road West
Westport, CT 06881
800/225-5800; 203/226-3571

Prentice Hall
113 Sylvan Avenue
Englewood Cliffs, NJ 07632
800/922-0579; 201/592-2000

Prentice Hall Law & Business
270 Sylvan Avenue
Englewood Cliffs, NJ 07632
800/447-1717

Princeton Architectural Press
37 East 7th Street
New York, NY 10003
800/458-1131

Public Citizen Publications
2000 P Street, NW
Washington, DC 20036
202/833-3000

Public Interest Publications
3030 Clarendon Boulevard, Suite 200
Arlington, VA 22210
800/537-9359

Publishers Distribution Service
6893 Sullivan Road
Grawn, MI 49637
800/345-0096; 616/276-5196

Publishers Group West
4065 Hollis Street
Emeryville, CA 94608
800/788-3123; 510/658-3453

Putnam Publishing Group
200 Madison Avenue
New York, NY 10016
800/631-8571; 212/951-8400

R. & E. Miles
707/442-5595

R. R. Bowker
121 Chanlon Road
New Providence, NJ 07974
800/521-8110; 908/464-6800

Rails-to-Trails Conservancy
Shipping Department
800/888-7747

Rainforest Action Network
450 Sansome, Suite 700
San Francisco, CA 94111
415/398-4404

Random House
201 East 50th Street
22nd Floor
New York, NY 10022
800/733-3000; 800/726-0600; 212/751-2600

Rawson Associates
See Macmillan

Real Goods Trading Company
966 Mazzoni Street
Ukiah, CA 95482
800/762-7325

Recycling Data Management
Box 577
Ogdensburg, NY 13669
800/267-0707; 315/471-0707

Redwood Alliance
P.O. Box 293
Arcata, CA 95521
707/822-7884

René Dubos Center for Human Environments
100 East 85th Street
New York, NY 10028
212/249-7745

Resources for the Future
1616 P Street, NW, Room 417
Washington, DC 20036
202/328-5086

Rivers, Trails and Conservation Assistance Program of the National Park Service
P.O. Box 37127
Washington, DC 20013
202/343-3780

Rocky Mountain Institute
1739 Snowmass Creek Road
Snowmass, CO 81654
303/927-3851

Rodale Press
33 East Minor Street
Emmaus, PA 18098
800/848-4735

Routledge
29 West 35th Street
New York, NY 10001
212/244-3336

Sage Press
524 San Anselmo Avenue, Suite 225
San Anselmo, CA 94960
800/218-4242

Salem Press
P.O. Box 1097
Englewood Cliffs, NJ 07632
800/221-1592; 201/871-3700

Scarecrow Press
52 Liberty Street
Box 4167
Metuchen, NJ 08840
800/537-7107; 908/548-8600

Scholastic
730 Broadway
New York, NY 10019
800/325-6149; 212/505-3000

School of Natural Resources and Environment at the University of Michigan
430 East University Avenue
Dana Building
Ann Arbor, MI 48109
313/763-3243

Schultz Communications
9412 Admiral Nimitz, NE
Albuquerque, NM 87111
505/822-8222

Sewall
145 Lincoln Road
P.O. Box 529
Lincoln, MA 01773
800/258-0559; 617/259-0559

Sierra Club
730 Polk Street
San Francisco, CA 94109
415/923-5653

Sierra Club Books
100 Bush Street, 13th Floor
San Francisco, CA 94104
415/776-2211

SilverPlatter
100 River Ridge Drive
Norwood, MA 02062
800/343-0064; 617/769-2599

Silvercat Publications
4070 Goldfinch Street, Suite C
San Diego, CA 92103
619/299-6774

Simon & Schuster
1230 Avenue of the Americas
New York, NY 10020
800/223-2336; 212/698-7000

Sinauer
North Main Street
Sunderland, MA 01375
413/665-3722

Skies America Publishing
9560 Southwest Nimbus Avenue
Beaverton, OR 97008
800/334-8152; 503/691-1412

Smiling Dolphin Press
4 Segura
Irvine, CA 92715
714/733-1065

Smithsonian Institution Press
470 L'Enfant Plaza, Suite 7100
Washington, DC 20560
800/233-1128; 202/287-3738

Social Issues Resources Series
P.O. Box 2348
Boca Raton, FL 33427
800/232-7477; 407/994-0079

Society for Conservation Biology
University of Nevada
Department of Biology
Reno, NV 89557
702/784-6188

Solar Energy Industries Association
122 C Street, NW, 4th Floor
Washington, DC 20001
202/383-2600

South End Press
P.O. Box 741
Monroe, ME 04951
800/533-8478

Southwest Research and Information Center
P.O. Box 4524
Albuquerque, NM 87106
505/262-1862

Special Libraries Association
Environmental Resource Management
Division
1700 18th Street, NW
Washington, DC 20009
202/234-4700

St. Johns Publishing
6824 Oaklawn Avenue
Edina, MN 55435
612/920-9044

St. Martin's Press
175 Fifth Avenue, Room 175
New York, NY 10010
800/221-7945; 212/674-5151

Stackpole Books
5067 Ritter Road
Mechanicsburg, PA 17055
800/732-3669

State University of New York Press
State University Plaza
Albany, NY 12246
800/666-2211; 518/472-5000

Storey Communications
Schoolhouse Road
Pownal, VT 05261
800/441-5700; 802/823-5200

Student Conservation Association
National Headquarters
P.O. Box 550
Charlestown, NH 03603
603/543-1700

SUN DAY
315 Circle Avenue, No. 2
Takoma Park, MD 20912
301/270-2258

Sustainable Agriculture Publications
University of Vermont
Hills Building, Room 12
Burlington, VT 05405
802/656-0471

Sustainable Energy Budget Coalition
See SUN DAY

Synergistic Technologies
3212 Quiet Mill Road, Suite B4
Raleigh, NC 27612
800/972-8501; 919/571-0444

Synerjy
P.O. Box 1854
Cathedral Station
New York, NY 10025
212/865-9595

TAB Books
P.O. Box 40
Blue Ridge Summit, PA 17294
800/233-1128; 717/794-2191

Taunton Press
63 South Main Street
Box 5506
Newtown, CT 06470
800/243-7252; 203/426-8171

Taylor & Francis
1900 Frost Road, Suite 101
Bristol, PA 19007
800/821-8312; 215/785-5800

Ten Speed Press
P.O. Box 7123
Berkeley, CA 94707
800/841-2665; 510/845-8414

Terra Firma Publishing
1216 State Street, Suite 607
Santa Barbara, CA 93101
805/962-0962

Terrene Institute
1717 K Street, NW, Suite 801
Washington, DC 20006
202/833-8317

Tilbury House Publishers
132 Water Street
Gardiner, ME 04345
207/582-1899

Tilden Press
1526 Connecticut Avenue, NW
Washington, DC 20036
202/332-1700

Touchstone Press
P.O. Box 81
Beaverton, OR 97075
800/877-2684; 503/652-1947

Tree Talk
P.O. Box 426
Burlington, VT 05402
800/858-6230; 802/863-6789

United Church Resources
800 North 3rd Street, Suite 202
St. Louis, MO 63102
800/325-7061

United Nations Environment Programme
Regional Office for North America
2 United Nations Plaza, Room 0803
UNDC Two Building
New York, NY 10017
212/963-8139

United Nations Publications
Publishing Division/Sales Section
2 United Nations Plaza, Room DC2–853
New York, NY 10017
800/533-3210; 212/963-8302

University of Arizona Press
1230 Park Avenue, Suite 102
Tucson, AZ 85719
800/426-3797; 602/621-1441

University of California Press
2120 Berkeley Way
Berkeley, CA 94720
800/822-6657; 510/642-6684

University of Idaho Library
Rayburn Street
Moscow, ID 83844
208/885-6534

University of Texas Press
P.O. Box 7819
Austin, TX 78713
800/252-3206; 512/471-7233

University Press of America
4720 Boston Way
Lanham, MD 20706
301/459-3366

Van Nostrand Reinhold
115 Fifth Avenue
New York, NY 10003
800/842-3636; 606/525-6600

VGM Career Horizons
4255 West Touhy Avenue
Lincolnwood, IL 60646
800/323-4900; 708/679-5500

Viking Penguin
375 Hudson Street
New York, NY 10014
800/331-4624; 800/526-0275; 212/366-2000

Visible Ink Press
See Gale Research

VisionLink Education Foundation
47 Calhoun Road
Waynesville, NC 28786
704/926-2200

Volunteer Monitor
Attention: Eleanor Ely
1318 Masonic Avenue
San Francisco, CA 94117

W & R Chambers
43/45 Annandale Street
Edinburgh EH7 4AZ
Scotland, United Kingdom
+44 031 557 4571

W. W. Norton & Company
500 Fifth Avenue
New York, NY 10110
800/223-2584; 212/354-5500

Waite Group Press
200 Tamal Plaza
Corte Madera, CA 94925
800/368-9369; 415/924-2575

Walker & Company
435 Hudson Street
New York, NY 10014
800/289-2553; 212/727-8300

Warner Books
1271 Avenue of the Americas, Room 964B
New York, NY 10020
212/522-7200

West Publishing
620 Opperman Drive
P.O. 64779
St. Paul, MN 55164
800/328-9352; 612/687-7000

West River Communications
RR 1, Box 161
Brattleboro, VT 05301
802/257-7300

Westview Press
5500 Central Avenue
Boulder, CO 80301
800/456-1995; 303/444-3541

Wild Forest Review
3758 SE Milwaukie
Portland, OR 97202
503/234-0093

Wilderness Society
900 17th Street, NW
Washington, DC 20006
202/833-2300

William Morrow & Company
1350 Avenue of the Americas
New York, NY 10019
212/261-6500

Williams & Wilkins
428 East Preston Street
Baltimore, MD 21202
800/527-5597; 410/528-4000

Wilson
see H. W. Wilson Company

Windcrest Books
See TAB Books

Wladyslaw Poniecki Foundation
8637 Arbor Drive
El Cerrito, CA 94530

Wooden Angel Publishing
P.O. Box 884
Harrisonburg, VA 22801
800/345-0096; 703/833-2801

World Bank
Office of the Publisher
1818 H Street, NW
Washington, DC 20433
202/473-1155

World Conservation Union
1400 16th Street, NW
Washington, DC 20036
202/797-5454

World Resources Institute
Publications
Box 4852, NW
Hampden Post Office
Baltimore, MD 21211
800/822-0504; 410/516-2596

World Wildlife Fund
Publications
P.O. Box 4866, NW
Hampden Post Office
Baltimore, MD 21211
410/516-6951

Worldwatch Institute
1776 Massachusetts Avenue, NW
Washington, DC 20036
800/825-0061; 202/452-1999

WriteWare
4785 Meredith Road
P.O. Box 51
Yellow Springs, OH 45387
513/767-7986

Yale University Press
302 Temple Street
New Haven, CT 06511
203/432-0960

Zed Books
See Humanities Press International

Index

Index

Index